The Young Lloyd George

David Lloyd George as a young M.P.

JOHN GRIGG

The Young Lloyd George

UNIVERSITY OF CALIFORNIA PRESS

BERKELEY AND LOS ANGELES

University of California Press
Berkeley and Los Angeles, California

ISBN: 0–520–02677–2
Library of Congress Catalog Card Number: 73–91067

© 1973 John Grigg
Second Printing, 1978

Printed in Great Britain

To Patricia

Contents

Illustrations

Acknowledgements and thanks are due to Topix for the frontispiece; to *The Life of David Lloyd George*, Vols I, II and III, by Herbert du Parcq (Caxton Publishing Co., 1912–13), for plates 1a, 2b and 3b; to *Lloyd George, 1863–1914*, by W. Watkin Davies (Constable & Co., 1939), for plates 1b, 2a and 2c; to J. L. E. Smith for plate 1c; to the Controller of Her Majesty's Stationery Office (photo by R.C.A.H.M. Wales) for plate 3c; to the Caernarvon County Record Office for plate 5; to the Gladstone Library, National Liberal Club, for plate 6a; to the National Library of Wales for plates 6b, 6c, 7a, 7b, 7c, 7d and 7e; to the National Portrait Gallery for plates 8a, 8b, 8d and 8e; and to *The Life of the Rt. Hon. Sir Henry Campbell-Bannerman*, by J. A. Spender (Hodder & Stoughton, 1923), for plate 8c.

Acknowledgements

My first thanks are due to Lady Olwen Carey Evans D.B.E., the late Lady Megan Lloyd George C.H., M.P., and Owen, the present Earl Lloyd George of Dwyfor, for their inestimable kindness and help. While taking me very fully into their confidence as a friend, they have never sought to restrict my independence as an author.

I am also specially indebted to Mr D. L. Carey Evans for the loan of documents, and to Mr R. R. Carey Evans D.F.C. for his generous interest in my work.

For permission to reproduce material of which they hold the copyright I am above all grateful to the National Library of Wales and to the First Beaverbrook Foundation.

Others to whom I am deeply obliged for similar permission, or for lending documents, or for information of exceptional value are Mr Nicholas Baring (on behalf of Baring Brothers); the Caernarvonshire County Record Office (Archivist, Mr Bryn R. Parry); the late Dr T. I. Ellis, and Mrs T. I. Ellis; Miss Gwendollen Evans; Councillor William George; Miss Elizabeth Humphreys-Owen; Mrs K. Idwal Jones; the late Frances, Countess Lloyd George of Dwyfor C.B.E.; the Hon. William Lloyd George; the National Liberal Club; the National Library of Canada; the National Portrait Gallery; Mr J. L. E. Smith; the late Viscount Tenby P.C.; and Mrs Enid Thomas.

Many people, at many institutions, have helped my research but I must mention in particular Mr David Jenkins (Librarian) and Mr B. G. Owens (Keeper of Manuscripts and Records) at the National Library of Wales; Mr A. J. P. Taylor F.B.A. (Librarian), the late Miss

Rosemary Brooks, and Miss Veronica Horne, at the Beaverbrook Library; and Mr D. Matthews (Deputy Librarian) at the London Library.

The text of this book was read in typescript by Mr Ian Gilmour M.P., Professor Alfred M. Gollin D.Litt., the Hon. Anthony Grigg, Dr Prys Morgan and Mr A. J. P. Taylor F.B.A. They were good enough to comment upon it in detail and to make extremely helpful suggestions, on most of which I have acted. My gratitude to them is immense.

Dr Prys Morgan, in addition, has translated many Welsh documents for me, and has given me the benefit of his profound and varied Welsh scholarship.

My publisher, Mr John Bright-Holmes, has shown great patience over a number of years, and has never ceased to give me his sympathetic encouragement. I am very grateful to him, and should also like to record my thanks to his most capable assistants, Miss Ann Mansbridge and Miss Mary Todd.

Finally, I must express my gratitude, however inadequately, to Miss Jean Walton, for typing the book and all the notes on which it was based, and for her constant friendship.

J.G.

Abbreviations

D.L.G.	David Lloyd George
M.L.G.	Margaret Lloyd George
N.L.W.	National Library of Wales

Preface

If Lloyd George had been killed by the hostile mob at Birmingham on 18 December 1901, one would still be justified in writing about him as a young politician of exceptional interest and promise. How much more so, seeing that his early life foreshadows one of the two outstanding Ministerial careers of British twentieth-century history.

The other outstanding career is, of course, that of Winston Churchill, and nobody seriously complains that the late Randolph Churchill devoted two very substantial volumes to the life of his father up to the outbreak of war in 1914, the first volume taking the story no further than to Sir Winston's election to Parliament in 1900. Yet Lloyd George has often been written about as though the whole time before he became a Minister in 1905 were of almost negligible importance – something to be disposed of in a few pages. Absurdly scant attention has been paid to his fifteen years as a very lively and significant back-bencher, while even his nearly nine years as a dominating figure in the pre-war Liberal Governments of Campbell-Bannerman and Asquith have received considerably less attention than they deserve.

For this error of perspective Lloyd George is himself partly to blame, because when he turned to autobiography in the nineteen-thirties he wrote only his *war* memoirs. One reason may have been that he had kept no proper files during his early years in politics, and was therefore short of raw material for a suitably detailed account of his efforts and achievements before he became a war leader. Whatever the reason, he undoubtedly failed to give any such account, and his failure has been matched, in varying degrees, by all who have written about him since.

Their task has, indeed, been abnormally complicated by problems of access to documents. Though far too little use has been made of public sources that have been readily available, there has, until recently, been a crippling dearth of private correspondence and other contemporary private records against which to check, and with which to supplement and season, the public record. Students have long been aware of the existence of a great collection of early Lloyd George material, formerly owned by Lloyd George's brother, Alderman William George (who died in 1967), and bequeathed by him to his son, the present owner, Councillor W. R. P. George. The treasures of this collection lie hidden: only twice have they been drawn upon for historical purposes, and only one outsider has been given even limited access to them – before the First World War. Councillor George wishes to go through the papers himself before opening them to the world at large, and one can understand his feeling. Unfortunately he is a very busy man.

Meanwhile, within the last decade, a new source has come to light, and one from which historians are not excluded. This may be termed the Carey Evans Collection, since it consists of documents presented to the National Library of Wales by Lloyd George's second daughter, Lady Olwen Carey Evans, and her son, Mr D. L. Carey Evans. Through their kindness I was able, five years ago, to work on these documents before they were deposited permanently in the National Library. It was tempting, then, to produce a book quickly, but I persisted in hoping – vainly, as it turned out – that I would, after all, be given access to the William George Collection.

By the beginning of last year it was clear to me that I would have to write about the young Lloyd George without the benefit of having consulted all the major sources known to exist, though still with advantages denied to every previous biographer. I would never, in any case, have aspired to write definitively on the subject, because there is no such thing as definitive history. The last word will never be written on Lloyd George, or on any part of his career. With the passage of time new facts will emerge, new explanations and interpretations will be offered.

The book that I have written is no more than an honest attempt to describe his origins, and his career up to 1902, at least on an adequate scale. I do not pretend to be an academic historian, and I have the possibly even worse defect of not being able to speak or read Welsh. On the credit side, I am a political animal, bred, unlike many academic historians, in a political atmosphere. Moreover, my father served Lloyd

George in the famous 'Garden Suburb' in 1921-2, remained a devoted admirer of his, and took me twice to lunch with him at Churt. (I therefore satisfy Dr Johnson's condition for writing a man's life, that one must have eaten and drunk with him.) Finally, I have the good fortune to have known, and to know, many members of the Lloyd George family.

Churchill said of Lloyd George: 'He was the greatest Welshman which that unconquerable race has produced since the age of the Tudors. Much of his work abides, some of it will grow greatly in the future, and those who come after us will find the pillars of his life's toil upstanding, massive and indestructible.' When I once asked Lord Beaverbrook to compare the two giants, he replied: 'Churchill was perhaps the greater man. But George was more fun.'

J. G.

March 1973

'How can I convey to the reader, who does not know him, any just impression of this extraordinary figure of our time, this syren, this goat-footed bard, this half-human visitor to our age from the hag-ridden magic and enchanted woods of Celtic antiquity?'

J. M. KEYNES

'He may possess qualities which appear to be those of a mystic, but his desires and ambitions are those of a realist every time . . . he is much more a Frenchman even than a Welshman.'

FRANCES STEVENSON

ONE
Not-so-humble Origins

David Lloyd George was a privileged child, born not to rank or riches but to a special historic opportunity. At the time of his birth Wales was experiencing a national revival, and the class to which his family belonged was providing the national movement with most of its leaders. Having regained its self-consciousness as a nation Wales was about to become a serious force in British politics, and a young man capable of exploiting Welsh grievances to the full, without losing sight of broader horizons, could hope to make his way almost as rapidly in late Victorian Britain as a young provincial of military genius in late Revolutionary France.

The Welsh people are, of course, descendants of the ancient Britons, diluted but still recognisable survivors of the race which dominated Western Europe before the rise of the Romans. In the British Isles there are three principal nations in what we call the 'Celtic fringe', and of these Wales, in at least one respect, has been the most successful in preserving its identity. While the Scots have almost completely lost their original language, and the Irish have been making frantic and rather futile efforts to revive theirs – which nearly died out in the last century – the Welsh language has remained very much alive and is still widely spoken in spite of many adverse influences, of which the most potent is that of modern mass communications. In one of his speeches Lloyd George gave a vivid illustration of the Welsh language miracle:

Two thousand years ago the great Empire of Rome came with its battalions and conquered that part of Caernarvonshire in which my constituency is situated. They built walls and fortifications as the tokens of their conquest, and they proscribed the use of the Cymric tongue. The other day I was glancing at the ruins of those walls. Underneath I noted the children at play, and I could hear them speaking, with undiminished force and vigour, the proscribed language of the conquered nation. Close by there was a school, where the language of the Roman conquerors was being taught, but taught as a *dead* language.[1]

In fact, the Romans never properly conquered Wales. They built forts and roads, but did not attempt to colonise the country as a whole, having little taste for campaigning, and still less for living, in its rainy, misty, hilly interior. The Normans and Plantagenets had a similar policy, building castles and fortified towns on or near the coast, and establishing English settlers in the towns, but leaving rural Wales and its inhabitants severely alone. It was thus that the Welsh language survived through the Middle Ages, but in more recent times it would have been doomed either to extinction or to degeneration into a number of base dialects, had it not been standardised, and thereby saved, when the Bible and liturgy were translated into Welsh.

This crucial event occurred in the reign of Queen Elizabeth I, whose ancestry gave her a certain interest in resuscitating Welsh culture. She was, however, very much more interested in uniting all her subjects in a homogeneous kingdom, and her decision to place Welsh Bibles and Prayer Books side by side with the English versions in all the churches of Wales was intended to benefit English rather than Welsh. It was hoped that the people might 'by conferring both tongues together the sooner attain to the knowledge of the English tongue'.[2] As it turned out, the local language was the chief gainer. Welsh was diffused throughout the Principality in a single, definitive form and became a language to be written and read as well as spoken. As such it gave a great impetus to the various movements which, over the next three centuries, combined to produce the national revival of Lloyd George's day.

Of these by far the most important was the religious movement. In Wales, as in England and Scotland, the Reformation triumphed, but the reformed Church in Wales did not emerge, like the Scottish Kirk, as a separate national establishment. It remained an integral part of the Church of England, the four Welsh dioceses belonging to the Province of Canterbury. Moreover, after the 1688 revolution it became customary

1. Quoted in W. Watkin Davies, *Lloyd George, 1863–1914*, pp. 162–3.
2. 5 Elizabeth, c. 28 (1562).

for Welsh bishoprics to be held by Englishmen, as minor preferment on the way to higher things. Most of these alien bishops spent as little time as they could in Wales; some never visited the country at all. From early in the eighteenth century until well on in the nineteenth no Welsh-speaking clergyman was appointed to a Welsh see. Inevitably, the religious instincts of an emotional and visionary people, gradually but profoundly stirred by the vernacular scriptures, found their outlet in Nonconformity rather than in the Established Church. To the older Dissenting sects were added, in 1811, the Calvinistic Methodists, who in that year broke away from the Church, and during the Victorian age Welsh Christianity was overwhelmingly Nonconformist in character. Religion provided a common inspiration for Welsh poetry and Welsh music in the art-form of the hymn, and Welsh hymns were sung with harmonious unction by an ever-growing number of chapel choirs.

Moreover, the political talent of Welshmen was nurtured by the chapels. The style of preaching which they encouraged had a natural application to politics, but it was not only a question of style. Dissent has generally been linked with social and political protest, and in Wales there were special reasons why it should be so. The Welsh gentry – though not English by race, like their counterparts in Ireland – became thoroughly anglicised after the Tudor period and were, for the most part, members of the Anglican Church. Opposition to their ascendancy could thus very appropriately be mobilised in and through the Dissenting chapels. The degree of radicalism might vary from sect to sect (the Methodists, indeed, were for a long time conservative in politics), but Nonconformity as a whole was estranged from the traditional squirearchy. Nor, as industry transformed the social pattern of Wales, did the Established Church compete successfully with its rivals in the new urban areas. At Merthyr, for instance, there were twelve Nonconformist chapels in 1840, but only one Anglican church. In the last century Nonconformity was the strongest unifying force in a Wales otherwise tending to become increasingly diverse.

Education, too, helped to unite a race whose hunger for learning was noticeable even in the Dark and Middle Ages. There were schools in Wales before St Augustine founded the first English school at Canterbury. The Reformation was initially disastrous because the mediaeval schools were associated with monasteries, whose fate they shared. During the Tudor period grammar schools came into being in the towns, but the language of instruction in them was English. The country districts were entirely neglected. Yet if Protestantism destroyed the old tradition of Welsh education, it created a new one; for it was through the zeal and resourcefulness of a Protestant clergyman that the Welsh-speaking people of rural Wales acquired the means to become literate. The Reverend Griffith Jones's circulating schools brought the rudiments of culture to over 150,000 children; and not to children only, because it was a striking feature of the Welsh educational revival that adults were as eager to be taught as to make the younger generation learn. Griffith Jones died in 1761, but the circulating schools lived on for a time, and the movement begun by him inspired another characteristic development in Welsh education, the Sunday schools, which also served as study groups for adults as well as Bible classes for children. The close link between education and Nonconformity may be seen in the fact that the pioneer of Sunday schools, Thomas Charles of Bala, was the very man who (reluctantly) led the Calvinistic Methodist secession from the Established Church.

Yet by the early nineteenth century Anglicans, aware of the threat to their position in Wales and anyway not impervious to the national mood, were competing with Nonconformists in the business of school-building. While the British and Foreign School Society built 'British' – i.e. undenominational – schools, the National Society built 'National' – i.e. Anglican – schools. Either way, the flavour and content of Welsh education remained almost exclusively religious.

In 1846 a Royal Commission was appointed to examine the state of education in the Principality, and its report had the effect not only of accelerating educational progress, but also, more dramatically, of arousing Welsh national pride and indignation. The Commissioners were English-men who neither spoke nor understood Welsh, and who allowed them-selves to be unduly influenced by English or anglicised witnesses. Consequently it was asserted in the report that the language of the ordinary people of Wales was the root cause of their backwardness, and of what was stated (without justification) to be their exceptional depravity. Naturally enough, these strictures were bitterly resented, but they also acted as a spur to Welsh ambitions. While holding fast to their own language, many Welshmen set out to master English as a means of proving that they were at least the equals of their ignorant, arrogant, insensitive neighbours. Indeed, before very long a Welshman set out to master England itself, and did so.

Cultural patriotism was stimulated not only by religion and the Welsh language, but also by antiquarian research and the Romantic movement. The rediscovery of Welsh folklore and the re-creation (or invention) of Welsh tribal rites were activities most congenial to expatriates living in England; but their example was gradually followed by the Welsh people at home. The Cymmrodorion, founded in London in the middle of the eighteenth century, is perhaps the best known of a number of Welsh societies, of which imitations were later formed in most Welsh towns. The Eisteddfodau, festivals of music and poetry which had almost petered out by the beginning of the eighteenth century, were revived towards the end of it, and in 1858 – five years before Lloyd George was born – the first National Eisteddfod was held. This annual event, itself the somewhat glorified product of a genuine tradition, incorporated the bogus Druidic ceremonies of the Gorsedd of Bards, which was a creature of Romantic fantasy. Romanticism also entered into the *political* thinking of Welshmen, at a time when Kossuth, Garibaldi and Mazzini were household names in Britain.

All the same, very few Welshmen have thought of their country as a completely separate and independent State, even when they have been most conscious of its identity. Unlike the Scots with their long memory of sovereign independence, or the Irish in their insular detachment, the Welsh had every reason to accept as a fact of life their country's organic connection with England. Even the great Llewelyn acknowledged a personal vassalage to the English Crown, and that was long before Henry VIII's drastic measures of assimilation, which imposed upon Wales the English system of law and the English pattern of government. In the eighteenth century Howel Harris, the outstanding prophet and instigator of the Welsh revival, displayed a no less fervent *British* patriotism during the Seven Years' War, when the country seemed to be threatened with a French invasion. He joined the militia and served at Yarmouth until the end of the war, helping to defend a coastline far removed from that of Wales. During the French Revolution, when the Irish rose in rebellion and a French expeditionary force landed in Ireland, Wales stood solidly with England, and an attempted French landing in Pembrokeshire, very near the farmhouse where Lloyd George's great-grandfather lived, was a total fiasco, owing to spirited local resistance.

Industrialisation made the idea of absolute Welsh autonomy less realistic than ever, since it created a grave unbalance between North and South Wales, without making it significantly easier to move from one to the other. The main railway lines from Gloucester to Milford Haven, from Shrewsbury to Aberystwyth, and from Chester to Holyhead, all emphasised the orientation of the Principality towards England. (In our own age Lloyd George's daughter, Megan, could still say that it was quicker to travel from her home at Criccieth in Caernarvonshire to her South Wales constituency of Carmarthen by way of London than by the more direct route.)

Between the beginning and the middle of the nineteenth century the population of Wales doubled, from over half a million to well over a million, but one quarter of the whole increase was in two southern counties, Glamorgan and Monmouth. The population of Cardiff rose (in round figures) from 1,800 to 18,000, of Swansea from 7,000 to 31,000, of Newport from 1,500 to 19,000, and of Merthyr from 7,500 to 63,000. Moreover, a high proportion of the new urban proletariat was of non-Welsh origin. Many unskilled labourers came from Ireland to work in the docks, the iron and steel works, or the mines. But the bulk of the immigrants came, as might be expected, from England.

In spite of the growing diversity of the people, and the division of the country between North and South – aggravated, rather than cured, by modern developments – the Victorian age nevertheless witnessed an extraordinary flowering of the Welsh national spirit. Indeed the physical and social changes that were taking place may have assisted the process, by making those Welshmen who valued their own culture cherish it all the more fervently. Their view of themselves, and of Wales, tended to be oversimplified, and is summed up in their concept of the *Gwerin* – of the Welsh people sharing the same way of life and the same values from time immemorial. The *Gwerin*, as they saw it, was a community of equals owing allegiance only to God, Beauty and Truth. Such a community has, of course, never existed, in Wales or anywhere else, and those who believed in its existence were idealising both the past and the present of Wales. But national movements are usually sustained by myths and, as myths go, the *Gwerin* was relatively harmless.

The Welsh patriotic *élite* into which Lloyd George was born was by no means representative of the whole Principality, nor were its ideals accepted even by all who were Welsh-speaking and ethnically Welsh. Like any other *élite* it was a class, but not a class in the English sense, because membership of it was determined by culture rather than wealth. To that extent it was egalitarian and democratic, and it made common cause with all 'true' Welshmen against the minority who spoke only English, who sent their sons to English schools and who aped the manners of Englishmen. Yet the Welsh *élite* was itself very keen to prove that loyalty to Welsh culture was no barrier to successful competition with the English in their own language and on their own ground. And it looked down on those Welsh people, whatever their material circumstances, who lacked the moral qualities appropriate to the *Gwerin*. Lloyd George once said: 'I do not believe in aristocracy, but I do believe in stock.'[1] The 'stock' that he was brought up to believe in was a mixture of race, language, religion, education and the desire for self-improvement. The people of whom it consisted might be engaged in quite modest occupations – might even be really poor. But in any case they would be authentically Welsh; they would speak, write and read Welsh; they would nearly always be chapel-goers; they would set much store by learning; and they would want to live useful lives. Their heroes would be teachers and preachers, their bogeymen landlords and licensees. They would seek equality with the English, not separation from England.

Such were the Lloyds, and such were the Georges.

In 1857 William George, a Pembrokeshire man, was appointed headmaster of a 'British' (undenominational) school at Pwllheli – a little out-of-the-way fishing port in the Lleyn peninsula, Caernarvonshire. During his two years in the job he met and married Elizabeth Lloyd, from the nearby village of Llanystumdwy, who was then in domestic service at Pwllheli. The couple moved to Newchurch, Lancashire, where their first child, Mary, was born. They were unhappy there and William's health began to fail, but he accepted a temporary post in charge of a big school in Manchester. So it came about that the most famous of all Welshmen was not a native of Wales. For their first son, David, was born in Manchester on 17 January 1863. His actual birthplace – 5 New York Place, Chorlton-upon-Medlock – has since been demolished, but a plaque recording the event is fixed to the wall of a council house now standing near the spot.[2] Early the following year William George gave up schoolmastering and took a small farm near Haverfordwest, in his home county of Pembroke. Within a few months he was dead. His second son, William, was born posthumously in February 1865.

David was less than seventeen months old when his father died, so

1. Speech at Maidenhead, 26 May 1905.
2. The site is in the neighbourhood of the University of Manchester. The plaque is inaccurately worded, referring to Lloyd George as 'Earl of Dwyfor'.

Wales

Railways in the 1890s

Amlwch
Llandudno
Holyhead
Colwyn Bay
Rhyl
ANGLESEY
Beaumaris
Conway
FLINT
St Asaph
Hawarden
Bangor
Llanrwst
DENBIGH
Caernarvon
Snowdon
CAERNARVON
R.Dwyfor
Llangollen
R.Dee
Nevin
Criccieth
Ffestiniog
Corwen
Lleyn Peninsula
Portmadoc
Bala
Lake
Bala
Pwllheli
Harlech
Llanstumdwy
MERIONETH
Barmouth
Dolgelley
Welshpool

Cardigan
Bay

Cemmaes
MONTGOMERY
Machynlleth
R.Severn
Newtown

Aberystwyth
CARDIGAN
RADNOR
Llandrindod Wells
R.Afon Teifi
R.Wye
Lampeter
Builth
Wells
Fishguard
BRECKNOCK
St David's
CARMARTHEN
PEMBROKE
Carmarthen
MONMOUTH
Merthyr Tydfil
Llanelli
GLAMORGAN
Newport
Tenby
Neath
Pontypridd
Caerphilly
Swansea
Port
Talbot
Cardiff

Bristol Channel

Miles
0   10   20   30

N S H

1. Wales

paternal influence, in his case, must have been the work of nature: responsibility for his nurture fell to another man. All the same, what little we know of William George suggests that some of his elder son's most important characteristics were inherited from him. The Georges were yeoman farmers, but William struck out on a new line in deciding to be a teacher. Moreover, he was a Welshman who spent most of his working life outside Wales, in London or Lancashire, returning to Wales for holidays – and to die. While he never abandoned his formal adherence to the Baptist Church, his mind was wide open to other opinions: close friends of his were the Congregational minister and educationist, J. D. Morell, and the eminent Unitarian, James Martineau. He was deeply interested in politics, a formidable arguer and a delightful, witty talker, 'much sought after by all, especially the well-educated families, throughout the whole of North Pembrokeshire'.[1] But he was ill at ease with the English industrial working class. At Newchurch the directors of the school were, he said, 'rough working men who had not the means to act liberally even if disposed to do so – and besides, my temperament is such that I would rather be the master of workpeople than their servant'.[2] Where, perhaps, he most differed from David was in lacking the driving force of ambition – or was it merely that he lacked opportunity? His son William hints, fraternally, at another difference. After recording that his father had an almost morbid addiction to the truth, he adds, 'This particular trait . . . which to a large extent I have inherited, was not, so far as I observed, transmitted in an undiluted state to his son Dafydd.'[3]

Though he had been in poor health for several years, William George's death was sudden. He caught a chill which turned to pneumonia, and died within a week. He was only forty-three (at which age David was to be a Cabinet Minister) and his widow was eight years younger. She was now left among strangers in a strange county, with two small children, another on the way, and no adequate means to support them. So she sent a telegram to her brother, Richard Lloyd, the master-cobbler of Llanystumdwy, and he came at once to Pembrokeshire. After helping them to dispose of their modest possessions he took the family back with him to North Wales, where his home became from then onwards their

1. Herbert du Parcq, *Life of David Lloyd George*, Vol. I, p. 10. The words are quoted from reminiscences by a niece of William George.
2. *Ibid.*, p. 9, quoting a letter from William George (undated).
3. William George, *My Brother and I*, p. 7.

home. To the George children he was the dominant figure in their lives, and to David more especially the man who early recognised his bright promise and spared no effort to make sure that it was fulfilled.

The character of Richard Lloyd – or Uncle Lloyd, as the family called him – has been described with such extreme piety, and with so little discrimination, that its subtler features have been lost to view. Certainly he was a providential guardian and mentor for Lloyd George, and as such deserves high praise. Certainly, too, he was a man of very consider-able virtue, whose Christianity was sincere without being narrow. Yet he was by no means the simple, selfless figure that he has been made out to be. Almost invariably he is presented as a man who sacrificed his own happiness to the task of bringing up his sister's children, and whose pure Christian idealism enabled him to launch Lloyd George on a career not of mere worldly success, but of militant philanthropy. We begin to wonder how the disciple of such a man can have brought himself to be a politician at all, rather than a missionary. The truth is that Uncle Lloyd was *not* such a man: he was both more and less. A proper look at him reveals complexities, even perversities, in his nature, which may impair his credentials as a saint but which add to his interest as a human being. They also help to explain his achievement.

Like the young Georges, he had the misfortune to lose his father at an early age, but there was no 'Uncle Lloyd' in his life and he was brought up by his mother, who was very much the managing type. She ran the little village shoemaking business until he was old enough to take it over. The Lloyds belonged to a Baptist sect of pristine simplicity known as the Disciples of Christ,[1] among whom it was a rule that they should have no paid ministry. When he was a very young man Richard Lloyd became an unpaid minister at the local chapel of the sect, and he stuck to his pastoral duties for nearly sixty years, until his death in 1917. He was a fundamentalist in belief and his personal code was puritan, but his attitude towards others was remarkably free from censoriousness. Him-self a total abstainer and non-smoker, he nevertheless kept away from Temperance meetings and did not lecture backsliders. According to his view of religion, prayer and example counted for more than precept.

Yet he was tolerant of the world not only because he felt that God alone should judge. Another reason was that the world fascinated him.

1. Also known as Campbellites, after the Irish–American revivalist, Alexander Campbell. Lloyd George is not the only political leader to have been a member of the sect. Another was President Lyndon Johnson.

It is impossible to understand him, or his relationship with his elder nephew, without realising that his character was to some extent that of a frustrated politician. As a Welsh patriot, deeply imbued with feeling for the *Gwerin* and all that it was supposed to stand for, he could hardly fail to take some interest in politics, when throughout the Principality the national resurgence was gathering momentum. But Uncle Lloyd's interest went far beyond the vague commitment to Welsh causes that might have been expected of anyone of his type at that particular time. His was the passionate, detailed interest of a connoisseur. During his childhood a schoolmaster had boxed his ears for talking Welsh in school, and for the rest of his life he was partially deaf in one ear. Such an experience must have added a touch of bitterness, however unconscious, to his desire that Wales's dignity should be asserted. Yet it would have been useless for him to enter the political arena himself, even if religion had not also called him. His English was bizarre, and even his Welsh slightly old-fashioned, so he lacked the verbal equipment for democratic politics. In the career of David Lloyd George, however, his political ambitions were vicariously satisfied, and he followed that career with an obsessive, unrelenting interest.

It is naïve to suggest that his devotion to Lloyd George was self-sacrificial. In what parents do for their children, or guardians for their charges, there is nearly always an element of self-gratification; but this was true in a special degree of Uncle Lloyd. The victim, if there was one, was not himself, but his younger nephew, William, who was brought up as an ordinary child while his brother was idolised. William was hardworking, conscientious and, by any normal standards, distinctly talented. It was no fault of his that he could not compete with David's brilliance, and Uncle Lloyd should have been at pains to show at least as much affection towards him as towards David. Instead, he made no secret of his preference for the elder boy, and later even went so far as to prevent William from adding the surname 'Lloyd' to the patronymic 'George' – a supremely wounding act, since it implied that of the two brothers only David was worthy to bear the name that meant so much to them both. While David went out into the world and became a legendary figure, William stayed quietly at home in North Wales, attending to the solicitors' practice which he and David had started together, and ministering reverently to Uncle Lloyd, who lived and died in his house. He must often have compared his lot with that of the dutiful, stay-at-home brother in the parable of the Prodigal Son.

That Uncle Lloyd made such a favourite of David was undoubtedly very hurtful to William, though he would have us believe that he was only a little jealous. Was it also harmful to David? William suggests that it was. 'He was the apple of Uncle Lloyd's eye, the king of the castle and, like the other king, could do no wrong. . . . Whether this unrestrained admiration was wholly good for the lad upon whom it was lavished, and indeed for the man who evolved out of him, is a matter upon which opinions may differ.'[1] Lloyd George himself used to maintain that he needed the unstinted praise and encouragement that Uncle Lloyd gave him, to keep his spirits up. As an old man he told Frances Stevenson that he lacked self-confidence but possessed 'the quality of love of approbation, which to a certain extent supplies the stimulus which lack of self-confidence needs'. Uncle Lloyd, he said, 'realised this failing in him, and for that reason sought to encourage him whenever he did well'.[2] Lloyd George's diffidence was never very obvious to the world at large, but his claim to suffer from it was not intentionally misleading. He *felt* that he was diffident, because the scale of his endeavours was such that even a man of his masterful temperament could hardly fail to have some qualms. A man's appetite for praise is usually as big as the tasks he undertakes, and Lloyd George's 'love of approbation' was proportionate to his ambition. From Uncle Lloyd he received hosannas not merely 'whenever he did well', but at all times. The old man's letters to him are almost without exception fan letters, and they never convey any serious criticism. When the news that David was Prime Minister was brought to Uncle Lloyd, his only comment was: 'The man is greater than his office.'[3]

Less doting treatment of him by the person he most respected might, in theory, have been better for Lloyd George's soul. In practice it would have made little difference, because his respect for Uncle Lloyd was largely conditional upon the latter's moral support for him being as predictable as it was. If that support had ever been withheld, Lloyd George's reaction would surely have been to turn against his uncle rather than to modify his own opinions or his own behaviour. There is an accepted myth that the politician who humbled domestic and foreign foes, and who mobilised the resources of a nation at war, never ceased to defer to the judgement of his first and best counsellor. Lloyd George himself did much to foster the myth. For instance, in a letter to his wife

1. William George, *My Brother and I*, p. 33.
2. Frances Stevenson, *Lloyd George: A Diary*, recording a conversation on 19 March 1934.
3. William George, *My Brother and I*, p. 37.

he said of Uncle Lloyd: 'All that is best in life's struggle I owe to him first. . . . I should not have succeeded even so far as I have were it not for the devotion and shrewdness with which he has without a day's flagging kept me up to the mark. . . . How many times have I done things . . . entirely because I saw from his letters that he expected me to do them. . . .'[1]

In reality, Uncle Lloyd's influence, even when Lloyd George was a child, should not be exaggerated, and his influence over the grown man was almost negligible. Beyond a doubt he stimulated the boy's interest in politics, but this interest itself was innate and the political climate would have stimulated it anyway. Uncle Lloyd encouraged him to read books, and to make an immediate written note of any useful information or idea that might occur to him while he was reading or thinking.[2] For a precocious boy in his teens it was most helpful to be talked to – and perhaps even more helpful to be listened to – for hours on end by an intelligent man who conversed with him on terms of equality. It was from Uncle Lloyd, moreover, that he acquired his lifelong veneration for Abraham Lincoln. When Lincoln was assassinated – very soon after the George children moved to Llanystumdwy – Uncle Lloyd bought a large picture of him and hung it in a place of honour, so that the martyred President became a tutelary presence in the home. The example of a country lawyer rising to national leadership would inevitably have appealed to Lloyd George sooner or later: as it was, he grew up with Lincoln's example vividly in mind.

Finally, Uncle Lloyd always advised him to concentrate his efforts upon the House of Commons – advice which he followed, very largely, during his early years in politics. In other respects, his susceptibility to Uncle Lloyd's influence was more apparent than real. As a reward for the old man's ceaseless adulation he paid him the compliment of pretending to set much store by his opinion; but in fact all that he wanted from Uncle Lloyd was what he unfailingly got – praise, more praise and still more praise.

The women in Lloyd George's childhood are shadowy figures compared with his uncle, but they evidently doted on him too. Uncle Lloyd

1. David Lloyd George to Margaret Lloyd George, 16 August 1902 (National Library of Wales). This letter was written from abroad, and obviously intended to be shown to Uncle Lloyd.
2. This habit, useful to Lloyd George as a politician, was also recommended by Samuel Butler to authors. 'The literary instinct may be known by a man's keeping a small notebook in his waistcoat pocket, into which he jots down anything that strikes him, or any good thing that he hears said, or a reference to any passage which he thinks will come in useful to him.' (*The Way of All Flesh*, ch. LXXIII.)

never married, but his mother, Rebecca, lived until 1868 and had time to initiate David into the habit of going for long walks, which he held to for the rest of his life. She would never allow him to be scolded. After Rebecca Lloyd's death, Elizabeth George kept house for her brother. She was rather frail and later became diabetic, but she looked after David well – perhaps too well. According to Frances Stevenson, she 'spoiled him – waited on him – he could never find his socks – and apparently was never made to do so'.[1] He remained extraordinarily helpless in small ways. A. J. Sylvester, his secretary for many years, has written: 'L.G. was one of the most clumsy of men when doing anything with his hands. He could never open a window at No. 10 without hurting his fingers, and although he must have passed to and from the dining-room thousands of times, he was never able to open the door himself. Always he would seize the knob and try to turn it the wrong way. This would go on for a few minutes until, finally losing his temper, he would stand and rattle the door until someone came to open it for him.'[2]

In 1917, visiting his old home with Lord Riddell, Lloyd George described his mother: 'Rather a small woman but with a good figure. She had a very soft sweet voice. She was a proud woman. The village boys used to go weed-picking for sixpence. I was anxious to join them, but she would never let me do so.' Had she a sense of humour? 'Yes, she could enjoy a joke, but she was shattered by my father's death. She never recovered. She was a very serious woman.'[3] A friend of the family remembered 'her calm face, meditative, extremely kind' and 'her slow, distinguished speech'. She was 'a gentlewoman in every gesture'.[4] Though she took little interest in politics, she was naturally pleased to see her son elected to Parliament, and twice re-elected. She died in 1896.

Llanystumdwy is a small village built on either side of a fast-flowing stream, the Dwyfor, which rises in the hills ten miles away and reaches the sea about a mile beyond the village. The focal point is an old stone bridge carrying the Criccieth-to-Pwllheli road across the Dwyfor, and Richard Lloyd's home was on the right-hand side of the road coming from Criccieth, a couple of hundred yards from the bridge. It was (and is) a two-up, three-down cottage with an adjoining workshop, and behind

1. Frances Stevenson, op. cit., p. 253.   2. A. J. Sylvester, The Real Lloyd George, p. 48.
3. Lord Riddell's War Diary, from the entry for 21 September 1917.
4. D. R. Daniel, unpublished memoirs of David Lloyd George (D. R. Daniel MSS., N.L.W.). Translated from the Welsh by Dr Prys Morgan.

it a fair-sized garden or orchard containing an earth closet which the family nick-named 'House of Lords'. The cottage itself is called 'Highgate'.[1] On the strength of his childhood spent there Lloyd George's rise to greatness was seen as the dawn of a new age, that of 'the cottage-bred man'. By English standards, however, the term was grossly misleading, because in England at that date a boy bred in a cottage would normally have been the son of an agricultural labourer. It was not until 1940, when Ernest Bevin became the second most powerful man in the country, that the cottage-bred man, in the English sense, came into his own.

Uncle Lloyd was very far from being an agricultural labourer. He was a master-craftsman, the Hans Sachs of Llanystumdwy, employing two or more hands in his workshop.[2] In addition to his earnings from the business, and to any savings that he and his mother may have had, Elizabeth George had an investment income of about £46 a year (roughly equivalent to £335 a year today). The family was probably the best-off in Llanystumdwy. Like Sachs, moreover, Uncle Lloyd was respected throughout the neighbourhood for his wisdom and integrity. People would see his lamp burning late at night and would know that he was still reading when others were asleep. During working hours, too, he always kept a book beside him, and he could easily he distracted from cobbling by a talkative friend or customer. Discussion was the breath of life to him. He presided over the informal village debating society which used to meet in the blacksmith's shop. The Lloyds were held in honour as a long-established local family: they were good stock. Richard Lloyd's grandfather[3] had been a friend of the major Welsh literary figures of his time, and Llanystumdwy was then the centre of cultural life in South Caernarvonshire. But Richard was honoured above all for his own merits. Among the literate, aspiring, nationally minded Welshmen of the district he was an uncrowned king, and his favourite nephew had the status, in their eyes, of a crown prince. He was known as 'David Lloyd' and much was expected of him.

Not long after his arrival at Llanystumdwy he started going to the

1. It now belongs to a trust administered by members of the Lloyd George family.
2. 'There were generally two men in the workshop. . . .' (William George, *My Brother and I*, p. 20). 'Richard Lloyd and his father before him had been master shoemakers, employing two or three workmen.' (Herbert du Parcq, *op. cit.*, Vol. I, p. 14.) '. . . he actually had a considerable shoe-making business, employing five hands. Some of these travelled through the Caernarvonshire countryside taking orders for the yearly requirements of many farms.' (Richard Lloyd George, *Dame Margaret*, p. 74.)
3. David Lloyd (Dafydd Llwyd), 1800–39.

village school – a short walk from 'Highgate', just the other side of the bridge. He was still under four when he went to school, and his brother William followed two years later.[1] The school was run by the Established Church – it was a 'National' school – but in education the character of an institution is never as important as the effect of an individual teacher, and Lloyd George's headmaster, David Evans, was a teacher of superlative quality. He was a good Latin and Greek scholar, as well as a sound mathematician, and he had a special interest in astronomy. But his outstanding gift was for holding the attention of the young and for arousing their enthusiasm. He could tell stories from the Bible in such a way that they came thrillingly alive to his audience, and it was doubtless from him that Lloyd George learned the narrative and mimetic techniques with which he later enthralled his own children – and many others. Teaching at the school was exclusively in English, and the subjects taught were Scripture, of course, and 'mainly the three Rs with a little geography and history thrown in. The elements of algebra and Euclid were taught in the upper standards.'[2] Lloyd George did so well in the infant class that at the age of seven he was promoted straight to the second standard, jumping over the first. Five years later he reached the seventh standard – the highest in elementary schools – but when he was thirteen he and two other boys received advanced tuition from David Evans in a class designated 7x. They sat at a table close to the headmaster's desk, so that he could keep in constant touch with their work. 'No pupil,' said Lloyd George in 1909, 'ever had a finer teacher'; and David Evans returned the Chancellor of the Exchequer's compliment: 'No teacher ever had a more apt pupil. He was always particularly good at doing sums; and now he is doing the big sum which we all have to pay!'[3]

Lloyd George was once asked by his elder son, when did he first become aware that he was 'a genius'? He replied, half-humorously, that the idea struck him, as a boy, while reading Euclid in the top branches of an oak tree.[4] Bertrand Russell found his first encounter with Euclid, at the age of eleven, 'as dazzling as first love',[5] and Lloyd George may have had a rather similar experience. Of course he was nowhere near Russell's class as a mathematician, but he was, all the same, a more efficient calculating machine than some of his political colleagues were

1. Their sister, Mary – or Polly, as they called her – went for a time to the village school, but was later removed from it and sent to a private school at Criccieth.
2. William George, *My Brother and I*, p. 39.   3. W. Watkin Davies, *op. cit.*, p. 16.
4. Richard Lloyd George, *Lloyd George*, p. 15.
5. Bertrand Russell, *Autobiography*, Vol. I, p. 36.

1a. Lloyd George's father, William George

1b. His mother, born Elizabeth Lloyd

c. His birthplace, 5 New York Place, Chorlton-upon-Medlock, Manchester, painted by L. S. Lowry

2a. Richard Lloyd ('Uncle Lloyd')

2b. David Lloyd George at the age of sixteen

2c. 'Highgate', Llanystumdwy – the cottage in which Lloyd George grew up (Richard Lloyd's workshop in the foreground)

prepared to admit.[1] Mathematics was definitely one of his best subjects. Another was geography: foreign countries always fascinated him and when he had the chance he soon became addicted to travel. History appealed to him, and he read a number of major historical works during his youth, including Macaulay's *History of England*, Rollin's *Ancient History* and Gibbon's *Decline and Fall of the Roman Empire*. He also became familiar with some of the classic works of fiction, especially Dickens's novels and Victor Hugo's *Les Misérables* (which, apart from the Bible, was probably the book which most deeply influenced him).[2] Napoleon bulked large in his imagination, as in Hugo's. There were a few well-thumbed books at 'Highgate', some belonging to Uncle Lloyd and some which had belonged to Lloyd George's father. The boy was encouraged to read, and one of his contemporaries described him as 'quite a book-worm'.[3] He was a rather slow reader, but – when he had the will to learn – a very quick learner. And whatever he learned, he was likely to retain. He had the ability to concentrate, a tenacious memory, a lively fancy and rare independence of mind. These were his paramount intellectual qualities, and they appeared early.

Proof of his independence of mind was his rejection, in childhood, of the religious beliefs with which he and all around him were indoctrinated. Llanystumdwy contained three places of worship – the Anglican church, a Congregational chapel and a Calvinistic Methodist chapel – but Uncle Lloyd's Disciples of Christ used to meet in a very small building at Penymaes, in the outskirts of Criccieth well over a mile away. On Sundays the family attended three services there, morning, afternoon and evening, covering the distance to and fro on foot. Even William George admits that they must have felt 'rather disgruntled'[4] at the way they spent their Sundays, though his orthodoxy was never seriously shaken and that of his sister, Mary, remained exceptionally strict, even bigoted. It was very different with David. When he was twelve his uncle baptised him in the little brook that runs beside the Penymaes chapel,[5] but during the night that followed he experienced a negative revelation. 'He meditated upon what he had done and confessed, his eyes staring

---

1. Loulou Harcourt said that he 'used figures as adjectives' – a remark which could have been meant as a compliment (because adjectives, like figures, may be exact or inexact), but which Harcourt, who disliked Lloyd George, certainly meant as a sneer.
2. He read it in Wilbur's translation, published by Routledge, price one shilling.
3. Quoted in J. Hugh Edwards, *David Lloyd George*, p. 26.
4. William George, *My Brother and I*, p. 33.
5. The chapel is now falling into ruins and the brook is choked with weeds.

into darkness, and saw all the heaven of his doctrine and his religious imagination of yore being shut before him. . . .'[1] He jumped out of bed and 'felt like a man who has been suddenly struck blind and is groping for the way. . . .'[2] We need not suppose that it all happened in one night, any more than that St Paul was immediately converted on the road to Damascus. The process of gaining or losing faith is usually gradual. All the same, it may be crystallised at a particular time and place, even when the person involved is much less given to self-dramatisation than a St Paul or a Lloyd George. The night of the soul which Lloyd George went through after his baptism made fully apparent to him something about himself of which he must already have had strong intimations.

After a time he confided his loss of faith to Uncle Lloyd who – to his surprise – 'was not in the least shocked, but seemed to understand perfectly well'.[3] Could there have been a small particle of the frustrated sceptic in Uncle Lloyd as well as a great deal of the frustrated politician? Whatever the truth about that, Lloyd George himself never returned to the original fold. He would gladly attend a chapel service to hear a good preacher, or to sing Welsh hymns. He was attracted by the Gospels, as by other Bible stories, but to him the founder of Christianity was a prophet of social reform rather than a personal redeemer. He accepted the Christian ethical code as a rough-and-ready guide to earthly conduct, but Christ for him had no supernatural authority. He could say that he had 'the religious temperament' – quickly adding that he would not be able to write down what his religious convictions were.[4] But his temperament was not, in fact, religious. He was a one-world-at-a-time man, living intensely in the present but lacking the transcendental sense. The deism that he returned to, after a short period of total atheism, was inspired by reading Carlyle's *Sartor Resartus*, and his attitude towards Jesus was finally shaped by Renan's *Vie de Jésus*. Prayer meant nothing to him, and his belief in God was only a vague belief in Destiny, which gave a semblance of meaning to history and, therefore, to his own career. It is no wonder that a man whose spiritual luggage was so light should have failed to hold the allegiance of British Nonconformists to the end of his days. The wonder is that he ever succeeded in becoming, as he did for a time, their acknowledged leader and champion.

The oddity of his position never unduly troubled his conscience, however, partly because it was not that sort of conscience, but also

1. D. R. Daniel, *op cit.*   2. Frances Stevenson, *op. cit.*, p. 77.   3. *Loc. cit.*
4. D. R. Daniel, *op. cit.*

because he regarded free thought as a logical extension of Nonconformity. Moreover, so long as he was chiefly concerned with Welsh affairs, he was able to identify Nonconformity with the national cause. The Established Church was a convenient target for attack, since it could plausibly be made to seem more obscurantist than any Dissenting Church, and anyway it was 'foreign'.

The most famous incident of Lloyd George's childhood was a demonstration against the Established Church, and it foreshadows many incidents in his adult political life. The school at Llanystumdwy being an Anglican foundation, there was an annual ceremony at which the children, nearly all of whom were from Nonconformist homes, were examined in the Creed and Catechism, with diocesan bigwigs present as well as the local parson and gentry. One year Lloyd George, who had heard his uncle inveigh against this ceremony,[1] organised his schoolfellows in a conspiracy of silence. When they were asked to recite the Creed, they all stayed dumb. The parson commanded, the headmaster commanded, but still they would not speak. Such a show of insubordination was disconcerting to the platform party and acutely embarrassing to poor David Evans. The ritual was not of his making but he had a job to do and he deserved better of the children than to be made to look foolish in front of his superiors. Eventually William George took pity on him and broke the silence with 'I believe'. All the others joined in – except David. He was furious at their weak-minded surrender and (according to one version) gave his brother a sound thrashing afterwards.[2] His treatment of the headmaster shows how well-equipped he already was with one quality most necessary in a controversialist – willingness to go all out for a public cause regardless of private interests and feelings. The demonstration achieved its object, in spite of apparent failure. The school managers never again required Nonconformist children to say the Creed.

Among those who witnessed the scene was Ellis Nanney, of Gwynfryn Castle, whose estate was the largest in the immediate neighbourhood of

---

1. The Lloyd children were the only Baptists in the village and it was a special grievance that they had to say they had received their names at baptism – though they were not yet baptised.

2. J. Hugh Edwards, *David Lloyd George: the Man and the Statesman*, Vol. I, p. 30. This version is corroborated by W. Watkin Davies, *op. cit.*, p. 25: 'The thrashing which he administered afterwards to his weak-kneed brother is remembered by the latter with terror down to this day.' But when William George came to write his own account of the incident (*My Brother and I*, pp. 42–4) he made no mention of the thrashing. Pride may have caused him to suppress what he was certainly best qualified to remember.

Llanystumdwy. He was a harmless, rather silly man, but to Lloyd George he was the embodiment of the anglicised landlord class that he detested. They were to meet again. Lloyd George's hatred of parsons and landlords might suggest that he was ill-natured, but actually his disposition was genial. Human beings of all kinds aroused his curiosity, and he was nearly always ready to be on good personal terms with an opponent. He was often ruthless, but seldom rancorous. His contemporaries admired his daredevilry – he stood up to bullies and was a leader on poaching expeditions[1] – but they also liked him for his high spirits and companion-ableness. Wherever he was, he could be relied on to enter into things with zest and to make the most of any opportunities for enjoyment. Yet at heart he found life at Llanystumdwy increasingly tedious. In later years he would speak of the 'terrible boredom' of his childhood, and he used to say that he would rather die than go back to it.[2] It was, in fact, only to die that he eventually returned to the village. When he felt his strength ebbing he settled there again, chose the site for his grave – over-looking the Dwyfor, where it rushes towards the bridge through a wooded ravine[3] – and chose a big boulder for his gravestone. But seventy years earlier he was thinking only of life, and of living it more abundantly. Llanystumdwy bored him; the world beckoned him.

He was offered a pupil-teachership at the school, with the added inducement that he would not at the outset be obliged to become a member of the Established Church. But Lloyd George's talents were not to be confined, like his father's, within a classroom. The Law seemed a suitable profession for him, with his quick wits and agile tongue, but to pass the Law Preliminary Examination he needed an adequate knowledge of two foreign languages. Latin counted as one of them, but the other decided on was French, which he studied at home through the medium of *Cassell's Popular Educator*, with Uncle Lloyd acting as his tutor and keeping one step ahead of him in the course. In November 1877 he went to Liverpool to sit the examination and a few weeks later heard that he had passed.[4] He was then introduced by one of his uncle's

---

1. Poaching was then the favourite recreational activity of rural Wales, to which the national revival gave patriotic overtones.
2. Frances Stevenson, *op. cit.*, p. 77.
3. The view from the grave has been marred by ugly new building in the fields opposite and by a concrete footbridge whose straight lines cut across the arches of the old bridge.
4. But he never learned to *speak* French or any foreign language (except English). One of the most disastrous mistakes of his career – his ardent support of General Nivelle in 1917 – was probably influenced by the fact that Nivelle spoke good English.

friends to a firm of solicitors, Messrs Breese, Jones and Casson, at Portmadoc, the next town east beyond Criccieth. In the summer of 1878 he started work with the firm, and early in 1879 – just after his sixteenth birthday – he was articled to the junior partner, Randal Casson. His family paid between £80 and £100 for his articles. At first he lived in lodgings at Portmadoc, returning to Llanystumdwy at weekends; but the following year Uncle Lloyd gave up his shoemaking business and the family moved to Criccieth. David was then able to live at home again, and to travel to work from Criccieth, by train or on foot. His mood as he turned his back on Llanystumdwy is well caught in the diary that he had begun to keep:

> May 9th 1880 – To Llanystumdwy. Slept there for the last time – perhaps – for ever.
>
> May 10th 1880 – Left Llanystumdwy without a feeling of regret, remorse or longing.[1]

1. Quoted in William George, *My Brother and I*, p. 73.

TWO
Fever of Renown

The town of Criccieth, which was Lloyd George's Welsh home for the greater part of his life, looks northward to Snowdonia and southward across the wide sweep of Cardigan Bay. It is an ancient borough with an essentially Victorian character. The dignified ruin of the castle – one of five built by Edward I to keep North Wales in subjection[1] – presides over a cluster of solid buildings mostly dating from the nineteenth century. Later accretions have left the visual impact of Criccieth very much what it must have been in Lloyd George's youth. The castle rock stands between two long beaches which have helped to give the town its modern prosperity. The British seaside first became fashionable during the Napoleonic wars, when people of money and leisure were temporarily cut off from the Continent. Such people were not very numerous at the beginning of the century, but their numbers grew rapidly as the industrial, commercial and professional bourgeoisie came into its own. A fashion set by the few was then, as usual, followed by the many, and scores of British seaside resorts were developed to cater for the mass of summer holiday-makers. North Wales was a natural playground for Lancashire and the West Midlands, but many people came there from further afield, attracted by the mountains as well as by a pleasant coast. The railway reached Criccieth in 1865, bringing a regular flow of visitors, including some who might be interesting for reasons other than their money. When Uncle Lloyd moved to Criccieth the family took in lodgers at their new home, Morvin House, during the summer season, and one of them was Rider Haggard (from whom David Lloyd George may have received his first

1. The others are Harlech, Caernarvon, Beaumaris and Conway.

colourful impressions of South Africa). Compared with Llanystumdwy Criccieth was quite a lively place, where an imaginative boy could feel, at least for part of the year, that he had some slight contact with the outside world.

Portmadoc, however, was a much livelier place, at the time when Lloyd George was working there. Named after its founder, the philanthropist W. A. Madocks – who, in the early nineteenth century, built a cob across the Glaslyn estuary, reclaiming thousands of acres of land – Portmadoc became a flourishing port and shipyard, where schooners of between a hundred and two hundred tons were launched to carry slates from the quarries at Blaenau Ffestiniog to ports in Northern Europe, such as Hamburg and Bremen. There the ships took on coal, with which they sailed to Italian ports; from Italy they crossed the Atlantic to Newfoundland with cargoes of salt; and from Newfoundland they returned home to Portmadoc with cargoes of dried codfish. In the streets of the little town Lloyd George was able to talk to men who had actually been to places that he had only read about in books or newspapers. Their first-hand accounts did something to satisfy his curiosity, while they also increased his *Wanderlust*. The eventual triumph of steam over sail, and the decline of the slate industry, reduced Portmadoc to comparative insignificance. Today it is just a tourist resort and a place to which people retire, like Criccieth. Madocks's cob is still the connecting link between Merionethshire and Caernarvonshire, over which motor-cars stream throughout the summer; and the light railway still crosses it on the way to Blaenau Ffestiniog, though the trains no longer bring loads of slate to a busy harbour. The harbour is long since dead, and Portmadoc has become an inward-looking town. But when Lloyd George was working there as an articled clerk it was still in its heyday as a trading and shipbuilding centre, and many local residents had part of their savings invested in its fleet of sailing ships.[1]

The office of Messrs Breese, Jones and Casson is a detached, mock-Tudor building in the main street of Portmadoc, on the edge of a small public garden. This was Lloyd George's place of work for over four years.

1. The British merchant service was slow to make the change from sail to steam. It was not until two years after Lloyd George was born that the amount of steam tonnage added to the U.K. register of shipping for the first time exceeded the amount of sailing tonnage in a single year. And for quite a long time the overall preponderance of sailing ships remained. In the eighteen-nineties Lloyd George's elder son could still count 'as many as thirty' of the Portmadoc windjammers 'making their way in and out of the bay at one time'. (Richard Lloyd George, *Dame Margaret*, p. 53.)

Sitting on a high stool he applied himself to a variety of humdrum tasks which, however irksome at the time, were of considerable value to him later. He became intimately acquainted with the legal aspects of rating, mortgages, fire insurance and other such mundane business – important to ordinary citizens – of which very few Parliamentarians of the period had a more than superficial knowledge. He was also initiated into the art of drafting legal documents, and received some practice in the even more subtle art of dealing personally with clients. 'We should study people as well as their conveniences,' he was soon noting in his diary, '. . . Let me try to make myself more affable towards everyone. . . . Clients are not to be gained by a "hitherto-thou-shalt-come-and-no-further" mien and attitude.'[1] His natural affability, enhanced by conscious effort, made him well liked not only by clients, but also by his principal, Randal Casson, who much enjoyed his company and treated him as a crony. William George, who followed his brother into the firm, contrasted the principal's demeanour towards himself – that of 'a standoffish headmaster in a posh private school' towards 'a shy country lad' – with the 'dining, gossiping, present-giving friendship' that existed between Casson and David.[2]

This friendship did not long survive David Lloyd George's emergence as a fully fledged solicitor. He passed his Intermediate examination in 1881, and his Final in 1884, after which he clearly expected to be taken into partnership. But Casson's attitude was 'hitherto-thou-shalt-come-and-no-further'. He regarded Lloyd George as a friend, but not yet as an equal – in the firm, at any rate. The most that he would offer was the position of managing clerk at the firm's Dolgelley branch. From a normal point of view the offer was tempting, because the family savings had been spent on the boys' legal education, and the Dolgelley job would have been quite a responsible one, with adequate pay and prospects, for a young man of just twenty-one. But Lloyd George did not want to go to Dolgelley. He wanted to get on, and quickly. Above all, he wanted to be his own master. So he decided to set up on his own, risking ignominious failure but also gambling on the chance of early, independent success. At first he worked from a back room of his home at Criccieth, with his brass plate displayed outside the front door. But soon his practice was based on Portmadoc, with branch offices at Pwllheli, Criccieth and Ffestiniog. And he got a certain amount of work in more distant places, even in England (through the Welsh expatriate network). William had the in-

1. Diary entry for 24 September 1879. Quoted in William George, *My Brother and I*, p. 108.
2. William George, *My Brother and I*, p. 121.

vidious experience of serving out his apprenticeship under a man who now saw Lloyd George as a professional rival, no longer as a friend. But when William in turn qualified as a solicitor (in 1887), he at once joined his brother in the firm, which thereafter went under the name of Lloyd George and George.

Whereas William qualified with first-class honours, David obtained only third-class honours. The difference, of course, was a measure not of their relative abilities, but of the elder brother's relative lack of interest in the Law. From the very beginning his passionate, overriding interest was politics. He was just old enough to remember the famous general election of 1868, which, thanks in part to Disraeli's Reform Act of the previous year, broke the Tory Party's traditional ascendancy in Wales. Out of thirty-three Welsh constituencies, twenty-three returned Members owing allegiance to the Liberal Party (though nearly all of them were, in fact, Liberals of the conservative, Whiggish sort). In Caernarvonshire a Liberal defeated the son of Lord Penrhyn, the local slate magnate. But voting was not yet secret, and after the election many tenant-farmers who had voted 'the wrong way' were evicted by their Tory landlords. This crassly oppressive behaviour intensified the feeling of Welsh patriots like Uncle Lloyd. Secrecy of the ballot was established by law in 1872, but in spite of it the deterrent effect of the evictions may have taken a little time to wear off. For this reason, perhaps, among others, the Liberals suffered an appreciable setback at the election of 1874. But the reaction was only an eddy in the current, not a reversal of it, and by the time Lloyd George was growing up conditions in Wales favoured another forward surge by the Liberals.

As a solicitor's clerk he was able to do some political work under the auspices of the firm, because the senior partner, Breese, was Liberal agent for Merionethshire and part of Caernarvonshire, and he made use of Lloyd George for registration and canvassing in the area. At the 1880 election all but four of the Welsh seats fell to the Liberals, and in November of that year Lloyd George's first newspaper article was published. He sent it in to the *North Wales Express*, where it appeared under his chosen pen-name of 'Brutus'.[1] The occasion for it was a recent speech at Taunton by Lord Salisbury, who was soon to succeed Disraeli as leader of the

---

1. There was a distinguished Welsh precedent for the use of this pseudonym. David Owen (1795–1866) was a well-known journalist and man of letters who wrote under the name of 'Brutus'. Ironically, he was a Baptist who reverted to the Established Church. He also attacked the Welsh language.

Conservative Party. The article begins with a general denunciation of Salisbury, in the quaint idiom of an adolescent experimenting with a foreign language:

> He is a relic of what he has been; the ruins of a character which, if not noble, at least seemed to be stable. . . . The prejudice and rancour of his unalloyed Toryism he still retains, but the consistency and integrity of character which whilom graced these propensities have departed.

In substance, this opening passage is fairly routine stuff, and so is the criticism of various remarks or phrases picked out of the speech, which occupies most of the rest of the article. All the more astonishing, therefore, is the final paragraph:

> Toryism has not been barren of statesmen – real and not charlatan – statesmen who prized the honour of England above the interests of party – who really hated oppression and demonstrated their detestation of it, not by pleading immunity from condign punishment for the instigation of foul and atrocious crimes, but by the laudable assistance which they rendered in the name of England to weak nationalities in their desperate struggles for Liberty – for freedom from the yoke of inhuman despots – for very existence. By so much was the Canning of ancient Toryism superior, nobler than the Salisbury of modern Conservatism.

Many who have written about Lloyd George have failed to mark either the extraordinary precocity of those words, or their startling relevance to his future career. The author was a seventeen-year-old boy, whose only formal education had been at an elementary school in a remote provincial village. True, he was widely read for someone of his age, and had been given every encouragement at home to study and improve his mind. As a child, he had discussed politics often and at length with Uncle Lloyd: there cannot have been many scions of the traditional ruling class who had been given as much opportunity to do so by their parents or guardians. All the same, Uncle Lloyd's knowledge was limited and his prejudices were strong. Tolerant he might be of error, even of sin, but he was quick to recognise both, and he had little doubt that the Conservative Party was a force of evil. Hatred of Toryism, and a highly coloured, demonological view of the Tory record, were almost obligatory among Welshmen of the type surrounding Lloyd George during his early years. That his own view was clearly more subtle and discriminating is further evidence of his power, even as a boy, to resist brainwashing. Just as he was able to question the religious orthodoxy of his environment, so was he able to question at least one facet of its political orthodoxy as well.

The passage quoted may suggest that, to him, the only good Tory was a dead Tory; but it also shows that, unlike most radicals, he could see redeeming features in the history of the Tory Party. It is striking that he chooses Canning as his example of what is praiseworthy in the Tory tradition – Canning who called a new world into existence to redress the balance of the old. In one sense that policy came to fulfilment when Lloyd George himself was Prime Minister. There is another anticipation of things to come when the future champion of the Boers and Belgians refers to the struggle of 'weak nationalities' for their liberty and survival. But the most pregnant reference of all is to 'statesmen who prized the honour of England' (England, incidentally, not Britain) 'above the interests of party'. There we catch a very early glimpse of the man who, in 1910, proposed a party truce to enable vital issues to be settled in the national interest; who, from 1916 to 1922, led a Coalition Government in war and peace; and who, for all his lifelong addiction to political argument, was never really satisfied with the slogans and oversimplifications of party. Historians have tended to interpret Lloyd George's career as a progression from narrow Welsh nationalism to world statesmanship. The interpretation is false. He *started* with a broad outlook, and with a number of basic ideas which remained remarkably constant throughout a long life. He always cared about Wales, but only in the much bigger context of United Kingdom and Imperial politics. His apparent preoccupation with Welsh affairs during the first phase of his career reflects a shrewd eye for tactics rather than a parochial mentality. It is surely most revealing that his first exercise in political journalism should have been an attack, not upon some local Welsh politician, but upon a major national and international figure.[1]

In November 1881 he paid his first visit to London. The occasion for it was his Intermediate Law exam, but he stayed on for a little sightseeing. The new electric light at Charing Cross station rather disappointed him ('sort of pale blue melancholy but unquestionably stronger than gas'[2]), and he also found the Houses of Parliament disappointing – understandably, because it was a Saturday and there were no politicians

1. The whole article is printed in Herbert du Parcq, *Life of David Lloyd George*, Vol. I, pp. 35–6.
2. Diary entry for 10 November 1881, quoted in William George, *My Brother and I*, p. 116.

around. What he saw was only a stage-set without actors. Yet his imagination brought life to the scene, and some inkling of a future star.

> Grand buildings outside, but inside they are crabbed, small and suffocating, especially the House of Commons. I will not say but that I eyed the assembly in a spirit similar to that in which William the Conqueror eyed England on his visit to Edward the Confessor, as the region of his future domain. Oh, vanity![1]

Lloyd George was eighteen at the time, with three years to go before he was a qualified solicitor; yet he was already dreaming of supreme power. Two months later he made his first speech at the Portmadoc debating society, on the payment of compensation to Irish landlords. When he sat down the chairman said: 'I do not know whether that was Mr George's maiden speech, but to say the least it was a very fair one.' Towards the end of 1882 he made a speech at the society which was reported with high commendation in the *North Wales Express*, and of which the *Caernarvon Herald* wrote that 'it would probably have gained praise had it been delivered in the House of Commons'. The speech was an indictment of Gladstone's policy in Egypt – the recent bombardment of Alexandria and the suppression by military force of Arabi Pasha's nationalist rebellion. It was not the use of force as such that Lloyd George denounced, but the wrongful purpose for which it had been used on that occasion. He was never a pacifist. Indeed, throughout his life he was fascinated by war, and he had already joined the local Volunteers.[2] When he later opposed the Boer War he did so not *a priori* because it was a war, but because he held it to be unjust and impolitic.

The extent to which he was recognised as a coming man even before he was of age is well illustrated by a feature which appeared in the *Caernarvon Herald* on 2 June 1883. Various people well known locally were presented to the readers with suitable quotations. Lloyd George

1. Diary entry for 12 November 1881, quoted in Herbert du Parcq, *op. cit.*, Vol. I, p. 40. According to Mr W. R. P. George, the entry no longer forms part of the original manuscript that he possesses. Du Parcq may perhaps have lost it while he was working on the family documents, but we can safely say that he could not have invented it.

2. The Volunteer Force was brought into being in 1860, when there was a war scare between Britain and France. Under the Cardwell reforms ten years later it was combined with other reserve forces, liable only for home service, in a comprehensive system based upon regimental districts throughout the country. A Volunteer was unpaid, but his uniform and equipment were provided. Lloyd George kept his uniform at Portmadoc so as not to offend Uncle Lloyd's anti-militarist feelings.

was one of them, and the quotation attached to his name was a verse
from Dr Johnson:

> When first the college rolls receive his name,
> The young enthusiast quits his ease for fame,
> Resistless burns the fever of renown,
> Caught from the strong contagion of the gown.

On which the 'young enthusiast' commented in his diary: 'titbit poetry . . .
referring to my thirst for renown etc. Perhaps (?) it will be gratified. I
believe it depends entirely on what forces of pluck and *industry* I can
muster.'[1]

In April 1884 he was in London again for his Final exam, and this time
he was able to witness a debate in the House of Commons, in which Lord
Randolph Churchill made one of his cheeky forays against Gladstone.
The spectacle naturally delighted Lloyd George, whose temperament
bore some resemblance to Lord Randolph's, and whose technique as a
Parliamentarian was unmistakably influenced by his.

When he started to practise as an independent solicitor – at the beginning
of 1885 – Lloyd George had three big advantages (apart from his native
talent): he was already well known in the neighbourhood, he had good
contacts through Uncle Lloyd, and he had some experience of public
speaking. Solicitors have the right to plead at petty sessions and in the
county courts, and Lloyd George brought to that side of his work the
forensic skill which he had already, in some measure, acquired as a
member of the Portmadoc and Criccieth debating societies,[2] and even in
discussions at the Llanystumdwy smithy. It is often suggested that he
graduated to the art of political advocacy from his experience as a legal
advocate. In fact, it was the other way round: he had spoken many times
on politics before he ever opened his mouth in a court of law. All the
same, from the moment he started practising on his own his legal interests began to react very favourably upon his political interests, and
vice versa. Between 1885 and 1890 it is virtually impossible to separate
Lloyd George the solicitor from Lloyd George the politician. Even as an
articled clerk he found that his work quite often had a political content.
When he became a practising attorney the overlap was much greater,
mainly because breaches of the law at the expense of landlords or the

1. Diary entry for 2 June 1883, quoted in Herbert du Parcq, *op. cit.*, Vol. I, p. 42.
2. He was chairman of the Criccieth debating society.

Established Church were regarded, in Wales, as acts of political defiance, and because successful pleading on behalf of some 'patriotic' law-breaker could give his attorney the status of a hero in Welsh eyes.

Most lawyers, however, had no inclination to be heroes. They were ready enough to earn their fees, ready enough to make their names, but not so ready to incur the displeasure of magistrates who were also their social superiors. George Borrow, walking through Wales in the mid-eighteen-fifties, met an attorney at Machynlleth who had come some distance to defend a man accused of spearing a salmon. The man was a local tenant-farmer whose landlord (a peer) presided over the bench which tried him. Fishing in the river belonged to another big landlord. Evidence against the farmer was given by two gamekeepers, who were also brothers. They deposed that they had been hiding behind a bush near the river a little before daylight, had watched the accused drive some cattle across the river, attended by a dog, and had then seen him put a spear on a stick, run back to the river and spear a salmon. After this, according to the witnesses, they ran forward and asked the man what he was doing. He threw the salmon and spear into the river and told them to go away. Borrow was admitted to the court and heard the attorney cross-question the witnesses, who were manifestly shifty and unreliable. They had been unable to recover the spear or the salmon, and they contradicted each other on one material point. But in essence they stuck to their unlikely story, which included asserting that the farmer was unaware of their presence before he speared the salmon. As the attorney was preparing to sit down, Borrow whispered to him: 'Why don't you mention the dog? Wouldn't the dog have been likely to have scented the fellows out even if they had been behind the bush?' But the attorney answered with a sigh: 'No, no! twenty dogs would be of no use here. It's no go – I shall leave the case as it is.' The accused was found guilty and fined £4 with costs.[1]

This sort of case often came Lloyd George's way, but he never resigned himself to defeat, as Borrow's attorney did. His policy was always to stand up to magistrates and, if necessary, to treat them with studied insolence. Of course, the passage of thirty years and the changed political atmosphere made it easier for him to act in that manner. All the same, his own contemporaries regarded his audacity as quite exceptional, and he was much admired for it. One of his first cases was defending a poacher at Portmadoc: he failed to get the man off but was complimented by the

1. George Borrow, *Wild Wales*, ch. 78.

chairman of the bench on his 'very able speech'.[1] His most pyrotechnical poaching case was in 1889, when he defended four quarrymen accused in front of the Caernarvon county magistrates of unlawful net-fishing in the Nantlle lower lake. The men had undoubtedly been fishing there with a net, but it was open to question whether the lake could be defined as a 'river' within the meaning of the Act, and it was also said that the public had been allowed to fish there for many years past. Lloyd George maintained that the bench had no jurisdiction, and when the chairman replied that this would have to be proved in a higher court, the following exchange occurred:

Mr George: Yes, sir, and in a perfectly just and unbiased court, too.
The Chairman: If that remark of Mr George's is meant as a reflection upon any magistrate sitting on this bench, I hope he will name him. A more insulting and ungentlemanly remark to the bench I never heard during the course of my experience as a magistrate.
Mr George: But a more true remark was never made in a court of justice.
The Chairman: Tell me to whom you are referring. I must insist upon you referring to any magistrate or magistrates sitting in this court.
Mr George: I refer to you in particular, sir.

The chairman then left the bench in a huff, and three of his colleagues did the same; but a little later they came back again and the case proceeded under a new chairman, without any apology having been extracted from Lloyd George. Two of the quarrymen were acquitted and the other two received token fines.[2] The episode recalls a much-quoted exchange between a county court judge and F. E. Smith, when the judge said: 'You are extremely offensive, young man', and F.E. replied: 'As a matter of fact we both are; the only difference between us is that I'm trying to be and you can't help it.' (No wonder Lloyd George and F. E. Smith became such friends in later years.)

But Lloyd George's demeanour in court was by no means invariably brash. No one could be more respectful or more quietly beguiling, if the circumstances appeared to favour that tone rather than one of fearless aggression. Brynmor Jones was a county court judge when, in June 1885,

1. Diary entry for 13 March 1885, quoted in Herbert du Parcq, *op. cit.*, Vol. I, p. 45.
2. Herbert du Parcq, *op. cit.*, Vol. I, pp. 62–3, and Frank Owen, *Tempestuous Journey*, p. 50.

'a particularly boyish-looking advocate, thin and rather pale', stood up to plead before him at Portmadoc.

> I was attracted by his youthful appearance and his talking voice, as well as by a certain earnest, eager, but yet restrained manner, and remember noticing as the hearing proceeded that his way of handling his case was in strong contrast with the inexperience which might be presumed from his youthfulness. A point of law arose, he was ready with his authorities, he asked no dangerous questions in cross-examination; he stuck to relevant points; he made no attempt at eloquence in his speech. I gave judgment for his client . . . and recollect the humorous look . . . in his eye when he asked for costs and got them. . . .
>
> When the case was over I said to the Deputy Registrar: 'What's the name of that young fellow?' He replied, 'David Lloyd George – only just admitted'. I said, 'Well, he did that case uncommonly well. He'll get on.'[1]

Actually, Lloyd George first appeared before Brynmor Jones at Pwllheli. We have his contemporary record: 'Pwllheli County Court. Brynmor Jones, Judge. Very shrewd and clever. Knows great deal of law. Sees point of case. Very courteous to advocates. If he continues like this, he is just the sort of fellow I'd wish. He'll stimulate you to carefully prepare your case, especially as regards legal points. He delights in these. Got my applications all right.'[2] Shortly beforehand, when he heard that Brynmor Jones was appointed to the Mid-Wales circuit, he noted that he was 'extremely gratified at this announcement'.[3] And the day after the Pwllheli session he was at the Portmadoc County Court: 'Never had a more successful field day. Won all my cases. . . . It will do a world of good to me.'[4] Obviously, he had Brynmor Jones well sized up in advance and knew the best way to handle him. They were later colleagues in Parliament.

In the summer of 1887 D. R. Daniel had his first encounter with Lloyd George, outside the police station at Portmadoc, and he describes his impressions:

> . . . a young boyish man, in simple clothes, a short shirt and a pair of Volunteer's leggings closed with laces on his legs. I remember his

1. Quoted in J. Hugh Edwards, *op. cit.*, Vol. I, pp. 80–1.
2. Diary entry for 23 June 1885, quoted in H. du Parcq, *op. cit.*, Vol. I, p. 46.
3. Diary entry for 13 June 1885, quoted in *ibid*.
4. Diary entry for 24 June 1885, quoted in *ibid*.

attractive smile and the incomparable brilliance of his lively blue eyes as though it were yesterday. . . . I remember going home and saying to my wife . . . that I saw in G. something that I had not found in any of the young Welshmen who were my friends then on the crest of the wave of political and social promise. He seemed nimbler in mind and bearing, more daring in his views, more heroic in his look (though he smiled most of the time) than any. We became instant friends.[1]

Daniel was a cultivated man who had visited America and was a close friend of T. E. (Tom) Ellis, most prominent of the younger Welsh nationalists. His friendship with Lloyd George lasted until the First World War, when they drifted apart. Daniel could not stomach the war policy to which Lloyd George was committed, but his admiration turned to sadness rather than bitterness. Soon after their first meeting they founded, with a few collaborators, a weekly Welsh-language newspaper called *Udgorn Rhyddid* (Trumpet of Freedom). Lloyd George chose the title and put up some of the £100 capital. The first issue appeared on 4 January 1888. To the second issue he contributed an article, in which he wrote: 'The place of greatest need is where men are suffering under greatest pressure: amidst the workers, labourers and farmers. It is an odd fact about all reforms that they have been brought about by persons outside the sufferers themselves. . . .'[2] The man who wrote that was not a man of the people, but a self-conscious reformer from the outside. Though he made the most of his 'cottage-bred' credentials, in his heart he knew very well that he was privileged.

Udgorn Rhyddid seems to have disappointed its sponsors. Its fatal defect may have been that the editing was carried on by a group rather than by an individual. At that time there was a plethora of Welsh-language papers; as early as 1870 two quarterlies, sixteen monthlies and ten weeklies were being published in the vernacular, with the support of Welsh Dissenting bodies. By far the most influential Welsh paper was the *Baner ac Amserau Cymru* (Banner and Times of Wales), edited and controlled by one man, Thomas Gee. Like so many Celtic nationalists, Gee was half-English; but he was born at Denbigh and devoted his life to Welsh national causes. An ordained Methodist minister, he had no specific cure of souls but used his genius for propaganda to arouse the fighting spirit

1. D. R. Daniel, *op. cit.* Lloyd George's sister and brother both had dark eyes. In the literal as well as the metaphorical sense, David was Uncle Lloyd's blue-eyed boy.
2. The article was unsigned, but Daniel could vouch for Lloyd George's authorship.

of Nonconformists throughout Wales. In particular, he became the leading champion of Welsh tenant-farmers against the payment of tithe for sectarian purposes, the insecurity of their holdings, and the alleged stiffness of the rents they had to pay.

Lloyd George threw himself into this land agitation. His first public (as distinct from debating-society) speech was in 1886, at a farmers' meeting in the town hall at Pwllheli; and for a time he acted as Secretary of the South Caernarvonshire branch of Gee's Anti-Tithe League. Soon he was much in demand as a stump speaker, audiences particularly enjoying the liveliness of his repartee. At one meeting a curate interrupted him to ask the crowd listening in the open air: 'Why do you listen to this little attorney? If you go to his office you'll pay six and eightpence for him to speak a word to you.' 'The reverend gentleman,' replied Lloyd George, 'is right when he says I'm a lawyer, a little lawyer, who tries to make a living with an occasional six and eightpence – sometimes less than that, sometimes a little more. . . . If you don't come to me I shan't ask you to pay me anything. But as for this man, whether you go to hear his sermon or not, you have to pay *him* just the same!'[1] Lloyd George's knock-about style was usually good-humoured as well as witty, and he had an ever-alert eye for conciliation and compromise. He believed in making his point strongly, and then being ready to negotiate. The novelist Berta Ruck, whose father was Chief Constable of Caernarvonshire, remembered a convivial occasion when a farmer was defying the law by refusing to pay tithe, and was threatened with distraint. Her father, the bailiffs and Lloyd George discussed the situation over a lavish tea provided by the farmer's wife.[2]

In 1886 Lloyd George had his first chance of being a candidate for Parliament. Though he was already interested in the constituency of Caernarvon Boroughs (his home ground, because one of the boroughs was Criccieth), he allowed friends of his at Harlech to put his name forward for the neighbouring county of Merioneth before the 1886 election. He attended a selection meeting at which, according to himself, he 'aroused a high pitch of excitement'.[3] Apparently he was well in the running to be nominated, but after all he decided to withdraw his name, ostensibly because he did not like to stand in the way of Tom Ellis, whose claims to the seat included being a Merioneth man. An entry in Lloyd George's diary, however, suggests that his underlying reasons may have

1. D. R. Daniel, *op. cit.*   2. Quoted in W. Watkin Davies, *op. cit.*, pp. 78–9.
3. Letter to his brother, quoted in William George, *My Brother and I*, p. 131.

been rather less Quixotic. 'I would not be in nearly as good a position as regards pecuniary, oratorical or intellectual quality to go to Parliament now as, say, five years hence. Would find myself in endless pecuniary difficulties; an object of contempt in a House of snobs. . . .'[1]

There was, moreover, another possible motive for hesitation, which he did not refer to. 1886 was a perplexing year for Welsh Liberals, because Gladstone's recent espousal of Irish Home Rule had brought him into conflict with Joseph Chamberlain who, as the arch-Nonconformist, had a big following in Wales, and whose radical ideas made a powerful appeal to Lloyd George, as to many others. It was feared that disunity would damage the party at the election, and Gladstone was, indeed, soundly beaten in the country as a whole. But not in Wales, where candidates of his persuasion – Ellis among them – were elected in overwhelming strength. Lloyd George took the hint and, whatever his private reservations, was thereafter a staunch Gladstonian for electoral purposes. His decision to stand aside in 1886 saved him from having to choose, as a candidate, between Gladstone and Chamberlain at a time when he might have made an ill-advised choice.[2] Even so, he would probably have been elected, and he would then have been an M.P. at the age of twenty-three (two years younger than the ultra-privileged Arthur Balfour when he was first elected to Parliament).

Anyone who met Lloyd George was likely to form the impression that it was only a matter of time before he embarked on a Parliamentary career. The legendary Irish agitator Michael Davitt came to address a meeting at Blaenau Ffestiniog and was so struck by Lloyd George's vote-of-thanks speech that he patted him on the back and predicted a bright future for him. The vote-of-thanks speech was fully reported and is of interest as a fine piece of radical invective which nevertheless avoids any commitment to land nationalisation – the policy that Michael Davitt

1. Diary entry for 20 June 1886, quoted in William George, *My Brother and I*, p. 131.
2. Harold Spender (no doubt echoing Lloyd George, upon whom he was for many years a faithful attendant) says quite definitely that, had he stood for Merioneth in 1886, Lloyd George would have stood as a Chamberlainite; but that he would have reverted later to the main body of Liberalism – like Sir George Trevelyan and W. S. Caine – and would not have followed Chamberlain into the Tory camp. (E. H. Spender, *The Prime Minister*, p. 46.) J. Hugh Edwards has a story that Lloyd George went to Birmingham to attend the inaugural meeting of Chamberlain's National Radical Union, but found, 'to his chagrin', that he had gone on the wrong day. On the right day his professional commitments made it impossible for him to return to Birmingham. (J. Hugh Edwards, *The Life of David Lloyd George*, Vol. II, p. 143, published in 1913. The story is not repeated in Edwards's later *Lloyd George: the Man and the Statesman*, published in 1930.)

and the chairman of the meeting, Michael D. Jones, were both advocating.[1]

In the course of 1888 the question of his candidature for the Caernarvon Boroughs came to a head. The seat had been lost to the Conservatives against the tide in 1886, mainly, it was thought, because the Liberal candidate was no good. By the summer of 1888 the three southern boroughs – Criccieth, Pwllheli and Nevin – had declared for Lloyd George, and in August he won over the leading Liberals in the cathedral city of Bangor. Conway and Caernarvon followed suit and in December he was chosen as the prospective Gladstonian candidate for the division. His eventual rivals were a Nonconformist minister and a professor from Trinity College, Dublin. Lloyd George was handicapped by what some regarded as his excessive youth, and he also had to reckon with the uneasiness that political talent of the highest order nearly always inspires in people of a certain sort, whatever their party label. Yet he scored heavily in being a local man whose capacity to fight an election was not in doubt, whose brand of advanced Liberalism and Welsh nationalism was becoming increasingly popular, and who was a household name not only in Caernarvonshire but also – by mid-1888 – throughout the whole of Wales. This dramatic boost to his reputation came from the Llanfrothen burial case.

Even to those who have it in them to succeed, luck is always an important, sometimes a vital, asset. Beyond question, Lloyd George was lucky in the Llanfrothen case, since he benefited from the insane bigotry of an Anglican parson and from an uncharacteristic lapse by a normally balanced county court judge. The circumstances of the case are, briefly, as follows.

In 1864 the churchyard at Llanfrothen, near Portmadoc, was enlarged by the gift of a piece of land, and the parishioners' thanks to the donors – a Mr and Mrs Owen – were recorded in the vestry book. Under an Act of Parliament passed in 1880 (the Osborne Morgan Burial Act) it became permissible for Nonconformists to be buried, according to their own rites, in parish churchyards, and the annexe to the one at Llanfrothen

1. When Michael Davitt died in 1906 Lloyd George said to D. R. Daniel that he (Davitt) would 'have a great place in the history of his country and among the reformers of the world'. (D. R. Daniel, op. cit.) But Davitt was a much more extreme character than Lloyd George. For instance, while they were both opponents of the Boer War, Davitt went to the length of withdrawing from Parliament and trying to organise foreign intervention on behalf of the Boers.

began to be used by and for Nonconformists as well as members of the Established Church. To the rector this was an abomination, and he persuaded Mrs Owen to make a new conveyance of the land with the proviso that people should be buried there only to the accompaniment of Anglican rites. In 1888 an old quarryman died, having asked on his death-bed to be buried beside his daughter in the ground presented by the Owens. The rector refused permission and locked the gate of the church-yard, at which the quarryman's family, advised by Lloyd George, broke into the place and buried the old man beside his daughter, according to the rites of his denomination. The rector sued the family, and Lloyd George defended them, in the Portmadoc County Court, where the jury found in their favour. The judge, however, after two months' delay, gave his verdict for the rector, making, into the bargain, an inaccurate note of the jury's findings. The family appealed to the High Court where the Lord Chief Justice and another judge quashed the verdict and gave judge-ment, with full costs, for Lloyd George's clients. The point at issue was whether or not the piece of ground had been validly transferred in 1864, so that it came within the scope of the Osborne Morgan Burial Act. The Appeal Court upheld the view of the Portmadoc jury that it had, and that Mrs Owen's later conveyance, with its restrictive provision, was therefore null and void.

The immediate legal effect of this *cause célèbre* was to enable two dead bodies to lie side by side in a country churchyard, but its more far-reaching effects were upon the living – notably upon the professional fortunes of the firm of Lloyd George and George, and upon the political fortunes of its senior partner. The case received enormous publicity and was seen by Welsh Nonconformists as a test case, in which their national and spiritual rights were opposed by the intolerable claims of an alien church. By fighting this case and, above all, by winning it, Lloyd George became a hero to the majority of Welshmen.

It has been alleged that the case did not come to him out of the blue, but was deliberately contrived by him; that he saw the potentialities of the situation (in view of the rector's attitude and Mrs Owen's second conveyance) and then went to work to engineer a confrontation, even to the extent of finding a suitably moribund Nonconformist and persuading him to request burial in the annexe. The allegation rests upon hearsay evidence and does not ring true. Lloyd George could be very ruthless, but he was not mean-minded. Of course he must have realised, as soon as the quarryman's family approached him for advice, that they were offering him a heaven-sent opportunity. He thereupon stiffened their mood of defiance and helped to elaborate their plan of campaign. He may even have had his eye on Llanfrothen for some time, and may have hoped that such a case would one day arise there. But it would have been out of character for him to sniff around until he found a dying man, and then to have put into the man's head the idea of asking to be buried beside his daughter. For one thing, Lloyd George always had a horror of illness and never, if he could help it, went anywhere near a sick person. But above all such behaviour was not in his style: he was a relentless fighter against the strong, not a callous exploiter of the weak.[1]

The year of the Llanfrothen case was also the year that county councils were introduced by Lord Salisbury's Government. This long-overdue reform gave the countryside the relatively democratic local institutions which had been given to large towns more than sixty years previously. In Wales the measure had a profound impact, since it transferred the control of most local affairs from the justices of the peace to the class of Welshmen through which the national revival was most conspicuously asserting itself. The first elections were held in January 1889, and the Liberals were returned with a two-to-one majority in the Welsh counties. Lloyd George was asked to be a candidate by four districts in Caernarvonshire, but declined so that he would be free to campaign for the Liberal Party throughout the county and throughout Wales. After the elections, the triumphant Caernarvonshire Liberals chose him as an alderman – the youngest in Wales – and he retained the position for the rest of his life. But he was obviously not cut out for parish-pump politics: his mind was on higher, or anyway larger, things. As a member of the Caernarvonshire council he moved a resolution calling for a Welsh county council association, which should serve as the embryo for Home Rule. Fifteen years later he mobilised the Welsh counties for his fight against Balfour's Education Act. But the humdrum work of a local authority bored him, and as time went on he became convinced that the units of British local government were too small to be effective.

1. The story appears in Donald McCormick, *The Mask of Merlin*, pp. 36–7, and the authority cited for it is Michael D. Jones (chairman of the Michael Davitt meeting referred to above), as reported, apparently, in a thesis on 'Nonconformity's Battle in Wales' by the Rev. Thomas Charles Williams. The thesis is not listed in the British Museum catalogue, there is no copy of it in the National Library of Wales, nor any reference to it in H. L. Williams's biography of Thomas Charles Williams – who was, in any case, a friend and strong supporter of Lloyd George. McCormick's evidence would suffer from being third-hand, even if it were less dubious on other grounds.

In his remarkable memorandum of August 1910, in which he proposed a coalition government and a programme to meet the most urgent needs of the nation, he wrote:

Our whole system of local government is on a very unsatisfactory basis. There are too many boards and there is no system of intelligent direction, such as is provided by the Burgomasters on the Continent. Whilst there are too many small boards and councils, there are too few large ones, and a good deal of work is cast upon the Imperial Parliament which could be much more efficiently discharged by local bodies on a large scale.[1]

Unfortunately, when he was Prime Minister he was too preoccupied with other work to put through the sweeping reform of local government which, if he had ever led the country under normal peace-time conditions, would have been part of his contribution to a modernised, but still Imperial, Britain.

As a mere candidate he was already behaving and talking like a national politician. In February 1889, at a demonstration in Liverpool, he defined the relationship of Welsh nationalism to the Liberal Party. It was not a hostile movement, but simply an intensification of Liberalism. Welsh people had to organise, however, because democracy depended far more than aristocracy upon organisation. And Wales should follow the example of Ireland: the Irish had shown how to secure justice and redress. It was all very well, he argued, to cry 'Excellent little Wales' and all that. At horse shows they sometimes saw a first prize of £10 given to one, £5 to another, while the third was 'Highly Commended'. That was the way that Wales had been treated by the Liberal Party. Ireland deservedly got the first prize (a series of splendid measures). Scotland took second prize. Wales, like a Welsh mountain pony, was sent empty away.[2]

A year later, in Cardiff, Lloyd George stated the case for Welsh Home Rule with unanswerable logic. All the arguments in favour of Home Rule for Ireland applied, he said, with equal force to Wales. The Imperial Parliament had the world on its shoulders and could not spare the time for provincial matters; nor would it have the necessary local knowledge, even if it had the time and inclination to attend to them. Wales was just as distinct a nationality as Ireland: more so, indeed, because the Irish had

1. The whole memorandum is set out in *The Age of Lloyd George*, introduced and edited by Kenneth O. Morgan, pp. 150–5.
2. Speech at the Hope Hall, Liverpool, 15 February 1889.

lost one of the title-deeds of nationality, their language. If it was true that Parliament had neglected Ireland, it was even more true that Wales had been neglected. Gladstone said of the Irish land reforms: 'We have not failed, but we have not finished.' Quite so, but in the case of Wales they had not even begun. As for the negative arguments – the arguments that Unionists put forwards against Irish Home Rule – these manifestly did *not* apply to Wales. 'Rome Rule' and the possible victimisation of Protestants were completely out of the question, so far as Wales was concerned. Equally irrelevant was the fear that Home Rule would be only the first step towards ultimate separation: no single passage in any speech by the most extreme Welsh nationalist could afford the slightest grounds for such a fear. Finally, whereas timid souls could object to Irish Home Rule as the surrender of loyal and law-abiding citizens to moonlighters, outrage-mongers and assassins, the same could never be said of *hen wlad y menyg gwynion* (the land of white gloves). There was no bloodstain on Wales's political record.[1]

Yet it was very much easier to state the theoretical case for Welsh Home Rule than to establish a practical basis for it in Wales. When Lloyd George tried, in 1889, to unite the Liberal Federations of North and South Wales he found – as he was to find more conclusively later – that Wales was not made for political unity. But his allegiance to Home Rule was not lightly given or lightly withdrawn. The vision of a Wales self-governing within the United Kingdom was slow to fade. At the same time he always realised that Welsh Home Rule was not a self-sufficient policy, and he combined his advocacy of it with a demand for social reform which, particularly in the industrial areas of the south, seemed more urgent than cultural or religious emancipation. After expounding the arguments for Home Rule he ended his Cardiff speech by relating Welsh local autonomy to the wider radical cause:

> You have pledged yourselves to a great programme – Disestablishment, Land Reform, Local Option. . . . But, however drastic and broad they may appear to be they after all simply touch the fringes of that vast social question which must be dealt with in the near future. There is a momentous time coming. The dark continent of wrong is being explored, and there is a missionary spirit abroad for its reclamation to the realm of right. A holy war has been proclaimed against 'man's inhumanity to man', and the people of Europe are thronging to the

1. Speech at Conference of the South Wales Liberal Federation, Cardiff, 4 February 1890.

crusade. . . . As a Welshman, I feel confident that, once it is afforded the opportunity, my country will act its part honourably in the conflict. . . .[1]

That peroration bears a strong family likeness to the closing words of the 1909 Budget speech, when Lloyd George said that he was introducing 'a War Budget . . . to wage implacable warfare against poverty and squalidness'. In 1905 Keir Hardie said of him that he was 'a politician with no settled convictions on social questions', and that such questions had hitherto 'lain outside the sphere of his orbit'.[2] By the time he said that, Keir Hardie – a carpet-bagger from Scotland – was one of the Members for Merthyr, but in 1890 South Wales was not yet *his* orbit, or he might have had a different impression of Lloyd George.

1. *Ibid.*
2. William Stewart, *J. Keir Hardie*, p. 222.

THREE
Husband, Father and M.P.

Shortly before he became involved in the Llanfrothen case, and about a year before his selection as candidate for the Caernarvon Boroughs, Lloyd George was married to Margaret Owen. In the course of his life he had many affairs, but only two real love affairs, and both of them resulted in marriage – though the second only after a long interval, during which, in fact if not in form, he was a bigamist. Margaret was his wife until her death in 1941, but after he had been married to her for nearly a quarter of a century he fell in love with a much younger woman, Frances Stevenson, who from 1912 until his own death in 1945 was his mistress and, eventually, his wife. These were Lloyd George's two great loves and, until death intervened, the second never completely supplanted the first. Each had a meaning for him, and each brought him comfort which the other could not supply. His deep, enduring attachment to Margaret and Frances should on no account be confused with the flirtations and casual amours to which he was always prone.

Lloyd George was very attractive to women, and they to him. His sexual impulses were abnormally strong and his nervous, driving nature made him all the more dependent upon the solace of female company. Puritanical repression often breeds a furtive addiction to sex, but there was nothing in the least furtive about Lloyd George's sexuality. He respected the Nonconformist conscience in others but, according to D. R. Daniel, 'there was never since the days of Charles the Second's roisterers a man with less of it'.[1] Perhaps, indeed, there was a little of it in his attitude towards alcohol: though he was never a teetotaller (he regularly drank

1. D. R. Daniel, *op. cit.*

wine and Irish whiskey), drunkenness always disgusted him and his advocacy of Temperance was no pose. There was also a touch of puritan-ism in his industrious habits and the earnestness of his desire to get on in the world. But his attitude towards sex was wholly unpuritanical. When he was only seventeen his sister Mary, whose Nonconformist conscience was of the strictest, felt moved to lecture him on his philandering. 'My sister gave it to me rather solemnly for flirting with J.M. Indeed, I am rather seriously disposed to give up these dealings . . . the realisation of my prospects, my dreams, my longings for success, are very scant indeed unless I am determined to give up what, without mistake, are the germs of the "fast life". Be staunch and bold and play the man.'[1] Yet he could never bring himself to act on this pious resolve for very long at a time: 'these dealings' remained a distinctive, though unimportant, feature of his life from adolescence to old age.

In Margaret Owen, however, he met a girl who for the first time en-gaged his emotions at a serious level. Her father, Richard Owen, was a substantial tenant-farmer who lived on the high ground above Criccieth. His holding of a hundred acres was large by Caernarvonshire standards, and he also had some money invested in the Portmadoc trading fleet. Once a year he used to drive sheep and cattle to Barnet fair, on the out-skirts of London, doing the journey both ways on horseback. He was one of Criccieth's most respected citizens, claiming descent from Owen Gwynedd (who ruled North Wales in the twelfth century). His wife, Mary, was of the same prosperous farming stock, known in Wales as *bonedd gwlad* and in France as *gros paysans*. She was a competent, spirited woman, but unable to write. Margaret was the Owens' only child, born on 4 November 1866. They doted on her and were determined that she should grow up with more education and polish than they had. So they sent her away to a genteel girls' school at Dolgelley, from which she emerged a regular little lady of the period – able to read and write, but with no aptitude for cooking or most other household tasks; a bit of an amateur artist; a passionate garden-lover, green-fingered; deeply self-confident, but without ostentation or side; at ease with all classes and noted for her capacity to put people at their ease. She was certainly in no ordinary sense a snob, yet she had intense pride of race, and a devotion to her ancestral ground which could hardly have been more pronounced in Owen Gwynedd himself. Criccieth, to her, was the centre of the universe. From her home, Mynydd Ednyfed, she had, on a fine day, one

1. Diary entry for 17 June 1880, quoted in William George, *My Brother and I*, p. 94.

of the most inspiring views in the British Isles, with St David's Head visible far across the Bay, to her left the mountains of Merioneth, below her the little town with its ruined castle, behind her the hills building up towards Snowdon. In such a setting even a down-trodden child, victimised rather than idolised by her family, might well have fancied herself, occasionally, the monarch of all she surveyed. But there was nothing downtrodden, nothing of the victim, about Margaret Owen. Her family environment, like her physical environment, ministered strongly to her self-esteem.

She and David Lloyd George were both spoiled children: her parents worshipped her, as Uncle Lloyd worshipped him. Both were brought up to feel that the world was their oyster, but the world that mattered to her was North Wales, whereas the world that mattered to him was – the world. Though she was much less clever than he was, her pride and wilfulness matched his own; and it was those qualities (or defects) in her that probably most attracted him in the first place. She, on her side, was fascinated, excited and amused by him, but not overawed or swept off her feet. And when they were married, she was never reduced to squawish subservience. On the contrary she often followed her own inclination when even the wife of an average husband would have felt bound to give priority to his interests. Since both of them had different ideas about how and where to live, and since both were in the habit of getting their own way, it was inevitable that tension should grow between them, and no wonder that in the long run they became partly – though never wholly – estranged.

It is not at all clear when they first met, but as children they must have seen each other in or around Criccieth, because the Campbellite chapel which the George children attended was on the edge of the town, and anyway David very often walked into Criccieth to collect the *Liverpool Post* for Uncle Lloyd. Margaret used to say that she remembered passing Rebecca Lloyd and her grandchildren on their way to chapel, and in particular 'the little lad, attired in knickerbockers and scarlet stockings, who, time and again, gave her the "glad eye" as they passed each other on the main road'.[1] But there seems to have been no serious contact between them until several years after Uncle Lloyd and his family moved into Criccieth. The first published reference by Lloyd George to his future wife

1. J. Hugh Edwards, *David Lloyd George: the Man and the Statesman*, Vol. I, p. 90. David and William were the only boys at Llanystumdwy school who wore knickerbockers.

is an entry in his diary, dated 10 June 1884, which records seeing 'Maggie Owen Mynydd Ednyfed' and describes her as 'a sensible girl without any fuss or affectation about her'. Eleven days later, after presiding at a *soirée* of the Criccieth debating society, he took her home the 'short way'.[1] At the end of the following year she received what appears to have been her first letter from him (or anyway the first that she kept). It was written from Morvin House on 30 December 1885:

Dear Miss Owen,

I enclose tickets for our Society's entertainment. The meeting commences at 7.30 p.m. punctual.

Young ladies need not arrange for any escort home after the meeting, as the Society provides efficient protection for them in this respect!

Kindly recollect this so as to avoid troubling anyone to wait for you from the meeting.

Yours sincerely
D. Lloyd George.[2]

The tone is affectionate and quizzical, but not yet that of an ardent suitor. By the following July, however, he was beginning his letters to her 'My dear Miss Owen', and ending with 'best love'. By September he was beginning 'My dearest Miss Owen', and early the next year (1887) 'My dearest love' and 'My little darling'. When he started addressing her by her Christian name it was in the diminutive form – 'My dearest little Maggie'. And so it remained.

Lloyd George is notorious for being an extremely bad correspondent, but in one respect the reputation is quite undeserved. However sparing he may have been of letters to colleagues, constituents and friends, he wrote very frequently and faithfully to his close relations. It has long been known that he was a punctilious letter-writer to Uncle Lloyd (though only a few extracts from the letters have so far been published, and the correspondence as a whole is not yet available for study). But until a few years ago nobody outside the family suspected the existence of well over two thousand letters written by him to Margaret Lloyd George before and after their marriage.[3] Instead of an almost total dearth of Lloyd George manuscript letters we now have a great mass of them, and more than half of this direct, contemporary, written evidence relates to

1. Diary entries for 10 June and 21 June 1884, quoted in William George, *My Brother and I*, p. 97. 2. Lloyd George correspondence, National Library of Wales. 3. See Foreword and Note on Sources.

the most neglected period of his life – his early career in Parliament. Over twelve hundred of the letters were written before he became a Minister, and they are on the whole the longer and the fuller ones, because he obviously had more time for writing letters when he was a back-bencher. They reveal much that is of strictly political interest, but above all they illuminate the mind and character of an extraordinary human being.

In so doing they make us vividly aware that the extraordinary is capable of being very ordinary – that what we call genius is not an all-embracing condition, but a rare, dynamic particle co-existing with much that is trivial and commonplace. This fact is perhaps a little exaggerated in the letters, because they are inevitably rather burdened with the small change of family life. Moreover, Lloyd George had an uncanny faculty for putting himself on the exact wavelength of anyone with whom he was communicating. When he wrote to Margaret he was writing ex-pressly to and for her, not with an eye to history or merely to exercise his own intelligence and wit. He was never the sort of man of destiny whose every word has to be carefully weighed lest it appear, in retrospect, to be unworthy of him. He wrote, as he conversed, spontaneously: no major statesman has ever been less pompous or portentous than he was. This virtue is reflected in his letters, giving them their freshness and convincing us that they provide a valid account of his reactions to people, experiences and events.

Though the Lloyd Georges habitually spoke Welsh in their family circle, the letters are nearly all written in English, with the odd Welsh phrase thrown in for explanation or effect. Occasionally Welsh is used for reasons of security – to cheat the prying eyes of Englishmen. Thus he writes in Welsh from the Law Courts in London: 'My dearest love, I must write in Welsh because there are four attorneys and one barrister sitting around me.'[1] And in another typical passage, written in Welsh, from the House of Commons, he says: 'You succeeded in giving me a really nasty clip on the ear by writing about Ellis Griffith [M.P.] and his wife. But no matter. You don't want some old baby like Ellis G. for a husband. Which would you prefer – a bit of a namby-pamby who would always be hanging at the hem of your petticoat, or a real old demon, though he would sometimes lose his temper with you? Tell me the truth, old Maggie.'[2]

1. D.L.G. to Margaret Owen, letter postmarked 23 February 1887 (N.L.W.).
2. D.L.G. to Margaret Lloyd George, 25 February 1896 (N.L.W.).

The highest incidence of Welsh seems to have been when, as Chancellor of the Exchequer, he was staying at Balmoral. For instance, in Welsh: 'I have arrived here and have had a chat with the King. He is very agreeable. He speaks about Germany and about the strikes. He is a very very small man and all his sympathy is with the rich – very little pity for the poor. . . . I am dressing for dinner.'[1] But on the whole Lloyd George wrote to his wife in English, partly no doubt because he was glad of the opportunity to practise it, but also maybe for security reasons at the receiving end – so that what he wrote would be less easily read by Margaret's Welsh servants.

The correspondence, as we have it, is largely one-sided. Too few of Margaret's letters to him are preserved in the Lloyd George Papers. Until Frances Stevenson took charge of his correspondence he kept hardly any letters, and after that Margaret was writing less. Not that she wrote anything like as often as he did, even in the early years. Over and over again he chides her for not writing, or for giving him too little news when she does write. There was a streak of indolence in her which made her a more restful companion than he could ever be, but which also made her sluggish about doing anything which she did not either want to do or positively have to do.

Their courtship had its ups and downs. It would have been impossible for two young people who meant so much to their respective families to get married at all without causing a lot of heartburning at home. How could Uncle Lloyd ever be satisfied that a girl was good enough for his David, or the Owens that any young man was good enough for their Margaret? But apart from that, there were special obstacles to a marriage link between the two families. The Lloyds and Georges were, as we know, Baptists; the Owens were Methodists. For all his tolerance, Uncle Lloyd would have preferred David to take up with a girl of his own denomination, and the Owens certainly regarded Baptists as an inferior religious species. There was a political difference, too. Methodists tended to be the most conservative of the Welsh Nonconformists, and Richard Owen, though a Liberal and a supporter of Disestablishment, was no radical and no friend to the nationalist cause. Moreover, on the Owens' side, ideological objections were reinforced by more down-to-earth doubts about Lloyd George. Would he be able to keep their daughter in the style to which she was accustomed? In the financial sense, he had very little behind him. Were his prospects any more solid? He was a clever

1. D.L.G. to M.L.G., 13 September 1911 (N.L.W.).

enough young man, and he did not seem to be afraid of work. But would his legal practice survive the damage that his reckless political views and activities were likely to inflict upon it? Finally, could they rely upon his personal steadiness and fidelity? There were disquieting rumours. In the last resort, the Owens could bear the thought of Margaret's being married to a Baptist and a radical. They could even bear the thought of her being married to a poor man. But the thought that she might be unhappy was too much for them.

The final doubt was the only one which Margaret herself in any degree shared. Like many mildly opinionated, but secure, children she reacted against her parents' beliefs. Lloyd George's shade of Nonconformity was a matter of indifference to her: even his scepticism held no terrors for her. She was also broadly in sympathy with his politics, though without, as we shall see, facing up to the inescapable consequences of his political ambition. As for his prospects of making a decent living, she was confident that he would get on well, and in any case her feelings for him were stronger than her (considerable) interest in money. But what of his feelings for her? Could she be sure that he cared for her enough to change his way of life after they were married, or would he all the time be hurting her with his attentions to other women? Had he really the makings of a family man? That doubt underlay her moods and hesitations during the two years of their courtship. He might suppose that she was uncertain merely on account of parental influence, and it was only natural that she should protect herself by giving him that impression. But in fact the trouble was in her own mind, and would have been there even if her parents' attitude towards him had been entirely favourable.

Of course, the things that she heard about him – and that he himself often made little attempt to deny – enhanced his glamour in the eyes of a young girl, eager for life, whose existence had so far been tediously sheltered. The 'roisterer' streak in him did not simply alarm her; it also contributed to the potent, if slightly caddish, charm which comes through to us in his letters. 'I am now at Drury Lane Theatre and write you this now between the acts. . . . A miserable singer is on now – so I can proceed. Saturday evening I went to the Lyceum – Faust was being acted. Irving personated Mephistopheles. . . . I am now out of theatre and standing by Chancery Lane pillar box to conclude this rigmarole. . . .'[1] 'I trust that you received due amusement and entertainment in the preaching meetings – instruction and edification you would scarcely dare to hope for in the

1. D.L.G. to M.O., date uncertain, but early – it begins 'My dear Miss Owen' (N.L.W.).

. Margaret Lloyd George, born Margaret Owen

3b. William George (David's brother)

3c. A general view of Criccieth, with the Castle

4. A group of family and friends including (l. to r.) Richard Owen (Lloyd George's father-in-law), Olwen Lloyd George, Mair Lloyd George, D. R. Daniel, Richard Lloyd George, Herbert Lewis, Margaret Lloyd George (*hidden*), Daniel Lloyd George, and Mary Owen (Lloyd George's

Association Games. Who won the buckle? Who raved most deliriously about the agonies of the wicked's doom and about the bliss of every true Calvinist's predestination?'[1] 'You can square your mother by reminding her . . . that Mr Gruffyd ap Arfon was an eminent Methodist divine who flourished before Christ and in fact initiated him into the principles of Calvinism. That ought to propitiate her.'[2] 'Make yourself as ill as possible – then you may evade tomorrow evening's service and I will come up with a liturgy proper for the occasion.'[3] 'Don't imagine angry things about me – that's a pet. I shall redeem all misbehaviour yet. Believe me, though I am bodily in the coffee room of the Belle Vue Hotel Trefriw with Parry Pwllheli by my side inditing a letter to one of his numerous sweethearts I am in mind at M[ynydd Ednyfed] with my sweetheart by me. I swear by the pen which I now hold in my hand that I shall not flirt nor even wink improperly at a girl. Parry is my surety as to that.'[4] (One can almost see him winking at Parry as he folds the letter!)

Towards the end of 1886 he was urging her very forcibly to stand up to her mother.

> I trust you will have something to report to me tomorrow of the result of an interview with your mother. As I have already intimated to you it is but of trivial consequence to me what your mother's views of me may be – so long, of course, as they do not affect yours. . . . You will appreciate my anxiety to bring the matter to an issue. . . . I somehow feel deeply that it is unmanly to take by stealth and fraud what I am honestly entitled to. It has a tinge of the ridiculous in it, moreover.[5]

Was he implying that he might compel her to marry him by the most time-honoured of methods? Or had there been some question of elopement? It would have been quite in character for him to throw out the idea of eloping, as a rhetorical flourish, but acting on it would have been as disastrous for him as it would have been unthinkable for her. He must have known very well that she would never do anything of the sort, so it was quite safe for him to offer the challenge. Though he was the one who, as it were, was on probation (since he was sure that he wanted to marry her, whereas she had yet to be convinced that it would be wise for her to

1. D.L.G. to M.O., written on his office paper, postmarked 8 August 1886 (N.L.W.).
2. D.L.G. to M.O., postmarked 25 September 1886 (N.L.W.).
3. D.L.G. to M.O., 11 December 1886 (N.L.W.).
4. D.L.G., to M.O., postmarked 18 July 1887 (N.L.W.). Trefriw was a small spa, then fashionable, on the river Conway, opposite Llanrwst.
5. D.L.G. to M.O., 8 December 1886 (N.L.W.).

Now once & for ever let us have an end of this long standing wrangle. It comes to this. My supreme idea is to get on. To this idea I shall sacrifice everything. Except I trust honesty. I am prepared to throw. Even love itself under the wheels of my Juggernaut if it obstructs the way. How I have told you over & over again that I consider you to be my good angel — my guiding star. Do you not really desire my success? If you do, will you suggest some course least objectionable to you out of our difficulty? I am prepared to do anything reasonable & fair you may require of me. I can not — earnestly — carry on as at present. Believe me & may Heaven attest the truth of my statement — my love for you is sincere & strong. In this I never waver. But I must not forget that I have a purpose in life. And however painful the sacrifices I may have to make to attain this ambition I must not flinch — otherwise success will be remote indeed

Write me your views candidly & in as good & earnest a spirit as I impart mine to you.

With fondest love

From your sweetheart

2. Facsimile of a passage in letter from David Lloyd George to Margaret Owen
(see opposite page)

marry him), he was nevertheless determined not to appear before her as a suppliant. He would take the war into her camp, gambling on the effectiveness of his masculine appeal.

It was probably at about this time – late 1886 – that he wrote her the first of two formidable letters, designed to make or break his chances. Neither letter is dated (except with the day of the week), but the first begins 'My dearest Miss Owen', the second 'My dearest Maggie' – which places it in the following year. Both are capital documents in the Lloyd George story. The first was written in pencil from Morvin House, at half past one on a Sunday morning:

> My dearest Miss Owen,
>
> Without any preamble or beating about the bush let's straight to the topic. Here I am under the very disagreeable necessity – through no fault of my own you must admit – of addressing you for the hundredth time during a not very protracted courtship in a remonstrative spirit. Appealing to the love I have for you or that you have professed for me seems to be but vanity itself in your sight. I am now going to appeal to your sense of fairness and commiseration. I have repeatedly told you that I am steeped to the lips in an accumulation of work. . . . You know how very important it is for a young fellow starting in business that he should do his work not only efficiently but promptly. Another thing you have been told is that clients from Criccieth and the surrounding districts can only see me in the evenings. . . . And yet . . . the only assistance you give me is this – that in the course of a *week's* time you have disappointed me in as many as THREE appointments made by you – and that at the last moment, when my business arrangements had been made to suit those appointments – that moreover you kept me on Friday evening to loiter about for about thirty minutes before you even took the trouble to acquaint me with your intention to make a fool of me at your mother's nod. . . .
>
> Now once and for ever let us have an end of this long-standing wrangle. It comes to this. My supreme idea is to get on. To this idea I shall sacrifice everything – except I trust honesty. I am prepared to thrust even love itself under the wheels of my Juggernaut if it obstructs the way – that is if love is such trumpery child's play as your mother deems courtship to be. Now I have told you over and over again that I consider you to be my good angel – my guiding star. Do you not really desire my success? Recollect my success probably means yours.

If you do, will you suggest some course least objectionable to you out of our difficulty. I am prepared to do anything reasonable and fair you may require of me. . . . Believe me – and may Heaven attest the truth of my statement – my love for you is sincere and strong. In this I never waver. But I must not forget that I have a purpose in life, and however painful the sacrifices I may have to make to attain this ambition I must not flinch – otherwise success will be remote indeed.

Write me your views. . . .

    With fondest love

From your sweetheart
D.LL.G.

You will probably get your ring straight from Birmingham. . . . It will afford you another opportunity to show your grit.[1]

The crisis passed, and he was able to give her the ring himself because it was after all posted to him. (Ironic that it should have come from Birmingham, in view of that city's later significance in his life.) But Margaret was still uneasy and suspicious. In early January 1887 she was taken for a short visit to London – perhaps to recover from the row – and two letters that reached her while she was there contain the premonitory rumblings of a second storm. 'As to the affair you refer to the reasons you give are . . . most weighty and entitled to respect and consideration. I only wish you had told them to me last night before I left you. I fear I have now committed myself. Anyhow you need not fear my in any way compromising you. . . . We shall fully and freely discuss this unfortunate business. . . . It undoubtedly requires tact and discretion – but honour must not be sacrificed.'[2] And two days later: 'I want to see you very particularly – about that breach of promise affair for one thing.'[3]

It appears that Lloyd George had agreed to represent a girl called Anne Jones in a breach of promise case. Anne Jones and her sister, Lizzie, were both members of his Chapel choir. Lizzie Jones had earlier taken a fancy to him, which he, no doubt, reciprocated. She was 'a dark-eyed damsel with a rich contralto voice'[4] and over two years previously he had recorded in his diary: 'Lizzie Jones sang some song with the burden "Oh,

---

1. D.L.G. to M.O. (N.L.W.). The words 'that is if love is such trumpery child's play as your mother deems courtship to be' and 'Recollect my success means yours' were inserted as afterthoughts.
2. D.L.G. to M.O., written from Caernarvon, postmarked 6 January 1887 (N.L.W.).
3. D.L.G. to M.O., from Morvin House, postmarked 8 January 1887 (N.L.W.).
4. William George, *My Brother and I*, p. 95.

where is my boy tonight?" Then she sang the last line "I love him still, he knows" – she gave me a glance.'[1] According to William George, that glance had its after-effects, and Margaret could hardly fail to be mistrustful of a professional involvement where there was already a fairly recent, and perhaps continuing, personal involvement. At any rate, the Jones affair provided the occasion for Lloyd George's second thunderbolt. Like the first, it was written in pencil, and from Morvin House:

My dearest Maggie,

Your ultimatum to hand and here I launch my protocol in reply.

What I wish to make clear is this – that whatever course you may think fit in your unfettered discretion to adopt has not been necessitated . . . by any dishonourable or disgraceful proceeding on my part.

What is the gravamen of your charge? Simply this: that I have deigned to permit myself to be entertained with a little harmless music by a couple of girls whom a bevy of dried-up, dessicated [sic] and blighted old maids object to. I am not sure whether their objection is not a recommendation. . . . My calls upon the girl were of a purely professional character – as witness the fact that prior to this breach of promise affair I was not on speaking – let alone visiting – terms with her. Now I could give you good reasons for my not objecting to a little music to finish up the consultations . . . were an Italian organ grinder to put anything in my way I would probably endeavour to please him at the risk of a little personal discomfort by asking him to display the musical qualities of his infernal machine. Now Miss Jones is to me a really good client – for if her case is fought out as it may be (and as it would be but for my regard to your anxiety for a settlement) my bill of costs would be a matter of between £50 and £100. There is moreover the notoriety of advertisement. . . . Well such a client, to begin with, is worth trying to please. Moreover whilst music is as innocent a recreation as you could possibly indulge in it always affords me unlimited pleasure. Furthermore the girls are members of the same Chapel as I am. And one of the few religious dogmas of our creed I believe in is – fraternity with which you may couple Equality. My God never decreed that farmers and their race should be esteemed beyond the progeny of a fishmonger and strange to say Christ . . . selected the missionaries of his noble teaching from amongst fishmongers.[2] . . . If

1. Quoted in *ibid*.
2. The father of Lizzie and Anne Jones kept a fish shop at Ty Mawr, Criccieth.

proof were required of the utter hollowness of what is known as respectable Christianity let him but study the silly scorn of classes for their supposed inferiors. . . . My preference for you rather than for those girls arises not from any social distinctions – these I have the utmost contempt for – but it arises entirely from your superiority in many endearing qualities.

. . . Even if it were a very improper and wicked thing to listen to the song of a fishmonger's daughter, it is now about a month since I heard the chime of her voice – except in Chapel. . . . You are like Blucher at Waterloo, you only appear on the field when the enemy has fled. You have been bombarding an abandoned fortress. . . .

You very kindly suggest that possibly I have committed a blunder in my selection. Well, I do make mistakes often, but as a rule it does not take me two years to find them out. And besides . . . my ideas as to the qualifications of a wife do not coincide with yours. You seem to think that the supreme function of a wife is to *amuse* her husband – to be to him a kind of toy or plaything to enable him to while away with enjoyment his leisure hour. Frankly, that is simply prostituting marriage. My ideas are very different – if not superior – to yours. I am of opinion that woman's function is to soothe and sympathise and not to amuse. Men's lives are a perpetual conflict. The life that I have mapped out will be so especially – as lawyer and politician. Woman's function is to pour oil on the wounds – to heal the bruises of spirit . . . and to stimulate to renewed exertion. Am I not right? If I am then you are pre-eminently the girl for me. . . .

As to setting you free that is a matter for your choice and not mine. I have many a time impressed upon you that the only bond by which I have any desire to hold you is that of love. If that be lost then I would snap any other bond with my own hand. . . .

You ask me to choose. I have made my choice deliberately and solemnly. I must now ask you to make your choice. . . . We must settle this miserable squabble once and for all.

Yours lovingly
Di [1]

Lloyd George's tough tactics worked. After his first outburst Margaret accepted an engagement ring; after the second, it was only a matter of

1. D.L.G. to M.O. (N.L.W.). The letter is dated simply 'Wednesday evening'. Di, Die, Dei and Dai are all familiar abbreviations of Lloyd George's Christian name which, moreover, is sometimes used in its Welsh form, Dafydd or Dafyd.

time before she accepted a wedding ring. Common prudence might have dissuaded her from marrying a man who had told her so clearly what he expected of her, and what she might expect of him. But she was in love. Besides, she was not a common character. When she married Lloyd George she knew that she was taking a big risk, but she followed her heart instead of playing safe. She may have blinded herself to the political implications, but she could not be blind to the human implications: he was sure to be a difficult husband. When he accused *her* of flirting – again on the principle that attack was the best form of defence – he was careful to reserve his own rights: 'Your letter . . . will justify all my flirtations for the past – and future – and teach me how to gloss them over when caught. Oh Maggie Maggie – you do know how to gloss over. Didn't I tell you the other day that cousins were very handy?'[1] The words 'and future' were put in as an afterthought, but that makes them all the more deliberate. Yet it was not three weeks since he had sworn to her, with 'Parry Pwllheli' as his witness, that he would 'not flirt nor even wink improperly at a girl'!

That autumn, the problem of her marrying outside her denomination seems to have been formally discussed by the elders of her Chapel, and Lloyd George boldly expressed the hope that she and her family would 'leave the Methodists and join the Independents'.[2] But the discussion could have no bearing upon her decision: so far as she was concerned, religion was never the real problem. Nor, in truth, was the attitude of her family – though it was doubtless an encouragement to her that her aunt became a strong supporter of Lloyd George, and that even her parents were to some extent influenced by his growing success.

The most effective resistance, however, had always been hers, and she alone could end it. Faced with his direct challenge she showed that she would not give him up. He told her to choose, and for good or ill she made her choice.

They were married on 24 January 1888, in the Methodist chapel at Pencaenewydd, a few miles from Criccieth. She was twenty-one, he just twenty-five. The service was in the morning, and was conducted jointly by Uncle Lloyd and the Methodist minister from Criccieth, with Uncle Lloyd performing the actual marriage ceremony, the minister reading the lesson and leading the small congregation in prayers. It is more than likely that this ecumenical arrangement would have been vetoed by some of

1. D.L.G. to M.O., written from London, postmarked 6 August 1887 (N.L.W.).
2. D.L.G. to M.O., postmarked 9 November 1887 (N.L.W.).

the Criccieth Methodists, which is probably the main reason why the service had to be held elsewhere. Another explanation is that the two families recoiled from the publicity of a Criccieth wedding. The Owens, indeed, insisted that the service should be private, and that it should take place in a Methodist chapel. In all the circumstances, the form and venue of the service represented the best compromise that could be worked out.

At midday Mr and Mrs Lloyd George left by train for London, where they spent their honeymoon. In spite of wet weather, Criccieth celebrated the occasion with a bonfire and fireworks.

When the couple returned from London ten days later they were met at the station by the Owens' carriage, which took them to Mynydd Ednyfed. This was to be their home for the next three years – until Richard Owen decided to give up the farm and build two houses, side by side, on the Portmadoc road out of Criccieth, facing the sea. One of these was for himself and his wife, the other he let to the Lloyd Georges, and they moved into it early in 1891. It was (and is) a fair-sized, semi-detached building, considerably larger than Morvin House – and a palace compared with 'Highgate' at Llanystumdwy. All the same, from Lloyd George's point of view it was hardly ideal that during the early years of his marriage he had to live, first *with* his in-laws, and then next door to them. He got on quite well with the Owens (he could usually get on with anybody if he tried), but a more genuinely independent home life would, of course, have suited him better. It would also have helped Margaret to make a more decisive transition from her rather pampered childhood to the status and responsibilities of a wife. In 1908, when the Owens were both dead,[1] the Lloyd Georges moved into a villa which they built on a well-chosen site overlooking Criccieth, not far from the little Penymaes chapel where David was baptised. But this became Margaret's house rather than his, and the garden with which she surrounded it was perhaps the finest achievement of her life.[2] Confusingly, they gave it the same name as their previous home – Brynawelon (the Hill of Breezes). Lloyd George used to go there for some of his holidays, and he entertained various colleagues there, including Winston Churchill

1. Richard Owen died in 1903, his wife in 1907.
2. When she died in 1941 the house passed to her daughter Megan, who at her death in 1966 left it to her nephew R. R. Carey Evans. In 1969 it was sold outside the family and its contents were dispersed.

(who came, on one occasion, in the Admiralty yacht *Enchantress*). It was always a pleasure to him to walk or to picnic in the country that he knew so intimately as a child. But in other respects Criccieth life did not appeal to him and he was never really happy even in the second Brynawelon. He would complain that it afforded him no privacy: he felt like the largest and most conspicuous fish in a goldfish bowl. Moreover, he detested the climate of North Wales.[1] His natural craving was for warm air and bright skies, and the house which he later built for himself at Churt, in Surrey, was called Bron-y-de (Bosom of the South).

The Lloyd Georges had five children, and Margaret made sure that they were all born at Criccieth. The first, Richard, was born early in 1889; Mair Eluned the following summer; Olwen in 1892; Gwilym in 1894; and the youngest, Megan, in 1902. Lloyd George's favourite was his eldest daughter, Mair, who seems indeed to have been too good for this world. As well as being intelligent and musical, she had an extra-ordinarily sweet nature. Her death from appendicitis in 1907 was the cruellest personal blow that Lloyd George ever sustained. Mair's special place in his affections was largely inherited by Megan, who responded with what was almost a father-fixation. The indulgence that might any-way have been shown to her as the 'baby' of the family was aggravated, in her case, as a result of Mair's death, and by the fact that her father was Prime Minister at the time when she was growing up. Sharing more noticeably than any of her brothers or sisters some of his temperamental traits – his caprice, his feverish vitality, his love of company, his passion for politics – she also shared the dubious benefits of his apotheosis. While he was flattered and fêted, she was flattered and fêted, too; when his star declined, hers declined with it. Most of her life was, therefore, a bitter anticlimax, further embittered by an indeterminate love affair of her own and by her father's love affair with Frances Stevenson – which she resented all the more because it was initially on her account that Miss Stevenson was brought into the family circle. (She was recommended by the head-mistress of Clapham High School as a suitable holiday governess for Megan during the summer of 1911.) Megan was so intensely fond of both her parents that their partial estrangement hurt her even more, perhaps, than it hurt either of them. Her father's second marriage affected her very

1. 'I know of no place where it rains so incessantly. Hundreds of well-known doctors go there and appear to die soon after. The air is too fresh, the water too pure and too much of it. If you wish to see an eclipse at any time, go to Criccieth.' (Fragment in Lloyd George's hand, N.L.W.)

deeply, and for a time she would not speak to him or have anything more to do with him. But they were reconciled before his death, and as he died she, symbolically, was holding one of his hands, Frances the other.

Megan was to some extent a victim of her family background. So was the Lloyd Georges' eldest child, Richard. Indeed, his case was even sadder than hers, because the eventual breach between him and his father was permanent. It was not only that he took his mother's side in the Frances Stevenson affair, though that was the main reason. Lloyd George on the whole preferred girls, and his first-born was perhaps made to feel a bit of a disappointment to him, even in childhood. 'Father and son . . . never got on' (Frances Stevenson has written), 'and personally I think that the trouble started when Dick was born. L.G. had passionately wanted a girl, and here was a boy. There was little sympathy between them, and when the Boer War came Dick was insulted and tormented by the boys at school, and began to resent his father.'[1] The loss of sympathy was far more gradual, in fact, than that passage suggests. There is no direct evidence that Richard resented his father's stand against the Boer War. On the contrary, he unequivocally endorses it in his own books, while admitting that it had unpleasant consequences for him, until he was moved from London to a school in Wales.[2] As a child, he may indeed have slightly resented Lloyd George's obvious preference for Mair, but he was very fond of her himself and there was also plenty of affection between father and son at that stage. Serious trouble began later, when Richard was unable to make a success of his life and so became a recurrent charge upon Lloyd George. With more ambition and force of character he might have done well as a civil engineer: he had the qualification, and his talents were certainly not mediocre. But he failed to develop and exploit them, he had an unhappy first marriage which ended in divorce, and he took to excessive drinking – a weakness that Lloyd George particularly despised. While his misfortunes alienated him from his father, they brought him closer, if anything, to his mother. She gave him moral support, and he supported her against Frances Stevenson, which in turn made matters even worse between him and his father. Thus what had begun, in childhood, as little more than a shadow, darkened and thickened into an impenetrable cloud. Lloyd George had no choice but to leave Richard the earldom which he accepted when he was almost on his death-

1. Frances Lloyd George, *The Years that are Past*, p. 275.
2. Richard Lloyd George, *Lloyd George*, pp. 74-82, and *Dame Margaret*, pp. 218-19.

bed; but he left him nothing else. And Richard later gave vent to his injured feelings in a book about his father which does justice neither to himself nor to the subject.

If Richard and Megan suffered from an excess of Sensibility, Olwen and Gwilym were blessed with an abundance of Sense. They also had the advantage of being placed in the middle of the family, rather than in the more exposed and vulnerable positions of eldest and youngest. They were neither wounded like Richard nor spoiled like Megan. Extrovert and easy-going, they were simply taken for granted as members of the team. Olwen was sent to Roedean and then for a year to Germany. During the First World War she married a promising young surgeon in the Indian Medical Service, Thomas Carey Evans, whose family lived near Criccieth. When they married he was serving with the Army in the Middle East, but after the war they spent several years together in India. For part of the time he was surgeon to the Viceroy, Lord Reading (Lloyd George's old friend, Rufus Isaacs). He was more than equal to the job, but in the circumstances felt that it was rather invidious. Later, when he was back in England, he established a successful private practice which made him completely independent of his father-in-law. In any case he, like Olwen herself, had a robust character and a no-nonsense, sceptical humour, so that he was able to help her to remain free from obsessive involvement in the Lloyd George magnetic field, without losing touch with, or affection for, either of her parents.

Gwilym went to a minor English public school, Eastbourne College. (Richard's briefer English school experience was at Dulwich, but they both went to Cambridge.) After war service with the Royal Artillery he became, in 1922, Liberal M.P. for Pembrokeshire, a seat which he held, with one interruption, until 1950, when he moved to Newcastle upon Tyne. It was fitting that he should represent 'George' country, while his father represented 'Lloyd' country. He was one of the best-liked politicians of his time, and his career took him gradually, by way of the National Government in 1931 and Churchill's war coalition, into the Conservative Cabinets of Churchill, Eden and Macmillan. When he retired from politics he added a second peerage to the Lloyd George name.[1] His make-up was in most respects the opposite of his father's, and he appeared to be just the sort of man whom his father always regarded as the enemy – a solid, good-natured, unimaginative, conventional English squire. Though apparently so different, however, he could

1. He was created Viscount Tenby in 1957.

also be accommodating. Lloyd George found him cooperative in business affairs, uncensorious in private affairs. Without being a hypocrite, he had the happy knack of being able to make the best of all worlds. He had his own life, his own family and, as time went on, his own career, but he never turned against his father any more than his father turned against him. There was no spirit of rivalry, no emotional tension between them: they treated each other as friends.

As great men go Lloyd George was not a bad father. His egocentricity and absorption in politics did not preclude his taking an intimate, continuing interest in his children, and he was interested not only in their general development but also in the small, everyday matters which other men of his eminence would have been likely to neglect. His letters show that, while he was performing his star parts in a much bigger theatre, he was constantly alive to the petty drama of home life. For long periods he was, indeed, away from his children, but for that Margaret deserves some of the blame, because she often kept the children with her in Wales while he, of necessity, was in London. On the other hand, he was often unnecessarily absent from home, more especially at Christmas time. He never forgot his children, however, and when he was with them he gave them full value, exerting himself to entertain, to amuse and to instruct. Instead of reading to them he would *tell* them stories from classical literature, using his gift of mimicry to impersonate the different characters. Richard describes his mesmeric power as a story-teller:

> Those were unforgettable evenings. With Mair and Olwen and Gwilym I used to sit spellbound as my father unfolded the thrilling narratives that Dumas, Hugo and Scott and other notables of a bygone age had written. . . . I am convinced any author would find himself in debt to my father – for telling his tale better than he wrote it. . . . The time at my father's disposal was limited, and curfew for us kids was strictly observed by my mother. But always my father managed to ring down the curtain when our suspense was at the peak! To hear what would happen next made us live for the following evening. Had there been cinemas in those days . . . you could not have seduced one of us away from those after-dinner tales.[1]

1. Richard Lloyd George, *Dame Margaret*, pp. 129–30. This and many other passages show how strong was Richard's admiration for his father, in spite of the breach between them. To the extent that he committed filial impiety in some of the things that he wrote – or dictated to a ghost-writer – about Lloyd George, he must have done so reluctantly and with very mixed feelings. (See Note on Sources for further discussion of his two books.)

Lloyd George was not aloof or condescending to his children, but they looked up to him and took no liberties with him, though he very seldom had recourse to corporal punishment. All the children were devoted to Margaret, who was certainly a most loving and attentive mother. At Criccieth they were also fussed over by their Aunt Polly, and they received no lack of affectionate notice from Uncle Lloyd. They were admitted alternately into the denominations of one or other of their parents – Richard a Baptist, Mair a Methodist, and so on. But the Lloyd George home atmosphere was hardly conducive to their setting much store by sectarian distinctions or niceties of doctrine.

Immediately after his marriage Lloyd George became immersed in the Llanfrothen case, and throughout 1888 and 1889 he was extremely busy with legal and political work. But since for most of the time he was able to return home in the evenings, there are few letters from him to Margaret during the two years before his election to Parliament; and such letters as there are consist very largely of sweet nothings. Thus we find him writing to her from the Court of Appeal in London, before the Llanfrothen hearing:

My dearest little round Maggie,

Case won't come on today by any chance. Fear it won't come on tomorrow. . . . Have been knocking about all day.

Take care of my little wife will you? . . . until I come down to look after her.

I anticipate with delight getting a long letter from you tomorrow.[1]

He probably anticipated in vain. On 15 March 1890 he wrote to her from Chester, where he had a case, suggesting that she join him there the following Monday so that they could go on together to London.

Four days later – on 19 March – Edmund Swetenham Q.C., Tory M.P. for the Caernarvon Boroughs, died suddenly of heart failure. Lloyd George, already the Liberal candidate, was presented rather sooner than he expected with his chance to break into the magic circle.

Fifty years later Dame Margaret Lloyd George recalled how they heard the news. She did not refer to the possible trip to London, but to a more modest arrangement – perhaps suggested by her as a substitute – that they should spend a day together at Caernarvon. That was as great a distance,

1. D.L.G. to M.L.G., postmarked 29 November 1888 (N.L.W.).

and as long a time, as she would have wished to be absent from her infant child. She was speaking, in 1940, to her friend Morgan Humphreys, and he·asked her first whether she thought, when she got married, that a political career lay before her. The exchange that followed is worth quoting both for its vividness and for the evidence that it provides of a myth in the making:

'No,' was the reply. 'I thought I was marrying a Caernarvonshire lawyer. Some people even then said he was sure to get on, but it was success as a lawyer that they had in mind. I am sure neither of us guessed then what lay before us. Even when he accepted nomination as the Liberal candidate for the Caernarvon Boroughs it did not seem to make any particular difference. I comforted myself that the general election was two years distant and that we had those two years in which to enjoy ourselves.'

'You were too optimistic.'

'Yes,' said Dame Margaret, smiling reflectively, 'and it was I who had to break the news to my husband. We had planned to go to Caernarvon for the day. My husband had gone to his office in Portmadoc and I was to join him on the train in Criccieth. It was a fine day, I remember, and I thought we should have a really enjoyable time. When I got to the station I was handed a telegram addressed to Lloyd George, and thinking it might be for me I opened it. All it said was "Swetenham died last night". . . . I knew what it meant. The sunshine seemed to have gone from the day. I did not book as I did not know what my husband would do under the circumstances. Presently his train came in and I saw him looking as if he were anticipating a pleasant holiday. I had to tell him the news, and his smile vanished. We decided to go to Caernarvon but we had a miserable day! The shadow of the coming election spoilt everything.'[1]

There is no reason to doubt that the scene on Criccieth station was as she described it. It was natural enough that she should have reacted as she did to the news of Swetenham's death, and no less natural that Lloyd George should have looked serious when he heard it or that their day in Caernarvon should have lost its carefree character. But the suggestion that she thought she was only marrying a Caernarvonshire lawyer when

1. Interview with Dame Margaret Lloyd George, April 1940 (Morgan Humphreys Collection, N.L.W.).

she married Lloyd George, or that people who predicted he would get on had only his success as a lawyer in mind, is the sort of myth that arises either from a deliberate intention to deceive or from unconscious self-deception. It would have been quite out of character for Margaret Lloyd George to falsify the record intentionally, so we have to conclude that she was doing so unintentionally – which means that she was deceiving herself. Margaret knew that she had spent long periods of time at Criccieth when her husband was begging her to be with him in London. She knew that her love for Criccieth had often vied with her love for him, and that her love for him had not always prevailed. Instinctively, she must have grasped at any explanation of her conduct which would set her own conscience at rest, by satisfying her that she had no responsibility for the flaws in their marriage. One such explanation (a relatively fair one) was that the interests of her husband had to be weighed against the interests of their children, whose health required that they should pass their tender years in the salubrious climate of North Wales rather than in the toxic air of London. But she was also able to persuade herself that she married Lloyd George, as it were, on a false prospectus – that she had no idea, when she married him, that he would become a national politician. If she had admitted to herself that his political destiny was manifest at the time of their marriage, then it would obviously have been more difficult for her to see her subsequent behaviour in a wholly favourable light, even assuming that the only motive for it was the children's welfare. When the truth is inconvenient fantasies are born, and Margaret's claim that Lloyd George's political career was a surprise to her (and to others who knew him in his bachelor days) was certainly pure fantasy. She could not, of course, have foreseen that he would be Prime Minister, but there was clearly no limit to his ambition and anyone could see that he was destined to be a politician rather than a lawyer, with the likelihood of being elected to Parliament at a fairly early date.

Even as a child he had shown unmistakably that he was a political animal. Uncle Lloyd's influence had merely confirmed his natural bent. While he was still only a solicitors' clerk he was writing articles on high politics, and people were tipping him as a future M.P. His favourite leisure activity was debating, and he soon became involved in serious political campaigning. When he was nineteen he was looking upon the House of Commons as the region of his future domain, and when he was twenty-one the local Press was commenting on his fever of renown. All of this (or most of it) must have been well known to Margaret when she began to go out with him, and very soon afterwards he came near to being adopted as Liberal Parliamentary candidate for Merioneth on the eve of a general election. If he had not decided to withdraw his name on that occasion he might well have been adopted and, if so, would almost certainly have been an M.P. *before* they married. Whatever the clinching reason for his withdrawal, nobody who knew him at all could have dreamed of its being due to any loss of interest in national politics, or to any desire on his part to spend the rest of his life practising the law in North Wales. But above all Margaret had the evidence of the blazingly candid letters that he wrote to her at two critical moments in their courtship. Even if there had been no other evidence to go on, these should have been more than enough to show her the sort of man he was and the sort of career he intended to have. He said that his supreme idea was to get on, and that he was prepared to thrust even love itself under the wheels of his Juggernaut if it obstructed his way – rather immoderate language, surely, if he was referring only to the process of getting on as a country attorney. He also said that he had a purpose in life, from which he must not flinch, and that he had mapped out his life as lawyer *and politician*. It would have been hard for him to serve clearer notice of his intentions. Perhaps she could not believe that he meant what he was saying, or perhaps she regarded him as a hot-headed youth whom time and experience would tame. Either way she was gravely mistaken, and if the consequences of her mistake were distressing to her the fault was at least partly hers, because he had given her fair warning.

The myth that she had no idea what she was taking on was given further currency by Richard Lloyd George in the book that he wrote about his mother. During his parents' courtship, he says, 'there was no hint of the shape of things to come'. Lloyd George was making a name for himself, but 'as an astute, resourceful, audacious lawyer', not 'as an embryonic politician'.[1] In *My Brother and I* William George emphatically states the opposite view, which corresponds with the known facts:

> When Maggie married my brother he was already actively engaged in promoting his acceptance as parliamentary candidate for the Caernarvon Boroughs, and she could not but have realised that his guiding ambition was to carve a career for himself in politics, with the inevitable consequence that the best part of his time would have to be spent in London. She had led a quiet life with her parents and she possibly did

1. Richard Lloyd George, *Dame Margaret*, pp. 86–7.

not realise what leaving the country for a life in London would mean to her.[1]

Unfortunately the mythical version seems, even now, to be rather more influential than the truth, with the result that the Lloyd Georges' matrimonial troubles have tended to be oversimplified, virtually all of the blame being ascribed to him, little or none to her. Worse still, the myth that he had no political ambition when he married has lent support to the more popular legend that he began as a 'small' man and grew, by slow degrees, into a 'big' man. In fact, he was always a big man, in the sense that from his earliest years he was thinking big.

The constituency of Caernarvon Boroughs – also, and more correctly, known as Caernarvon District – had returned a Member to the House of Commons since 1536. It was one of the borough constituencies established by Henry VIII when he assimilated Wales to the English political system. Originally composed of five boroughs – Caernarvon, Criccieth, Pwllheli, Nevin and Conway – it was completed by the addition of Bangor at the time of the great Reform Act of 1832. By 1890 it was already something of an anomaly, since its population was under 30,000 while the average for Welsh constituencies was over 45,000. When the county division of Caernarvonshire (with which the borough division must not be confused) was split in 1885 into two constituencies, each of them had a larger electorate than the Boroughs. South Caernarvonshire, or Eifion, then contained nearly 43,000 people; North Caernarvonshire, or Arfon, over 45,000. The number of electors in either case was about 9,000, while the number of electors in Caernarvon District was under 5,000. Anomalous though it was, the Boroughs or District division survived until the redistribution of 1948, and it was ironic that Lloyd George, the champion of democracy, should throughout his career have represented a seat which so flagrantly violated the principle of one vote, one value.[2]

The tradition of the constituency since 1832 had been middle-of-the-road: it had certainly not been radical. The shopkeepers and professional men of whom the electorate largely consisted were hardly the type to be over-zealous for social reform, but they now included many actual or

1. William George, *My Brother and I*, p. 101.
2. The principle has never, in fact, been fully implemented, and representation in the House of Commons is still based on a compromise between the numerical and territorial principles, though the former has gained some ground.

potential enthusiasts for the cause of Welsh nationalism. Until the recent past, moreover, the constituency had a tradition of conspicuous loyalty to its Member, and when it elected Lloyd George the tradition was renewed. In the 108 years between 1837 and 1945 two men – William Bulkeley Hughes and David Lloyd George – together represented Caernarvon District for a total of ninety-four years. W. B. Hughes (another lawyer) was first elected as a Conservative, defeating a member of the noble house of Paget. But ten years later he changed his label to that of Liberal Conservative, under which he held the seat comfortably until 1859, when he fought as a full-blown Liberal and was temporarily put out by another man calling himself Liberal Conservative. In 1865 he regained the seat as a Liberal and held it as such until his death in 1882. It was then won by T. L. Jones-Parry, who had scored a famous victory for the Liberals in 1868, when he captured the Caernarvon *county* seat from the Tories. But Jones-Parry was better at winning seats than at holding them. His popularity as a local worthy could not quite make up for his ineptitude as a politician and public speaker. Having won the county division in 1868, he lost it at the next election, in 1874. And having won the Boroughs in 1882, he lost them to the Tory, Edmund Swetenham, in 1886. Disenchanted with Jones-Parry, the Liberals of the constituency looked for another candidate and chose Lloyd George.

Such, then, was the background to the bye-election contest in March–April 1890. Since his adoption as candidate, Lloyd George had had about fifteen months to prepare for it. He knew the Boroughs extremely well. One of them was his home town, and with all of them he had close professional and political contacts. He had secured financial backing for his campaign from a rich Methodist in the neighbourhood. (This enabled him, after the election, to refuse the offer of a public fund to cover his election expenses, which amounted to about £250. But in future elections, until he became a Cabinet Minister in 1905, he allowed the Liberal Association in the Boroughs to find the money for his campaigns, which they were glad enough to do.) He was well known and much admired for his prowess as an advocate, more especially for his recent triumph in the Llanfrothen case, and his reputation as an orator was already considerable. As a noted scourge of the Established Church he could be sure of powerful support from his fellow-Nonconformists – though one of the Boroughs was the cathedral city of Bangor, containing an extra-large number of Church people. He realised that his best issue would be Welsh nationalism, which to some extent cut across the sectarian line.

The previous general election, and most of the bye-elections which had since been held in Wales, proved beyond a shadow of doubt that the tide was running strongly in favour of Gladstonian Liberalism and Welsh nationalism.[1] The county council elections told the same story. There was, indeed, more resistance to the nationalist current in North Wales than in South Wales, but even in the north Lloyd George stood to gain by campaigning, first and foremost, as a Welsh patriot.

The Conservatives, having lost their sitting Member, were in the disadvantageous position of having to choose someone at short notice to face a Liberal who had been nursing the seat for over a year. In that respect, the tables were turned. If Lloyd George had had to fight Sweten-ham at the next general election, his chances of success would have been more problematical. Even as it was, he had no illusions of a walkover: the struggle, he knew, would be hard and close. The candidate chosen to stand against him was none other than Ellis Nanney, the squire of Llanystumdwy (who had been present in the school there when Lloyd George staged his demonstration against the Creed and Catechism). Nanney was most reluctant to accept the nomination, and was persuaded to do so only with the greatest difficulty. Poor health was the reason he gave for his diffidence, but it was amply justified on other grounds.

Yet he was a local man, and even those who had no time for his opinions or his class tended to like him personally, while to those who were alarmed by Lloyd George's youth and brilliance he must have seemed reassuringly middle-aged and mediocre. In a division whose traditional allegiance was to a rather conservative brand of Liberalism, Nanney was capable of appealing not only to Conservatives but also to a few of the more hidebound Liberals. On the other hand, he was really not of the calibre to stand for Parliament at all, let alone against Lloyd George. He had stood for the Caernarvonshire division in 1880, and for the South Caernarvonshire (Eifion) division in 1885, but he was not a man who could ever be convincingly projected as a national politician. His supporters were reduced to the dangerous tactics of ridiculing Lloyd George for the scale of his talents and political interests. Sir John Puleston M.P., a leading Welsh Tory, said during the campaign: 'The intelligence, the magnificent intellect of Mr George does not confine him within the nar-

1. 'In seven vacancies, seven Liberals were returned, all comparatively young, all Welsh-born and Nonconformist, and all in some sense representative of the nationalist fervour coursing through Wales.' (Kenneth O. Morgan, *Wales in British Politics, 1868–1922*, p. 112.) On 20 February 1890, the constituency of Mid-Glamorgan returned S. T. Evans, unopposed, as a Gladstonian Liberal, in place of a deceased Liberal Unionist.

row limits of the small Principality of which we are so proud: his ideas are as boundless as the Empire itself.'[1] The observation was strikingly true, but it could only serve to draw attention to the rather modest intellect of Nanney. It could not, at that stage of his career, throw any serious doubt upon the sincerity of Lloyd George's commitment to Wales.

Moreover the Liberal candidate was able to exploit to the full the symbolism of the confrontation between himself and Squire Nanney of Gwynfryn Castle. His most effective speech during the election (which prompted the chief Tory agent for Wales to report that the seat was as good as lost) contained the famous passage about 'the cottage-bred man':

> . . . I see that one qualification Mr Nanney possesses . . . is that he is a man of wealth, and that the great disqualification in my case is that I am possessed of none. . . . I once heard a man wildly declaiming against Mr Tom Ellis as a Parliamentary representative; but according to that man Mr Ellis's disqualification consisted mainly in the fact that he had been brought up in a cottage. The Tories have not yet realised that the day of the cottage-bred man has at last dawned.[2]

The misunderstandings created by the key phrase in that passage have already been discussed, but it would not have been misunderstood by Lloyd George's immediate audience. The electors of Caernarvon District were very far from being proletarians, and they knew that Lloyd George was a good bourgeois, like themselves. Above all they knew that, as a member of the *Gwerin*, he had cultural wealth which more than counterbalanced his material poverty. The rich-man-in-his-castle poor-man-at-his-gate image was very useful to Lloyd George later on, when he was the standard-bearer of radical Liberalism in national politics. But in North Wales, at the time of his first election, the class-war overtones of his challenge were social and cultural, rather than economic. The men whose votes he was seeking were, for the most part, less well-off than Ellis Nanney, but they were rich compared with many others, who lacked the property qualification to vote. Such resentment as they were able to feel against Nanney was against the grandeur and Englishness of his ways, rather than against his wealth as such.

Lloyd George's election address, issued on 24 March, was skilfully

1. Quoted in W. Watkin Davies, *op. cit.*, p. 81. Puleston was to be Lloyd George's next opponent.
2. Quoted in Malcolm Thomson, *David Lloyd George*, p. 89, and in other works on Lloyd George. But a *Daily News* special correspondent covering the election reports the phrase as 'hamlet lads' (7 April 1890).

adapted to the business in hand. There was the necessary ritual genuflexion to Irish Home Rule, but the emphasis was upon Wales. Graduated taxation was mentioned, but casually and incidentally: no hint that the author of the address would one day introduce into the British fiscal system the tremendous innovation of super-tax. Gladstone signified his approval of the candidate's policy statement. The veteran Thomas Gee came to speak in support of his young disciple, and among others who spoke for him were Sir Wilfrid Lawson, the Temperance reformer, and Arthur Dyke Acland, an English Liberal M.P. who showed an interest in Welsh education. But the best spokesman for Lloyd George was, of course, himself. He also had the benefit of his early experience of registration work, when he was an articled clerk. Tom Ellis (who could not take part in the campaign because of illness, but sent a warm letter of support) had written to him soon after his adoption urging him to attend to the register, which was, he said, 'the great mine to work'.[1] The advice would not have been lost on Lloyd George.

Polling in the bye-election was on 10 April and the result was declared, after two recounts, the following day. It was:

| Lloyd George | 1,963 |
| Ellis Nanney | 1,945 |

Lloyd George was, therefore, elected by the slender margin of eighteen votes. In the fifty-five years that he held the seat he was never again returned with such a small majority.

After the declaration of the poll there were tumultuous scenes, and Lloyd George indulged in the hyperbole that is normal on such occasions. 'The County of Caernarvon,' he cried, 'today is free . . . the Boroughs have wiped away the stain.' Within a week he was in London. The Boroughs' actual achievement was to send to Parliament one who would leave a more decisive mark upon the British State than any man since Cromwell.

1. T. E. Ellis to D.L.G., 8 January 1889, quoted in Herbert du Parcq, *op. cit.*, Vol. I, p. 97.

FOUR
In at the Deep End

The new Member for Caernarvon District belonged to a class of which Edmund Burke particularly disapproved – 'obscure provincial advocates . . . country attorneys, notaries and the whole train of the ministers of municipal litigation, the fomenters and conductors of the petty war of village vexation'. Such people, he thought, were over-represented in the *Tiers Etat* when the States-General met at Versailles in 1789, and were responsible for much of the trouble that ensued. He would, therefore, have given a very guarded welcome to a young Welshman of the same type arriving at Westminster just over a century later, and in one respect rightly so: for Lloyd George had little of Burke's reverence for the oligarchic structure of government established at the Glorious Revolution, and none whatever for the House of Lords serving as 'a natural rampart' for the protection of property. While he fully shared Burke's hatred of individual tyranny, and of collective tyranny in the form of mob rule, he was, unlike Burke, equally hostile to the selfish exercise of power by a privileged minority. His view of Britain's hereditary ruling class may have been unduly jaundiced, just as Burke's was unduly rosy; but on the assumption that it was right for the British Constitution to become more democratic, one has to admit that Lloyd George's bias was preferable to Burke's.[1]

However that may be, Lloyd George's first concern was to make his mark in the House of Commons and to acquaint himself very thoroughly

1. The quotations are, of course, from Burke's *Reflections on the Revolution in France*, the 'peg' for which was a sermon preached by Dr Richard Price, an untypically revolutionary Welshman. Lloyd George always had a deep admiration for Burke.

with its procedure, without neglecting the public outside. For nearly ten years he concentrated upon Welsh affairs and kindred issues, not because they were his only interest but because he knew that Wales alone could give him political leverage. Though his ulterior ambitions were boundless, he was well aware that nobody could hope to storm the citadel of power from the outside without a very substantial following; and in his case the followers most readily available were Welshmen. This is not to say that his Welsh nationalism was insincere, or that he ceased to care about Wales when other subjects claimed his attention more urgently. He could not restrict his political life's work to Wales, but Wales was never very far from his thoughts even when he was most preoccupied with other business; and the fact that he came to dominate United Kingdom politics made him a much greater practical asset to Wales than he could ever have been as the permanent leader of a tribal faction. The tribe, however, did provide an indispensable base for his assault upon the summit, and he remained conscious of what he owed to his fellow-countrymen – more conscious than they were, eventually, of their debt to him. When he was Chancellor of the Exchequer he said to D. R. Daniel: 'I never had a hand stretched to me from above . . . but I've had hundreds of zealous and faithful friends pushing me from behind. . . .'[1] It is just as wrong to suppose that Lloyd George was *only* interested in Wales during his early years in Parliament, as it is to suppose that he lost interest in Wales when his activities became more diversified. In both phases of his career he showed the same outstanding quality, which Winston Churchill defined as his 'power of living in the present without taking short views'.[2]

One result among many of Gladstone's conversion to Home Rule was that the Liberal Party became, from then onwards, excessively dependent upon the Celtic fringe. England is a conservative country and the Liberal Party only once again secured a majority of the English seats – in the freak election of 1906, when its opposition to Tariff Reform provided it with a good conservative issue. Gladstone's infatuation with Irish Home Rule, and his increasingly arbitrary, capricious methods in old age, cost his party most of the Whig element led by Hartington[3] and much of the

1. D. R. Daniel, *op. cit.*
2. Winston S. Churchill, *The World Crisis 1916–1918*, ch. XLV.
3. Spencer Compton, Marquis of Hartington, had been offered the Premiership in 1880, but had stood aside in Gladstone's favour. He refused to join Gladstone's 1886 Government, since he was opposed to Home Rule. In 1891, he became 8th Duke of Devonshire. He died in 1908.

English radical element led by Joseph Chamberlain. After the election of 1886 (which followed the defeat of the first Home Rule Bill in the House of Commons) England showed a two-and-a-half to one majority of M.P.s opposed to Gladstone, while Scotland supported him in a ratio of three to two, Ireland in a ratio of four-and-a-half to one, and Wales in a ratio of five to one. Parnell and the Irish Party were his allies for obvious reasons of self-interest, and Scotland's marginal preference for him is fairly easy to explain. His family origins were Scottish, he represented a Scottish seat, and he had given the Scots their own Department of State presided over by a Cabinet Minister.

But Wales's sweeping allegiance to him is rather more of a mystery. He had, it is true, widened the franchise for rural voters and protected them against victimisation by making the ballot secret; he had given some support to educational and Temperance reform in Wales; he had appointed the first Welsh-speaker since the eighteenth century to a Welsh bishopric; above all, he was known to be generally sympathetic to the struggle of subject nations for greater freedom and dignity. Yet he was also, in a sense, everything that Welsh Nonconformists could be expected to dislike and distrust – a High Churchman, married into a family of anglicised Welsh gentry, owning a large landed estate in Wales, and living in a castle.[1] He was no longer, as formerly, strongly opposed to Welsh disestablishment, but was not yet committed to it, and he was distressingly silent on the tithe question which was convulsing many parts of the Principality. Besides, it was very clear that he would sacrifice Welsh and any other interests to his Irish policy. Chamberlain, on the other hand, was a Nonconformist, with a whole-hearted belief in disestablishment, and a scheme for devolving power to national councils which, though it might not have permanently satisfied the Irish, would almost certainly have been enough to satisfy the Welsh.

Lloyd George, of course, was a very reluctant Gladstonian. In most respects he was Chamberlain's disciple. His social radicalism was manifestly derived from Chamberlain, and his concept of Home Rule All Round was influenced by Chamberlain's devolutionist ideas. He continued to believe, privately, that Wales ought to have followed Chamberlain rather than Gladstone in 1886. In his view, 'while the action of the Welsh people then was noble and generous, it would have been far better for

1. Mrs Gladstone was born Catherine Glynne, and when her unmarried brother, Sir Stephen Glynne, died in 1874, the castle and estate of Hawarden, in Flintshire, became Gladstone's property.

them to have told Gladstone that they declined to support him in a course which would lead to the disruption of the party and the consequent loss of Welsh disestablishment for a long time'. He considered that, if they had done that, Gladstone would have given way and Parnell would have accepted a different sort of Bill, which would have fitted into a pattern of Home Rule All Round.[1]

Certainly, Chamberlain was able to do nothing for Welsh causes as an ally of the Tories, but Lloyd George's point was that if the Welsh had followed him in 1886 he would never have been forced into alliance with the Tories, and the Whig–Liberal–Radical coalition which the Home Rule controversy shattered might then have achieved what a Liberal rump was obviously quite unable to achieve. Lloyd George's personal decision to follow Gladstone after 1886, and his subsequent campaigns against Chamberlain, must not, however, be written off as cynical opportunism. He could never have entered into a working partnership with the Tories, as Chamberlain did, on the single issue of Irish Home Rule, at a time when the power of the House of Lords was still unbroken and when Tory policies, in general, were anathema to him. His objection to Chamberlain was essentially the same as his objection to Gladstone – that he became a monomaniac. (But at least Gladstone did not go over to the enemy: he merely made the enemy a present of a decade of power.) Chamberlain seemed, to Lloyd George, as unbalanced in sacrificing everything to defeat Home Rule, as Gladstone was in sacrificing everything to promote it. Later, Chamberlain's monomaniac tendencies were seen in his determination to crush the Boer republics, and above all in his crusade for Tariff Reform, which even led him to support the unreformed House of Lords in the constitutional struggle over Lloyd George's 1909 Budget. Lloyd George's coalition project in August 1910 was comprehensive in scope, and he eventually became an ally of the Tories only when the nation's life was at stake. After the war, in 1918, he believed that coalition was still necessary to deal with an immense range of unprecedented problems at home and abroad, and it could

---

1. Conversation on the way to Thomas Gee's funeral, recorded in Herbert Lewis's diary, entry for 3 October 1898 (Herbert Lewis Papers, N.L.W.).

To some extent Lloyd George's view is endorsed by a great Liberal historian, G. M. Trevelyan: '. . . it is difficult to say whether the cause of Irish conciliation was retarded or advanced by Gladstone's proceedings. . . . The Home Rule question broke up the Liberal Party and greatly weakened it. . . . Above all, Gladstone's acceptance of Parnell's claim to have Protestant Ulster as a part of the new Ireland was more than an error in tactics. It flew in the face of racial and political possibilities.' (*History of England*, Bk VI, ch. IV.)

hardly be denied that the case for his remaining in partnership with the Tories then was much stronger than Chamberlain's for entering into partnership with them in 1892, more especially as Lloyd George had the additional advantage of being Prime Minister.

The long-term consequences of Gladstone's decision on Irish Home Rule, and of Wales's support for him in 1886, are, therefore, wide open to argument. But the immediate consequences were unquestionably advantageous to Wales. The Liberal leadership became more susceptible than it had ever been to pressure from the Welsh Members, who for the first time began to look like 'a coherent and distinct party'.[1] Even Lord Salisbury's Tory Government was prepared to take the Welsh more seriously, partly as a means of embarrassing Gladstone. The Tories were inflexibly opposed to disestablishment, but they were willing to legislate on tithe – an issue on which the Liberals had no agreed policy. The Government also gave its blessing and practical assistance to an important Private Member's Bill establishing a system of intermediate schools, which were to fill the gap between the elementary schools and the new Welsh university colleges. The Welsh Intermediate Education Act of 1889 was remarkable not only for putting Wales ahead of England in the development of public education, but also for treating the subject undenominationally and for setting a major precedent of separate Welsh legislation.[2] At the same time, the Welsh Members were working hard to get the Liberal Party committed to Welsh disestablishment. By the end of 1887 it was thought that all but two of the former Liberal Ministers would accept it in the party programme, but one of the two uncommitted was Gladstone himself. When a motion calling for disestablishment was debated in the House of Commons in May 1889, Gladstone was absent, and his speeches in the country, though increasingly sympathetic in tone, were still maddeningly evasive in substance. That year, the Liberal Party was formally pledged to disestablishment, but its leader was not; and, bearing in mind the way Irish Home Rule had become Liberal policy, nobody could doubt that it was Gladstone's will that really counted.

The Welsh Parliamentary Party, when Lloyd George arrived to join it, had recently acquired a new leader. Until 1888 it was led (to the

1. Kenneth O. Morgan, *Wales in British Politics, 1868–1922*, p. 112.
2. The ease with which the measure passed the House of Lords shows that that Chamber was not indiscriminately hostile to progress. Its hostility was, on the whole, reserved for measures which appeared to threaten the fundamental order in Church or State, to tamper with the rights of property, or to damage the interests of the Tory Party.

extent that it was led at all) by Henry Richard, the senior Member for Merthyr. Richard, who spent most of his adult life in England, was a radical internationalist rather than a Welsh nationalist. A friend of Cobden, he devoted himself to the cause of world peace and paid visits to foreign statesmen, urging them to resort to arbitration instead of war. But, though he shared Cobden's idealism, his talents were of a lesser order and his influence abroad was negligible. In Wales, he was essentially a spokesman for the Liberation Society, an organisation of English origin whose aim was disestablishment for the whole country, not just for Wales. Like Thomas Gee, he was a Nonconformist minister turned politician, but to the younger generation of Welsh patriots he had little to say. When he died, leadership of the Welsh Members passed to Stuart Rendel.

Rendel is one of the more interesting minor figures in Victorian politics, whose Life has yet to be written, and who is surprisingly neglected even by the *Dictionary of National Biography*. Old Etonian, Oxonian and High Churchman, he was a close associate of Gladstone in the final phase of the latter's career, and one of his daughters married one of Gladstone's sons. Yet his devotion to the G.O.M. was combined with shrewd, even cynical, insight. Pondering why the Gladstones stayed with him so often, he said: 'I think it was because Mrs Gladstone desired to promote the friendly relations of her children and mine, with the not infrequent maternal motive in such cases. Mr Gladstone liked my company well enough, but in such matters was accustomed to yield to his wife's wishes.'[1] From a mercenary point of view Rendel was certainly worth cultivating. Like Gladstone, he was the son of a self-made man. His father, James Meadows Rendel, son of a Devon farmer, became one of the outstanding civil engineers in an age when Britain led the world in engineering. His work brought him into contact with W.G. (later Lord) Armstrong, a scientific entrepreneur of genius who was, among other things, a pioneer in the manufacture of modern armaments. As a result, three of J. M. Rendel's sons, including Stuart, became partners in the firm of Armstrong's. Stuart was for some years the London partner – the firm's headquarters were at Newcastle upon Tyne – but he also had a strong taste for politics, which his wealth enabled him to gratify. In 1880 he succeeded, partly by means of lavish expenditure, in breaking the Wynn family's traditional hold on the Montgomeryshire seat. Of all Liberal

1. *The Personal Papers of Lord Rendel.*

victories in the 1880 election, Rendel's was the most costly.[1] It was also one of the most significant politically. Though a carpet-bagger and an ethnic outsider, Rendel soon became known as 'the Member for Wales'.

It was his belief that the Welsh Members should work together for specifically Welsh causes, but within the framework of the Liberal Party. The policy which seemed to him to arouse the widest support in •Wales, and the least antagonism in England, was disestablishment. The land agitation worried him, as did some of the political rhetoric of the younger Welsh nationalists, because he feared that the English might come to regard Wales as another Ireland. But in his view disestablishment was a viable issue, and he was impatient of the Liberation Society's demand for nation-wide disestablishment. He sought 'religious freedom' for Wales only, and exerted himself to liberate Welsh politics from remote control by English Nonconformists. Instead of a Wales dependent upon the Liberation Society, he hoped for a Liberal Party so dependent upon Wales that it would have to attend to Welsh grievances.

Such, indeed, was the situation after the 1886 election, and he lost no time in exploiting it. Before the annual conference of the National Liberal Federation, in the autumn of that year, he elicited from John Morley (an acknowledged pace-setter in the party) the admission that Wales had 'subsisted long enough on general expressions of sympathy', and the personal opinion that Welsh disestablishment was a reform which could 'no longer be kept out of the active objects of the Liberal Party'. In time, it was hoped, Rendel's links with Gladstone would bring the leader to the same point of view.

Meanwhile, as the prime mover of the Intermediate Education Bill, Rendel showed his deep concern for the cultural side of Welsh life,[2] and his remarkable skill as a Parliamentarian. A. G. Edwards who, as Bishop of St Asaph, was the liveliest opponent of disestablishment, wrote long afterwards of Rendel:

He was rich, he was clever. He read the Welsh character in its strength and weakness. The Celt in Wales, as in Ireland, may in his embryonic

1. According to one account, Rendel spent £12,000 in the election, his opponent, C. W. Williams Wynn, £20,000. (Kenneth O. Morgan, *Wales in British Politics, 1886–1922*, p. 40.) Rendel himself told T. E. Ellis in 1895 that he began his career with an outlay of £8,000 in 1880 and had since devoted twenty per cent of his annual expenditure to politics. (Stuart Rendel Papers, N.L.W.)

2. He was also a major benefactor of the University College at Aberystwyth, and later presented a site above the town for the National Library of Wales.

stage have multiplied by spontaneous fission. . . . When Mr Stuart Rendel appeared the Welsh party were without form and void – split up into small groups. . . . He set before them one objective, the Church problem. This meant unity of action and ultimately discipline and obedience.[1]

In fact, there was not too much of either in the Welsh Party, even under Rendel's leadership. The Welsh Members were more united, certainly, but they were still far from being a well-drilled fighting force, like Parnell's Irish Party. When Rendel was chosen as leader two Whips were at the same time appointed, but they had no power other than that of persuasion, and collective decisions of the party were never binding on individual members. Rendel had to make the best use he could of such imperfect machinery, and to hold the balance between conservatives and radicals.

Among the latter, the most colourful and beguiling figure in the 1886 Parliament was Thomas E. Ellis, the new Member for Merioneth (where Lloyd George had withdrawn in his favour). Ellis was the son of a tenant-farmer, who ran the complete gamut of formal education in Wales – British school, grammar school, university college at Aberystwyth – before reading Modern History at New College, Oxford, where he took a second-class degree and was on the committee of the Union. After going down from Oxford he acted as private secretary to the Liberal M.P. and industrialist, John Brunner. A man who approached politics in a highly idealistic spirit, Ellis was perhaps over-susceptible to visionary concepts, such as the nationalism of Mazzini or the imperialism of Cecil Rhodes. He was a politician who inspired an unusual degree of affection, though insufficient fear; and he was further handicapped by recurrent ill-health, after being struck down by typhoid on a visit to Egypt in 1889. In many ways he was close to Lloyd George, but Ellis's Oxford period had left him with a somewhat delusive sense of identification with the English élite, which Lloyd George never shared. Ellis was less hard-minded than Lloyd George, as well as less talented.

Between 1886 and Lloyd George's election in 1890, there were two important additions to the radical wing of the party – S. T. Evans and D. A. Thomas. Evans was a grocer's son who, like Ellis, had studied at Aberystwyth. With a London external LL.B. degree he entered the legal profession, first as a solicitor; but after his election to Parliament he was

1. Archbishop A. G. Edwards, *Memories*, p. 150.

called to the Bar (and ended his career as a very distinguished judge, from 1910 onwards). He was returned as M.P. for mid-Glamorganshire in February 1890, shortly before Lloyd George. The two men cooperated in many Parliamentary battles, and they were also cronies during their early years in London. Evans as a recent, and distinctly merry, widower was possibly not the best of influences during Lloyd George's frequent periods of grass widowerhood. (Yet Lloyd George hardly needed to be influenced to do anything that he fancied.) Between him and Evans the friendship was insecure, and eventually lapsed. Whereas Ellis's nature was free from the demons of jealousy, Evans's was not entirely so, and he had, in common with other barrister-M.P.s, a sense of professional superiority which aggravated his resentment of Lloyd George's success.[1]

D. A. Thomas, who was elected for Merthyr in 1888, came to resent it even more bitterly, but partly for a different reason. Though in practical talent he was the most formidable of Lloyd George's Welsh contemporaries, he was a poor speaker and a bad Parliamentarian. Like Evans, he was the son of a grocer, but a grocer turned mining speculator, who sent him to an English school – Clifton – and then abroad, with £300 in his pocket, to broaden his mind. Returning to England, he went as a scholar to Caius College, Cambridge, where he was idle and only got a second in Mathematics. In spite of a Congregational upbringing, he developed a free-thinking outlook very similar to Lloyd George's. His wife, however, who was an orthodox Anglican, insisted that he go through the religious motions, and he once wrote to her, charmingly: 'I'm afraid I haven't got much more faith now than I had before I went to church regularly; perhaps it is because I have so much faith in you . . . that I haven't any to spare for anything else.'[2] From his father he inherited a share in the colliery firm of Thomas, Riches and Co., but his ideas were too dynamic for his partners and he moved for a time to England. In 1887, when one of the Riches died, he was recalled to Wales and, after his election to Parliament the following year, combined politics with big business. Though his acquaintance with Welsh was very limited, he was elected as a 'Young Wales' enthusiast, the most ardent supporter to date of Tom Ellis. Later, he sabotaged the nationalist movement, his personal rivalry with Lloyd George both reflecting and intensifying the

1. In 1891 Lloyd George himself toyed with the idea of becoming a barrister, but decided against it. His brother, who advised caution in the matter, reflects that 'very rarely, if at all, do careers at the Bar and in Parliament go well together' (William George, *My Brother and I*, p. 134).   2. *D. A. Thomas, Viscount Rhondda*, by his daughter and others, p. 21.

rivalry between South and North Wales. His English education, and the time he spent in England as a young man, left him with a social and cultural ambivalence which was bound to complicate his relations with Lloyd George. Their quarrel in the nineties did not, however, blind Lloyd George to his great potential as a man of action, and in the 1916 Coalition he was given – and fully justified – the chance to prove himself in two challenging Ministerial posts.[1]

Rendel, Ellis, Evans and D. A. Thomas were, in their different ways, probably the most significant members of the Welsh Party when Lloyd George joined it, but they were by no means its only personalities of note. Among the older members the most impressive was George Osborne Morgan, author of the Burials Act which gave rise to the Llanfrothen case. Morgan was a scholar of such precocity that he won the Oxford Craven scholarship while still a schoolboy at Shrewsbury, and when he reached the university covered himself with further academic glory. He then became a barrister, and in the famous election of 1868 was returned to Parliament for Denbighshire. In Gladstone's 1880 Ministry he held the modest office of Judge-Advocate-General, in which, however, he did the country a good turn by abolishing flogging in the Army. In the 1886 Government he had to be content with the Under-Secretaryship for the Colonies. He gave Rendel strong backing in his work for Welsh education, and worked hard for disestablishment though himself an Anglican.

Another senior Liberal Member from Wales was the English naval architect, Sir Edward Reed, who sat for the very large and cosmopolitan constituency of Cardiff. He was a volatile politician, at one time rejecting Welsh Home Rule as unthinkable, at another supporting the idea of a completely independent Welsh Party. In 1886 he held lowly office as a Lord of the Treasury. By contrast with Reed, William Abraham (nicknamed 'Mabon') was so authentically Welsh that he had difficulty in making himself understood when he entered the House of Commons in 1885, as M.P. for the Rhondda. He was a miners' representative – the first from South Wales – who had worked for twenty years underground, and he was also a fervent Methodist who, when the normal resources of oratory were exhausted, would captivate an audience by singing to it. Finally, John Bryn Roberts, elected Member for the Eifion

---

1. Thomas, later Lord Rhondda, was in part the model for Lord Raingo in Arnold Bennett's novel of that name, in which the Prime Minister, Andrew Clyth, is modelled on Lloyd George.

(South Caernarvonshire) division in 1885, was one of the most indi-
vidualistic of all the Welsh Members. He was, indeed, rather too
'awkward' to succeed, in the worldly sense. In spite of having a good
political mind he was never a Minister, and in spite of being an excellent
lawyer he was never more than a county court judge. He and Lloyd
George were usually at loggerheads on Welsh issues, and their mutual
antagonism may have been sharpened by the barrister–solicitor syn-
drome. During the Boer War, however, they took the same unpopular
line.

These were by no means the only Welsh Members of above-average
quality. Man for man, the Welsh parliamentary group, though less
numerous and less disciplined than the Irish Party, was also considerably
more varied and more interesting – even before Lloyd George appeared
upon the scene.

For a politician intent upon making his mark at Westminster there are
obvious advantages in being returned at a bye-election. As he takes his
seat the spotlight is momentarily upon him, whereas if he arrives after
a general election, along with a platoon of other new Members, his
entry into the Chamber is relatively undramatic. Lloyd George had the
further advantage of being able to take his seat on Budget Day. Polling
in the Caernarvon bye-election took place during the Easter recess, but
Parliament reassembled on 15 April, and on the 17th George Joachim
Goschen[1] introduced his fourth Budget. After Questions, and before the
Budget statement, the new Member was introduced by Arthur Acland
and Stuart Rendel. From an eye-witness we have this record of the
occasion:

> It was a striking sight, the closely packed benches, the Chancellor of
> the Exchequer with many little volumes of notes, bracing himself up
> for a grand effort; while immediately below the venerable figure of
> Lord Cottesloe stood the young M.P. for the Caernarvon Boroughs,
> nearly seventy years his junior, pale with excitement and the thoughts
> of the career opening before him, waiting for the last answer to be
> given before taking his seat.
>
> He had plenty of time to study the scene of his future labours and
> to weave golden dreams if he chose, for the Boulak Museum, the

1. Goschen, a financier-politician of German extraction, was a right-wing Liberal Unionist
who joined the Salisbury Government as Chancellor of the Exchequer when Lord Randolph
Churchill resigned, suicidally, in December 1886.

Portuguese Imbroglio and the Indian Factory Law still blocked the way.

When at last the young Member, with his sensitive face and slight, boyish figure, advanced to the Table, between Mr Stuart Rendel and Mr Arthur Acland, the cheers were loud and hearty; and they had scarcely subsided when Mr Goschen had risen and was congratulating the House upon the state of the national balance-sheet. . . .[1]

While Goschen was speaking, Lloyd George wrote to Margaret:

This is the first letter which I write as an introduced member of the House of Commons and I dedicate it to my little darling.

I snatch a few minutes during the delivery of Goschen's budget to write her.

I was introduced amid very enthusiastic cheers on the Liberal side. . . .

Cymru Fydd [Welsh nationalists] came to the station to meet us. Mr Alfred Davies a member of the London County Council had his carriage ready to drive us to the House. A very small 'landau'.

Sir John Puleston came up to me and very kindly invited me to dine with him at 7.30. . . .[2]

The new Member had dinner with Puleston, who had spoken against him during the election and was to stand against him at the next one. Thus he lost no time in showing his willingness to consort amicably with people on the other side. In platform speeches he would express mock-indignation that on his first night in the House of Commons he saw leading members of the Tory Government hobnobbing with Irishmen, whom they publicly denounced as criminals. Yet such behaviour was, in fact, congenial to him and he normally did his best to emulate it. Towards Puleston, however, his attitude did soon change, because he came to regard him as a *faux bonhomme* and very much resented his appointment, in July, as Constable of Caernarvon Castle.

Goschen's Budget was on the whole popular with his supporters, though even they noted with some regret that the surplus which he had to distribute was largely due to the increased consumption of alcohol. Moreover, towards the end of his speech he announced a scheme for buying up a certain number of public houses, with compensation to the

1. Eye-witness account by a Mrs Verney, quoted in the *Caernarvon Herald*, 'Town and Country Notes', 2 May 1890.
2. D.L.G. to M.L.G., dated 'Wednesday evening' (N.L.W.).

owners out of money raised from the liquor taxes. 'As he uttered the words,' wrote one Tory M.P., 'we who were sitting immediately behind him looked in each others' faces, with wonder at the first moment, and dismay at the next.'[1] A rather similar scheme had been included, two years previously, in the County Councils Bill, but had had to be withdrawn under heavy fire from opposite quarters – brewers and publicans fearing the consequences of being placed under the control of popularly elected councils, Temperance reformers rejecting the principle of compensation for licensees. The new proposals might be more acceptable to the trade, but Tory M.P.s rightly apprehended another furious outcry from the Temperance lobby. It was on the 'compensation' issue that Lloyd George was to make his maiden speech, but he was in no hurry to make it, explaining his reasons in a letter to Uncle Lloyd: 'I shan't speak in the House this side Whitsuntide holidays. Better not appear too eager. Get a good opportunity and make the best of it – that's the point. Let the cry against compensation increase in force and intensity: then is the time to speak.'[2]

Meanwhile he made his first formal utterance in Parliament – apart from taking the oath – when, on 24 April, he asked the Leader of the House (W. H. Smith) whether the Government intended to bring in legislation to carry out recommendations of the Town Holdings Committee, in favour of leaseholders acquiring the freehold of their own homes 'and to the effect that all religious bodies to whom land has been granted on lease . . . should be empowered to purchase the fee. . . .' Smith replied in the negative, pointing out that the Committee had not yet completed its work.[3] Question Time was a feature of Parliamentary life which had been developing very rapidly in recent decades. Questions were first printed on the notice paper in 1835, and after 1869 a special part of the paper was devoted to them. Until 1886 they were put to Ministers orally, but by the time Lloyd George entered Parliament the modern procedure had been adopted, whereby a Member simply rises in his place and calls out the number of his question. Back-benchers had been discovering the value of Question Time, not so much as a means of eliciting information, but rather for the purpose of drawing attention to themselves, their constituents or their pet hobby-horses. Consequently the number of questions had roughly doubled within the last ten years,

1. Sir Richard Temple, Bart, M.P., *Life in Parliament*, ch. VIII.
2. Letter to Richard Lloyd, 16 May 1890, quoted in H. du Parcq, *op. cit.*, Vol. I, p. 102.
3. Hansard, Third Series, Vol. CCCXLIII, col. 1284.

and on one day in 1889 there were as many as in a whole session forty years previously.

Lloyd George's first important speeches as an M.P. were made from public platforms, not in the House of Commons. Indeed, he had established himself in England as an orator before he delivered his maiden speech. On 7 May he spoke at the Metropolitan Tabernacle, at a meeting organised by the Liberation Society and presided over by Henry Campbell-Bannerman who, fifteen years later, appointed him to the Cabinet. The subject was disestablishment and Lloyd George's speech, though it came at the end of the evening, seems to have been well received. On 4 June he made a triumphant appearance at the Free Trade Hall, Manchester. His theme was the compensation of publicans, and he argued that those who infringed the provisions of their licences should be punished as rigorously as Irishmen who, in other ways, broke the law. The publican demanded equity, and should therefore be judged by the 'grand old maxim in Equity. . . . "He who comes to Equity must come with clean hands".' The liquor trade should show the hand with which it proposed to grasp compensation. 'It reeks with human misery, vice and squalor, destitution, crime and death.'

In a letter to his wife he described the audience's reaction:

> Your old Die scored the greatest success of his life at the Free Trade Hall last night. The Hall was packed with an audience numbering several thousands. . . . Immediately I got up the audience cheered again and again. . . . This set me up. When I said I was a native of Manchester they renewed their cheer. . . . I spoke for half an hour amid continued and long continued cheers. . . . I never saw a people more profoundly impressed. . . . During my closing sentences a hush fell over the whole place. I spoke fiercely – feeling myself mind you intensely every word I uttered and charging my sentences with all the intensity of my heart . . . when I sat down there came a sight which I shall never forget – the whole dense and immense audience seemed for a moment stunned but recovering they sprang up as one man and flung hats handkerchiefs sticks . . . anything they could get hold of. . . . I trembled like a leaf with passion for a long while. I was overwhelmed with congratulations. . . . The Tabernacle was nothing to it in point of delivery and effect. I am asked to go to all sorts of places now. . . .[1]

1. D.L.G. to M.L.G., 5 June 1890 (N.L.W.).

Lloyd George's accounts of his speeches never err on the side of under-statement. His rhapsodical appreciation of them recalls that of an author whom he specially admired, Victor Hugo, for the speeches which he delivered in the French Assembly. These, collected in his *Actes et Paroles*, he adorned with parenthetical notes describing how his fellow-legislators reacted to them (*bravos, murmures, clameurs, vive et profonde agitation, explosions de rire, hilarité bruyante, tumulte inexprimable*, and so on). In this, as in some other respects, Lloyd George resembled Hugo.[1] In letter after letter he shows that he can outdo the most enthusiastic Press reports of meetings that he has addressed.

On 13 June he seized a good opportunity for making his maiden speech. Arthur Acland had moved a wrecking amendment to the Local Taxation Bill, aimed at diverting to educational purposes the money earmarked for compensating publicans, and it was on this that Lloyd George decided to speak. New Members either go in, as it were, at the shallow end, with maiden speeches composed of innocuous platitudes, or – much less frequently – address the House for the first time in an aggressively controversial spirit. Most novices prefer the safer course, but Lloyd George characteristically took the plunge with a speech containing sharp criticism of two Parliamentary giants, Lord Randolph Churchill and Joseph Chamberlain. (In 1929 another young Welshman, Aneurin Bevan, made a similar maiden speech, in which he attacked Winston Churchill – and Lloyd George.) Apart from its audacity, the speech has no particular interest or merit; but it was evidently well-judged and well-delivered, so that it caught the fancy of the House. The personal attacks were administered with a wit which now seems rather laboured, but which at the time may have served to mitigate disapproval of the speaker's brashness. The following day he wrote to Margaret:

My very dearest Maggie,

Shortly after I wrote my letter of yesterdays [*sic*] to you I got up and spoke for the first time in the House of Commons . . . there is no doubt I scored a success and a great one. The old man and Trevelyan, Morley and Harcourt appeared delighted. I saw Morley shortly afterwards and he said it was 'a capital speech – *first rate*' and he said it with marked emphasis. He is such a dry stick that he wouldn't have said anything unless he thoroughly believed it.

1. They were also very much alike in sexual behaviour. The reference to Hugo's comments on his own speeches is taken from 'The Oratory of Victor Hugo' in *Biographical Essays 1790–1890*, by Sir Edward Boyle, Bart (father of Lord Boyle of Handsworth).

I have been overwhelmed with congratulations both yesterday and today. I was in the Library of the House getting up statistics . . . and several Irish members who happened to be there came up . . . and said my speech was all the talk. Tom Ellis – who is *genuinely* delighted because one of his own men has succeeded – told me that several members had congratulated *Wales* upon my speech. Stuart Rendel said I had displayed 'very distinguished powers'. . . . There is hardly a London Liberal paper or even provincial paper which does not say something commendatory about it. I send you some of them. . . .

> Your loving old
> Dafyd[1]

The Press was, indeed, very favourable, and Gladstone was reported to Lloyd George as being 'exceedingly delighted'.[2]

Early in August he was preparing Margaret for an even bolder sally. He would be objecting, he said, to a vote of £2,000 'for providing gilt breeches or something of that sort for a fellow who, happening to be Lord-Lieutenant of Ireland, imagines he ought to ape royalty'. The short speech he was planning to make would 'not be particularly sweet to those who adore the peacockism of royalty'.

> S. T. Evans and I intend objecting to making some Princeling of Royal lineage a Knight of the Garter at an expense of £400 to the country. . . . Don't you think old Maggie I ought to have a fling at them even if the Tories howl me down and brand me as a wild revolutionary fanatic. D——n the whole brood (and that is damning a good lot for they are exceedingly numerous).[3]

Nor was it only Tories who would be outraged by what he had to say:

> It is frightfully difficult to get up in this House at all especially on a question like this when all the gentility of even your side is against you.[4]

The speech was delivered on 13 August on a motion by Lloyd George to reduce the vote for 'Miscellaneous Advances'. It was good knock-about stuff:

> I think it absolutely monstrous that we should be paying these sums for what is absolutely worthless to this country, when there is so much

1. D.L.G. to M.L.G., 14 June 1890 (N.L.W.).
2. H. du Parcq, *op. cit.*, Vol. I, p. 107. The campaign against the 'compensation clauses' was successful. The Government withdrew them at the end of June.
3. D.L.G. to M.L.G., 7 August 1890 (N.L.W.).
4. D.L.G. to M.L.G., 9 August 1890 (N.L.W.).

suffering . . . among our working classes. Shortly before this Supplementary Estimate was issued, the Report of the Sweating Committee appeared, and what a ghastly comment are the main features of that Report upon this expenditure. The Report shows that thousands of hard-working, thrifty people are living a life of hopeless, ceaseless toil, and yet we are asked to spend hundreds in decorating a foreign Prince [Henry of Prussia], and thousands in adorning a mere supernumerary. These items represent principles of expenditure which do a vast amount of harm in this country. . . . I do not believe that this gorgeousness, and this ostentation of wealth, is necessary in order to maintain the Constitution. On the contrary, I think it does far more to repress than to promote sentiments of loyalty.[1]

He was satisfied with the effect that this speech produced. 'There was a very good House . . . and everyone listened with great attention. I think I scored. . . .'[2]

Lloyd George was never a serious republican, but he had mixed feelings about the Monarchy. The symbolism of the Crown appealed to his imagination, and when he was in power he showed how well he understood its appeal to others. At the same time he felt that some royal personages were unworthy of their privileges, and he also detested the kind of snobbery and flummery which Courts have a habit of breeding, and to which, he felt, the English were almost morbidly prone. In attacking some incidental features of royal and viceregal life he was, therefore, deliberately attacking aspects of the English character which, as a Welshman, he found objectionable. And he did so in the knowledge that an offensive strategy was more likely to succeed with the English than a policy of tame submission. 'The Englishman,' he said, 'never respects any fellow unless that fellow beats him: then he becomes particularly affable towards him.'[3] It was on that principle that he acted from the moment he set foot in the House of Commons, but his offensiveness was carefully calculated. He did not, as a rule, insult either persons or institutions in a reckless way, and he certainly never believed in insulting the Monarchy as such. When, at a Mansion House banquet which they were both attending in May 1892, Sam Evans refused to stand up and drink the loyal toast, Lloyd George was annoyed – all the

1. Hansard, Third Series, Vol. CCCXLVIII, cols 904–6.
2. D.L.G. to M.L.G., 14 August 1890 (N.L.W.).
3. D. R. Daniel, *op. cit.*

more so as he became involved in guilt by association, the incident being used against him during the election the following month.

On arrival in London Lloyd George first stayed with R. O. Davies[1] and his wife at their house in Acton. Margaret came on a brief visit a fortnight later (when he was able to try out on her his speech for the Metropolitan Tabernacle), but she did not stay with him in London for any length of time until the following year. Her dislike of London, always strong, was at its strongest when she was expecting or nursing babies, and Mair was born early in August 1890. That year, after leaving the Davieses, he stayed at a succession of digs or at the National Liberal Club. Reluctance to travel home to Criccieth for the weekend when Parliament was sitting was soon apparent, and became more marked with the passage of time. It was, admittedly, a long and tedious journey, but that was not the only reason: another was that he loved the big city and had no taste for small-town life. Immediately after Mair's birth he spent 'a very ungodly and rather unprofitable Sunday':

Who should come into my room at 10.30 in the morning . . . but S. T. Evans. . . . We looked up the 'preachers for tomorrow' in the Saturday papers and finding there was no one we cared for we took a boat up the river to Kew Gardens. It was a bright day and the ride was a pleasant one. We returned on the top of an omnibus. When we were half way to London the horses stuck and would not proceed an inch and there we were in the middle of a crowded street with numbers of people massing to gaze at us looking like a lot of idiots. . . .

After changing buses twice they arrived, in drenching rain, at the St James's restaurant, Piccadilly, where they had 'soup and steaks'. Lloyd George then went to the House of Commons and worked at his speech (on Prince Henry of Prussia etc.) 'until one o'clock in the morning'.[2] Margaret reacted sharply to this letter, because he had pleaded work as the excuse for not coming to Criccieth. But he defended himself:

. . . there is a great deal of difference between the temptation to leave your work for the pleasure of being cramped up in a suffocating

1. Not to be confused with Alfred Davies who met him at the station and drove him in a landau to the House of Commons.
2. D.L.G. to M.L.G., 10 August 1890 (N.L.W.).

malodorous chapel listening to some superstitious rot . . . and on the other hand the temptation to have a ride on the river in the fresh air with a terminus at one of the loveliest gardens in Europe.[1]

She was, perhaps, too ready to nag him – a self-defeating habit, more especially when practised at long range.

His social circle in London was, at first, almost exclusively Welsh, and it remained so to a large extent even when he could count many English politicians as friendly acquaintances. Among Welshmen who had established themselves in London at that date several were prominent in the drapery business, with names that are still very familiar to Londoners. Soon after his arrival he was dining with Mr and Mrs D. H. Evans:

> . . . Evans is a young Welshman who keeps a drapery establishment in Oxford St. Although he is only 33 yrs of age and started worth £500 now he has already amassed a large fortune. He lives in a small house in Regent's Park. He showed me one of his pictures – a Landseer picture of a dog – which cost him £800!! He had also a Turner which must have cost him some hundreds . . . he is a lightheaded feather-brained fellow with some good nature and much practical shrewdness . . . she is clever but purse proud and consequently contemptible. Of course she was alright with Thomas[2] and I [sic] – we are M.P.s and therefore fit company for a beatified draper's wife but I hated and despised her from the moment she talked about the Welsh Society in London being 'led by drapers' assistants'. I asked fiercely – 'Why not drapers' assistants? Every great movement has been initiated by men of that class'. . . .[3]

Lloyd George never had much to do with the D. H. Evanses, but as time went on he became the frequent companion of another Welsh draper, Timothy Davies – and of Mrs Davies.

At the end of 1890 he was keen to move out of lodgings and into a family flat. He urged Margaret to come up in the New Year, bringing the children. Fogs, he said, would have disappeared long before Parliament resumed. Early in 1891 he took for £70 a year's lease on a set of rooms in Verulam Buildings, Gray's Inn, and did his best to commend them to Margaret. 'With a porter at the gate and two housekeepers on the premises and your own chambers double-doored and the windows

1. D.L.G. to M.L.G., 13 August 1890 (N.L.W.).   2. Alfred, not D. A., Thomas.
3. D.L.G. to M.L.G., postmarked 10 June 1890 (N.L.W.).

iron-barred you surely ought to feel very secure until your husband comes home.'[1] About a week later she did join him in London, accompanied by the infant Mair, but not by Dick. They stayed with him until May. When they went back to Criccieth he failed to see them off at Euston, pleading afterwards rather lamely: 'I hate all partings and leave takings. They always were an aversion of mine.' But he complained pathetically of the solitude when they were gone. 'We are in for an all-night sitting this evening. I don't mind it at all. I would prefer sleeping on one of the soft benches in the Upper Lobby here to returning to that deserted lonely haunt of mine in Verulam Buildings.'[2] Margaret was up again – with both children – for a few weeks in June and July, but thereafter she was expecting Olwen (who was born the following April), and she was not in London at all throughout 1892. In August of that year he gave up Verulam Buildings, but expressed the hope that they would be able to find 'decent chambers' for the following year 'when *we* come up'. And he added in Welsh: 'Remember old Maggie that you and the children will have to come up next time.'[3]

During the long months that they were apart she kept him supplied with country produce – eggs, butter, fruit and flowers. And he often asked her to send him books or other documents that he needed for the preparation of speeches. 'I want you to send me by tomorrow's post *without fail* a book or pamphlet called "Fabian Essays in Socialism". In that book there are some notes I took of the attendance at the parish churches in England and *I want those*. If you send me those notes you needn't send me the book.'[4] In return, he sent presents to the family: for instance, snow shoes for his mother-in-law, toys for the children. And when he could remember he sent his clothes home to be washed. 'I haven't changed my drawers for a whole fortnight. Please send me a pair per parcels post.'[5] After such an admission it is a little hard to understand how he managed to have a reputation for cleanliness and spruceness. But he certainly had.

When Lloyd George was a young M.P. each year's session began in February and ended in July or August. It was rare for Parliament to be

1. D.L.G. to M.L.G., 2 February 1891 (N.L.W.).
2. D.L.G. to M.L.G., 14 May 1891 (N.L.W.).
3. D.L.G. to M.L.G., 9 August 1892 (N.L.W.).
4. D.L.G. to M.L.G., 21 January 1891 (N.L.W.). The 'Fabian Esssays' were published in 1889.
5. D.L.G. to M.L.G., 27 May 1892 (N.L.W.).

kept sitting even into the late summer. But Lloyd George never spent the whole of the long recess at Criccieth. After his Manchester triumph he was much in demand as a platform speaker up and down the country, and he was soon also kept away from home by business commitments, as well as by the growing volume of his legal work outside Wales. At the end of September 1890 he spoke in support of John Morley at St Helen's. Most of the speech was quite wittily polemical at the expense of the Government's Irish policy, and of Arthur Balfour (Chief Secretary for Ireland) in particular. This went down well at the time, but one passage catches the eye in retrospect: 'The great battles of Europe were fought in Belgium. They were fought, not for the independence and freedom of Belgium, but for the liberty of Europe against some despot or other.'[1] At Sheffield, in November, he warned English Liberals that unless Welsh disestablishment was given 'precedence' they could no longer count on the loyalty of their Welsh brethren. 'Pious opinions' would no longer do.[2]

At this time the political world was convulsed by the O'Shea divorce case, which ruined Parnell and split the Irish Party. Parnell's fall was due to his being disowned by Gladstone, who feared the political effects of outraged puritanism in Britain; and the Irish split was due to his refusal to stand down when Gladstone disowned him. Lloyd George had a sneaking admiration for Parnell, but also felt that he had no right to sacrifice the Irish cause to his personal vanity ('He must be a base selfish wretch'[3]). Moreover, he took Parnell's fate as a warning to himself, and over twenty years later, when inviting Frances Stevenson to become his mistress, he was careful to explain that he could not make her his wife, because no man had 'a right to imperil his political party and its objectives for the sake of a woman – which meant that no divorce was possible'. To illustrate his point, he gave her a copy of Kitty O'Shea's book on Parnell.[4]

He was very active, early in 1891, on the Committee stage of the Government's Tithe Bill, which was designed to make tithe payable by the owner of land, rather than by the occupier. One of Lloyd George's amendments (defeated) was to the effect that appeals from tithe valuations

1. Speech at St Helen's, 29 September 1890.
2. Speech at Sheffield, 20 November 1890.
3. D.L.G. to M.L.G., 28 November 1890 (N.L.W.).
4. Frances Lloyd George, *The Years that are Past*, ch. 4. What he said was the truth, but not the whole truth. Apart from the need to protect his career, he was also reluctant on other grounds to end his marriage with Margaret.

should be to the county court, because the Commissioners were, he alleged, as a rule local landowners, whose impartiality was necessarily in doubt.[1] Another of his proposals (also defeated) was that in any penal or criminal proceedings arising out of the Bill defendants should have the right of trial by jury and, in summary cases, the right of appeal to Quarter Sessions. 'Something was said the other night about juries in Wales being carried away by their sympathies when trying cases arising out of the present tithe agitation. But I would point out that the Registrar, on whom the duty of selecting the jury would fall, would not select persons who were likely to be carried away by their feelings.' In the county of Caernarvon, he said, five of the six Registrars were Conservatives, and he believed that the sixth was a Liberal Unionist. County court judges were not ardent partisans, but the same could not be said of magistrates.[2] He intervened repeatedly on the Bill, gaining useful practice in the technique of Parliamentary discussion. Already he was showing his mastery of the pithy Committee speech, short, to the point, yet with no opportunity missed for a good generalisation. And he was also quite prepared for give-and-take in the re-wording of amendments. His efforts (and S. T. Evans's) were written up in the Press, and the Attorney-General[3] congratulated Lloyd George on his 'acuteness'. The Bill eventually passed, but after considerable delay and with the Welsh Members voting against it by twenty-five to five. Moreover, Lloyd George was able to claim that about one-third of his and Evans's amendments had been incorporated.

Reference to one Tory argument on tithe gave him a good debating point the following month, when the Member for Cardiganshire brought in a Welsh local option bill, which was unexpectedly carried by six votes on Second Reading. Speaking on it, Lloyd George said:

The attitude of hon. gentlemen opposite . . . on this question affords a strange contrast to that which they took up in regard to the tithe question. They said it was necessary to deal with [that] because of the scenes of disorder which occurred in Wales arising out of the collection of tithes; but the amount of disorder that arises in connection with tithes is as nothing compared to the disorder that arises in connection with public houses.[4]

1. Hansard, Third Series, Vol. CCCXLIX, cols 1540–1, 2 February 1891.
2. *Ibid.*, Vol. CCCL, cols 63–5, 5 February 1891.
3. Sir Richard Webster, later Lord Alverstone.
4. Hansard, Third Series, Vol. CCCLI, cols 1340–2, 18 March 1891.

In June he had another chance to beat the Welsh Nonconformist drum, when the Government's Education Bill was introduced. This was essentially an enlightened and progressive measure, in that it established the principle of free elementary schooling. But the chief motive for it seems to have been a partisan desire to safeguard the voluntary (Church) schools. It was feared that, unless the Tory Government made it possible for fees to be abolished in *all* elementary schools, the next Liberal Government would abolish fees for the Board schools without providing in any way for the Church schools, so making the latter's position untenable. In a long Second Reading speech Lloyd George attacked the Bill's sectarian aspect. The fact that Ministers had accepted the principle of free education ought not to blind Members on his side of the House to the 'dangerous and insidious' features of the Bill. Passing over in silence his own lucky experience at a Church school, he gave many examples tending to show that the Board schools were superior to those in the denominational system. Politically, his immediate object – as, later, in the big controversy over the 1902 Education Bill – was to air a Nonconformist grievance. Educationally, his ideal was a secularised system, and his underlying impatience with religious bickering in politics is manifest in his peroration:

> Why should you perpetuate these grievances? Your Church gains nothing thereby. Every grievance redressed adds force to Conservatism in its higher sense. . . . England requires the services, the energies, the enthusiasm of men now devoted to the redress of wrongs for other and important national matters. You have in Wales the best men on either side – Churchmen and Nonconformists – devoting their energies to this deplorable struggle, and meantime you have the population reduced to such a condition that, on January 1st, one person in every nineteen of the population was in receipt of parish relief. We want, I say, the energies of our people devoted to raising the social condition of the nation. I urge the Government to take this opportunity to give free education in a generous form, free from denominational trammels, and worthy of its name.[1]

In Committee he proposed an amendment to the effect that managers should not stipulate membership of any particular denomination in appointing or retaining teachers. It was supported by Harcourt, Acland, Ellis and Trevelyan, but opposed by Joseph Chamberlain. In another

1. Hansard, Third Series, Vol. CCCLIV, cols 1301–3 and 1315–23, 23 and 24 June 1891.

amendment he suggested that when the grant to a school exceeded the amount paid in fees the surplus should be applied to educational purposes. 'I desire that [the surplus] shall be used to secure greater efficiency of education instead of relieving the friends of voluntary schools. . . . I would urge that the money might be used for providing technical instruction.'[1] Both amendments were lost.

Lloyd George's most brilliant display of gamesmanship in his first Parliament came in long debates on the Clergy Discipline (Immorality) Bill, which was first introduced at the end of July 1891, but then withdrawn and re-introduced in a shorter and, as it was hoped, 'not contentious' form in the spring of 1892. It was, indeed, a relatively blameless measure to facilitate the removal of criminous clerks from their livings, but Lloyd George and S. T. Evans realised that it gave them abundant scope for filibustering. On Second Reading Lloyd George moved an amendment 'that this House, whilst deploring the circumstances which have occasioned the introduction of this Bill, considers that it is no part of the functions of the State to attend to matters of spiritual discipline'. Speaking second in the debate, he denied any intention of enforcing disestablishment through the perpetuation of scandals in the Church. But he could see no urgent need for the remedial action proposed 'while there is other legislation of the foremost importance to the mass of the people waiting to come on'. Moreover, Parliament was not fitted to deal with such matters. It was 'elected by people two-thirds of whom are not adherents of the Church of England, and it is elected for secular purposes – for dealing with questions of finance, of peace and war, and for solving great social problems. . . .' The next speaker was Gladstone himself, who paid a very young Member the compliment of replying laboriously, and at some length, to his arguments. There was no lack of irony in the situation – organised religion meaning so much to Gladstone, so little to Lloyd George. S. T. Evans opposed the Second Reading on three grounds: that disestablishment was the proper remedy, that 'clergymen' in the first clause did not include bishops and archbishops, and that some offences were not covered in the Bill. All the same it was, of course, read a second time, and Lloyd George's amendment was heavily defeated.[2]

The Bill was then referred to the Standing Committee on Law, and Gladstone arranged to be a member of it so that he could carry on the

1. *Ibid.*, Vol. CCCV, cols 46 and 597–9, 1 and 7 July 1891.
2. Hansard, Fourth Series, Vol. III, col. 1585, 28 April 1892.

fight. Lloyd George admired his relentless spirit: '. . . he would just sit and shake his head at us when we moved an amendment, and glare at us with his fierce eye – ah! how fierce when you were fighting him.'[1] When the Bill returned to the floor of the House, Lloyd George and Evans, with fairly steady support from Ellis, kept discussion going for over eight hours, moving and seconding amendments mostly on technical points speciously adduced as matters of principle, though some were valid in their own right and accepted. A typical amendment, moved by Lloyd George, was to leave out the word 'shall' and substitute the words 'may, if he think it to be to the interest of his parishioners' – in a context which enabled him to appear more Anglican than the Anglicans.

> As the Bill stands at the present moment, the Government propose to compel a bishop to re-institute a clergyman whenever the mercy of the Crown is extended to him. I can conceive of several cases in which a bishop would not consider it in the interests of the parishioners to re-institute such a man. After all, we must not forget that this Bill is not intended to protect the parsons, or even to punish them, but . . . to purify the Church to the greatest possible extent. . . . Take the case of a clergyman who gets a free pardon on the ground that he was of weak mind at the time of the offence. . . .

The amendment was carried. Altogether, Lloyd George intervened thirteen times on Report, and the Speaker commented: 'I have never known a Bill on Report debated in this way. I have never known such elementary and long speeches made on every amendment. . . .' And the Attorney-General, who made vigorous use of the closure, called the House's attention to the fact that 'there are no fewer than twenty-three amendments put down in the names of two hon. Members'.[2] It was just the way for opposition back-benchers to cut a figure on the eve of a general election.

The Clergy Discipline Bill was the occasion for Lloyd George's first major encounter with A. J. Balfour, who became leader of the House of Commons at the end of 1891, after the death of W. H. Smith. Balfour moved the Second Reading of the Bill, and Lloyd George was the next speaker. The careers of these two men were to be closely intertwined, and they had far more in common than superficial appearances suggested. Both had come into politics young, as privileged representatives of a

1. Quoted from the *Daily Chronicle*, 19 May 1892 (Herbert du Parcq, *op. cit.*, Vol. I, p. 129).
2. Hansard, Fourth Series, Vol. V, cols 464–518, 2 June 1892.

class (though not, of course, the same class); both had a fundamental belief in the British Empire, and both had an activist approach to politics. Lloyd George was not the rugged plebeian who might have been expected to emerge from a country cottage; nor was Balfour the etiolated patrician that it suited his opponents – including Lloyd George – to make him out to be.[1] Certainly Balfour was half a Cecil (Lord Salisbury, the Prime Minister, was his maternal uncle), and one of his grandmothers belonged to the firmly rooted Scottish family of Maitland. But the Balfours themselves were comparatively new rich. The family fortune was made by A. J. Balfour's grandfather, as a military contractor in India. In any case, there was nothing soft about the new Leader of the House. He got the job not because he was the Prime Minister's nephew, but because Tory Members much preferred him to Goschen or any other possible candidate. He was a professional politician of commanding intellect and exceptional ruthlessness, between whom and Lloyd George there was a bond of understanding and mutual respect which grew stronger with the passage of time, as each became more fully aware of the other's formidable qualities.

Lloyd George had the rare distinction of being equally successful as a Parliamentarian and as a platform speaker. Those who excel in one *genre* do not necessarily excel in the other, and some leading politicians excel in neither; but Lloyd George unquestionably excelled in both, and the varied merits of his style as a popular orator may be seen in three of the speeches that he delivered in the country, during the period of his first Parliament.

At Rhyl he deployed his arts of sarcasm and ridicule in an attack on the Church of England, and more especially its doctrine of Apostolic Succession:

Some virtue from Peter has been transmitted through ages and generations and is now running in the veins of Welsh parsons. All that I can say is that, on its way down, it must have passed through some very muddy channels. . . . We are asked to believe that the unction which has oozed out of the fingers of a succession of profligate

---

1. Even when they were no longer opponents Lloyd George could still say that Balfour, in history, would be 'just like the scent on a pocket handkerchief' (Thomas Jones, *Whitehall Diary*, entry for 9 June 1922). But he did not really mean it. He was sacrificing truth to the momentary lure of a phrase.

pontiffs and unrighteous prelates is more potent in its influence for good than the inspiration which comes straight from heaven as the result of the prayers of good and holy men. But I fear that the mediums through which this Apostolic Succession has passed have injuriously affected its recipients. . . .

They are the successors of Peter, the plain, bluff, honest old fisherman. If he had turned up at the Church Congress the other day, there is not a prelate or a prebendary or a dean amongst them who would not have shunned him. They might have handed him over to some convenient curate to be proselytised, who would have warned him against the pernicious habit of attending conventicles to listen to an ordinary carpenter's son – a man without the true sacerdotal succession in his veins.

Can you picture him coming down to attend the Church Congress in a special train, with a man in buttons dancing about him, carrying a jewelled crozier, and marching in a brilliant procession to attend the conference? Can you portray him driving up in a brougham to the door of the House of Lords, lolling on its scarlet benches, and in his most archiepiscopal twang drawling out a series of speeches in favour of county-courting and imprisoning his fellow-religionists for refusing to pay a tribute to which they have conscientious objections? Can you imagine him dwelling in a stately mansion with a host of menials ministering to his luxury? Can you fancy him drawing a salary large enough to have kept the Temple going for months? And all this with the poor rotting in misery at his very palace gates.[1]

The target was wide, but the aim uncommonly sure.

On the theme of social justice, he used an historical argument to buttress his indictment of the comfortable classes:

These classes receive their quota of the national wealth in return for services which they are supposed to render, but do not perform. The land of this country was distributed amongst its owners, the predecessors of its present holders, for the express purpose of enabling them to organise and maintain a military system in the country for the defence of its coasts, and even for aggressive purposes when necessary. The land was also to maintain royalty, and to bear the expense of dispensing justice and preserving law and order. Now what has happened? The land is still in the possession of a privileged

1. Speech at Rhyl, 10 November 1891.

few, but what has become of the burden of maintaining the army, law, order and royalty? It has been shifted upon the shoulders of the toilers of this country. . . .

. . . Things must be equalised. This deplorable state of things cannot go on for ever. But let no working-man make a mistake: the party which is dominated by . . . plutocrats and millionaires is not the one which is likely to assist them in attaining such a desirable consummation.[1]

There was force in the historical argument, but Lloyd George's lifelong vendetta against landowners caused him to overlook their virtues as a class, while somewhat exaggerating their vices. Feudal burdens had, indeed, been drastically reduced over the centuries, but the sense of feudal obligation lingered on and found expression in various forms of unpaid public service as well as in an attitude towards dependants which, though seldom generous and normally unenlightened, was seldom exactly callous. *Noblesse oblige* is a French saying, but the habit of acting on it has, perhaps, been rather more noticeably English. In his efforts to mitigate the inequality of society Lloyd George had to contend with a sentimental conservatism which was not wholly irrational, and which was certainly not confined to the rich.

Finally, a speech must be quoted in which he expounded his faith as an Imperialist in the Lord Durham tradition:

It was a maxim of Roman jurisprudence that slaves should have no country. . . . The statesmen of ancient Rome knew well that even slaves, if animated by the ardour of patriotism, could no longer tolerate their shackles. . . . The Tory chiefs know too well that when Irishmen, Englishmen, Scotsmen and Welshmen are stimulated by a proud belief in the future of their respective nationalities, all bondage will be at an end and freedom alone will be possible. So they oppress the national spirit in Ireland, jeer at it in Wales, cajole it in Scotland, and pervert it in England. . . . As Welsh Liberals we are Imperialists because we are nationalists, and we are also Liberals for the same reason. We know that by honouring our native land we shall best respect ourselves . . . and that by the sum of the success, prosperity and happiness attained by little Wales, the great Empire of which she is a part will be the more glorious.[2]

1. Speech at Bangor, 21 May 1891.
2. Speech at Caernarvon, 29 May 1891.

The young man who spoke those words could be accused of wishful thinking, but could hardly be described as a blinkered little provincial. At least his view of Empire would have commended itself to Burke.

FIVE
Gladstone's Last Fling

The Parliament elected in 1886, and joined by Lloyd George in 1890, was dissolved on 26 June 1892. Lord Salisbury's overall majority had been cut almost in half since his Government took office, and the country had moved into a trade depression. Circumstances, therefore, favoured the Liberals, but they were handicapped by a policy which was too sweepingly radical in theory, and which in practice was mortgaged to Gladstone's messianic obsession with Irish Home Rule. At Newcastle the previous October the National Liberal Federation voted for a programme which, in addition to Irish Home Rule, included disestablishment for Wales and Scotland, local option, 'one man one vote', Triennial Parliaments, taxation of land values, cottage-building for the countryside, extension of small-holdings, abolition of entail, district and parish councils, employers' liability, and (more vaguely) limitation of working hours and payment of M.P.s. The 'Newcastle Programme' has been claimed as the first outstanding success for the Fabian Society's technique of permeation.[1] But, whatever the truth about its genesis, its endorsement by Gladstone was only a formal gesture and the more radical items in it were alarming without being altogether credible (a bad combination).

1. Bernard Shaw wrote, many years later: 'The first Fabian Socialist programme on which a general election was fought and won, in 1892, was drafted by Sidney Webb; but it was called the Newcastle Programme and put forward as the programme of the Liberal Party. It was in fact fobbed on it by me at an obscure meeting of an obscure branch of the Liberal Association, in a speech of which the reporters and the Liberal Parliamentary candidate who seconded me (the whole audience) did not understand a single sentence. . . .' (From 'Sixty Years of Fabian Socialism', quoted in *Shaw: An Autobiography, 1856–1898*, selected from his writings by Stanley Weintraub.)

In the country at large Home Rule was regarded as the one serious issue of the campaign.

Not in Wales, however. The serious issue there was disestablishment, which Gladstonians and Chamberlainites were at one in demanding, and to which, it seemed, Gladstone was at last committed. Early in 1891 he had retreated from his position that the Welsh Church could not be separated from the Church of England. And in his speech following Lloyd George's on the Second Reading of the Clergy Discipline Bill he had indicated as clearly as he ever could that he accepted disestablishment for Wales.

Lloyd George himself went into the election with disestablishment as the first point in his election address, and during the campaign he dealt exclusively with Welsh issues. He had the advantage of being the sitting Member, famous already for his aggressive role in Parliament, and appreciated by his constituents as a keen promoter of their local interests. He had a new election agent, R. O. Roberts – the previous one, he thought, had rubbed people up the wrong way – and he had recently become one of the sponsors of a new Press combine based on Caernarvon, the Welsh National Press Co. Ltd.[1] In Sir John Puleston, however, he had a more substantial opponent than Ellis Nanney. Puleston had been M.P. for Devonport for nearly twenty years, but he belonged to an old Welsh family and had a house near Pwllheli. As Constable of Caernarvon Castle he was able to put some electors under an obligation by giving them the use of the Castle for public or private functions.[2] In his early years he had spent some time in the United States, where he worked in banking and journalism before taking part in the Civil War as an honorary colonel in the Federal army. His credentials as a devotee of Abraham Lincoln were superior even to Lloyd George's, and he had scarcely less good credentials as a Welsh cultural patriot. But on the issue that really mattered he was swimming against the tide. As a Churchman opposed to disestablishment he would have been unlikely to win in 1892, even

1. This company, formed in January 1892, took over the copyright and goodwill of three newspapers, *Y Genedl Gymreig*, *Y Werin* and the *North Wales Observer and Express*. The manager was Beriah G. Evans, later secretary of the 'Cymru Fydd' movement. The board of directors was representative of the whole Principality, and Tom Ellis, S. T. Evans and 'Mabon', as well as Lloyd George, were among those who signed the Memorandum of Association.

2. When he died, in 1908, Lloyd George succeeded him as Constable, and made more spectacular political use of the Castle when he stage-managed the Prince of Wales's investiture there in 1911.

with an adversary less redoubtable than Lloyd George. Polling in the Caernarvon Boroughs was on 8 July, and the result was declared two days later:

Lloyd George   2,154
Puleston   1,958

Lloyd George thus retained the seat with a majority of 196. The Liberal Club at Caernarvon was lit up with gas jets and a huge procession formed behind a banner inscribed 'The Victory of Young Wales'. At Bangor, a Liberal procession was attacked by Tories and, in return, the Conservative Club there was 'riddled with stones'.[1]

In Wales as a whole Gladstonians scored an overwhelming triumph. All but three of the Welsh seats fell to them, and those three were border seats. But the national result was very different. In the new Parliament Gladstone's supporters and their Irish allies had a majority of only forty over the Conservative/Liberal Unionist alliance. This meant that Gladstone was just as dependent upon the Welsh as he was upon the Irish. Though the Welsh group was much the smaller (thirty-one M.P.s, compared with the Irish eighty-one), the defection of either group would be enough to destroy his majority. The only difference was that the Welsh would have to vote with the Tories, whereas the Irish could bring him down merely by abstaining. Lloyd George was quick to drive home the lesson of the figures, and to forestall any tendency on the part of his colleagues to be over-accommodating. At a celebration meeting in Conway he told Gladstone what was expected of him in the bluntest language:

It is very important that Liberal statesmen should understand clearly why Wales is so overwhelmingly Liberal at the present moment. It is not to install one statesman in power. It is not to deprive one party of power in order to put another in power. It has been done because Wales has . . . demonstrated its determination to secure its own progress. . . . The Welsh Members want nothing for themselves, but they must this time get something for our little country, and I do not think that they will support a Liberal Ministry – I care not how illustrious the Minister may be who leads it – unless it pledges itself to concede to Wales those great measures of reform upon which Wales has set its heart. Wales has lived long on promises. She has in hand a

1. *North Wales Observer*, 15 July 1892.

number of political I.O.U.s from the leaders of one or other of these great parties in the State. One of these debtors is at the present time in a position to take up the note, and Wales is in a splendid position, by the exigencies of the electoral results, to insist upon prompt payment.[1]

He was speaking shamelessly – but, all things considered, quite sensibly – as a blackmailer. It was clear to him that the Welsh Members must be as bloody-minded as the Irish, or they as individuals, together with their cause, would go down in ignominy. It was also clear to him that the biggest obstacle was still Gladstone, so he addressed a deliberate and personal threat to the Grand Old Man. In doing so, he knew that Liberals in England and Scotland were, on the whole, more sympathetic towards Welsh disestablishment than towards Irish Home Rule,[2] and that it might perhaps be slightly easier for the Tories to change their ground on the first than on the second, more especially since Joseph Chamberlain was their ally. His threat to Gladstone was, therefore, combined with an unmistakable hint to the other side. His best hope may have been that Gladstone would be forced to repair the breach between himself and Chamberlain, and that Liberals who believed in the Newcastle Programme would work together to that end. Alternatively, he may have felt that the Welsh Members could achieve more as an independent group than as predictable supporters of either big party. In any case, he was determined to make life very difficult for Gladstone unless and until a firm guarantee was extracted from him that Welsh disestablishment would be brought on immediately after Irish Home Rule.

Among the new Welsh Members elected in 1892, two require special notice in any study of Lloyd George's life – Frank Edwards and Herbert Lewis, who became his most intimate and faithful friends in politics. They are early examples of his power to win the devotion of people very unlike himself. Edwards was a Churchman, an old boy of Shrewsbury and a graduate of Oxford, who was nevertheless a keen Liberal and advocate of disestablishment. He represented his home county of Radnorshire on and off from 1892 until 1918, and he also served as a magistrate, deputy-lieutenant and high sheriff. Genial, uncomplicated

1. Speech at Conway, 22 July 1892.
2. He had attended the meeting of the National Liberal Federation at Newcastle, when the party programme was formulated, and his speech on that occasion, pressing the case for Wales, had been received with enthusiasm.

and not very clever, he attached himself to Lloyd George without a thought for his own advancement. The same was true of Herbert Lewis, who was, however, a politician of rather more weight, as well as a more earnest character. Like Edwards, he was a graduate of Oxford, but in addition, he had attended McGill University, Montreal; and he was a Methodist, not a member of the Established Church. By profession he was a solicitor, like Lloyd George. Throughout his life he took a deep interest in education, and he came into politics by way of local government. After serving as the first chairman of the Flintshire county council, he was Member in turn for Flint Boroughs and Flint County from 1892 until 1918, when he transferred to the Welsh University seat.

Edwards and Lewis were both small squires, but they were redeemed in Lloyd George's eyes by their fidelity to Liberalism, to Wales – and to himself. For this they were rewarded with his friendship, but not by any marks of favour disproportionate to their abilities. However unscrupulous he may have been in the bestowal of honours, he was more scrupulous than most Prime Ministers in the bestowal of offices. It is significant that he never made Frank Edwards a Minister, and never promoted Herbert Lewis to a senior Ministerial post, whereas he gave top jobs to his old rival, D. A. Thomas.

Another rather interesting new Welsh Member in 1892 was Major Rowland Jones – always known as 'the Major' – who, like Puleston, had fought for the North in the American Civil War. He was, indeed, a veteran of the battle of Gettysburg. Recently he had been acting as American consul at Cardiff. Though his Parliamentary career was brief (he was defeated at the next election), and though he was never very close to Lloyd George personally or politically, he was a co-sponsor with him of the Welsh National Press Co. Ltd, and was also associated with him in another business venture.[1]

Salisbury did not resign as soon as the election results were known, but decided to face the new Parliament. On 11 August his Government was beaten on a vote of no confidence in the House of Commons. He then resigned, and Gladstone was invited to form his fourth – and last – Ministry.

Even under the comparatively leisurely conditions of Victorian politics the task might have daunted a man in his eighty-third year. But Gladstone throve on power, even when the degree of it was inadequate. His

1. *See* below, ch. 7.

disappointment at not obtaining the landslide victory which he had irrationally expected (aggravated, as it was, by a very poor result in his own constituency of Midlothian) soon gave way to his natural zest and sheer enjoyment of the great game. He did not, however, find the actual business of forming the Government very enjoyable. Lord Rosebery, whom he asked – with strong and just misgivings – to be Foreign Secretary again, played very hard to get and had to be entreated (by the Prince of Wales and others) to accept the post. It would have been better if the entreaties had failed, because Rosebery had the wrong opinions for a Liberal Foreign Secretary, and anyway the wrong temperament for exercising authority. In opinion, he was anti-French, pro-German and bent on a policy of Imperial expansion; in character, he was moody, touchy, brittle and neurotic. His distinction as orator, wit, bibliophile, student of history and literary stylist could not atone for his defects as a practical statesman.

Gladstone also had trouble with Sir William Harcourt who, like Rosebery, was reappointed to the post he held in the 1886 Government – in his case, that of Chancellor of the Exchequer. There was nothing brittle about Harcourt, but he, too, had an awkward temperament and a notable capacity for antagonising colleagues. His views on foreign and Imperial affairs were much closer to Gladstone's than to Rosebery's, but he did not at all agree with the Prime Minister on domestic priorities. It appalled him that Irish Home Rule should be given overriding precedence, in spite of the manifest lack of electoral support for it in Great Britain, while other items in the Newcastle Programme, of much less questionable benefit to the party, were postponed to an uncertain future. At one point Harcourt threatened that he would not serve as Gladstone's second-in-command in the House of Commons unless the implementation of reforms for Great Britain was promised. But he failed to carry out the threat.

'The People's William' (as Gladstone was nicknamed) had a marked partiality for the landed gentry, and what he himself called 'a sneaking kindness for a lord'. It grieved him more that the Home Rule controversy had cost the Liberal Party most of its Whig grandees, than that it had alienated Chamberlain and many other radicals. Talking to Rendel early in 1892 he said that Hartington's defection had resulted in 'the permanent severance of its aristocratic and landowning section from the Liberal Party. . . . The Liberals might now have some forty peers, but they had but four or five peers who were large landowners . . . in fact, probably nine out of every ten acres in the United Kingdom were now in Tory hands.'[1] It was not only that he regretted the loss of their money, and of their influence in the county seats (which, even after the Ballot Act, was still far from negligible). He also, and even more sadly, missed the tone and dignity which they brought to the Liberal Party, and without which it might soon be at the mercy of tradesmen and rootless demagogues. 'Gladstone,' remarked Lloyd George some years later, 'was always a Tory at heart. He belonged to the worst section of the middle class – that section which thinks itself aristocratic.'[2] His snobbery, however, was not confined to the landowning class; it also embraced intellectuals from the older universities (preferably Oxford) regardless of their social origins. This category took in his friend and future biographer, John Morley, who returned to the Irish Chief Secretaryship in the new Administration. And it took in the only new member of it whose appointment could be described as sensational – Herbert Henry Asquith, who was brought straight from the back benches to be Home Secretary.

Asquith was not yet forty, and had been in Parliament only six years, at the time of his elevation. But it was he who moved the vote which brought the previous Government down. His father was a Congregationalist woolmaster in a small way of business in Yorkshire; but he died early in his son's life and for various reasons Asquith was sent to the City of London School. Thence he took a classical scholarship to Balliol College, Oxford, where he became one of the brightest stars in the Jowett firmament. After Oxford he was called to the Bar and, with the help of a fellow-barrister influential in the Lowlands, R. B. Haldane, secured election to Parliament as the Member for East Fife. As a barrister he made little impact until, in 1889, he had the good fortune to serve as junior counsel before the Parnell Commission of Enquiry, when he was able to share some of the credit for exposing the Piggott forgeries, and so for clearing Parnell of the charge that he was a party to terrorism.

In Asquith's career the Parnell Commission had a significance roughly analogous to that of the Llanfrothen case in Lloyd George's. The two

---

1. *The Personal Papers of Lord Rendel*, diary entry for 19 January 1892. Hartington was leader of the Liberal Unionists in the House of Commons until he succeeded his father as 8th Duke of Devonshire in December 1891. Chamberlain then became leader of the group.
2. Herbert Lewis diary, entry for 27 December 1907 (Herbert Lewis Papers, N.L.W.). In the same conversation Lloyd George went on to say: 'His [Gladstone's] sympathy with Ireland was largely based upon his sympathy with the Old Church. Supposing it had been Nonconformist Wales that was similarly circumstanced, he would never have done what he did for Ireland.' This was an unfair comment.

men were also alike in having a Nonconformist background and in having come to politics young, without financial or social advantages. But there the resemblance ended. In other ways they were not at all alike, though the precise nature of the difference between them is often misunderstood. Many believe that Lloyd George was volatile and romantic, Asquith solid and 'Roman' – and they are encouraged to do so by the fact that one was a Welshman and a spell-binder, the other a Yorkshireman and a Latin scholar. But in reality there was no lack of romanticism in Asquith, no lack of solidity in Lloyd George. Indeed, it could be said that Asquith was the more romantic; he was a connoisseur of English poetry and for that reason, among others, more susceptible than Lloyd George to the charm of traditional England. Certainly Lloyd George had more imagination, but Asquith had a finer aesthetic sensibility and was, therefore, in some respects more vulnerable. The ethnic difference may have had something to do with it, too, because the English are more romantically inclined than the Celts, in spite of superficial appearances to the contrary. It was true, moreover, that Asquith had a mind capable of reflection unrelated to action – a mind cultivated in the city of dreaming spires – whereas Lloyd George's reflective faculties were harnessed almost exclusively to his talent for creative action.

Without belittling Asquith's abilities and merits, one is bound to say that he would not have been promoted so fast if the Home Rule split had not deprived the Liberal Party of a substantial section of its leading personnel. Luck, however, is an indispensable quality in politics as in generalship, and Asquith deserved his luck. Though not a Home Secretary of the calibre of Robert Peel or R. A. Cross, he turned out to be a thoroughly competent one, and was thereafter regarded as a likely future leader of the Party. Even his opponents were impressed by his 'drastic, caustic, masterly manner' in debate.[1] His appointment gave satisfaction to the Welsh Members, who felt that they could count on him to do his utmost for disestablishment, seeing that he was a son of Nonconformity who had been active on behalf of the Liberation Society. They were also pleased that Arthur Acland was appointed Vice-President of the Council, a post which at that date carried responsibility for public education.

Only one Welsh Member actually joined the Government, however, and he was Tom Ellis. Rendel was not invited to join, though Gladstone

---

1. Sir R. Temple, *Life in Parliament*, p. 357.

stayed at his house, 1 Carlton Gardens, while forming the Government.[1] Subsequently, he excused his failure to offer Rendel a job on the pretext that he believed Rendel's business commitments would make it impossible for him to accept. But the true reason, surely, was that he needed Rendel as an experienced intermediary and shock-absorber between himself and the Welsh Members, at a time when shocks were likely. If Rendel could not hold the group steady, nobody could. Osborne Morgan refused his old job as Judge-Advocate-General, and Sir Edward Reed refused a minor post. But Tom Ellis, after much heart-searching, agreed to become Deputy Whip. Lloyd George's view of his acceptance is not entirely clear. On 16 August he wrote to Ellis (in Welsh): 'The greatest expectation exists concerning the association of Wales and the Ministry. If it is not honourable, I know that you will not join it at all.'[2] And on the 21st Ellis was writing to Lloyd George:

I have received many congratulations . . . but yours were the most generous and the most thoughtfully appreciative. . . . This is an experiment which I undertake relying upon the goodwill of my colleagues and their trustfulness that in this new sphere my ideals and loyalty shall be Welsh. . . . Your letter deepens the conviction which our steadily growing friendship has planted in me that you will be my steadfast friend and sympathetic and outspoken counsellor.[3]

Obviously Lloyd George had expressed warm, if perhaps slightly qualified, approval of Ellis's decision to join the Ministry. Yet we are also told that 'Lloyd George's disappointment over Tom Ellis's decision to accept . . . was accentuated by a foreboding that, should it so happen that the political interests of Wales were found to clash with the exigencies of the Government, Ellis would not be in a position to enforce the just demands of the Welsh people'.[4] And another biographer says that he viewed Ellis's acceptance 'with dismay'.[5] There is evidently a contradiction between his judgement of the matter as conveyed to Ellis at the time, and as conveyed to others subsequently.

1. It was also from this house that Gladstone, in November 1890, wrote his famous letter explaining that Parnell's continuance as leader of the Irish Party 'would be productive of consequences disastrous in the highest degree to the cause of Ireland'. (1 Carlton Gardens is now the official London residence of the Foreign Secretary.)
2. Lloyd George to T. E. Ellis, written from Criccieth (Ellis Papers, N.L.W.).
3. T. E. Ellis to Lloyd George (Ellis Papers, N.L.W.).
4. J. Hugh Edwards, op. cit., Vol. I, p. 161.
5. Malcolm Thomson, David Lloyd George: the Official Biography, p. 108.

The difference is, in fact, largely accounted for by the passage of time. In August 1892, Lloyd George was feeling optimistic about Gladstone's intentions. 'Tell Uncle,' he wrote to Margaret, 'that Gladstone has given us better pledges on Disestablishment than even we ventured to anticipate.'[1] Whatever the 'pledges', Lloyd George's satisfaction with them proved impermanent; but while it lasted, he could naturally have felt that Ellis's acceptance of office was quite consistent with his personal honour and the interests of Wales. Later, when Gladstone's intentions were once again suspect, it was equally natural that Lloyd George should forget his temporary euphoria and convince himself that he had been suspicious all along. In the process he would almost automatically convince himself that he had always thought it was wrong for Ellis to take office. Even at the outset, however, some allowance has to be made for mixed motives. Lloyd George was genuinely fond of Ellis, but without being blind to the fact that he was a rival. In ability and eloquence Ellis might be no match for his younger colleague, but his personal qualities, above all his dedication, gave him the authority of a leader. So long as he was free from Ministerial restraints he would obviously be the leading exponent of Welsh nationalism, but if he were imprisoned in the silence of the Whips' office the field would be open to another challenger. In fairness, we should not assume that this was Lloyd George's principal reason for welcoming and endorsing the step that Ellis took, but it would be naïve to suppose that the idea never entered his mind.

In September Gladstone paid a theatrical visit to North Wales, hoping, no doubt, to reduce his troublesome supporters there to a mood of grateful, awe-struck acquiescence. The ostensible purpose of the visit was to open a public footpath leading to the summit of Snowdon, and he stayed with the donor, Sir Edward Watkin, at a nearby chalet. Lloyd George and Ellis were asked to dinner to meet the Gladstones,[2] and at the beginning of his *War Memoirs* Lloyd George describes the occasion, in one of the all-too-rare glimpses that he gives us of his early life:

It was a small party. . . . Mr Gladstone did practically all the talking . . . and the rest of us, only too thrilled to meet and hear this great figure from a past world, were naturally content to listen in silence.

1. D.L.G. to M.L.G., 11 August 1892 (N.L.W.).
2. Mrs Gladstone wrote to Mrs Rendel: 'Then imagine to yourself Mr George following us here to dinner, and Mr Ellis, and my awe, remembering our talks.' (*The Personal Papers of Lord Rendel*, p. 201.) It is interesting that Lloyd George is mentioned first. He had met Gladstone before, but never in such an intimate and privileged way.

... He was vital. His deep vibrant tones were music to the ear whatever he said. That evening he was at times gay and merry.

His conversation ranged over a curious variety of topics. He talked for some time on the development of transport in the country and the improvement in the habits of the people who were associated with it. . . . To illustrate this theme he told us one or two quite amusing stories of his experiences in the old coaching days. . . .

He then gave us a dissertation on corrugated-iron roofing, and the difficulties which had been encountered in keeping buildings of this kind warm in winter and cool in summer. The last subject was suggested by the fact that the chalet was built of this material. He then diverged to other reminiscences . . . recalled with regret the prohibitive price of sugar candy when he was a boy. . . .

He then launched out into a wonderful panegyric on the people of France. I think it arose out of a reference to the Channel tunnel which Sir Edward Watkin was then promoting. Mr Gladstone made it quite clear that in his judgement the French were a much more enlightened, broadminded and civilised people than those over whose destinies he was at the moment privileged to preside. . . .[1]

As he talked that evening in Snowdonia he could not have guessed that one of the two young Welsh M.P.s who were hanging on his lips would one day play a decisive part in saving the liberties of France.

Among those who witnessed the opening of the footpath was Lloyd George's brother, William, and long afterwards he still remembered it vividly:

News of the meeting had spread abroad and a large crowd had congregated on the mountainside. . . . The opening ceremony took place on a piece of level ground flanked by a protruding rock which served as a platform for the speaker. The view from the heights to which we had now attained was a magnificent one . . . but everyone's main passion was to see and hear the most heroic figure in Welsh eyes. . . . And see him and hear him we did as he stood on the granite platform silhouetted against the mountain-side behind him, bending forward slightly as he addressed the eager crowd beneath him.

Looking upwards at him . . . gave me the impression that he was stouter and more stocky . . . than I had pictured him to be . . . and, like the rest of the crowd, I was surprised at his agility in walking up

1. David Lloyd George, *War Memoirs*, Vol. I, pp. 3–5.

the steep climb to the rock and afterwards mounting it to address the gathering. . . . I remember that his deep sonorous voice carried magnificently, as he stood there, towering over the crowd with his silvery locks waving in the breeze . . . he announced his intention to appoint a Royal Commission to investigate and report upon the Land Question in Wales . . . the surrounding rocks re-echoed the applause which this important announcement produced.[1]

After Gladstone's speech a vote of thanks was moved by Bryn Roberts, the Member for Eifion, which Lloyd George seconded in response to the crowd's demand. He spoke very briefly, in a light-hearted vein, ending with the boast that it was since Gladstone came to live in Wales (i.e. at Hawarden) that he had 'developed the Liberal statesmanship which had placed him at the head of the Liberalism of the world'.[2] When the Prime Minister arrived at Caernarvon the day before, Lloyd George met him at the station and took the chair at a meeting in the Castle Square, at which Gladstone said a few words. Altogether, the Member for Caernarvon Boroughs extracted the maximum political advantage from the visit.

In his Snowdon speech Gladstone was less specific, even on the land question, than William George remembered him to have been. His references to all Welsh issues were studiously vague, but the tone of the speech encouraged Welshmen to believe that he meant business. Actually, he took some persuading to set up a Royal Commission on Welsh agriculture. His first intention was merely to appoint a select committee which would sit in London, and Rendel agreed with him. But Ellis contended strongly that nothing less than a Royal Commission taking evidence in Wales would satisfy Welsh opinion. Not until December did Gladstone give way, but he then agreed to a Royal Commission – itself a time-honoured device for postponing executive or legislative action.[3] By the time the Commission reported the Liberals were out of office. On the Welsh Church question Gladstone equally resorted to delaying tactics. During the autumn of 1892 it was decided that instead of introducing a disestablishment bill in its first session the Government would prepare the ground for it with a suspensory bill, placing the emoluments

1. William George, *My Brother and I*, pp. 161–2.
2. *North Wales Observer*, 16 September 1892.
3. The same device was used for putting another 'burning' issue into cold storage. Gladstone set up a Royal Commission, with the Prince of Wales as a member, to inquire into the system of poor law relief. It reported in 1895 and had no practical effect.

of the Welsh dioceses under Parliamentary control. This was a far cry
from giving disestablishment a priority second only to Home Rule, and
in a speech at Liverpool shortly before the Queen's Speech in January
1893, Lloyd George used menacing, even seditious, language. After
quoting Burke to the effect that it was 'the first duty of a statesman to
study the temper of the people whom he governs', Lloyd George said
that Wales was 'prepared, if need be, to sacrifice her political connections,
her devotion to great statesmen, *and even her respect for law*, in order to
ensure the freedom and equality upon which her soul [was] bent.' He
added that he did not care what the House of Lords did to a disestablishment bill. 'By throwing it out the peers will be doing their own order
more harm than they can possibly inflict upon our movement. . . . The
more good bills they reject the merrier, and they will soon be overwhelmed in the debris of beneficent measures that they have wrecked.'[1]

After moving out of the rooms in Verulam Buildings, Gray's Inn, Lloyd
George stayed at first, again, with the Davieses at Acton, but this was
inconveniently far from the centre of London and he soon moved to
the National Liberal Club. Towards the end of 1892 he took for £25
a six-months' furnished lease of Sam Evans's rooms in the Temple,
5 Essex Court.

Meanwhile he had his first experience of foreign travel when, at the
end of August – just before Gladstone's visit to North Wales – he and
Evans attended a conference of the Inter-Parliamentary Union in Switzerland.[2] Speaking engagements had already taken him on extensive travels
inside Britain – including one to the Scottish Highlands the previous
autumn[3] – but this was the first of many trips abroad. Before leaving
the Alps he wrote to Margaret from Chamonix:

> Never did I pass through such imposing scenery. I hope some day to
> bring you here to view it. I thought of that constantly on my journey
> whenever I came to a good bit. I thought the glimpses of Snowdon

1. Speech in the Hope Hall, Liverpool, at a meeting in support of disestablishment presided
over by Thomas Gee. Reported in *Liverpool Mercury*, 20 January 1893. Author's italics.
2. This was the fourth annual conference of the Union, which was founded in 1888 by an
unofficial group of British and French parliamentarians, 'to promote personal contacts' and
'with a view to strengthening and developing democratic institutions'. The conference
was held in the Swiss Parliament House, Berne, which Lloyd George described as more
simple than 'many a Methodist chapel' he knew. As well as himself and Evans there were
three or four English M.P.s on the U.K. delegation – 'very good fellows all of them'.
3. When he stayed with, among others, Andrew Carnegie, who became one of his warmest
admirers and settled £2,000 a year on him for life in recognition of his war services.

in driving up the pass of Llanberis very fine but they sink into utter insignificance when you contrast them with Mont Blanc. Imagine a vast expanse of rock crag and glacier partly covered with snow thousands of feet above your head and penetrating far away into the clouds beyond your view altogether. The road was sufficiently striking in itself. Cut into the solid rock it hung over terrific ravines and gorges through which a furious stream quite grey and swollen with the storm rushed and roared. . . .[1]

He also noted with interest that a tunnel cut through the rock contained traces of a tunnel cut by the Romans.

During the autumn of 1892 he became involved in a business venture which, over the next few years, was to make heavy demands upon his time.[2] This took him on a short trip to Paris in November, and provided a further excuse – in addition to his legal and political commitments – for staying in London and avoiding the nine-hour train journey to Criccieth. Margaret was in London intermittently during the first half of 1893, and on one most unusual occasion he wrote a letter from Criccieth to her in London.[3] But normally she was at Criccieth with the children, while he was in London on his own. His evening amusements included a good deal of theatregoing: for instance, he went with Tom Ellis and Sam Evans to *The Second Mrs Tanqueray*, which he described to Margaret as 'a terrible play'.[4] He also dined quite often with friends (mostly Welsh) at restaurants such as the Criterion and Frascati's. But he was at pains to reassure Margaret as to the innocence of his diversions, and one way of doing so was to complain of Evans's frivolity. One day he writes: 'Sam has made a firm resolve to foreswear evil habits. I fear this virtuous determination will not survive the onslaught of the first temptation.' And the next day: 'Sam is gallivanting around with Mrs Pedr Williams and her sister. He is going to take them to a music hall tonight. Mrs Pedr has asked him to do so – that's what Sam has just told me! Pedr is from home! There will be business there.'[5] The hidden message in these reports (explicit in some others) is that his own virtue was unsullied.

1. D.L.G. to M.L.G., written from Chamonix but posted from Geneva, 4 September 1892. Lloyd George's letters from abroad are full of detailed descriptions which are seldom entirely free from the sub-romantic clichés familiar to readers of Victorian travel guides. He is at his best when recording incidents or describing people: his landscapes without figures are apt to be rather commonplace. 2. *See* below, ch. VII.
3. 30 April 1893 (N.L.W.). 4. D.L.G. to M.L.G., 24 July 1893 (N.L.W.).
5. D.L.G. to M.L.G., 4 and 5 September 1893 (N.L.W.). Who escorted the sister?

If Margaret could have believed him – if she could have even pretended to believe him – their marriage would have been a happier one. Unfortunately she could neither trust him when her back was turned, nor show indifference to the misdemeanours of which she suspected him. Her only remedy would have been to stay with him constantly in London, but this remedy seemed to her even worse than the disease. Disease in the literal sense was one reason for her prolonged absences. London was then a very unhealthy place (a House of Commons cleaner died of cholera in 1893), and Margaret's reluctance to expose her children to the hazards of living there was understandable. The corollary should, however, have been a philosophic acceptance of the rather different hazards of leaving a husband like Lloyd George alone in the metropolis for months on end. He certainly wanted her to be with him and persevered in the attempt to establish a family home in London, so that they could be together during the Parliamentary sessions. In August 1893 he was house-hunting, with Herbert Lewis, in the Kensington area, and in the late autumn he took a flat there – 30 Palace Mansions, Addison Road – which became his London base for the next six years. He wrote of it enthusiastically to Margaret: it was 'very charming . . . on fourth floor, with a good view – and there is a lift. Children would see cabs, omnibuses etc. rolling along. Hippodrome close by.'[1] The only snag was that it was half an hour by underground ('a horrid method of travelling') to the House of Commons. The rent was £90 a year.

It has been well said that Gladstone's last Government 'could do nothing for Ireland and nothing without Ireland'.[2] The Prime Minister had to hold the support of the Irish Party or he would immediately lose his majority. Yet it must have been obvious to him that there would never be the slightest chance of enacting an Irish Home Rule Bill so long as the powers of the House of Lords remained intact. By bringing in a Home Rule Bill before tackling the Lords he would simply be wasting his own, and Parliament's, time. All the same, the Queen's Speech on 30 January 1893 announced that a Bill would be submitted 'on the earliest available occasion, to amend the provision for the government of Ireland . . . to afford contentment to the Irish people, important relief to Parliament, and additional securities for the strength and union of the Empire'. The 'earliest available occasion' was less than a fortnight later. Gladstone's

1. D.L.G. to M.L.G., 15 November 1893 (N.L.W.).
2. Herbert Paul, *A History of Modern England*, Vol. V, p. 272.

second Home Rule Bill was introduced on 13 February and read a first time on the 17th. In one respect it was a distinct improvement on its predecessor. The 1886 Bill, while transferring only very limited powers to an Irish Parliament, would have removed Irish elected representatives altogether from the Parliament at Westminster. Since the powers reserved to Westminster would have included fiscal policy, the principle of 'no taxation without representation' would have been violated. That the Irish Members were prepared to accept such a flagrantly unjust measure can only have meant that they did not regard it as permanent.[1] Under the terms of the 1893 Bill the Irish were to remain at Westminster, but with their number cut from 103 to 80 (a reform in any case long overdue, since their existing number was based on the pre-Famine population), and with the right to vote only on Imperial questions or questions affecting Ireland. The differential voting clauses proved, in the event, almost as big an embarrassment to Gladstone as the total exclusion provided for in the first Home Rule Bill. They gave rise to so many technical difficulties that it was necessary, at length, to abandon them; and the Government was then open to the charge that it was allowing the Irish to have it both ways – to govern both themselves and the rest of the United Kingdom and Empire. Gladstone's speech introducing the Bill impressed Lloyd George as a *tour de force*. At 6.30 p.m. he added this postscript to a letter to Margaret: 'Old man's speech just over. Marvellous performance.'[2] Another witness was the young Winston Churchill, sitting in the Distinguished Strangers' Gallery.[3]

It was not until after Easter that the Second Reading could be taken and when the Committee stage began it soon became clear that, if the Bill was to be disposed of within the year, the Session would have to be extended. A time-limit (known as the 'gag') was proposed at the end of June, but even with this expedient freely used, in Committee and on the Report stage, eighty-two days were spent discussing the Bill before it was read a third time on 1 September. Then the Lords, sitting at a

1. At a late stage Gladstone offered to reconsider the exclusion of Irish Members from Westminster, but by then the harm was done.
2. D.L.G. to M.L.G., 13 February 1893 (N.L.W.).
3. In 1940, at a dinner to celebrate his golden jubilee as an M.P., Lloyd George said that this was the only occasion he could remember when chairs were placed on the floor of the House, to accommodate Members for whom there was no room on the crowded benches. (Private information from Sir Dingle Foot Q.C., who was present at the dinner.) But chairs were also put there on 11 August 1892, when Joseph Chamberlain spoke in the debate on the Address before the Salisbury Government fell. (Sir R. Temple, *Life in Parliament*, ch. XI, p. 360.)

season normally devoted to other activities, turned their attention to it and rejected it by a ten-to-one majority. The verdict, if not the scale of the adverse vote, was undoubtedly in accordance with British public opinion, and of course it also reflected the will of the Scots–Irish community in Ulster. Gladstone's personal exertions during the long debates on the Bill were as magnificent as they were futile. He intervened repeatedly, adding to the inordinate length of the proceedings but also setting the final crown upon his reputation as a Parliamentarian. His resilience as he fought for the Bill is well conveyed by Morley, who was his Chief Secretary for Ireland at the time:

> One day when a tremendous afternoon of obstruction had almost worn him down, the adjournment came at seven o'clock. He was haggard and depressed. On returning at ten we found him making a most lively and amusing speech upon procedure. He sat down as blithe as dawn. 'To make a speech of that sort,' he said in deprecation of compliment, 'a man does best to dine out; 'tis no use to lie on a sofa and think about it.'[1]

Lloyd George later described how the old man could appear, in the Home Rule debates, 'a shrunken figure, huddled up and torpid', until roused by some worthy antagonist, when he would stand forth again as 'an erect athletic gladiator, fit for the contest of any arena'.[2]

The Home Rule Bill took up so much Parliamentary time that there was virtually no hope for any other legislation in the spring or summer of 1893. The Welsh Church Suspensory Bill was introduced by Asquith at the end of February, and Gladstone made a spirited speech in the debate on First Reading. But the Bill was never read a second time and in September it was formally withdrawn. Meanwhile the Welsh Church issue was providing the main theme for Lloyd George's platform oratory. At Shrewsbury he said that the Bishop of St Asaph in a recent speech had 'simply Latinised the tirades of an irate washerwoman'. And he developed his case against the Anglican record in Wales, in terms which seem to anticipate the Chester–Belloc:

> The Roman Catholic Church, according to the admission of ecclesiastical historians themselves, faithfully and honestly administered their

1. John Morley, *Life of Gladstone*, Vol. III, p. 502.
2. Lloyd George, article in *Young Wales*, July 1898, quoted in H. du Parcq, *op. cit.*, Vol. I, p. 188.

trust to the poor as long as the endowments were in their hands – to such an extent, indeed, that no poor law was ever required in the realm until the ecclesiastical endowments were transferred to the Reformed Church. Since that event, for more than three centuries, the portion of the poor has been absorbed by the bishops and their clergy, and, when the poor venture through their representatives to prosecute the matter in the High Court of Parliament for the recovery of their lost inheritance, they are told by the pillagers themselves that they are simply animated by greed and cupidity.[1]

At Swansea he attacked a recent speech by John Owen, Dean of St Asaph and later Bishop of St David's:

What Dean Owen wants is a 'national' religion – not a religion of the people which will fight against intemperance and promote the welfare of the people, but a religion the priests of which shall grace every regal puppet-show and pronounce a benediction on every filibustering expedition which leaves these shores to rob and to massacre our fellow-men in other countries.[2]

Owen, in fact, was a scholarly man of high character, but that sort of polemical flight by Lloyd George was not meant to be taken personally. If anyone offered him a target he could hardly resist having a shy at it, as when young Lord Powis described the Church as 'the mother of the Welsh nation'. 'Why,' said Lloyd George, 'Lord Powis seems to have forgotten the very simple fact that mothers are not born after their children.'[3] In another speech he referred to 'the poodle-hugging dames of the Primrose League'.[4] Such phrases may have been a little cheap, but they were good for the box-office. Besides, his speeches contained plenty of more solid material: for instance, he could quote constitutional historians, such as Stubbs, Taswell-Langmead and Gneist, on the background to the tithe question.

In Parliament he was relatively silent throughout 1893, but he did intervene strongly when Major Jones brought in a Welsh local option

1. Speech at Shrewsbury, 22 February 1893 (reported in *Shrewsbury Chronicle* two days later). A Church Defence Conference had recently been held in the town.
2. Speech at Swansea, 4 April 1893 (reported next day in the *Cambrian Daily Leader*). Lloyd George was delighted with this meeting. 'Finest ever held in Swansea so I am told on all hands.' (D.L.G. to M.L.G., 5 April 1893.)
3. Speech at Newtown, 28 April 1893.
4. Speech at Leeds, 19 April 1893.

Bill – a more stringent version of the liquor control which, in accordance
with the Newcastle Programme, Harcourt was simultaneously proposing
for the whole country. Major Jones, who had been successful in the Private
Members' ballot, regretted that chance 'should have placed a Bill of such
deep interest and far-reaching importance in his 'prentice hand'. He may
also have had inner doubts as to the merits of the prohibitionist case, and
he certainly had good reason to doubt his own qualifications for espous-
ing it. The following spring he was absent from a meeting of the Welsh
party, at which he was expected to second a resolution, because he was
'stupidly drunk about the House' and had to be taken home. A week
later he was still *hors de combat* 'recovering . . . from his attack of
dipsomania', and his wife said that 'when he had these attacks on he
could not be restrained – there was only one thing to be done and that
was to keep him from appearing too much in public'.[1]

However dubious the Major's right to deplore the evils of intemperance, Lloyd George's conscience in the matter was clear. He may once
have got drunk while attending a Volunteer camp in his Portmadoc
days, but as a rule he was most careful not to drink to excess. His speech
in the 1893 debate was an uncompromising plea for prohibition. An
earlier speaker had said that it was better to teach people to resist temptation than to remove it from their path. Lloyd George replied that he
could not understand why the State should not do both. When questions
arose affecting the interests of the Tory Party, did Tory Members then
'depend on moral suasion – on appeals to the good sense of the people?'
No, they brought in coercion acts. All that Lloyd George and his friends
were contending was that where they could 'get the cooperation of a
majority of the people in the forcible removal of temptations to
intemperance from their midst', they should 'avail themselves of it'. In
his home district there were fifteen parishes with no public houses, in
which there was only one pauper to forty-one of the population,
compared with one to eighteen in parishes which had pubs. The North
American experience of local option would not necessarily be matched
in an old country like Britain. 'I do not want to go to Maine or Canada,
for within a day's journey of this House hon. Members can test the effect
of prohibition.' Much had been said about depriving publicans of their
property, and the £20 million paid to slave-owners was a favourite
illustration. But 'slaves were the absolute legal property of their owners',
who, moreover, fed and clothed them, whereas the publicans 'stripped'

1. D.L.G. to M.L.G., 25 and 31 April 1894 (N.L.W.).

and 'despoiled' the slaves of drink, 'destroyed them body and mind, and reduced them to beggary and starvation'. The slave trade at least built up the cotton and sugar industries but the drink trade had no such constructive effect. Publicans took a chance on the annual renewal of their licences, and must abide by the result. Their record was iniquitous: 160,000 convictions for drunkenness, fifty per cent of all pauperism attributable to drink, and ninety per cent of all crime. 'Let the Welsh people grapple with this evil, which has been the despair of the past and which casts a gloom over the future of democracy.'[1]

It was a well-argued speech, and the bill's Second Reading was carried. But, like Harcourt's measure, it then sank without trace. The British people are very firmly opposed to any attempt by the State to make them more abstemious than they have a mind to be. Resistance to such attempts may have been slightly less vigorous in Wales than in England, but even the Welsh have never been prepared to go anything like as far on the road to compulsory temperance as Lloyd George would have wished.

As it became apparent that even the Welsh Church Suspensory Bill would never be passed, the Welsh Members grew increasingly restive and Lloyd George proposed that a letter should be sent to Gladstone. Only Bryn Roberts was against the idea, and on 26 June Rendel sent a letter, drafted by Lloyd George. On 5 July: 'Gladstone has replied to our letter. He pleads the Home Rule Bill as an excuse for not giving a definite answer just now. He promises to give a further reply after it is substantially through. I don't care for the nature of the reply and we must press him hard. He will try to get out of it if he can. . . .'[2] The snag in Gladstone's reply was that he declined to give Welsh disestablishment the highest priority after Irish Home Rule. Disestablishment was merely 'an essential part of the Liberal policy and plans'. This was not good enough for Lloyd George. 'If there is a row with Gladstone I must stump Wales.'[3] But he was in no hurry to bring the row out into the open. On 28 July Rendel wrote a second letter (again, Lloyd George's work) requesting that disestablishment be given top place in the Govern-

1. House of Commons, 15 March 1893 (Hansard, Fourth Series, Vol. X, cols 116–22). D. R. Daniel helped him to make his point about the 'dry' parishes. On 8 March he wrote to Daniel: 'There are 15 parishes in Lleyn without a pub. . . . Can you find out for me the condition of man and beast in these localities? Is the area which is devoid of pubs a large one? It is very interesting and would tell in the House of Commons.' (D. R. Daniel Papers).
2. D.L.G. to M.L.G., 5 July 1893 (N.L.W.).
3. D.L.G. to M.L.G., 21 July 1893 (N.L.W.).

ment's programme for the next session. Gladstone replied on 8 August, promising a disestablishment bill without firmly committing himself on the question of priority. 'But,' the letter ends, in a passage so sublimely obscure that one almost suspects the author of deliberate self-parody, 'the important and enlightened body of gentlemen, on whose behalf you write, may rest assured that at the first moment when deliberations of reasonable solidity on the subject of priority become possible, we shall approach the question with the firm intention so to handle it as, amidst competing and conflicting claims, to avert whatever might threaten to deprive Wales of the advantages which I have described as attaching to the position she has acquired.'[1]

Within a week the South Wales Liberal Federation was passing a resolution calling upon the Welsh Members to break loose from the Liberal Party unless disestablishment were made the top Government priority for 1894. And D. A. Thomas soon issued a public threat that the Welsh Members might withdraw their support for Irish Home Rule. Lloyd George was tempted to take a similar line, but consulted Rendel who, on 26 August, wrote to him from the Isle of Skye advising caution. A threat of revolt might, he argued, enable the Government to put them in the wrong, and would leave them with 'no reserve at the critical moment'. Withdrawal of support was their 'one trump left'. 'We must not play it too soon. What we have now to do is to give a perfectly frank and clear warning. We ought not in my judgement at present to do more.'[2] To some extent, Lloyd George may have been influenced by this argument and in any case it would not really have suited him to become involved in a full-scale political campaign at a time when business affairs were claiming much of his attention. He wanted to have the credit for being militant, without having to face any immediate practical consequences; and that is exactly what he achieved.

When the Welsh Members met, on 1 September, to consider their position, he helped to defeat an out-and-out 'independence' motion and,

1. When Gladstone was only thirty, Macaulay wrote of his style: 'There is no want of light, but a great want of what Bacon would have called dry light. Whatever Mr Gladstone sees is refracted and distorted by a false medium of passions and prejudices. His style bears a remarkable analogy to his mode of thinking, and indeed exercises great influence on his mode of thinking. His rhetoric, though often good of its kind, darkens and perplexes the logic which it should illustrate. Half his acuteness and diligence, with a barren imagination and a scanty vocabulary, would have saved him from almost all his mistakes. He has one gift most dangerous to a speculator, a vast command of a kind of language, grave and majestic, but of vague and uncertain import. . . .' (Essay, 'Gladstone on Church and State', *Edinburgh Review*, April 1839.)   2. Rendel Papers, N.L.W.

though he ostensibly supported D. A. Thomas's motion proposing independence if the Government failed to give definite assurances about the next session, it was no disappointment to him that this, too, was defeated. When the others had failed, it was his turn to propose a compromise resolution – which Ellis seconded – to the effect that the Welsh Members should think again about supporting the Government if disestablishment were not 'in such a place in the Ministerial programme for the next session as will enable the House of Commons to carry it through all its stages, and send it to the Lords before the session is over'. This was carried by a three-to-one majority, though it was not extreme enough for some of the Members from South Wales, and still too extreme for Bryn Roberts.

Lloyd George reported his success to Margaret. The meeting, he said, lasted three hours, but the result was 'an overwhelming majority' for his resolution. 'Ellis and I stuck together all through' and 'Rendel was also with us'.[1] With Lloyd George's help Rendel and Ellis had, in fact, handled the situation with much skill. Gladstone's second letter, for all its obscurity of language, was tantamount to a pledge that disestablishment would be brought on in the next session; and the limits of effective militancy within the Welsh party had been correctly judged. In the autumn Rendel wrote to Gee: 'Your own straightforward reliance upon Mr Gladstone is the attitude I should humbly wish Wales to assume towards the English Liberal Party and the present Parliament. There is no occasion for Wales to scream in order to be heard and still less occasion to bluster or bully in order to be thought sincere.'[2] The attitude recommended by Rendel did not survive intact until the end of the Parliament, but it did survive for what remained of the G.O.M.'s Premiership.

Gladstone had said that his one reason for staying in public life at his advanced age was his desire to settle the Irish Question, and he meant what he said. But however one looks at it he set about his task the wrong way. Even had he been justified in concentrating upon Home Rule to the virtual exclusion of other issues, it should still have been obvious to him that to carry Home Rule by a small majority in the House of Commons would be useless so long as the Lords were unconverted and

1. D.L.G. to M.L.G., 1 September 1893 (N.L.W.).
2. Rendel to Gee, 15 October 1893. The above account of relations between Gladstone and the Welsh Members through the summer of 1893 is largely based upon K. O. Morgan, *Wales in British Politics, 1868–1922*, and upon the Rendel Papers in the National Library of Wales.

in full possession of their powers. His attempt to settle the Irish Question without first tackling the Constitutional Question was a plain case of putting the cart before the horse. Yet it was essential to fight the Lords on a popular issue. Reform of the Constitution – to make the people, as Gladstone put it, truly self-governing – should, no doubt, have been a sufficiently popular issue in itself. But the British nation lost very little sleep over theoretical flaws in the Constitution, and a showdown aimed at removing the Lords' veto would arouse public enthusiasm only if it took place in circumstances highly prejudicial to the Lords. It was difficult to be sure of the right issue, but most Liberals could see very clearly that Home Rule would be the wrong one.

After a holiday of less than six weeks Parliament was recalled at the beginning of November to consider legislation delayed by the Home Rule Bill marathon. The measures in question were the Parish Councils Bill and the Employers' Liability Bill. At a more normal time they would probably have encountered little opposition, but party feeling was running so high at the end of 1893 that the Tories could hardly be expected to give the Government any quarter. The Parish Councils Bill was a logical pendant to the County Councils Act passed by the Salisbury Government in 1888 (thanks to which Lloyd George was a Caernarvon-shire alderman). Even so the Tories, after accepting the Bill in principle, obstructed its passage by interminable discussion in Committee, so that it did not become law until 1 March 1894.[1] But at least it got through, which is more than could be said for the Employers' Liability Bill. The Minister responsible for this, Asquith, would not accept a Lords' amendment providing that workmen should be free to contract out if they were covered by an alternative form of insurance; and the Bill was therefore dropped. Asquith's biographers have defended his action rather too glibly, claiming that the amendment would have wrecked the Bill.[2] Actually, the contracting-out proposal was by no means entirely unreasonable and had some support from Liberals. If it had been accepted the Bill would still have been well worth passing. The reason

1. Both the 1888 and the 1894 Acts were, strictly speaking, Local Government Acts; but they are commonly known by their more descriptive unofficial titles. The second brought district councils into being, as well as parish councils.
2. 'The House of Lords . . . mangled the measure so seriously (especially by permitting contracting out of its benefits) that it was dropped.' (J. A. Spender and Cyril Asquith, *Life of Lord Oxford and Asquith*, Vol. I, p. 80.) '. . . an Employers' Liability Bill, to which he had devoted great effort during the session, had been so mangled by the Lords that abandonment seemed the better course. . . .' (Roy Jenkins, *Asquith*, p. 68.)

for its rejection was not that it would have frustrated the whole purpose of the Bill, but rather that the Government was under pressure from the trade unions and the ideological Left, who wanted an all-or-nothing solution.

The prolonged debates on Parish Councils and Employers' Liability kept Parliament sitting right through the winter. For the first time Lloyd George was not at home on Christmas Day: he spent it with his friends at Acton. Soon it became a bad habit with him to be away for Christmas.

While M.P.s debated, a secret struggle was going on inside the Cabinet. Gladstone was at loggerheads with his colleagues over the naval estimates, but this was really only a symptom of the more fundamental fact that they had lost confidence in his leadership and were tired of being at the mercy of his whims. In the naval argument, the demand of the Sea Lords (of whom the Third was a certain Jackie Fisher) for a stronger Navy was endorsed by the First Lord of the Admiralty, Spencer, and by most of the Cabinet; while Gladstone resisted it as wasteful and militaristic. 'I shall not,' he said, 'break to pieces the continuous action of my political life, nor trample on the tradition of every colleague who has ever been my teacher.'[1] Gladstone was not, as is often suggested, concerned with morality to the exclusion of any interest in national power. He believed, certainly, that morality was a vital ingredient in British power, without which the country would not deserve to be powerful. That belief was justified. But there were other ingredients which he recognised as valid without, however, making a correct assessment of their relative importance. In particular, he overrated economics and underrated armed force. As the last great Peelite, survivor of the generation of politicians which had established the 'Free Trade' system, he saw that system not only as the principal cause of British dominance in the modern world, but also as something good in itself – an economic expression of the higher verities.

It did not, apparently, occur to him that the system had worked to Britain's advantage for a variety of reasons, few of which were purely economic, many of which were morally indefensible, and all of which were likely to prove impermanent. Even with her spectacular, but temporary, lead in industrial development Britain could not have done so well out of 'Free Trade' without the concurrent assets of an invincible Navy and vast Imperial possessions. The first, obviously, protected the

1. Memorandum dated 20 January 1894, quoted in Peter Stansky, *Ambitions and Strategies: the Struggle for the Leadership of the Liberal Party in the 1890s*, p. 30.

sea-routes upon which Britain's economic life depended; the second ensured privileged access to raw materials and enabled markets to be rigged in favour of British manufacturers. Rows about the scale of naval armaments were to be a recurring feature of the Liberal Government before the First World War, and Lloyd George, as Chancellor of the Exchequer, was then an exponent of economy. But his attitude towards the Navy – and, for that matter, towards the Empire – was by no means Gladstonian. He never doubted that British power rested upon both, and he wished, without being extravagant or oppressive, to maintain them in full vigour.

In January 1894 Gladstone withdrew to Biarritz, leaving his colleagues in a state of perplexity and exasperation. Finding that he could not bend them to his will over the naval estimates, he suggested instead (in a letter to the Chief Whip) that they should dissolve at once and go to the country on the issue of Peers versus People. But they would not defer to him on this either, because they considered that an election would, in the circumstances, be disastrous. The Party was not ready, the Lords had not yet made themselves sufficiently unpopular, and in any case the naval question would have to be settled first. So Gladstone could see that the game was up. He returned to London on 10 February and, after keeping his colleagues a little longer on tenterhooks, he resigned on 3 March, pleading the state of his eyesight and hearing. In its end-of-an-age symbolism the event was comparable only with the death of Queen Victoria seven years later. Serious-minded eccentric, worldly idealist, anxious Christian, Gladstone embodied more of the character and flavour of Victorian England than any other individual.

After his resignation he submitted Rendel's name for a peerage, and in any case Rendel had already indicated to Ellis that he wished to stand down as chairman of the Welsh Party. Writing from his villa in the South of France on 2 March, he said:

> The future is to you and to such as yourself. I am determined to leave before I am left. . . . My work was a special one and such as it was it is accomplished . . . it is best now, both for the cause and for my credit in connection with it, that I should go. And so, with the warmest gratitude and good wishes, I say farewell, and to no Welshman with more deep feeling than yourself – the child of my aspiration for Wales and in a sense the crown of the humble efforts of such as myself.[1]

1. Stuart Rendel to T. E. Ellis, 2 March 1894 (Ellis Papers, N.L.W.).

Rendel may have been fonder of Ellis than of any other Welsh Member, but he certainly also had a great admiration for Lloyd George and regarded him as a man of the future. Over ten years later, looking back at the time when Lloyd George was first in Parliament, Rendel said that he had 'noted at once his quickness of perception, his alertness in seizing a point.' Some older members of the Party 'wanted to sit upon him', but he (Rendel) stood by him and backed him up, 'seeing in him qualities that were essentially Welsh'. He had hoped that 'the emancipation of Wales from political thraldom' would produce such a man, and he added 'I am thankful to have lived to see it'.[1] In saying this he was perfectly sincere, and not unduly influenced by hindsight. Though Lloyd George's gadfly activities often irritated him, he never mistook them for the antics of a natural outsider. He could see the statesman behind the *frondeur*, and during the negotiations with Gladstone in the summer of 1893 he took Lloyd George very closely into his confidence.

Respect was mutual. In spite of youthful impatience and intermittent complaints of 'Rendelism', Lloyd George was never really blind to the difficulties of Rendel's position, nor did he fail to appreciate all that 'the Member for Wales' had done for the Principality. When a Welsh bishop attacked Rendel as an alien, Lloyd George warmly defended him: 'He is not an alien in his sympathy. . . . There was an old law in Wales that a stranger who rescued a Welshman from bondage should be for ever a naturalised citizen of Wales. This Mr Rendel has done.'[2] Apart from his services to Wales, Rendel had another strong claim on Lloyd George's esteem: he was a technocrat of the sort that Lloyd George always admired, and that he recruited for high office when he was Prime Minister. Incidentally, Rendel was also the original source of a remark often quoted by Lloyd George, and commonly attributed to him – that in politics there are no friends at the top.[3] Perhaps the idea was suggested to Rendel by his own association with Gladstone, for his loyalty was shamelessly exploited – and ill-requited – by that marvellous, maddening, old man.

1. Herbert Lewis diary, entry for 8 January 1905 (Herbert Lewis Papers, N.L.W.).
2. Speech at Newtown, 28 April 1893.
3. 'L.G. said that Lord Rendel had told him, almost at the outset of his (L.G.'s) political career, that when he got into office, he would find there were no real friendships at the top. L.G. found that this cynical remark was quite true.' (Lord Riddell's War Diary, entry for 20 August 1915.)

SIX
Play-acting Rebel

Rendel's maxim was supremely well illustrated in the period between Gladstone's resignation and the fall of the Liberal Government fifteen months later. The Government's two leading members disliked each other so intensely that they could hardly work together at all. The root cause of the trouble was that the wrong man succeeded Gladstone as Prime Minister. Rosebery, for all his brilliance, had temperamental defects which unfitted him for any high executive office, let alone the Premiership. He also had the disadvantage of being a peer, and of having very little knowledge of, or interest in, home affairs. To be Prime Minister in the House of Lords was quite normal at the period, but for a Liberal Prime Minister it was undesirable, because in an overwhelmingly Tory House he was isolated from his Parliamentary supporters. Moreover, it was vital that any Prime Minister in the Lords should have as Leader of the House of Commons a man with whom he could work amicably and confidently. Salisbury, who shared Rosebery's preoccupation with foreign and Imperial policy, was nevertheless at pains to ensure that he would have a good working relationship with his chief lieutenant in the Commons. (His only failure, in this respect, was with Lord Randolph Churchill – and it was short-lived.) To do Rosebery justice, he was aware of his own unsuitability and tried fairly hard to dissuade the Queen from sending for him.[1] But when pressed to form a Government he did not, in the end, refuse. It was in the nature of his psychological case that he

1. See his letter to the Queen's Private Secretary, Ponsonby, dated 2 March 1894 – the day before Gladstone formally resigned. (Quoted in Robert Rhodes James, *Rosebery*, pp. 322–3.)

disliked being in, but at the same time did not really want to be out. He became Prime Minister because it was, on the whole, the will of the Cabinet and of the Liberal Press that the job should go to him, and because his own will to resist it was not strong enough. The consequences were predictably bad. Only a leader of quite exceptional quality could have rescued the Liberals from the mess that Gladstone had left them in: with Rosebery as their leader they were bound to get into an even worse mess.

If the Queen had asked Gladstone for advice as to his successor, he would have recommended Spencer. Apart from being a peer and a grandee, Spencer was about as different from Rosebery as anyone could be – a man of dull wits and steady character. If the Queen had asked him to form a Government he would almost certainly have declined and advised her to send for Rosebery, so the eventual result would have been the same. In any case, the Queen did not ask Gladstone for his opinion. The man who should have been the new Prime Minister was Harcourt, and he would probably have been the choice of rank-and-file Liberals. Sir William Vernon Harcourt was a political all-rounder: he had been Solicitor-General and Home Secretary as well as Chancellor of the Exchequer, and before he went into politics had been a professor of international law. He was almost as well qualified to deal with foreign as with domestic affairs, and he was a superbly good House of Commons man, his Parliamentary talents being matched, moreover, by his excellence as a platform speaker. Above all, he was a man who might conceivably have healed the rift between the Liberal Party and the Chamberlainites. Though he did not share Chamberlain's radicalism – Harcourt was essentially Whiggish – his personal *rapport* with Chamberlain had survived the Home Rule schism. 'These two thoroughly liked one another in an uncovenanted manner less difficult than sworn friendship and so often more lasting.'[1] For Rosebery, on the other hand, Chamberlain's feelings were cool and rather contemptuous: there was never the slightest human understanding between them, in spite of their common interest in Imperial expansion, which Harcourt did not share. If, as some thought, it was above all the personality of Gladstone that prevented Chamberlain from returning to his old party allegiance, then it was surely possible (though, one must add, unlikely) that the disappearance of Gladstone and the advent of Harcourt might have set the stage for a

1. J. L. Garvin, *The Life of Joseph Chamberlain*, Vol. II, p. 492.

reconciliation which would have transformed Liberal prospects. No such possibility existed when Gladstone was succeeded by Rosebery.

It was Harcourt's misfortune that an abrasive manner tended to conceal his basic good nature, whereas Rosebery's charm tended to conceal the misanthropy which, in him, was never far below the surface. As a result, Cabinet colleagues formed a mistaken judgement of their relative merits. Harcourt, moreover, suffered from the intrigues conducted on his behalf by his devoted son Lewis (Loulou), which put him in a rather false, unpleasant light – and with nothing, after all, to show for it. He was understandably resentful that Rosebery was chosen rather than himself. When he first entered Parliament Rosebery was still a boy at Eton, and when he was Home Secretary Rosebery served for a time as his junior Minister. Granted the situation, it would have been better if either or both of the two men had realised at once that they would never be able to cooperate, and had thus avoided an attempt at joint leadership which was doomed from the start.

On at least one very important matter Rosebery and Harcourt were, however, in agreement. Both regarded Irish Home Rule as a liability. The Government, however, still depended upon the votes of the Irish Members, so that the problem was how to get rid of Home Rule without bringing down the Government. Rosebery's handling of the problem was a masterpiece of ineptitude. Having told his followers that there would be no change of policy or principles, and more especially that the Government was bound to Home Rule 'by every tie of honour', he then made a speech in the House of Lords in which he stated that before Home Rule could be conceded 'England, as the predominant member in the partnership of the three kingdoms, will have to be convinced of its justice'.[1] This extraordinarily maladroit remark infuriated the Irish and appeared to justify the Lords' rejection of Home Rule. A few days later he had to explain away what he had said,[2] but meanwhile the Government had the humiliation of being defeated in the Commons on an amendment to the Address, denouncing the power of the Lords.[3] This was, in effect, a vote of censure on Rosebery, who was made to look even sillier when the Government, in order to negative the amendment, had to vote against, and then re-introduce, its own Address. In spite of his attempted

1. House of Lords, debate on the Address, 12 March 1894.
2. Speech at Edinburgh, 17 March 1894 (St Patrick's Day).
3. 13 March 1894. The amendment was moved by Labouchere and supported by Redmond, the Parnellite leader.

explanations, Rosebery's attitude to Home Rule cost him the support of some Irish Members, and the Government's majority dwindled from forty to twenty. At the same time he failed utterly to regain the confidence of Liberal Unionists. He would have been wiser to keep his mouth shut, or to speak of Home Rule – to the extent that he had to speak of it at all – with Delphic ambiguity. In practice the issue was shelved until a Liberal Government was once again dependent upon Irish votes, and until the Lords' veto was abolished.

The biggest achievement of the Rosebery Government owed nothing at all to Rosebery. The 1894 Budget, containing a proposal for the introduction of death duties, was framed by Harcourt without any help from, or prior reference to, the Prime Minister.[1] The innovation consisted not in taxing inheritance (it was already taxed, at a flat rate), but in substituting a graduated system applicable at identical rates both to realty and personalty.[2] When Rosebery saw the proposals he objected strongly to graduated death duties, arguing that they would make the division between parties 'horizontal' and that they would antagonise men of property. If so, Harcourt retorted, the Liberal Party would 'share the fate of another Party which was founded 1,894 years ago'. At the same time he hinted that Rosebery was against the idea because he had 'great possessions'. Actually, the two men differed in this matter only on tactics (apart from their natural disposition to quarrel). Harcourt was a younger son, whose interest in hereditary wealth was less direct and personal than Rosebery's.[3] But no one could have been less of a social revolutionary than Harcourt. He traced his descent from the Plantagenets and was very conscious of the fact: as a don at Cambridge he decorated his rooms with heraldic devices. The motive for his reforming efforts was primarily conservative, though stupid conservatives could not see that he was on their side. When he was Home Secretary he was bitterly attacked by landowners for his Ground Game Act, which gave the occupiers of land protection against hares and rabbits, and established an equality between

1. One of the strongest influences behind the adoption of death duties was Alfred (later Lord) Milner, Chairman of the Board of Inland Revenue at the time.

2. Gladstone's comments on the latter feature are of some interest. Speaking of Harcourt's Budget to Rendel, on 4 February 1895, he suggested that the new system was unfair to landed property. 'Land had long borne an exceptional taxation annually (personalty escaping rates), which was the excuse for easier Death Duties. Its assimilation with personalty in regard to Death Duties seemed to Mr G. to involve an equal degree of assimilation in reference to local burdens.' (*The Personal Papers of Lord Rendel.*) Since 1925 duty has been levied at a reduced rate on agricultural land.

3. Though in fact he eventually inherited the family estates, in 1904, from his nephew.

landlord and tenant in the right to kill ground game. The effect of this
measure was to remove a major grievance of tenant-farmers, and so to
reconcile them to the game laws in general.

The rationale of his death duties scheme was very similar. By subjecting
inherited capital to a form of taxation which, though still very modest,
was not exactly derisory, he sought to disarm the enemies of large-scale
private property. A glance at the pattern of ownership in Britain nearly
eighty years later shows how well he succeeded. Rosebery's objections
to the scheme were not those of a stupid conservative, but his judgement
of the social (and therefore political) reactions to it proved erroneous.
Harcourt agreed to modify the scale of graduation, but would not budge
on the principle. The Budget passed both Houses and did something to
restore the Government's credibility. But it aggravated the already deplorable relations between the two leaders.

If Harcourt got his way over the Budget, Rosebery exercised a more
or less free hand in external policy. Though he did not, like Salisbury,
combine the offices of Prime Minister and Foreign Secretary, he installed
in the Foreign Office a Secretary of State – Kimberley – who broadly
shared his outlook and upon whom he could rely to be sufficiently
accommodating. A pledge had been given that Harcourt would be consulted on foreign and Imperial affairs during the formative stages of
policy, but the pledge was repeatedly broken. During Gladstone's last
Ministry Rosebery made a habit of acting on his own quite independently
of the Cabinet, and in 1894-5 the practice was continued even more
shamelessly, with the added advantage (to Rosebery) that he was Prime
Minister. For instance, he did not think twice about signing a treaty
with Belgium, or declaring a protectorate over Uganda, without a word
to his colleagues, who were simply presented with a *fait accompli*. His
policy was essentially the same as Salisbury's, except that he was even
more anti-French and rather more pro-German.

For the Welsh Members the main point of interest in the new regime
was that Tom Ellis was promoted to the office of Chief Whip.[1] Ellis
thus assumed overall responsibility for party discipline at a time when
Lloyd George was deciding that it was expedient to be more rebellious.
To Lloyd George it was obvious that the Government was for all practical
purposes a dead duck. With such a small majority and such a record of

1. The previous holder, Edward Marjoribanks, succeeded his father as 2nd Lord Tweed-
mouth the day after Gladstone resigned.

failure, with a confident, unreformed House of Lords to block their measures, and in the absence of Gladstone's prestige – to say nothing of the unsatisfactory and divided character of the new leadership – how could the Liberals hope to retrieve their fortunes *as a party*, within the lifetime of the Parliament? Surely they could only hope to do so *as individuals*, by winning for themselves an independent popularity which would atone for the unpopularity of the Government. This was clearly Lloyd George's view throughout the brief interlude of the Rosebery Administration, and it provides a logical explanation of his conduct.

On 8 March he and Frank Edwards had a 'private' interview with Ellis, at which they asked for a definite assurance that the new Government would carry a Welsh disestablishment bill through the House of Commons before the end of the coming session. An account of this interview appeared next day in the *Caernarvon Herald*, and the report stated that unless the required pledge were given it was 'understood that ten or a dozen of the younger and more advanced representatives of the Principality' would 'not hesitate, if necessary, on some early and critical occasion, to withhold their support from the Ministry'.[1] Four days later, after the Queen's Speech had been read in the House of Lords, the Welsh Members met in Committee Room 7. Their first business was to elect a new chairman in succession to Rendel, and their unanimous choice was Osborne Morgan – a respected but rather *passé* figure, with neither the popular appeal of the young nationalists nor Rendel's privileged access to the party leadership. His function could be no more than that of a stopgap. Herbert Lewis and Frank Edwards were appointed joint whips, but their behaviour in the months ahead was singularly unwhiplike. Their loyalty was to Lloyd George and the Welsh national cause as they saw it, rather than to the Parliamentary group. In any case, the Welsh Party whips had none of the disciplinary powers normally associated with the job.

The Queen's Speech had foreshadowed 'measures dealing with ecclesiastical establishments', but with no indication that a Welsh bill would be given the highest priority. Lloyd George, therefore, proposed that the Welsh Members should 'wait upon Sir William Harcourt on the earliest day convenient to him', to obtain 'his personal assurance' that a Welsh disestablishment bill would be 'pushed to completion in the House of Commons during the present session'. The motion was carried with only one adverse vote, and one or two abstentions. Harcourt received

1. *Caernarvon Herald*, 9 March 1894.

a deputation of Welsh Members, including Osborne Morgan, Lloyd George, S. T. Evans and Major Jones, on 16 March, when he assured them that their bill would be carried, that the Government would not be content with the empty gesture of a Second Reading debate, and that he *thought* the bill could be passed during the session. This was not exactly the copperbottomed pledge demanded in Lloyd George's motion, but, according to a newspaper with which he had close links, the interview was 'considered to be satisfactory'.[1]

Very soon, however, an event occurred which changed his mind, convincing him of the necessity for open revolt. At the end of March there was a bye-election in Montgomeryshire (caused by Rendel's elevation to the peerage), at which the Liberal vote dropped very sharply and the Party's candidate, A. C. Humphreys-Owen of Glansevern, had quite a struggle to be returned. Humphreys-Owen was a cautious Liberal, educated at Harrow and Cambridge, a barrister, a landowner, and nearly sixty. Lloyd George, who spoke for him at the election, was quite sure that the extent of the setback was due to the type of candidate, and that Liberals of the Humphreys-Owen type had no future in Wales. As he wrote to Margaret: 'The Montgomery election was a narrow shave wasn't it? I had calculated upon a reduction in the majority – but not to that extent. . . . These respectable moderate men who never make mistakes they are not liked at all. People as a rule prefer harem scarem chaps who occasionally say and do wild things.'[2] Fellow politicians assured him that it was only his intervention that had saved the seat. 'One of the Tory members for Shropshire . . . who had been down to Montgomery told me that everybody said I was the member for Montgomeryshire and not Humphreys-Owen. . . .'[3] The message was clear: to safeguard his own position at the next election he must act, meanwhile, in a 'harem scarem' manner, saying and doing 'wild things'. Having read the signs, he was quick to show that he had heeded their warning.

At the Reform Club, Caernarvon, on 14 April, he addressed a meeting of his constituents and won their support for a personal declaration of independence. After reviewing in some detail (but with a light touch) the Liberal Government's cavalier treatment of Welsh issues since it came into office, he referred to the meeting with Harcourt on 16 March. 'Sir William Harcourt,' he said, 'declined to give a pledge' that

1. *North Wales Observer*, 23 March 1894, reporting interview with Harcourt on 16 March.
2. D.L.G. to M.L.G., date illegible but, in rough terms, obvious from the context (N.L.W.).
3. D.L.G. to M.L.G., 4 April 1894 (N.L.W.).

IN THE WITCHES' CAVE.

WITCH LLOYD-GEORGE:
 Now hath dawned the longed-for hour!

WITCH D. A. THOMAS:
 Now at length we've got the Bill!

WITCH FRANK EDWARDS:
 Sooth, it was high time—high time!

WITCH GEORGE:
 Round about the cauldron go—
 In our choice amendments throw!
 Though we have at last the Bill,
 We are discontented still.
 Mother Church shall get it hot—
 In with all to the damned pot!

ALL:
 Gabble, gabble, bawl and babble—
 Rob the Church to please the rabble!

WITCH EDWARDS:
 Fairness isn't on our list—
 How the cauldron glowed and hissed!
 In we hurl our flaunting phrases—
See the stench the mixture raises!
 Curses boil the pot full soon—
 How it bubbles 'neath the moon!

ALL:
 Gabble, gabble, bawl and babble—
 Rob the Church to glut the rabble!

WITCH THOMAS:
 Preachers' spite and chapel screw—
 In the pot the venom strew!
 Nonconformist conscience next,
 Zedekiah's special text!
 Plundering threats of pious thieves—
 How the filthy mixture heaves!
 Church and clergy, soon you'll weep,
 Drinking from our cauldron deep!

ALL:
 Gabble, gabble, bawl and babble—
 Rob the Church to feed the rabble.
 Let the Government delay—
 Every dog must have his day!

3. 'In the Witches' Cave', *Western Mail*, 3 May 1894

disestablishment would be carried through all its stages during the current session. What, then, were the Welsh Members to do? It was obvious that disestablishment would not be carried, unless it were given a higher place in the Government's programme, or unless there were an autumn sitting. Moreover, he did not know what the Government's disestablishment bill would contain, but 'if the outline given in the newspapers was anything like correct, it would be better that they should wait five years more and get, if possible, a better measure'. The English regarded the Welsh as parasites, but he wished to show that they were mistaken. The Cabinet was 'a Cabinet of Churchmen'. There were some 'who were originally Nonconformists, but they left their Nonconformity behind immediately they came in contact with the atmosphere of London society'. The Welsh Members must 'stand on the ground of independency and tell the Government that they would not receive Welsh support to break their pledges to Wales'.

After the speech, one questioner asked Lloyd George whether the whole of the Welsh Party was prepared to support him in taking independent action. He replied that his colleagues had voted by twenty-one to five to act independently if the Government failed to give a satisfactory pledge on disestablishment. Another questioner asked if he was 'going to do his utmost to turn this Government out and thereby give a chance to let a Tory Government in'. His answer was that Wales must face the consequences of standing up for her national rights. He had paired for the Budget and for the Registration Bill, but 'as for voting on anything else, I will not, whatever may be the consequences'. His action and attitude were endorsed by the meeting with only one dissentient and few abstentions.[1]

Frank Edwards immediately threw in his lot with Lloyd George. 'Frank is a "sticker". . . . He is fully satisfied with the situation and feels that we are standing on a rock.'[2] D. A. Thomas took the same independent line, though he naturally regarded himself as the standard-bearer from South Wales, rather than as Lloyd George's henchman. After some vacillation Herbert Lewis joined the rebels at the beginning of May, and thereafter they were known as "the Four".

Meanwhile the Government had introduced its bill for disestablishing and disendowing the Church in Wales. From 1 January 1896, the Church was to be disestablished in the thirteen Welsh counties; the Welsh bishops

1. Report in *North Wales Observer*, 20 April 1894.
2. D.L.G. to M.L.G., 23 April 1894 (N.L.W.).

were to be excluded from the House of Lords, and the Welsh clergy from Convocation. Tithe was to be vested in the county councils and devoted to public and charitable objects. Burial grounds were to be assigned to the new parish councils. Only property conferred upon the Church since 1703 would be left intact. A commission of three would be made responsible for maintaining cathedrals and other Church buildings. Pensions would be paid to incumbents, but not to curates. Asquith introduced the Bill on 26 April, and Lloyd George spoke on it after the weekend, on the 30th.

He dealt first with the argument that the Church and Nonconformity were about equally divided in Wales. If that were true, it meant that at the last election tens of thousands of Churchmen must have voted for disestablishment. He challenged those who said that Wales had never had a separate national existence. The Tories were prepared to recognise Wales as a separate entity for intermediate education and even for Sunday closing – but not for disestablishment. He attacked the compensation clauses. The treatment of the clergy was 'too indulgent and too generous'. Whenever the Government discharged officials it compensated them 'for any loss they might suffer by being thrown upon an overcrowded market', but he had 'never heard of any Government assuming that officials in the prime of life were so thoroughly handicapped against obtaining other appointments that they ought to be provided with the full measure of their income for the rest of their lives'. A clergyman's life interest had no market value, because it was not disposable; yet it was proposed 'to give the same liberal compensation for the loss of it as . . . if it were an unencumbered and perfectly fair life interest'. In a florid peroration Lloyd George said that the Church was now 'stimulated into activity' by forces which 'rendered its existence unnecessary', and he protested against 'extending exceptional indulgence to an establishment the priesthood of which, during their whole career, had simply had one record of betrayal of [Wales's] highest interests'.

Balfour, who was the next speaker, remarked acidly that while the details of the Bill had been expounded with 'masterly lucidity' by Asquith, the defence of its principles had apparently been 'left to the honourable gentleman who has just sat down'. What did the Home Secretary think of his argumentative methods? On the statistical question, he merely said that he did not intend to enter into a wrangle about figures, because 'our decision ought not to depend upon the relative numbers of the various denominations concerned'. But he taunted the

Liberals with refusing 'the religious census for which we have constantly asked'. Dealing with Lloyd George's history he tried to be loftily dismissive: '. . . it does not require one to be a competent historian to know that the honourable Member has drawn entirely upon his own fancy when he has pictured his independent Wales as existing at some period unknown and unspecified in the remote darkness of the Middle Ages. The honourable gentleman did not give us . . . one single date or one single authority, except a stray reference to an Act, which I confess I had never heard of before, which he described as the Act of Union with Wales.' Balfour said that he had asked a friend to fetch a copy of the Act (Henry VIII's) from the Library, and he quoted from the preamble in support of his own view that Wales had never been recognised as a separate entity. He deplored the tone of Lloyd George's peroration: 'I do not mean to follow the honourable gentleman through the embittered controversy which he initiated, and certainly I am not going to use towards the Nonconformist bodies in Wales epithets and phrases which he was not ashamed – though he ought to have been ashamed – to use towards the members of that great communion which he was attacking.' Two years previously a chairman of the Welsh Nonconformist Conference had described disestablishment and disendowment as 'a low aim for the Church of the living God'. This was a handy weapon for Balfour. 'It is not my business . . . to express agreement or disagreement with a statement made upon the authority of the chairman of this Nonconformist meeting, but at all events it may teach, it should teach, the honourable gentleman and his friends some greater humility of statement than he has permitted himself today.'[1]

In mid-May Lloyd George obtained backing for the rebellion at a lively meeting in the Penrhyn Hall, Bangor. He and his friends were only, he said, asking for a specific pledge that disestablishment would be passed through all its stages during the existing session, even if it were necessary to make Parliament sit in the autumn. If the Government gave them that undertaking, they would at once return to their allegiance.[2] On 23 May Rosebery declared at Birmingham that the Government would not go to the country until disestablishment had been passed by the Commons, and two days later the Welsh Members recorded what was, in effect, a

---

1. Hansard, Fourth Series, Vol. XXIII, cols 1690–1718. Lloyd George was, as usual, well satisfied with his performance. 'Think I succeeded wonderfully. Held House much better than Balfour who followed me. . . . Heaps of members trooped out after I sat down.' (D.L.G. to M.L.G., 30 April 1894, N.L.W.).   2. Speech at Bangor, 16 May 1894.

vote of confidence in him, rejecting the 'Four's' demand for a more militant reaction. Lloyd George, encouraged by old Gee's fervent support,[1] felt that the pressure must be kept up. Rosebery's speech he took to be an indication that they were 'winning'.[2] On the day of the Welsh party meeting Humphreys-Owen wrote to Rendel:

> I am getting to the bottom of the Welsh revolt. Lloyd George asked me how one could expect men who were getting big Treasury briefs to do anything to inconvenience Government. . . . He went on to say he will not be satisfied with anything but an organization like the Irish pledged to take no favours – money or office – from the Government. . . . He repeated to me his views that we should be just as well off with a Tory as with a Liberal administration and said he was completely indifferent so long as he got money for his constituents whether it was paid as blackmail or not. In short he is a real irreconcilable and though we are great friends I am afraid we shall have a fight. Our meeting was very short. . . .[3]

Lloyd George did not mind being in bad odour with most of his colleagues, but he was anxious not to incur displeasure in Wales by what might appear to be churlish treatment of Ellis. He made it known, therefore, that he fully understood 'the acute difficulty' of Ellis's position, and that no one would be more willing than himself to pay a 'cordial tribute' to the Chief Whip.[4] Incidentally, Uncle Lloyd seems to have had some doubts about the revolt, but this did not trouble Lloyd George at all. 'Uncle must not worry. Surely he can trust me to the extent of knowing what is best to be done under the circumstances.'[5] So much for the idea that Uncle Lloyd was his Svengali.

1. D.L.G. to M.L.G., 23 May 1894 (N.L.W.).
2. D.L.G. to M.L.G., 24 May 1894 (N.L.W.).
3. A. C. Humphreys-Owen to Lord Rendel, 25 May 1894 (Glansevern Papers, N.L.W.). Another interesting glimpse of solicitors' resentment of barristers, and vice versa. Sam Evans was among those who were strongly opposed to Lloyd George at this time.
4. Manchester Guardian, 25 April 1894 (quoted in H. du Parcq, op. cit., Vol. I, p. 161). Lloyd George regarded Ellis's position as intolerable, quite apart from anything that he himself might have done to make it more so. 'I am afraid that Ellis is not getting on at all. . . . He is sometimes compelled to submit to the grossest personal insults. There is a fellow called Captain Fenwick, a brewer who got in as a Liberal for a Durham constituency. Ellis stopped him the other day as he was walking into the Tory lobby. He turned round and said "Don't you think I know how to vote without your telling me – you damned Welshman?" Isn't that abominable?' (D.L.G. to M.L.G., undated, N.L.W.).
5. D.L.G. to M.L.G., 30 May 1894 (N.L.W.).

He was determined not to truckle to Rosebery who, he said, had referred to the Welsh as 'natives of the Principality' – 'as if he were referring to a tribe of Wahabees in Central Africa'. This was the sort of indiscretion that Lloyd George loved to exploit. He had been 'reading of how Stanley and his followers gave the natives empty jam-pots. . . . The policy pursued towards the "natives of the Principality" was one of empty jam-pots. Others had the jam; they had the pots.'[1] On 6 June Rosebery achieved one of the few successes of his Premiership, when he won the Derby with his horse, Ladas II. At the Eisteddfod the following month Lloyd George had this to say: 'What the bull-fight is to the Spaniard, the carnival to the Italian, and horse-racing to the Englishman, the Eisteddfod is to Wales. Ladas for England, Elvet for Wales!'[2] But Rosebery was at the same time under fire from the opposite quarter. Churchmen were outraged by the Disestablishment Bill, if not by the Prime Minister's frivolous recreations. When, at the Christ Church gaudy (reunion dinner) soon after his success at Epsom, he quoted a passage from Juvenal in which Ladas is mentioned, a clergyman present turned to his neighbour and said: 'Why doesn't he finish the quotation – "Because I persecuted the Church of God"?'[3] The clergyman need have felt no serious anxiety about what the Government would or could do to the Church. In July the Disestablishment Bill was withdrawn until the following year when, after further discussion, it shared the Government's own fate.

Since it was obvious that the Welsh Church would never be effectively 'persecuted' so long as the House of Lords was capable of protecting it, an atmosphere of unreality surrounded the disestablishment controversy in 1894–5. Asquith regarded his Bill as part of the process which he described as 'ploughing the sand', and which others more hopefully described as 'filling up the cup' (of popular wrath against the Lords). Moreover, the controversy was unreal for another reason: it was, at least partly, a sham fight. Intelligent men on both sides were aware that moderation and commonsense would eventually have to prevail. Many Churchmen knew that the Church would have to be disestablished, and were only concerned to negotiate favourable terms. Many Nonconformists –

1. Speech at Cross Keys, Monmouthshire, 29 May 1894.
2. Speech at Eisteddfod, Caernarvon, 13 July 1894. Elvet was the Rev. Dr Howell Elvet Lewis (1860–1953), well-known in Wales as bard, romantic poet and hymnologist: later arch-druid.
3. 22 June 1894. (*Seventy Years at Westminster*, with other letters and notes of Sir John Mowbray, Bart, M.P , edited by his daughter, Edith M. Mowbray.)

especially crypto-secularists like Lloyd George – were keen to get the religious question out of the way so that there could be more united support for other Welsh policies, and for wider social causes.

There was also a growing awareness among all but the most bigoted Nonconformists that the Church was no longer the corrupt, down-at-heel institution that it had been in the eighteenth century, when parsons acted as estate agents to boorish landowners, and when it was not unknown for a vicarage to be let off as a public house. In late nineteenth-century Wales the Church was once again on the up-grade. Its numbers were increasing at a relatively faster rate than those of the Nonconformist sects, though of course its total strength was still much less than theirs.[1] But above all its spiritual integrity had been largely regained, and it was also well on the way to regaining its Welsh identity. The gibe that it was an 'alien' Church, though still freely used, was ceasing to correspond with the facts, because Welsh clergymen were tending to be just as Welsh in culture and spirit as their Nonconformist counterparts, and no less ardent for the promotion of Welsh national interests.

The new state of affairs was epitomised in the relationship between the two most vigorous campaigners for their respective sides – Lloyd George for Nonconformity, and A. G. Edwards, Bishop of St Asaph (since 1889), for the Church. These two men went for each other hammer and tongs in public, but in private they soon came to like and understand each other very well. A typical Lloyd George remark about the Bishop was that he was 'the unique specimen of a shepherd who holds in contempt the flock he shears'.[2] But he did not mean it, and the Bishop soon knew that he did not mean it. Lloyd George, in fact, 'regarded this staunch supporter of the claims of the Establishment with respect, and the friendship formed between them is one of the brightest features of religious controversy in Wales'.[3] A quarter of a century later they were the joint architects of a settlement generous to the Church, and enduring. Meanwhile they tried to settle the question, but failed. According to Edwards, Chamberlain examined the Disestablishment Bill and 'found that Mr Lloyd George was in favour of making concessions'. Chamberlain outlined a compromise scheme which 'proved of no small value' in the eventual negotiations.[4]

1. In 1895 the Church claimed nearly 115,000 Easter communicants, while the total strength of Welsh Nonconformists at that date is estimated at nearly 417,000.
2. Interview given by Lloyd George to the *Caernarvon Herald*, 14 September 1894.
3. Herbert du Parcq, *op. cit.*, Vol. I, p. 166.
4. A. G. Edwards, *Memories*, p. 170. He adds that 'at that early date Mr Lloyd George . . . was recognised by Mr Chamberlain as pre-eminent among the Welsh party'.

But at the time it was a waste of effort, as was the so-called 'Bangor scheme' put forward by a group of Churchmen possibly with Lloyd George's direct encouragement and collusion.[1] Circumstances were not auspicious for a deal, and when Parliament resumed in the New Year (there had been no autumn sitting) the Government brought in another Disestablishment Bill which differed hardly at all from that of the year before.

Lloyd George spoke in the Second Reading debate, on 26 March. He got up at about half-past ten in the evening and spoke for over an hour. The Welsh had come to Parliament, he said, to ask for a readjustment of property in favour of those who were meant to be the beneficiaries. 'If that were pillage and robbery, all he could say was that there was hardly a month when the Court of Chancery did not sanction a scheme of pillage and robbery almost identical. . . .' The Church in Wales had nine-tenths of the wealth, yet its religious efforts 'sank into insignificance when compared with those of the poorer Church of the small tradesman, the small farmer, and the labourer'. It was argued that if the Church were disendowed there would be no resident ministers in three or four hundred Welsh parishes. But the Nonconformist churches did not depend upon resident ministers: they had itinerant ministers, and they also had elders who, as a rule, were 'men of unblemished character' and 'superior intelligence', selected to look after the interests of the Nonconformist flock. He described the situation in one remote parish 'cut off from the surrounding country by a range of hills', where the only resident minister was the Church of England parson whose congregation consisted of his own son, while the Nonconformists had a chapel with seventy members and a Sunday school with about seventy-five members. He ended with an emotional appeal to the House 'to apply [Welsh] national property for better, holier and more Christian ends, in assuaging suffering, in succouring distress, in relieving and, if possible, redeeming their people, by giving them that training and discipline which would enable them to overcome those . . . evils which the present system encouraged'.[2]

It seemed to him that this was one of his most telling speeches in the House. When he got up the Chamber was nearly empty, but by the time he sat down 'every available Member' was there. 'Balfour . . . came in hurriedly as if someone had told him and he remained to the end except for ten minutes' absence. . . .' (He had gone up to the Peers' Gallery to

1. K. O. Morgan, *Wales in British Politics, 1868–1922*, p. 148.
2. Hansard, Fourth Series, Vol. XXXII, cols 247–59.

speak to the Bishop of St Asaph.) When the peroration began 'a hush fell over the House which was quite solemn and when I sat down there was by far the biggest cheer given to anyone except possibly Asquith and it was quite as good as his'. Afterwards Lloyd George was 'overwhelmed with congratulations', and he noted with pleasure that Members 'trooped out' as soon as the speech ended. He had got his 'sea legs in the House' and felt that his position there would soon be secure.[1]

During the Committee Stage Lloyd George and D. A. Thomas embarrassed the Government by moving amendments of a Welsh nationalist character. For instance, on 20 May Lloyd George proposed that instead of the three-man commission which, under the Bill, was to be set up to administer secularised endowments, the fund should be administered by a national council to be set up, in accordance with the 1888 Local Government Act, as a body elected by the Welsh county councils. He had no special quarrel with the commissioners who had been named, except that it did seem 'rather remarkable that there was only one who was a Welshman, and not one who was a Nonconformist'. His point was that it could not be desirable for 'a purely local fund' to be 'administered by a number of gentlemen who might be utterly out of sympathy with the people to whom the property belonged'. He did not wish to transfer the commission's judicial functions, only its more general duties of administration. Asquith at first refused to budge, but at length agreed to reconsider the points on a later clause. Lloyd George then announced that he would not press his amendment.[2]

A month later, on 20 June, the Government had a majority of only seven on one clause of the Bill, and the following day it was defeated on a quite different issue (the supply of cordite to the Army). As a result of that defeat, it resigned. Opponents of Lloyd George subsequently blamed him for the Government's fall, and the charge has received some support from a distinguished historian of modern Wales.[3] The anti-Lloyd George case was made at the time in Y Goleuad, a Methodist paper close to Bryn Roberts, who strongly opposed Lloyd George's national council idea. The paper alleged that Lloyd George had intrigued with the Opposition to force the Government to accept his ideas; and that Asquith, having

1. D.L.G. to M.L.G., 27 March 1895 (N.L.W.).
2. Hansard, Fourth Series, Vol. XXXIII, cols 1632–43, 20 May 1895. Actually, Lloyd George had to vote against his own amendment, because Tory Members would not allow it to be withdrawn.
3. K. O. Morgan, Wales in British Politics, 1868–1922, pp. 155–8.

eventually done so under duress, was then content that the Government should be beaten on cordite rather than have to act against its principles on the Disestablishment Bill. Dr Morgan argues that the 'real' defeat of the Government was the day before, when its majority fell to seven. By contrast, the cordite vote was 'trivial'. Though it was actually D. A. Thomas who was making the running on 20 June, Lloyd George's activities 'did materially weaken his own government, even if the charge of consorting with the Opposition remains unproved'. Ellis later defended Lloyd George, but Asquith, in a near-contemporary letter to Ellis, more or less corroborated the *Goleuad* version.

The truth, surely, is that rebel manœuvres on the Disestablishment Bill were almost as incidental as cordite to the real sources of Government weakness. The Rosebery Government fell because it was hopelessly divided at the top, because it had no coherent strategy, and because it was at the mercy of the House of Lords. Whatever happened, there was no question of disestablishment going through: it was bound to be rejected by the Lords, even if it passed the Commons. The Bill was no more than a histrionic gesture, and all who took part in the debates on it were play-acting after their own fashion. Asquith was doing so no less than Lloyd George, but since his interest in the matter was substantially different he struck a different attitude. He had no interest at all in the Welsh national-ism which was Lloyd George's dominant theme at the time. As an Englishman representing a Scottish seat, Asquith wanted to keep the Welsh movement under strict control, because he was afraid that the majority of British voters might see in Wales (however mistakenly) a repetition of what had happened in Ireland.

Lloyd George, on the other hand, wanted to make the most of a tide which was potentially of great benefit to himself, and against which – as the Montgomeryshire bye-election had shown – it was dangerous for any Welsh politician to swim. His intention was not to be swept away by it, but to be the engineer who would harness it. If he conspired with the Tories (and there is no proper evidence that he did) he was merely acting in accordance with a doctrine that he had openly proclaimed – that the Welsh Members, having received less from the Liberal Government than from its Tory predecessor, should now act independently in the interests of Wales. His conduct, on the least charitable view, is morally preferable to Asquith's the previous year over the Employers' Liability Bill, because to make his propagandist point Lloyd George did not torpedo a bill which would otherwise have become law in a quite useful and beneficent form. He was merely attitudinising at the expense of a bill which was anyway totally doomed.

To Lloyd George disestablishment was only one aspect of the more general cause of devolution, to which he was now giving most of his time, talent and energy. *Cymru Fydd*[1] began as a cultural movement, initiated by Welshmen living in England. By the early nineties it was spreading throughout the Principality, though it had only recently started to catch on in South Wales. Tom Ellis, inspired by Continental and Irish nationalism, felt that the movement should be orientated towards politics as well as towards culture; and before he was disqualified by becoming a Minister (more especially a Whip) he was the leader of *Cymru Fydd* in its more politically active form. Lloyd George then took over and during the next few years the movement had first claim upon his formidable powers of oratory and organisation. *Cymru Fydd* branches proliferated (their membership consisting very largely of Welsh Liberals and Nonconformists under another name), and in 1894 it was proposed that they should federate in a *Cymru Fydd* League. In August of that year representatives of all the branches met at Llandrindod Wells and adopted a constitution for the federal body.

The aims of the movement, as set out in the League's constitution, show very little trace of separatism, and also show that the politicisation of *Cymru Fydd* did not mean that its original, cultural mission was abandoned. The more important of the aims were: to confederate all existing *Cymru Fydd* societies into an organisation for the furtherance of Welsh national objects, and to establish branches in every town and village in Wales; to secure legislation for Wales conceived with due regard to its national aspirations, and its special needs and circumstances; to promote a movement in favour of obtaining a national system of self-government for Wales;[2] to ameliorate by legislation and other means the condition of the labouring classes of Wales; to take steps for bringing the claims of Wales to the notice of electors in the United Kingdom, and to organise the Welsh vote in centres outside Wales; to enforce the principles of the League in the election and administration of county, district, parish and municipal councils, and other public bodies in Wales; and (finally) to preserve the Welsh language, to foster the cultivation of literature, art and music, to encourage the founding of libraries and of a national

1. The name is variously translated 'Wales of the Future', 'Wales-to-be' and 'Young Wales'.
2. i.e., within the United Kingdom.

museum, and to ensure the preservation of national monuments and antiquities.

It was further provided that the League should have five officers – a president, two vice-presidents, a treasurer and a secretary – who would be elected annually by a National Council of the League. The National Council was to be composed of 'at least 111 representatives', three assigned to each Welsh Parliamentary division (and to each of the three expatriate 'divisions' of London, Liverpool and Manchester), together with the officers, who would sit *ex officio*. Ordinary meetings of the Council were to be held at least every six months, and the Council was to have exclusive responsibility for the funds and policy of the League. In addition, there was to be an annual convention, the first to be held in January 1895.

All this looked rather splendid on paper, but the League soon ran into difficulties. Earlier attempts to unite the Welsh for political action were fair warning of what was likely to happen. Lloyd George himself, before his election to Parliament, had been involved in an abortive attempt to combine the Liberal Federations of North and South Wales in a single body. On that occasion the initiative came from South Wales, and it was the North which was reluctant, fearing domination and absorption by the South. But a few years later the rôles were reversed, and instead of a show of mass solidarity at the beginning of 1895, the leaders of the South Wales Federation refused to cooperate, demanding that the two most populous counties, Monmouth and Glamorgan, should have virtual autonomy within *Cymru Fydd*, and that the National Council should be ornamental but powerless.

D. A. Thomas controlled the South Wales Federation, and his jealousy of Lloyd George made what would anyway have been an improbable union impossible. On the other hand, the North Wales Liberals were persuaded – though some of them were reluctant – to merge with the League, and a pretence of national unity was achieved by the election of another Thomas from the South – Alfred – as the League's President (and of Beriah Gwynfe Evans, also from the South, as its Secretary). But Alfred Thomas was no substitute for D.A. Though comparable in wealth, he lacked the other man's strength and independence of mind. A Baptist, a large-scale contractor in Cardiff, and for eleven years a member of the borough council, Alfred Thomas was elected to Parliament in 1885 as the Member for East Glamorgan. People liked him, and quite respected him, but he was never a commanding figure. Lloyd George, though four years his junior in Parliament and nearly a quarter-century his junior in age, soon established an ascendancy over him which cannot have escaped the notice of their fellow Members. In 1892 Alfred Thomas introduced a bill calling for the appointment of a Secretary of State for Wales and the establishment of a Welsh National Council (consisting of the thirty-four Welsh M.P.s and sixteen representatives of county and county borough councils), which D. A. Thomas significantly opposed because, for one thing, it would have given too much weight to the smaller counties. This was a foretaste of what happened three years later, when the Constitution of *Cymru Fydd* was open to a similar objection, and when the election of Alfred Thomas as President must have appeared to his namesake, and to many other Liberals in the South, as a cover for the effective leadership of Lloyd George. At any rate, the South Wales Liberal Federation refused to join the League.

The movement's fundamental disunity did not, however, unduly cramp Lloyd George's style. Wherever he went he could be sure of an audience, and most of his audiences were very enthusiastic. In October 1894, he told the Cardiff branch of the League that for an aggregate period of fourteen years out of twenty-six Liberal Ministries had been in power, dependent for most of the time upon the loyalty of their Welsh supporters. Yet during that period Wales had not obtained from a Liberal Government one single measure of reform dealing with any of her special interests. It was not enough to put the blame on Tory obstruction. England always got what she wanted, whichever party was in power. And, among the Celtic nationalities, Ireland had 'even shot ahead of England in the number of drastic and comprehensive measures which [she had] succeeded in forcing from the Imperial Parliament'. The reason was clear. Ireland was the only Celtic nationality which had 'organised or drilled the whole of her progressive forces . . . into one compact league'. Wales had not yet made the necessary effort, but the time had come for them to bring all the resources of the Principality 'into one general organisation which shall cover the land'. Nothing had been accomplished for the subject races of Europe except through the spirit of patriotism, which had been 'like the genie of Arabian fable'. It had 'burst asunder the prison doors and given freedom to them that were oppressed . . . transformed the wilderness into a garden and the hovel into a home . . . helped to drive away poverty and squalor, and brought riches and happiness in its train . . . raised the destitute into potentates and bent monarchs to its will'.[1]

1. Speech at Cardiff, 11 October 1894. The i. ensity of Lloyd George's work at this period may be judged from a note from the *North Wales Observer* (12 October 1894): 'On Tuesday last

5. Gladstone addressing a great open-air meeting on the slopes of Snowdon, 13 September 1892

6a. William Ewart Gladstone in 1894

6b. Stuart (later Lord) Rendel

6c. T. E. Ellis

In its programme and propaganda the League aimed to enlist the support of the industrial masses of South Wales, and it unquestionably did make quite a strong appeal to them – an appeal both reflected in, and reinforced by, the adherence to *Cymru Fydd* of the veteran trade unionist M.P. from the Rhondda, William Abraham ('Mabon'). But 'Mabon' was no separatist, in either the national or the party sense. He wanted Wales to remain integrated with the United Kingdom, and the Welsh Party loyally attached to the British Liberals. Lloyd George was wholly in agreement with him on the first point, but not on the second. He could see no advantage in a formal alliance which restricted Wales's bargaining power, and which, as the evidence proved, had been barren of rewards and benefits for Wales. He could also see (but this, of course, was a reflection which he kept to himself) that a solid bloc of Welsh M.P.s under his leadership would give him, personally, a position at Westminster strictly comparable with Joseph Chamberlain's. He would be an independent leader who could make his own terms with the big parties, and though his natural preference would be for the Liberals he would not shrink from negotiation with the Tories if the Liberals would not go his way. Thus, there was no contradiction between his belief that Wales should be part of the United Kingdom and his desire for a separate, independent Welsh party. Both were relevant to his ambition to do the best that he could for Wales while exercising power within the much larger British spheres of nation and Empire.

The formula which seemed to meet all requirements was that of Home Rule all Round – Chamberlain's idea originally, but dropped by him and then taken up by Lloyd George. In January 1895 Rosebery gave it his blessing when he addressed the National Liberal Federation meeting – as a gesture to Wales – at Cardiff. And on the same occasion Lloyd George made a short but very telling speech, when he seconded a motion on Irish Home Rule proposed by C. P. Scott, editor of the *Manchester Guardian*. Two years before, he said, the people of Ireland, Wales, Scotland and nearly half of England had declared that Home Rule should be conceded to Ireland. They were now told that the policy had been

---

he addressed a great gathering at Llanrwst at the inaugural meeting of the local branch of the Cymru Fydd League. On Wednesday he was engaged all day in a game case at Pwllheli. On Thursday he was "Cymru Fydding" at Cardiff, on Friday at Swansea. On Saturday he addressed a Temperance meeting at Cardiff; on Sunday he conducted a religious meeting at Cardiff; and on Monday he addressed the Congregational Union at Liverpool.' (The Liverpool meeting was, in fact, on the previous Monday.)

dropped not because two or three million people had changed their minds, but because 'a ricketty old institution called the House of Lords' had voted against it. Three nations and a half cornered by one crack of a lordly whip! What a picture of British pluck! He seconded the motion 'with a lively sense of favours to come'.[1] Tom Ellis, who was on the platform, was so carried away by Lloyd George's eloquence that he 'lost control over himself and shouted out repeatedly, in pure Cymraeg: "Da iawn, fy machgen i, da iawn!" '[2] Two months later there was a debate on Home Rule all Round in the House of Commons, on a resolution moved by Henry Dalziel. (Dalziel was a Scottish Member, a future newspaper magnate, and soon to become one of Lloyd George's cronies.) In his speech seconding the motion Lloyd George began by saying that Wales had no intention of setting up 'a separate and independent republic'. They did not want an army and navy, only the measure of devolution foreshadowed by Chamberlain, whose words on the subject he quoted. He said that before any small nationality within the United Kingdom could get its grievances attended to it had 'to resort to something in the nature of lawlessness' – which was regrettable. He gave as instances the Scottish Crofters' Bill, the Irish Arrears Bill of 1887, and the settlement of the tithe agitation in Wales. His speech ended with an appeal to 'foster the spirit of local patriotism'.

> Honourable Members opposite [he said] are rather too fond of treating that idea with contempt. I notice that our military men discovered its value long ago. In the army there were Welsh troops, Scotch troops, Irish troops. Why? Because our men of action know that there is nothing that brings out the best and most soldier-like qualities of their men like an appeal to their enthusiasm for the honour and the fame of their country. What is true of warfare against foreign foes is equally true in the war which is being waged against social evils. It is one way to stir up men to fight against those evils, which are much more dangerous than any foreign foe.

John Redmond, the Irish Parnellite leader, spoke next and showed his displeasure that the resolution put Ireland on a par with the other Celtic nationalities, instead of giving the prime, unique place to Irish Home Rule. He said that Dalziel's and Lloyd George's speeches were 'scarcely equal

1. Speech at National Liberal Federation meeting at Cardiff, 17 January 1895.
2. "Well done, my boy, well done!" (Report in *South Wales Daily News*.)

to the magnitude of the subject', and suggested an amendment, which Dalziel accepted, that devolution to Scotland, Wales and England should follow the establishment of a national Parliament in Ireland. One Minister spoke – Sir George Trevelyan, the Scottish Secretary – and he referred to Lloyd George as 'really admirable in his exposition of the Welsh case'. He supported the idea expressed in the resolution, but left the vote free.

Balfour poured the coldest of cold water upon the whole affair. He could not share Trevelyan's belief in the value of such Friday-evening debates on theoretical subjects. Home Rule all Round seemed to him a disastrous idea. 'Look at the process by which Italy has been converted from a geographical expression into a national reality. Look at the process by which German unity has been built up. . . . I say that the process of change, the movement, the progress . . . has been to bind together, and not to loosen.' He quoted Morley as saying that one of the great benefits of the French Revolution was that 'it stamped out the very last remnants of those divisions which even the power of the French Monarchy had been unable to efface'. And he ended:

> Surely we shall not add to our dignity in the view of the public if – after three hours' discussion, in the absence of a very large number of the most important Members of the House, with the Government Bench unadorned by the leading members . . . in a House compared with its whole numbers relatively small – we are to pass a resolution which, if it means anything, means this: . . . that we are to introduce a complexity into our affairs, which at the best must produce inevitable friction, and which at the worst will prove a centrifugal force. . . .[1]

In spite of Balfour's intervention the resolution was carried by twenty-six votes. The victory had no political significance, but the debate gave the subject a good airing and Lloyd George was very pleased with his own performance. 'Never spoke better in the House of Commons in my life. Admitted on all sides. One member . . . absolutely clapped his hands when I sat down – of course it was out of order to do so but he was quite beside himself. . . . I have been overwhelmed with congratulations.'[2] It was only two days since he had reported in equally rhapsodical terms the success of his Second Reading speech on Welsh disestablishment. The

1. Hansard, Fourth Series, Vol. XXXII, cols 523-60, 29 March 1895.
2. D.L.G. to M.L.G., 30 March 1895 (N.L.W.).

two speeches undoubtedly mark a further step forward in his Parliamentary career.

Margaret hardly came to London at all in 1894. She was expecting
Gwilym, who was born at the beginning of December. As a result,
Lloyd George let the Palace Mansions flat towards the end of the year and
stayed, when in London, at the National Liberal Club until the following
April. He complained of being left on his own: 'I like London right
enough when you and the little ones are up but it is a bore in this fashion
of living.'[1] In fact, he liked London anyway, but would have liked it
better still if his family had been with him. In the summer of 1894 he
went to Switzerland with Herbert Lewis, Frank Edwards and their
wives. Margaret stayed at home in Wales, to his evident chagrin. 'I
cannot tell you how exceedingly sorry I am to learn . . . that you cannot
come with us. . . . I had really looked forward to getting your company
on this journey and pointing out to you the objects of interest I had been
talking to you about. It really went to my heart that after all you have
made up your mind that it is not safe for you to come.'[2] All the same,
he enjoyed the trip which, he told Uncle Lloyd, 'effected quite a marvellous transformation' in him, so that he 'could jump over the moon'.[3] The
party travelled by train to Berne, then on to Thun, where they embarked
in a boat and crossed the Thunersee, completing the journey to their
destination – the Grand Hotel Victoria, Beatenberg – by funicular. At
the hotel they were surprised to find Welsh acquaintances, 'Mr and Mrs
Cadwaladr Davies and Miss Hughes (the Philosopher, whom Daniel
was so frightened of)'.[4] The days were spent walking in the pine woods
or climbing local heights, from which they could admire the glories of
Nature. Mrs Lewis had brought a spirit lamp and kettle for making tea,
which they consumed either in their rooms or out of doors, in convenient beauty spots. On Sunday they gave way to nostalgia. 'After all
the visitors at the hotel had left for their respective strolls we the little
Welsh gang congregated in the drawing room and after Frank had sung
one or two little things Mrs Mary Davies enchanted us with a series of
the loveliest songs. When she sang Cwynfan Prydain . . . my throat
choked. . . . There were one or two English and French visitors present

1. D.L.G. to M.L.G., from the National Liberal Club, 9 March 1895 (N.L.W.).
2. D.L.G. to M.L.G., 25 July 1894 (N.L.W.).
3. D.L.G. to Uncle Lloyd, 7 August 1894 (N.L.W.).
4. D.L.G. to M.L.G., 2 August 1894 (N.L.W.).

but altho' they could not possibly have understood a line of the words tears filled their eyes. . . . Frank and Mrs Edwards and I are now off to the English Episcopalian service.'[1] In his long letters to Margaret, Lloyd George reproached her for the shortness of hers, and she must have made a spirited retort, because he was at pains to mollify her:

> Don't you make any mistake at all. There are no letters I love to get and read more or a tithe as well as yours. And if I complain of their shortness it is because every additional line affords me such delight. There is no pleasure at Beatenberg which affords me half the enjoyment I derive from perusing your letters. This afternoon in coming down [from the mountains] I was parched even to the point of torture but what I was thinking most of in coming down was of the letter from my pet which would be awaiting me on my return . . . so no more frowning hen gariad. . . . I am very sorry to hurt you in the slightest degree.[2]

The soft soap worked, because she decided to come up to London to meet him on his return the following weekend. Herbert Lewis put his flat at their disposal (their own being let). For the rest of August, and all of September, Lloyd George was at Criccieth with hardly an interruption.

After that, he was very busy until September of the following year (1895). *Cymru Fydd* campaigning, intense Parliamentary activity, a general election, and a fair amount of legal and other work, left him very little time for home life in Wales. But he did not forget his family. 'I had started writing to the *Guardian* but I saw a neat little chap walking in his mother's hand along the road. That made me think of the pets at home. I dropped the *Guardian* and started writing this [letter].'[3] However tiring his days, he usually had the energy and inclination to write to Margaret. One typical day at this period began with a visit to the Law Courts, which involved a row with some official there lasting several hours. 'He became quite impertinent thinking evidently from my

1. D.L.G. to M.L.G., dated only 'Sunday' but from internal evidence obviously 5 August 1894 (N.L.W.).

Dr Mary Davies (wife of Cadwaladr) was a keen exponent of Welsh folk-song. *Cwynfan Prydain* ('Britain's Lament') is a mournful dirge to words written in 1695 by Hugh Morris, and was a favourite of nineteenth-century ballad-singers.

It is revealing that Lloyd George, the free-thinking Baptist, was prepared to accompany the Anglican Edwardses to their church, whereas the Methodist Lewises appear to have preferred no church to the wrong church.

2. D.L.G. to M.L.G., 'Monday' (6 August) 1894 (N.L.W.). 'Hen gariad' means 'old darling'.　　　　　　　　　3. D.L.G. to M.L.G., 17 February 1895 (N.L.W.).

appearance that I was a boy. I soon brought him to his knees. I told him that I would stand none of his impertinence and that he must not talk in that fashion to me. I threatened to report him. They would do nothing at first – but after that they were all too ready to do everything.' After this, Lloyd George went to the House of Commons, where he wrote part of 'a long article' for the *Manchester Guardian*, arranged a meeting of the Welsh group for later in the week 'to consider the question of amendments' (to the Disestablishment Bill), entertained two constituents from Caernarvon to dinner, finished his *Guardian* piece, put down a question for the next day but one, and then started his letter home – to which he added a characteristic postscript, asking Margaret to send him a clean nightshirt.[1]

Rosebery's abrupt resignation after the 'cordite vote' brought the Conservatives back to power for a decade. When the Liberals were next given the chance to form a Government, Lloyd George immediately became a Cabinet Minister. Meanwhile he had plenty more to do as a back-bencher, and one of the biggest storms of his career, the Boer War, to weather. His first task was to retain his seat at the general election which Salisbury, the new Prime Minister, was quick to hold. This was a less difficult task than he made it out to be. The fact that he was branded as a rebel against the Liberal leadership was no handicap, but a positive advantage to him. In the circumstances of the last year or so rebelling had become the key to electoral survival. That was why he had done it. He had acted not from any moral compulsion, but in response to what he took to be the clear lesson of the Montgomeryshire bye-election. Since then it had been increasingly obvious that his independent line was popular in Wales, with the result that, at the general election, 'discipline' was as much of a pretence as 'rebellion'. Instead of Lloyd George making his peace with the official leaders of the Welsh party, they showed that they were almost pathetically anxious to make their peace with him, realising that they needed his support more than he needed theirs. Ellis came and spoke for him during the campaign, and he himself was asked to speak for the chairman of the Welsh party, Osborne Morgan – an invitation which he accepted with amusement and relish.[2] Discipline should be made of sterner stuff.

1. D.L.G. to M.L.G., 3 April 1895 (N.L.W.).
2. '. . . there is a certain irony in the fact that the leader of the Welsh party has to send hysterical telegrams to the rebel chief for his assistance. At the commencement of the

It was not the Welsh split, or his own part in it, that endangered Lloyd George in the Caernarvon Boroughs, but rather the split in the Liberal leadership and the continuing trade depression, which together made it virtually certain that 1895 would be a 'Tory year'. Like every other anti-Tory candidate he had to resist the prevailing trend, but his strong local credit, enhanced by his apparent heroism on behalf of Wales, gave him an exceptionally good chance of doing so. The Liberal Party went to the country without a coherent national policy. Rosebery stood for tackling the House of Lords, Harcourt for local option, Morley for Irish Home Rule. None of these policies was likely to appeal to the English electorate – which was largely indifferent to the House of Lords issue, and actively hostile to Temperance and Home Rule – but in Wales all three were relatively popular.

Besides, Wales had its own pet issue of disestablishment, which now appeared to be a firmer article of Liberal Party faith than Irish Home Rule itself. There was also the exciting, but much vaguer, demand for Welsh Home Rule, which most Welsh Liberal candidates fought shy of but which Lloyd George included in his programme. Shortly before the change of government he made a resounding speech in which he claimed that Wales should be ruled by her own sons and daughters and not by 'groups of Englishmen three hundred miles away . . . whose knowledge of Wales was drawn entirely from their morning perusal of *The Times* or from an occasional flying visit to Llandudno or Tenby, whence, because they could be served with a chop or steak without resorting to the device of drawing a picture of a cow and a frying-pan, they rushed back to England with the cry that Welsh was no longer spoken'.[1] This was not a call for sovereign independence or anything remotely approaching it. It was simply the *Cymru Fydd* theme with Lloyd Georgian grace-notes. But the best political artists know how to make an essentially modest demand sound dramatic, and Lloyd George certainly made the most of *Cymru Fydd* in his election campaign.

The Conservatives helped him by choosing Ellis Nanney to stand against him a second time. It was hardly to be expected that a candidate who, in spite of much local goodwill, was unable to beat him when he was five years younger and a newcomer, would be able to beat him as

---

struggle he gave me a nasty stab under the rib which had he any strength at all would have finished me. Now I am having my revenge in rushing to the rescue of the man who tried to down me.' (D.L.G. to M.L.G., 24 July 1895.)
1. Speech at Blaencwm, 6 June 1895.

the sitting Member and an established Parliamentarian. Lloyd George took the offensive at once, attacking the commission proposed in the Disestablishment Bill.

> It is a custom to appoint Commissioners to manage the property of lunatics, but I am not willing to acknowledge that Welshmen are a nation of lunatics . . . and the insult is aggravated by the announcement that two of the proposed Commissioners are either Englishmen or Scotsmen, both of them dubious Liberals, the only Welshman being a Tory and all three being Churchmen.

Should a vacancy occur under a Tory Government another Tory would be appointed, and then 'the property of the Welsh nation, a nation of Liberals and Nonconformists, would be managed by English Tory Churchmen'.[1] A Welsh national council must, he insisted, be brought into being, first to administer Church property, and then to take increasing control over Welsh affairs. Throughout the campaign he fought on the scarcely veiled assumption that the Salisbury Government would be confirmed in power, and this gave him a neat answer to those, like Bryn Roberts, who were reproaching him with having made life so difficult for Liberal Ministers. 'If I have been sometimes rather troublesome to a Liberal Ministry in the cause of Wales, I will be a hundred times more so to a Tory Government.'[2]

The cordite vote provided him with a line of attack on Chamberlain, which was to feature more prominently in the next election.

> Mr Chamberlain says that there should be four hundred cartridges . . . for every soldier, and on that question the Government has been thrown out. Mr Chamberlain is anxious to know whether the Government has given sufficient orders to a firm called Kynoch & Co. of Birmingham. What is the history of that company? The chairman is Mr Chamberlain's brother. There are four Chamberlains who have large holdings in the firm. . . .

In response to a heckler, he added emotional colour to the charge. 'The reason why the Disestablishment Bill has been thrown out and the Government has been defeated is because Mr Chamberlain complained that there were not enough powder and bullets to kill people.' The

1. Speech at Caernarvon, 26 June 1895. In the same speech he denied a published statement that he intended to desert the constituency and look for a seat in South Wales.
2. Quoted in J. Hugh Edwards, *op. cit.*, Vol. I, p. 180.

heckler: 'It was to support home industries.' 'Then our home industries are bullets! If you are going to support home industries, I will do the same, my friend. We have industries in Wales – religious equality, social reform, Temperance reform, something that will uplift the people and not mangle and mutilate them. Support home industry! Then let them have bullets for Birmingham, and we will have freedom for Wales.'[1]

Chamberlain was now Colonial Secretary in the Salisbury Government. His estrangement from the Liberal Party was complete, and for the next fifteen years British politics were to be complicated by the fact that the two outstanding exponents of radical reform were on opposite sides in the party battle. One reform which Chamberlain had already advocated – old age pensions – Lloyd George made an issue in the Caernarvon contest. He declared himself strongly in favour of old age pensions, and suggested that the £5 million needed for them should be raised by the proper use of tithe (to help the poor, rather than the parsons), by increasing death duties, by taxing ground-rents and by taxing royalties.[2] When Nanney replied that lawyers' bills should be taxed, Lloyd George glibly retorted: 'Mr Nanney knows well enough that they are taxed and that his own agent is the taxing-master. . . . I have no objection to lawyers' bills being taxed, but I will say that it is high time to tax the landlords' rents.'[3] When asked his opinion on One Man One Vote, he said that he would give men as many votes as they had heads. 'The squire has only one head; I would give him one vote. We want to give votes, not to property, nor land, nor business, but to brains.' On the same occasion, when asked if the Liberal Government was responsible for the depressed state of trade, he gave a strikingly fatalistic answer: 'No, the Government is no more responsible for the trade of the country than it is for the rain which is now falling.'[4]

While the election was in full swing Lloyd George went to Liverpool to consult a specialist about his ears. A robust constitution did not, in his case, exclude a lifelong tendency to hypochondria, and when he found that he could not hear the tick of a watch three inches away, his immediate impulse was to consult a leading medical authority outside Wales, even at the risk of losing the momentum of his campaign. The specialist informed him that the wax in his ears was 'as hard as nails' and removed it from the left ear, advising him to return to Liverpool after the election to have the right ear attended to. Recovering from this 'little operation',

1. Meeting at Bangor, 4 July 1895.   2. Speech at Caernarvon, 5 July 1895.
3. *Ibid.*, 16 July 1895.   4. Open-air meeting at Bangor, 13 July 1895.

at the North Wales Hydropathic at Rhyl, Lloyd George heard the first election results, with the startling news of Harcourt's defeat at Derby.

> The first results came in last night. We have lost 5 and gained 1. Harcourt who got 2,000 last time is now out by 300. That is of course a staggering blow. It will have the effect of putting heart into the Tories and of depressing our people. I must apply myself next week to rousing them to a final effort. If I succeed then we win. If not then I shall apply myself for the next six years to Criccieth and business.[1]

He would, of course, have done nothing of the kind, but the problem never arose because, when the Caernarvon Boroughs went to the poll (in a thunderstorm) on 22 July, Lloyd George emerged a comfortable winner. The figures were:

Lloyd George	2,265
Ellis Nanney	2,071

His majority of 194 was only two less than he had scored at the previous election. 'The wave of Toryism,' he said, had 'dashed itself in vain against the rocks of Eryri [Snowdonia].' And next day he added that if his opponents could not improve on their rate of progress it would take them five hundred and fifty years to wrest the seat from him.[2]

There was no denying the impact of the Tory wave upon the country at large. The Conservatives came back with a majority of 152 in the House of Commons, and the Liberals sustained the worst defeat for either party since 1832.[3] Even in Wales the Tories gained six seats, including Frank Edwards's in Radnorshire. He was the only one of the 'Four' to be defeated, and his defeat is partly attributable to the special character of Radnorshire – one of the least 'Welsh' of Welsh counties.[4] Herbert

---

1. D.L.G. to M.L.G. (i) 12 July 1895, (ii) the following 'Sunday' and (iii) undated, but obviously the same weekend. Polling in British general elections was not uniformly conducted on a single day until 1918. The statutory life of a Parliament was still seven years, but in practice elections usually occurred, as they do still, a little before they became obligatory: hence Lloyd George's reference to 'the next six years'.

2. Few words spoken at Rhyl station, 22 July 1895. Ellis Nanney had the consolation of being created a baronet, as Sir Hugh Ellis-Nanney, in 1897, but since his only child was a daughter the baronetcy died with him in 1920.

3. The swing of votes, however, was only about 4½ per cent.

4. There seems also to have been a local issue which affected him adversely. 'The election at Radnor was fought upon a most peculiar question – one upon which the Tories were greater authorities than we were . . . the lunatic asylum.' (Lloyd George at Rhyl, 25 July 1895.)

Lewis was returned for Flint Boroughs, and D. A. Thomas got in again for Merthyr, though with a drastically reduced majority. Lloyd George's victory was seen as a major personal triumph, and so in a sense it was. The chances of his being ousted by Nanney were admittedly small, and he would have been a hard man for even a much stronger Tory candidate to beat. All the same, the ease of his victory was impressive. He had proved that he could hold his seat even in a record Tory year, and he had also proved the truth of his maxim that humdrum Liberalism would not win elections.

SEVEN
Elusive Eldorado

Lloyd George's constituents were proud of him, as most Welshmen were, for his ability to play a conspicuous and at times even a commanding role in the Englishman's world at Westminster. They were also proud of him, more specifically, as a local boy made good, and pleased with him for using his reputation and influence to further their interests as a community. An M.P. was not then expected, as he is now, to act as a welfare officer attending to the multifarious needs and wants of his constituents as individuals. It might be wise for him to do a good turn here and there to people who 'mattered', but in general it was accepted that an M.P.'s function was at the national level and it was not regarded as scandalous if he paid only infrequent visits to the place he represented in Parliament. Today an M.P. may neglect his wife and family, but he cannot afford to neglect his constituents. In Lloyd George's youth it was possible to do both.

This was very fortunate for a man who loved the idea of Wales but rather disliked the reality, and whose reluctance to deal with correspondence amounted almost to a disease. Lloyd George had little desire to see his constituents, and less still to receive letters from them. In his view, any letter from an outsider – that is to say, anyone outside his circle of close relations and intimate friends – was an intrusion, and he naturally tended to leave it unanswered, even if he bothered to read it. He would rather, he said, submit to a dozen interviews than write one letter.[1] He once asked Herbert Lewis to go to his locker in the House of Commons to fetch some document, and when Lewis opened the locker hundreds of

1. Interview with *Caernarvon Herald*, 14 September 1894.

letters fell to the floor. 'Most of them will have answered themselves by now,' was Lloyd George's casual comment.[1] He himself describes a similar incident, in one of his letters to Margaret. He was looking for a telegraphic code (nothing whatever to do with his political work, but relating to his business affairs). 'I have just been engaged for an hour and a half cleaning out my locker! I filled three wastepaper baskets to the intense amusement of the bystanding policeman. . . . After wading through [a] dunghill of newspapers, circulars, letters and documents I got hold of the missing code – to my intense relief.'[2] Other letters make it clear that, if his London home was empty or let, he did not arrange for mail to be forwarded to the House of Commons or the National Liberal Club or wherever he might be staying. On one occasion, returning after an absence of some weeks, he could hardly open the door at Palace Mansions for the mass of mail which had accumulated behind it.

That his extraordinary attitude towards correspondence did not, apparently, damage his career in its early stages is the measure of his value as a politician, and of the extent to which people were prepared to accept him on his own terms. It must soon have been common knowledge that there was very little hope of getting at him through the post, and that personal contact was the only reliable method, either directly or through a third party. As soon as he became a Minister in 1905 he had a staff to handle his official correspondence, but it was not until Frances Stevenson became his confidential secretary, as well as his mistress, in 1912 that his more private letters – including letters concerned with public affairs, but not intended for the eyes of civil servants – were systematically dealt with and filed. His failure, as a back-bencher, to preserve more than a tiny fraction of the letters he received is something that historians will always regret. But apart from the offence against history, was his disregard of letters in other respects wholly wrong? Too much of the average politician's time, even in his day, must have been spent answering letters of no particular importance. Dealing with correspondence can surely be a vice as well as a virtue. Lloyd George was no slacker, but he felt that writing to strangers or even colleagues was nearly always a waste of time. Though he could express himself with great force and facility on paper, he never mistook words for deeds. A fault which Winston Churchill imputes to Curzon[3] – that of believing that he had achieved a concrete result when he had merely stated a case – could never be im-

1. Quoted in Frank Owen, *Tempestuous Journey*, p 70.
2. D.L.G. to M.L.G., 10 August 1893 (N.L.W.).   3. In *Great Contemporaries*.

puted to Lloyd George. For one so articulate, he was singularly free from that sort of verbal vanity. Besides, his practical sense might have warned him against giving too many hostages to fortune, in the form of letters, even if it had been his natural disposition to write them.

The people of Caernarvon Boroughs do not appear to have been unduly resentful of the epistolary silences and prolonged absences of their Member, and their resentment would in any case have been softened by the fact that his wife was living among them for so much of the time. In that way her addiction to North Wales was a boon to Lloyd George. Normally, she was the member *in* Caernarvon District, while he was the Member *for* it. But if Lloyd George was seldom accessible to his constituents as individuals, he was very useful to them collectively. With great persistence he would raise and press constituency points, either at Question Time or behind the scenes; and his skill in negotiation, allied to his growing reputation as a controversialist, enabled him to get results. Representing as he did a string of little coastal towns, he was particularly active on their behalf in matters such as foreshore rights, harbour improvements and communications. On the landward side, he was most attentive to the interests of local quarrymen. In 1891 he told Margaret that his work on railway rates and quarry royalties was probably doing him more good than anything in the Boroughs.[1] Even so, he did less for his constituency than a modern M.P. would be expected to do, not only because the public then had a different conception of an M.P.'s duties, but also because the State's recognised sphere of responsibility was so much narrower than it is today. The life of the community proceeded, on the whole, without State intervention, and the scope for lobbying of and by M.P.s was strictly limited.

Another pertinent fact was that M.P.s were not then salaried servants of the State. They were unpaid (until 1911), and as a rule it was they who financed their constituency associations, rather than *vice versa*. Lloyd George could not have afforded to do this, and his association bore the cost of his elections (£400 in 1895, subscribed by eighty of his supporters). Until he was a Minister he received no salary for his political work, and his earnings from other sources were modest and fluctuating. For the year 1893–4 his income was assessed at £338, on which the tax demand was £6 4s 7d.[2] Since he had no capital, that income had to

1. D.L.G. to M.L.G., 27 July 1891 (N.L.W.).
2. Notice of First Assessment under Schedules D and E of the Income Tax Acts, on D. Lloyd George Esqr., Solicitor, of Criccieth and Portmadoc (N.L.W.).

cover the cost of two establishments, the feeding and clothing of a wife
and three children, and much of the expense involved in a busy political
life. Even when one allows for the change in the value of money – £338
in 1893 was the equivalent of about £2,650 in 1973 – Lloyd George's
income as a young M.P. was cramping to one who, in D. R. Daniel's
words, had a 'luxurious nature'.[1] It also went against the grain with him
that he was, at this period, excessively beholden to his brother.

William George was the junior but – after Lloyd George's adoption as
a Parliamentary candidate – the more assiduous and gainful partner in
the firm of Lloyd George and George. From that time onwards he could
honestly claim that the main burden of the partnership fell on his
shoulders, and that he became 'the bread-winner for two families'.[2]
Lloyd George continued to practise as a solicitor, in spite of the ever-
increasing demands of politics, but the briefs which he handled, in London
and other parts of England as well as in Wales, were marginal compared
with the volume of work handled by William. It might be true that the
fame of a well-known politician was an asset to the firm, as Lloyd George
and Margaret liked to believe: 'You are quite right about the practice.
Will would never have worked it up. He keeps it together very well
but my name helps him materially to do so. Anyone would tell him
that.'[3] But William was an able and hardworking lawyer, who would
certainly have made his way in the profession even with a less glamorous
partner. His conscientious toil was worth 'materially' more to his brother
than his brother's prestige was worth to him. In 1897 Lloyd George
established a London partnership with another Welsh solicitor, Arthur
Rhys Roberts, with an office first at No. 13 Walbrook, later at No. 63
Queen Victoria Street. This became moderately prosperous (though it was
hard hit by Lloyd George's unpopularity during the Boer War), with the
result that he gradually became less of a charge upon the firm in North
Wales. All the same, as late as the first quarter of 1899 his net drawings
from Lloyd George and George amounted to £276 12s 1d, which
included his household expenses at Criccieth, the rent (paid to his father-
in-law) for his house there, and two quarters' rent for Palace Mansions.

Once he had made his mark in politics he began to be able to supplement what he received as a solicitor with fees paid to him for journalistic
work. His quick reactions and vivid phraseology gave him a natural
aptitude for journalism, which first revealed itself when he was only a

1. D. R. Daniel, *op. cit.*   2. William George, *My Brother and I*, p. 86.
3. D.L.G. to M.L.G., 21 July 1893 (N.L.W.).

boy. Newspapers could hardly fail to be interested in a politician who was glad of the chance to write for them, and who combined a distinctive outlook with a bright and lively style. The first English newspaper to approach him seems to have been the *Star*, for which, in February 1892, he was engaged to write 'a weekly article . . . of about a column and a half in length'.[1] The following year he started writing for the *Manchester Guardian*, whose illustrious editor, C. P. Scott, later became one of his closest allies and confidants in the national Press. The *Guardian* had recently launched a special Welsh edition, said to be the first localised edition of a daily newspaper published on this side of the Atlantic. It contained, among other things, regular Welsh features from London, and most of Lloyd George's contributions were probably to the Welsh lobby notes, though some may have been to the London Letter. In 1893 he contributed, in all, 140 paragraphs, and earned a total of £57 12s od[2] – a little more than one-sixth of his income for that year.

As well as journalism, he did some paid lecturing on the work of the House of Commons, or on politico-historical subjects such as 'Llewelyn the Great', or (later) on foreign countries that he had visited. The fee was usually five guineas per lecture, and this enabled his enemies to hint, in 1895, that he was paid for his *speeches*. He replied indignantly – but without mentioning the lectures – that no man had spoken more than he had on behalf of Wales, that in doing so he had sustained financial losses and neglected his business as a solicitor, and that the people who scurrilously attacked him were 'cads'.[3] When he made political speeches in the country he was seldom out of pocket, because his travelling expenses were normally covered either by his hosts or by some sponsoring organisation (Temperance or Nonconformist) in London.

Yet when every fringe item has been taken into the reckoning it remains true that Lloyd George depended for his livelihood, during at least the first ten years of his political career, upon his brother William and the firm in North Wales. William helped him on the political side as well, because he, like Margaret, was far more closely in touch than Lloyd George with the people of Caernarvon District. The two brothers were poles apart temperamentally, but their partnership, though often irritating to them both, was fruitful. In the process of enabling David to get

1. D.L.G. to M.L.G., 16 February 1892 (N.L.W.).
2. David Ayerst, *Guardian: Biography of a Newspaper*, pp. 290–1.
3. Speech at Ferndale, 20 May 1895. An anonymous letter in the *South Wales Daily News* had said that the promoters of *Cymru Fydd* were 'men who received four or five guineas for every speech they delivered'.

on William did not entirely forfeit the chance of getting on himself, but he undoubtedly made sacrifices, and it may be significant that he married late.[1] By 1892, however, he had enough money to build a good-sized house in Criccieth – standing at the end of a drive, in its own grounds – which he named 'Garthcelyn' ('Holly Garden') and which became his mother's, his sister's and Uncle Lloyd's home as well as his own. One way and another he was supporting the whole family.

Lloyd George entered politics with big advantages, of which, as a realist, he must have been fully conscious. Apart from the inborn privilege of genius, he belonged to a national community – revived from a long torpor – which sent thirty-four Members to the Imperial Parliament, and to a religious category of intense political significance not only in Wales, but throughout Great Britain. Moreover, as a professional man, he belonged to an occupational grouping which, in recent years, had become the second largest in the House of Commons. In 1875 land-owners and rentiers held 32 per cent of the seats, the professions 24 per cent, and commerce and industry also 24 per cent. Over the next decade the first grouping had declined to 16 per cent, while the professions had increased to 32 per cent, commerce and industry to 38 per cent.[2] Solicitors might not be regarded as the cream of the professions, but there was considerable solidarity among professional men of all sorts, vis-à-vis the rest of society, and as a grouping their political weight was evidently fast increasing. Lloyd George, therefore, had a very large catchment area in which he could hope to mobilise support. As for his schooling, it had been at least as good as that of the average public-school boy, and if he had not attended a university, neither had Disraeli – who, into the bargain, had to face a much greater degree of ethnic prejudice than Englishmen felt against Welshmen, without the compensating advantage of a Jewish contingent, thirty-four strong, in the House. Besides, Lloyd George had got into Parliament much younger than Disraeli, and in politics it definitely helps to make an early start.

So far, so good – but there was one respect in which Lloyd George

1. On 24 July 1910. His wife was Anita Williams of Fishguard, a nursing sister at the Royal Northern Hospital, London. Lloyd George, Chancellor of the Exchequer at the time, arrived late for the service at the Hermon Baptist Chapel, Fishguard. The minister, who was uttering a prayer of thanksgiving, saw Lloyd George standing in the porch and impro-vised: 'And we thank Thee O Lord for his worthy brother who has just arrived.' This was reassuring to the thousand-strong congregation.
2. W. L. Guttsman, *The British Political Elite*, p. 82.

knew that he was at a serious disadvantage compared with most M.P.s. He was not financially independent. Whereas most of the men he saw around him at Westminster had substantial private fortunes, which they had either inherited or made, he, destitute of capital, was forced to lean upon his brother and upon his constituency association. Money never interested him for its own sake: he was after power, not pelf. But he craved the freedom of action, the freedom from worry, and the freedom from a nagging sense of obligation to others, which money alone could confer. He wanted to be able to concentrate upon politics without being bothered about how his household bills were to be paid, and he wanted to enjoy a standard of living which was luxurious without being sybaritic. Since there was no immediate prospect of office, his thoughts naturally turned to business, and to the type of business in which the maximum profit might be achieved in return for the minimum effort. It was thus that he became involved in the Welsh Patagonian Gold Fields Syndicate Limited.

The man who started him on this venture was David Richards of Harlech, a mining engineer who had spent some time in the Chubut province of Patagonia, where there was a Welsh colony founded in 1865 largely on the initiative of Michael D. Jones (principal of Bala College and chairman of the Michael Davitt meeting at Ffestiniog in 1886, when Lloyd George moved the vote of thanks). For several years there had been gold fever in the area and Richards had ostensibly acquired a concession there, which he lacked the capital to exploit. No doubt he thought of Lloyd George as someone who could help to raise money in North Wales, while at the same time securing the interest of some of his political friends in London.

Anyway, that was exactly what happened. Towards the end of 1892 Lloyd George threw himself into the business heart and soul. Before long he had interested several M.P.s including, more especially, Major Jones and Dr G. B. Clark, the Member for Caithness since 1885. Clark was a doctor of medicine who had attended three universities – Glasgow, Edinburgh and King's College, London. Initially a Marxist, he had been connected with the British section of the First International. When he first got in for Caithness it was as a crofters' candidate standing against the official Liberal; but by 1892 he was sitting as a Gladstonian. Later he served as Consul-General for the Transvaal Republic, and this may have been one reason why he lost his seat in 1900 and never sat in Parliament again. His interest in Patagonian gold has to be reconciled, as best it may, with his modest reputation as one of the pioneers of British working-class politics.[1]

Richards's proposal was that his exploring and mining rights in the area known as Corcovado Mica and Teca gold fields should become the property of a syndicate, in which he would hold half of the equity. This seemed to Lloyd George a perfectly fair proposal, all the more so as Lloyd George and George were to act as lawyers in the deal. It was decided that the initial capital should be £10,000, half of which had to be raised from outside sources (the other £5,000 being the value of Richards's shares, and the assumed value of the assets which he was vesting in the Syndicate). On 11 November 1892, the memorandum of association was signed and the new company registered. Those whose signatures appeared on the memorandum were five M.P.s – Lloyd George, Ellis, Clark, 'the Major' and S. T. Evans – together with David Richards, Michael D. Jones and Edwyn C. Roberts (who, like Jones, was one of the founders of the Welsh colony in Patagonia).[2] A week later Richards signed an agreement transferring his Patagonian rights to the Syndicate in return for fifty per cent of the initial and future equity. The Syndicate accepted the evidence of title which he provided (certificates apparently granted by the Argentine Government the previous July), and he accepted liability for all the legal and other costs of the new company 'up to the incorporation thereof'.[3] But on the same day he signed an agreement with Lloyd George and George under which they were to indemnify him for the preliminary expenses. The *quid pro quo* was that he undertook to give them five hundred of his five thousand shares if their obligations were duly performed – their obligations to include not only the legal work but also using 'their best endeavours to induce persons to apply for shares in the Company'.[4]

A number of small options were taken up but the promoters needed bigger money if they were to raise the necessary £5,000 as quickly as they desired. Clark got in touch with a group of French financiers who, it was hoped, would come in for £2,500. In mid-November Lloyd George and Clark were in Paris negotiating with them, but at the

1. Lloyd George and Clark had been fellow-delegates to the conference of the Inter-Parliamentary Union in Switzerland, in September 1892 (*see* above, ch. 5).
2. Memorandum of Association registered 11 November 1893 (Public Record Office ref. BT 31/5434/37535).
3. Agreement dated 18 November 1892 and registered 2 January 1893 (Public Record Office ref. BT 31/5434/37535). The condition that Richards would receive fifty per cent of future equity was later expunged, by mutual consent.   4. *Loc. cit.*

beginning of December they turned the proposal down. This should have prompted second thoughts about the whole business, but there is no evidence that it did. While awaiting the French decision Lloyd George persuaded T. J. Hughes, 'a moneyed chemist' at Bethesda, to 'take his chance with half the remaining shares' if the Frenchmen refused to come in.[1] By 5 December £3,200-worth of shares had been taken up, and Hughes underwrote the balance.[2] Three days later Lloyd George was able to report that all the shares were allotted, and that applications had been received for more than were available.[3] The official summary of capital and shares, issued early in the New Year, gives the names of thirty-four shareholders and the size of their holdings. Apart from Richards, Hughes was the largest with 1,100 shares, but Lloyd George and William George had 1,600 between them (1,000 and 600 respectively). Clark had 500, and though 'the Major' had only 50 his company secretary, Fred Woodman – who also became secretary of the Syndicate – had 380. Most of the remaining holdings were for £100 or £50 or less, but W. J. Parry, the journalist and trade union leader, was in for £250.[4]

Meanwhile the Syndicate had entered into an amazing new agreement with Richards. He was to place his services at the company's disposal for eighteen months – which the company could extend, if it wished, to two-and-a-half years – and was to go at once to the Argentine, where he was to spend a fortnight in Buenos Aires 'for the purpose of attending to matters relating to the titles', and then another fortnight in Chubut 'to purchase various necessary articles for the exploration'. He was then to proceed to the gold fields, where he was to 'investigate and examine' the Syndicate's 'tract of country', and report on the most likely methods of obtaining good results from it. He was to keep a regular diary showing 'the disposition of his time', and was to send home a copy of the diary, together with a statement of accounts, quarterly. In consideration of these

1. D.L.G. to M.L.G., 29 November 1892 (N.L.W.).
2. D.L.G. to M.L.G., 5 December 1892 (N.L.W.).
3. D.L.G. to M.L.G., 8 December 1892 (N.L.W.).
4. Summary of Capital and Shares of The Welsh Patagonian Gold Fields Syndicate Limited, made up to 19 January 1893, and registered 10 February 1893. In 1892 the North Wales Quarrymen's Union, of which Parry was the first general secretary, presented him with an illuminated address and a cheque for £440. This testimonial 'was widely supported in the press and among the patrons . . . were the officials and General Council of the Union. . . .' (J. Roose Williams, 'Quarryman's Champion: the life and activities of William John Parry of Coetmor', Transactions of The Caernarvonshire Historial Society, Vols 1963–6. This article, which appeared in three instalments, contains no reference to the Welsh Patagonian Gold Fields Syndicate Ltd.)

services he was to receive a salary of £450 for the first eighteen months (£100 cash down, £4 per month until the end of the contract, then the balance). He was also to receive two hundred additional shares in the company (half of them at once, the other half at the end of the contract). The agreement could be rescinded if he failed to carry out his duties as specified.[1]

It was ominous that the promoters of the venture should instruct him to attend to 'matters relating to the titles' – a euphemism, surely, for *verifying* the titles – so soon after binding themselves legally to accept the validity of proofs supplied by him. Moreover, any shareholder who saw the agreement must have reflected that Richards's knowledge of the area, when he acquired the concession, had obviously been rather superficial. Nevertheless, he was given a rousing send-off when, with W. J. Parry and one or two others, he sailed from Liverpool on 4 January 1893. During the train journey back to London Lloyd George wrote to Margaret: 'Well we saw our Patagonian friends off. Parry looked as happy as an April morning and the others were almost as elevated. High hopes seemed to possess them all.' He added that a mining expert had come to the conclusion, 'after a long and searching examination of Richards', that they had 'hit upon a very good thing'.[2] The 'mining expert' referred to was probably a man called Hoefer, who left for the Argentine a few days later, apparently with instructions from the Syndicate to send an independent report.

The company's office was at Effingham House, Arundel Street, off the Strand, from which 'the Major' conducted his paper, the *Shipping World*. He charged £10 per month for the office accommodation. There were five directors, who received three guineas per meeting if they lived in London, or five guineas if, like Lloyd George, they could plausibly claim to be country members of the board. Thomas Lewis M.P. became chairman, and Lloyd George vice-chairman – an arrangement which was explained to Margaret (if to no one else) in very frank terms: 'We made T. P. Lewis Chairman – at my special request. He is a good blind to the public. Myself they made deputy chairman.'[3] Lewis was M.P. for Anglesey at the time, and a prosperous flour merchant, who had become known as Thomas *Palestina* Lewis because he gave so many lectures on his travels in the Holy Land. The other directors were 'the Major', R. O. Davies,

1. Agreement dated 31 December 1892 and registered 3 January 1893.
2. D.L.G. to M.L.G., 4 January 1893 (N.L.W.).
3. D.L.G. to M.L.G., 5 January 1893 (N.L.W.).

Lloyd George's Acton friend, and Vincent Evans, lobby correspondent of the *South Wales Daily News*, secretary of the Chancery Lane Land and Safe Deposit Company, and a prominent figure in the world of Welsh culture – whose relations with Lloyd George, before and after, were by no means always so comradely. One can tell from Lloyd George's letters that William was unhappy about the project and a reluctant participant, but he went along with it all the same and assured his brother that Uncle Lloyd would not be told about it.

In August the directors had bad news. '*Confidential*. Patagonia is I fear a failure. . . . Hoefer wires that "the property falls short of representations". He will be here in a month and will let us know whether it is worth our while going on. . . . Will and I may be able to save ourselves to a great extent by a stiff lawyer's bill but we must of course lose a lot of money. Just like our luck.' Then in Welsh: 'Not a word to anyone, remember, but to Will. . . .'[1] This was the time when the Welsh Members were badgering Gladstone about disestablishment, and when Rendel was constantly seeking Lloyd George's help in drafting letters. When Hoefer arrived: 'News no better than his telegram. He has now ordered Jim Roberts to drive an adit into one vein and the only question now is whether that will improve as it goes down. We are likely to hear from Jim in October. Hoefer praises Parry very much. He says R^{ds} [Richards] is more of a fool than a rogue.'[2] Two days later: '. . . Hoefer simply assayed the surface. There is a chance that the stuff may improve as you go deeper. . . . There is gold there but Hoefer did not think that it would pay to work it unless the quality of the quartz improved.' Already they were looking for a way out. 'We have just been discussing a scheme to sell all our shares out at Buenos Ayres [*sic*]. The Spaniards there are getting up an excitement about the business and it would be easy to feed that excitement and dispose of the whole thing to them. . . . The Company has money in hand still and it is proposed to utilise it for that purpose. . . . The Argentinos can manage the business out there better than we can from here.'[3] Not, perhaps, saying much.

Then, for no discernible reason, 'gold' came to the Syndicate in the form of fresh equity finance. A Bangor concern called the Andes Exploring Company first appeared with an offer 'to take 1,000 shares at 10/–

---

1. D.L.G. to M.L.G., 16 August 1893 (N.L.W.).
2. D.L.G. to M.L.G., 19 September 1893 (N.L.W.). Jim Roberts was presumably a member of Richards's party. An adit is a horizontal entrance to a mine.
3. D.L.G. to M.L.G., 21 September 1893 (N.L.W.).

premium in our Coy. . . . If this can be arranged' (wrote Lloyd George to Margaret) 'and we manage to raise another £1,000 ourselves we propose sending Hoefer or somebody else out to prospect the country around. . . . You may rely upon it that I am not going to risk another penny piece.'[1] Terms seem to have been agreed with the Andes people, but three months later, while Lloyd George was spending the Christmas holiday in London with the Davieses, an even more exciting offer turned up. On Boxing Day he went to the Club to see if there were any letters for him, and found a telegram and a letter from Patrick Chance M.P., who had been in touch with the Syndicate on behalf of stockbrokers in Dublin. The telegram offered 'to put £5,000 in the Company', and the letter gave more details: the Dubliners would take 3,300 shares at 30/– each. 'Now isn't that glorious for a Xmas present. It means a present of £120 at the least to me, for it will keep the affair going for 18 months even if we get no further funds. But we'll have no difficulty now in raising another £2,000. People are much more apt to take shares if they know that you don't particularly care whether they do or not. With £5,000 behind us and fifty per cent premiums there will be a boom in these shares.'[2] Before the end of the year Chance's cheque had arrived, and he was offering to find another £10,000 on the same terms. 'Fancy money being pressed upon you,' wrote Lloyd George exultantly.[3]

But there was still no news of any Patagonian gold to justify the investors' faith. At the beginning of March the Syndicate agreed to send W. J. Parry 'forthwith' to the Argentine 'in the capacity of general Agent and Manager'. He was to stay there for at least seven months. His salary was to be £50 per month, and he was also to receive four hundred more shares in the Syndicate.[4] His mission was a failure and the agreement proved a financial disappointment to him.[5] Meanwhile the summary of capital and shares, as at 30 March 1894, shows how the company had developed (in one sense) financially. The nominal capital has increased to £50,000, and the list of shareholders reflects the Syndicate's arrangements with the Andes group, and with Chance's contacts: there are additional names from North Wales, and 3,300 shares are held in the names of two Dublin stockbrokers. Five Argentinian names also appear

1. D.L.G. to M.L.G., 28 September 1893 (N.L.W.).
2. D.L.G. to M.L.G., 26 December 1893 (N.L.W.).
3. D.L.G. to M.L.G., 30 December 1893 (N.L.W.).
4. Agreement signed 3 March 1894, and registered 6 March 1894.
5. See Coetmor Papers (Bangor University College).

in the list. Lloyd George has disposed of 90 of his original shares, reducing his holding to 910, but Uncle Lloyd now has 10 shares and Margaret 15. (Uncle Lloyd was told about the Chance deal, so by then he knew of the Patagonian venture. When he was first informed is a mystery.) William's holding is unchanged at 600. Hughes, the 'moneyed chemist,' has sold 110 of his shares, and Parry has got rid of 115 of his (though 40 may have been transferred to his wife and sister, who appear with 20 each). David Richards has managed to offload 518 of the shares allotted to him as payment for the Corcovado Mica and Teca concession. If he was 'more of a fool than a rogue', he was a lucky fool. The allotment of 380 shares to Fred Woodman has been cancelled, but 'the Major's' own holding of 50 shares stands.[1] The following June Lloyd George told Margaret that they were intending to move the business out of 'the Major's' office. 'In all he has received £200 out of it and has only grossly neglected it.'[2]

One interesting new shareholder is Henry Labouchere, outstanding Liberal back-bench M.P. and editor/proprietor of *Truth*, who had befriended Lloyd George from his earliest days at Westminster. On the face of it, taking 200 shares in a highly speculative company was just another act of friendship. As a rich man 'Labby' could afford it, though rich men are not always so generous. He liked Lloyd George and regarded him as a kindred spirit, in spite of belonging to a different generation (they were separated by more than thirty years). Both men were radicals who disliked the Whiggish element in the Liberal Party and deplored the breach between Gladstone and Chamberlain. Both were natural adventurers, but at the same time very shrewd and down-to-earth politically. It is said of Labouchere that 'his scepticism and realism were of the French rather than of the English cast'[3] (he was, in fact, of Huguenot extraction), and Frances Stevenson, in her diary, makes a similar comment on Lloyd George: 'He may possess qualities which appear to be those of a mystic, but his desires and ambitions are those of a realist every time. He must have the concrete . . . he is much more a Frenchman even than a Welshman. . . .'[4]

1. Summary of Capital and Shares of the Welsh Patagonian Gold Fields Syndicate Ltd made up to 30 March 1894.   2. D.L.G. to M.L.G., 7 June 1894 (N.L.W.).
3. *Dictionary of National Biography*, 1912–21, p. 317 of the standard edition.
4. Frances Stevenson, *Lloyd George: A Diary*, entry for 9 February 1917. Elsewhere in the diary she records: '. . . he says there is a tremendous similarity between the Welsh and the French peasant, their thrift, their religious side which nevertheless does not debar them from ribaldry and even obscenity. "The garden and the midden are very close together with the Welshman and the Frenchman", he said. . . .' (Entry for 24 April 1934.)

Labouchere's talents were not of the same order as Lloyd George's, yet he probably deserved – as he certainly wished – to be given his chance either as a Cabinet Minister or as Ambassador in Washington. But he had made too many enemies, including the Queen, and he lacked what Lloyd George possessed – a political following to reinforce his personal merits. Consequently his hopes were disappointed. He was a born gambler, who incurred £6,000-worth of debts while he was at Cambridge. The Patagonian Syndicate may have appealed to the gambler in him, quite apart from his goodwill towards Lloyd George. It may also have reminded him of an amusing incident which brought his early career, in the Diplomatic Service, to a close. When the Foreign Secretary (Lord John Russell) offered him the post of Second Secretary at Buenos Aires, he replied that he would gladly accept it if he could perform the duties at Baden-Baden, where he happened to be staying. He was dismissed the Service.

Between the summer of 1894 and early 1896 there is hardly a reference to Patagonia in Lloyd George's letters to his wife. He was very busy with the 'rebellion', disestablishment, electioneering and *Cymru Fydd*. But in February 1896, he writes that a message has been received from 'one of our men' on the spot, reporting that 'the men who are now endeavouring to buy it from us have been there inspecting it' and have said it is 'very good property'. And Lloyd George adds, rather puzzlingly: 'It struck me that they were rather keen about it. That is why I drove such an excellent bargain with them.' He gives no indication who the men were, nor any details of the bargain.[1] In July he begins to refer to 'the voyage' and it soon emerges that he is going to the Argentine. Nearly three years before he had toyed with the idea: 'I have a good mind to pair . . . and run over to Buenos Aires to see our title complete – that is of course if the Coy pay my exes and some remuneration for the job.'[2] It certainly would have been better if somebody had given proper attention to the Syndicate's title at that stage, or indeed earlier. But for one reason or another the idea came to nothing, and the next year Parry was sent. In 1896 Lloyd George did go, with Herbert Lewis and Henry Dalziel as his companions. Lewis was probably his most devoted friend and Dalziel – proposer of the motion on Home Rule all Round which he had seconded, and later founder of *Reynolds News* – was a new friend of his. Neither was a foundation shareholder in the Syndicate, nor did

1. D.L.G. to M.L.G., 2 February 1896 (N.L.W.).
2. D.L.G. to M.L.G., 8 August 1893 (N.L.W.).

either's name appear even in the March 1894 list. But they must have become involved more recently, because they took part in Syndicate negotiations when they reached the Argentine, and Lloyd George clearly set particular store by Dalziel's business acumen and City contacts.

On 4 August (after telling Margaret that he longs to press his 'bony hard face' against her 'soft and sweet one') he writes: 'I am endeavouring to arrange with the Liquidator for payment of my exes out to Buenos Aires. They will mount – between exes out there and equipments for voyage – to not far short of £100.'[1] Mention of a liquidator explains the sudden sense of urgency. Lloyd George had to try, where others had failed, to perform a miracle in the Argentine. He and his two friends sailed from Southampton, on R.M.S. *Clyde*, on 21 August.

His first long letter from the ship reports that he has been suffering from seasickness and homesickness, but has been got down by neither. Dalziel has been trying to disguise his seasickness with bravado. The ship put in at Vigo, where they witnessed the unveiling of the statue of some local dignitary, paid for by himself.[2] Next day, 'off Lisbon' (which they visited): 'Tonight we put out to sea and make tracks straight across the Atlantic. The only land we sight at all will be Teneriffe. Barring that we see nothing but salt water and sky for nine days. All the better I think. These visits ashore altho' very interesting and helpful in breaking the monotony of the voyage are not particularly useful from the point of view of health. . . . The ozone is much preferable to the breezes wafted across putrid offal.'[3]

The ocean-crossing was chronicled in a series of letters, here briefly digested:

Tuesday, 25th. 350 miles south of Lisbon. Delightful day. Not a cloud. Refreshing breeze. Has seen his first flying fish. 'I have been lying on deck on my chair all day reading one of Lever's novels. . . . When I have finished this I shall proceed to finish Thucidydes.' Herbert 'took a Kodak view of my slumber' on deck. Prodigious appetite.

Wednesday, 26th. Sailing between the Canaries. The peak of Teneriffe towers to the right. Has done nothing but lie on deck all day reading Lever and Thucidydes.

1. D.L.G. to M.L.G., 4 August 1896 (N.L.W.). He also sent her his newly acquired cummerbund to hem.
2. D.L.G. to M.L.G., 23 August 1896 (N.L.W.).
3. D.L.G. to M.L.G., 24 August 1896 (N.L.W.).

Thursday, 27th. Now in the tropics. One day like another.

Saturday, 29th. Mentions playing shovelboard. People tell him how much better he looks. 'I cannot tell you how weak I felt when I drove you to Euston. . . . Today I showed my photos to Mrs Clarke . . . the lady who leaves her children for 3 years in order to join her husband. She was delighted with Dick's photo. Thought Mair bach's face so sweet. When she saw yours she said you were the very girl for me. . . . She is so nice. Poor woman.'

(We can imagine Margaret's reaction to that letter!)

Monday, 31st. 'Now within a few miles of the line. . . . Yesterday we had an interesting service on board . . . conducted by the captain and chief officer . . . in the saloon. . . . The captain sat at the head of the table with hymn book and Common Prayer set in front of him on a cushion covered with the Union Jack. . . . We all sang best we could. The singing was the poorest part of the performance. . . . No parts.' A disagreeable feature of ship life is that 'your only choice is between draughts and suffocation. If you close your portholes at night you feel like sleeping in a Turkish bath. If you open them your cabin is like a winnowing chamber.'

Tuesday, September 1st. 'Stormy. . . . Last night we had a sailors' concert downstairs. . . . We passed the island of Fernando this afternoon . . . a Brazilian convict establishment. . . . On Sunday we passed a beautiful sailing ship. They are so much more sightly than these steamboats.'

Saturday, 5th. Ship 'rolling and pitching under the impulse of a south-easterly gale. . . . Yesterday we had lovely weather. The sea calm and placid. But his is not the only placid face that I have known to sulk. Is it hen gariad?' Went ashore, not at Pernambuco, but at Bahia. Then 'sailed through the whale region'. Saw 'huge monsters sporting around some within a stone's throw of the ship. One colossal whale followed by a smaller one came quite close and sprang clean out of the water.' *3.45 p.m.* Has been on deck since lunch 'wrapped up in my macintosh and rug. . . . The storm is distinctly on the increase . . . far and away the worst weather we have had. . . . I rather like it. You know how my spirits always rise with a storm.'

Wednesday, 9th. Most of the passengers left at Rio, and he is glad the journey is nearing its end, much as he has benefited from it. 'I want to get into this Patagonian business to see whether there is anything really to be made out of it. If there is not then it must be dropped altogether.' He praises shovelboard as a form of exercise on board ship.

'Herbert is at it incessantly and . . . gets as excited over it as he does over obstructing a Government measure in the House of Commons. Dalziel is too lazy to practise much shovelboard.'

Wednesday night. Thick fog. Engines slowed down to half speed and foghorn 'moaning at the darkness every two minutes'.

Thursday morning, 10th. 'Fog lifted this morning. . . . We sighted land about 10. . . . [Captain] will get us into Monte Video this afternoon. . . . A pampero blowing savagely in our teeth. You can hardly stand on deck. It is bitterly cold.'

They arrived in Buenos Aires on 12 September, and the following evening Lloyd George wrote a long letter from the Royal Hotel. After describing the formalities which they had to go through before they were allowed to land, he says they were met and looked after by a young Welshman running the Central Argentine Railway, and by 'Mr Bowers', whom he describes as the local manager of Baring Brothers.

Bowers is a big man out here and we are going to ask him to put us in the way of settling our business. . . . He has influence with some leading Government men.[1] We have already got to know fairly well how the affair stands. . . . As near as I can see there is a general scramble going on for our property and the only thing that has saved it for us is that the thieves cannot agree as to the division of the swag. . . . Whether we can set matters to rights goodness alone knows. We have an appoint-

1. The man referred to is obviously Nicolas Bouwer, who was Barings' agent in Buenos Aires from 1876 until 1890 – the year when Barings' nearly went bust and had to be saved by the Bank of England. Bouwer's activities were considered to have played some part in bringing the firm into such straits, and in 1890 – six years before Lloyd George met him – his allowance was stopped and his agency ceased. He continued, however, to have influence in the Argentine, since he remained a partner in his father-in-law's firm, Hale and Co.

Bouwer's character is described in most uncomplimentary terms by two representatives of Barings' writing from Buenos Aires after the crisis. A. Bowden Smith, Bouwer's successor as agent, wrote privately to John Baring (later the 2nd Lord Revelstoke) on 23 June 1891: 'The other day I went over Bouwer's new house at Belgrano with the architect. There is still all the internal decoration to do, and he informs me that it will have cost over $200,000 by the time it leaves his hands. It certainly is one of the most sumptuous looking edifices outside in the country. . . . The insolent and unfair way in which Bouwer has talked to and treated this poor fellow since the crisis began is perfectly shameful, but his manner to everyone is atrocious. . . .' And Essex E. Reade wrote to John Baring on 1 November 1891: 'Bouwer is a disagreeable chap to deal with. He is pretty intolerable at most times, but sometimes it is quite impossible to put up with him, as he can't differ without becoming personally rude.' (Letters preserved in the archives of Baring Bros.)

Even when allowance is made for Barings' natural desire, in 1891, for a scapegoat, it would seem that Bouwer was not likely to be the ideal counsellor for Lloyd George in 1896.

ment with Von Heyking [a mining man who seems to have been acting for the Syndicate] tomorrow morning. . . . From him we'll get to know at any rate one side of the story. We have already heard the other side. We shall then be in a position to place the facts before Bowers and ask his advice on it. We have also arranged to see Mr Haskold the head of the Mining Department either tomorrow or Tuesday.

The letter is continued next day: 'This morning . . . we saw Von Heyking. He is very sanguine about the whole business. He is of the mining type – smart, plausible and capable. I think he is fairly straight as mining men go but I would not trust the best of them out of my sight. At the present moment he is entirely in our hands.' The Syndicate had sent Von Heyking power of attorney, but it had never arrived. Fortunately Lloyd George had obtained power of attorney in his own name. He had come not a moment too soon, because the parties who were trying to 'jump' the Syndicate had got the Mining Department to issue final notice giving the Syndicate four weeks to protest or (presumably) forfeit the property. Von Heyking, however, said that the 'jumpers' had bungled the job, neglecting necessary formalities. He would take Lloyd George, at his expense, to see his lawyer – a former Minister to the United States – and he also suggested that a man called Gilderdale should be sent straight to Chubut 'to attend to the essential preliminaries'. Probably Von Heyking wanted to get him out of the way, because when Lloyd George saw Gilderdale later the same day he said that the jumpers were 'very good people'; that one group was a syndicate in which Rothschild had an interest, and under the direction of 'a relative of Rothschild's' who would 'have nothing to do with Heyking'. But for that, it should be possible to come to terms with the other syndicate. Lloyd George now felt it was a pity they were 'bound hand and foot to Von Heyking legally and morally'. But on Tuesday the 15th, just before posting the letter, he scribbled a few lines to the effect that Gilderdale was trying to get the jumpers to come to terms.[1]

In his next letter he begins with a complaint about having not yet heard from Margaret. He is getting 'agonising fits of homesickness' and has almost come to the conclusion that he is 'not the man to travel far from home'. Then he turns to business. The previous night they had a meeting with Haskold, chief of the Mining Department, at his private residence. 'He lives with his brother. The chief is a staid executive

1. D.L.G. to M.L.G., 13, 14 and 15 September 1896 (N.L.W.).

but most agreeable old gentleman. The brother is 20 or 30 years his junior and a perfect contrast in every respect. He is a harem-scarem chap – wild, impulsive – dissolute I fear – but with flashes of genius. He entertained us with music.' First he played 'Elizabeth's Prayer' (from *Tannhäuser*) 'with wonderful feeling and pathos'. Then he sang 'a barely decent old English song', self-accompanied on the guitar. Both men seemed anxious to help the Syndicate. In Lloyd George's view, they hated the jumpers because they were Germans, and the Haskolds prided themselves on being English. The younger brother advised that the Syndicate should lodge protests at once, giving them the name of a lawyer trusted by the Department. He further said that, although they might 'technically' have forfeited their claims by not working them, they could still place such obstacles in the jumpers' way that it would not be worth their while to proceed, but would suit them better to come to terms.

The following morning the three M.P.s saw Von Heyking again. He now had the idea that they should pool a large number of mining rights in different parts of the country and form one syndicate for the lot, with a capital of, say, £50,000. The money would be spent on developing the mines up to the point where they could be reported on favourably by 'an expert' and then put on the market one by one. Lloyd George thought this 'an excellent idea', and Dalziel, he said, 'could get hold of the men who would find the capital to carry it out'. So even if the Chubut mines proved useless, at least one other mine would be a success and they would be repaid 'for loss of time and for trouble and expense'. But he assured Margaret that he would not, personally, be incurring any more liabilities.

When, next day, they saw the lawyer recommended by the Haskolds, he told them that he would probably be able to persuade the Cabinet to give them a year's extension to work the mines. They also saw Von Heyking again. The following day they decided abruptly not to go to the Welsh colony, but to go 'up country' instead: 'free first class passes sent us – with sleeping and dining saloons'. And they were planning to return to England in a fortnight's time on a ship called the *Magdalena*, in spite of a rumour that she was 'overrun with bugs'.[1]

On the 19th they visited the Argentinian Senate where the President, General Roca, invited them to sit below the gallery, and where – after

1. D.L.G. to M.L.G., 16, 17 and 18 September 1896 (N.L.W.). Lloyd George was also at this time having tooth trouble, which involved two long sessions with a local dentist. During the first he 'squirmed a good deal . . . and once or twice looked out for a hand to grasp – but it was 8,000 miles away'.

listening to a debate on the revision of foreign treaties – they talked in the lobby to Dr Pellegrini, a former President of the Republic, who was a a relation of John Bright and spoke very good English. The next afternoon they went by train to Quilmer, where they dined with 'the Boisdevals' and met some Welsh people from Cardiff and Swansea.[1] Before they left for Cordova Lloyd George was able to report to Margaret that Pellegrini had agreed to become chairman of their local board of management, and that Roca had sent word he would do all he could for them.[2] A week later he wrote again, describing the Cordova trip. They had had 'a great time' in the mountains. For three days they rode through the valleys – Lloyd George feeling a little nervous at first, because he was unaccustomed to riding. But he soon got the hang of it and then 'galloped about at a great rate'. The exotic surroundings fascinated him.

> The glens were lovely – clothed with palms mimosa and cactus. Parrots – flights of them chattering around and an occasional humming bird. . . . The scent of the mimosa accompanied us everywhere. Each day we picnicked out under the shade of a rock . . . or under the foliage of some fine native trees – as a rule on the banks of bright little streams. The peons who guided us lit up a fire of dry sticks and roasted a kid. . . . High up above us huge condors hovered ready to pounce on the refuse. . . . After lunch we bathed in a pool. . . . We had one moonlight ride which was most picturesque.[3]

Herbert Lewis says that on their way to and from Cordova they passed through clouds of locusts. There were 'millions in the air', and it was said that they had 'fallen in one of the squares in Buenos Aires and covered it 3 ft deep'.[4] Lloyd George seems to have been oblivious of the locusts.

He was also averting his eyes from the human locusts who were devouring the Syndicate's property. The week in the mountains was obviously a delightful experience, but hardly relevant to the matter in

1. Herbert Lewis's diary, entries for 19 and 20 September 1896 (Herbert Lewis Papers, N.L.W.).
2. D.L.G. to M.L.G., 21 September 1896 (N.L.W.). In the same letter he says that they were taken the night before to 'the principal club here the Progresso – a magnificent club'. This appears to conflict with Herbert Lewis's account of how that evening was spent, though it is possible that they were taken to the Progresso late at night, when they returned to Buenos Aires from Quilmer. The M.P.s were made temporary members of the club – 'now' (according to Lewis) 'a Reform Club in name only', comprising 'men of all parties', but with 'fine reading, writing and billiard rooms'.
3. D.L.G. to M.L.G., 29 September 1896 (N.L.W.).
4. Herbert Lewis diary, entry for 21 September 1896 (Herbert Lewis Papers, N.L.W.).

hand. It seems to have been arranged by Bouwer, who may have been playing a deep game of his own. There is certainly nothing to show what advice, if any, he gave on the future of the Syndicate. Lloyd George's failure to see for himself what was happening in the gold fields is perhaps the most egregious of all his errors of omission and commission in the Patagonian affair. Having travelled so far, it was absurd that he never went to Chubut, but merely listened to what other people told him. At that rate he might just as well have stayed in London. The nearest he got to Chubut was when he met (in Buenos Aires) the Governor of the area, who made flattering remarks to him about the Welsh colony there.[1] Before the three M.P.s left the Argentine 'a grand dinner' was given in their honour, which Pellegrini, Roca and 'several influential Senators' attended.[2]

There is no account of the M.P.s' last days in Buenos Aires or their return journey, except a bizarre story told by Lloyd George's elder son more than sixty years later. According to this, Lloyd George's attentions to the wife of a successful Argentinian business man provoked the husband into challenging him to a duel, which – for the sake of his family and political career – he was unwilling to fight. He therefore took refuge in 'an obscure hotel' and was persuaded to shave off his moustache, because the husband had 'hired sleuths to track him down'. After a few days his friends were able to 'smuggle him out of the country, shorn but intact'. On his return, however, his moustachelessness caused a stir, and the story of his escapade 'was all over town, in the clubs and drawing rooms; Fleet Street caught echoes of it and Margaret learned all the facts'.[3] The story is not inherently incredible, though the book in which it appears is a dubious source.[4] Lloyd George was a man of indefatigable gallantry, which the guitars, mimosa, etc., of the Argentine could only have served to excite. He might not have realised that the attitude towards women in a Spanish Roman Catholic community was more restrictive than even in Nonconformist Wales, so that a misadventure such as the one described could quite possibly have befallen him. On the other hand, he was also the sort of man to whom such stories were readily – often too readily – attached, and in the absence of corroborative evidence they should be treated with scepticism. Moreover, Lloyd George's moustache must have

1. Quoted in H. du Parcq, *op. cit.*, Vol. I, pp. 195–6, from an interview given by Lloyd George to the *Western Mail*, which appeared in that paper on 15 September 1899.
2. D.L.G. to M.L.G., 30 September 1896 (N.L.W.).
3. Richard Lloyd George, *Lloyd George*, pp. 54–6.   4. *See* Note on Sources.

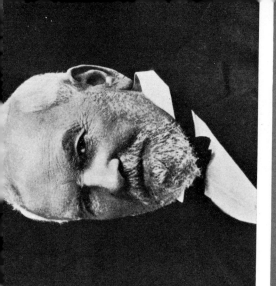

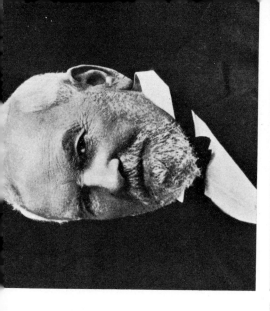

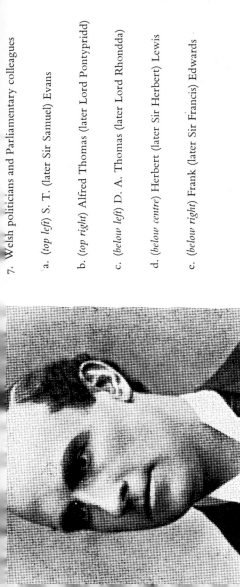

7. Welsh politicians and Parliamentary colleagues

a. (*top left*) S. T. (later Sir Samuel) Evans

b. (*top right*) Alfred Thomas (later Lord Pontypridd)

c. (*below left*) D. A. Thomas (later Lord Rhondda)

d. (*below centre*) Herbert (later Sir Herbert) Lewis

e. (*below right*) Frank (later Sir Francis) Edwards

8a. (*top left*) Lord Rosebery, by Harry Furniss

b. (*top right*) Sir William Harcourt, by S. Car-ruthers Gould

c. (*below left*) Sir Henry Campbell-Bannerman

d. (*below centre*) Joseph Chamberlain, by J. S. Sargent

e. (*below right*) Arthur James Balfour, by Sir Lawrence Alma-Tadema

regained some of its normal luxuriance during an Atlantic crossing, and anyway a plausible excuse for its removal could surely have been invented. Contemporary London gossip would be of little value as evidence, even if it were indeed such as the story suggests: retailed long after the event it is of practically no value. Finally, while it is true that Lloyd George and Margaret had a quarrel soon after he got back, there is nothing in the letters to show that it was due to occurrences, or supposed occurrences, during his stay in the Argentine.[1]

What is certain is that he was back in London at the beginning of November, after a week or so with his family at Criccieth. And he now had another plan for rescuing the Patagonian venture. A new Syndicate was to be formed, in which there would be 9,200 shares for the old one, including 2,300 for Dalziel and himself to cover their recent journey, and a further 2,500 which would be allotted to each of them, over and above their portion of the 9,200. Lloyd George calculated that he and William would thus have 1,150 plus 2,500 plus 920 (their shareholding in the old company) – in all, 4,570 shares in the new concern. But where was the money to come from? Dalziel was off to Scotland to talk to 'his friends', and Lloyd George was hopeful of persuading the Dubliners to make a further investment. His and William's shares would then 'with average luck' have 'some marketable value'. But, he added philosophically, 'it may come to nothing like most of my florid anticipations of good things to come'. He wished to goodness that the venture would 'turn up trumps', so that they would all be placed 'above anxiety'.[2]

But he wished in vain. Four days later he met Chance and Mack (one of the Dublin stockbrokers who had put money into the Syndicate) and the result was negative.

No good I fear. Chance gave me some valuable hints as to how to proceed. But he did not seem anxious that Mack shd. come into the business at all. I must therefore look elsewhere. Dalziel has gone into the City now to meet a friend who might assist but he is rather looking forward to finding the coin in Scotland. It will be a very difficult thing to pull off. There is a great depression in all mining matters now. . . .[3]

The rescue operation called for £7,500, which was evidently not forth-

1. Richard Lloyd George was probably confusing this trip with another, when Lloyd George *did* shave his moustache. (*See* below, p. 261.)
2. D.L.G. to M.L.G., 2 November 1896 (N.L.W.).
3. D.L.G. to M.L.G., 6 November 1896 (N.L.W.).

coming, because the new syndicate was never formed. As late as May of the following year Lloyd George could still write 'I hope we may do something.'[1] But nothing could be done to save the Welsh Patagonian Gold Fields Syndicate Ltd. On 6 December 1900, a formal meeting was held to wind up the company. No member of the Syndicate bothered – or had the heart – to attend. Finally, on 5 November 1907, notice of its dissolution appeared in the *London Gazette*.

Lloyd George kept very quiet about the Patagonian fiasco. There is no hint of it in any book about him hitherto published. Most of his biographers refer to the Argentine trip as a 'holiday',[2] and William George makes no mention of it, or of the Syndicate, in *My Brother and I*. Herbert Lewis's anyway very laconic diary of the trip gives no indication that any business affairs were involved. It is understandable that Lloyd George and his associates should have chosen to be reticent, because if the story of the Syndicate had become public knowledge they would have been bound to appear in a ridiculous light, and not everyone would have interpreted their actions so charitably. They had, after all, themselves invested, and encouraged others to invest, in a piece of property whose development value was extremely speculative, in a remote part of another continent, and the man who vouched for its mineral wealth was a by no means disinterested witness. When they began to have doubts about him, and even about the validity of their title, they still encouraged people – many of them small tradesmen and professional men in North Wales – to put their money into the Syndicate. The promoters at least got something out of it to set against their capital losses: they received fees for their negligent and incompetent services. The firm of Lloyd George and George was paid for its legal work, and for pushing the Syndicate's shares, while Lloyd George himself was paid at the preferential rate, as a 'country' director, for his attendance at board meetings. Admiration for him was used as a bait to draw people into a venture of which they might otherwise have been chary.[3] In allowing his good name to be so exploited he showed unscrupulousness and a certain lack

1. D.L.G. to M.L.G., 21 May 1897 (N.L.W.).
2. Malcolm Thomson calls it 'his first trip abroad' (*David Lloyd George: the Official Biography*, p. 121). Actually, he had been on three trips abroad before he went to the Argentine.
3. There is no explanation why the Irish stockbrokers took shares in the company. But Patrick Chance, who brought in the Irish money, was a reckless character. A solicitor by profession, he sat for South Kilkenny from 1885 until 1894, when he resigned his seat. He was close to Tim Healy, and crops up later in Lloyd George's career.

of self-respect. His motive – to be able to fulfil his destiny in politics without financial anxiety – was perfectly honourable. But the same cannot be said of his methods.

The Syndicate's failure, and the proof that he had no talent for business, did not deter him from dabbling in further speculative projects. In the summer of 1897 he was deep in a scheme to buy the Dorothea slate quarry in the Nantlle Valley, Caernarvonshire.

> I must stick here all through August and put my back into this Quarry business. This afternoon I met Clough [Liberal M.P. for Portsmouth] and Druckner [Tory M.P. for Northampton] to discuss a plan of operations. . . . Druckner, who is a wealthy chap with a following in the City, liked the thing immensely and said it was the sort of thing he wouldn't mind taking up himself. . . . He is prepared [subject to valuation and accountants' report] to buy the Quarry at £160,000. That leaves £30,000 to be divided between four of us and L. G. Roberts & Co. [Lloyd George's London partnership] would get £7,500. I must have all my wits free and unhindered. So for God's sake 'Don't talk to the man at the wheel'.[1]

In spite of Margaret's evident misgivings, Lloyd George was again confident that he would make his fortune. But not for long: a fortnight or so later: 'There is not exactly a hitch in the Quarry business but it looks much more doubtful than it did.'[2] And two days later: '[If] we hear . . . that the owners of the Dorothea decline to extend the time . . . I am sorry to say the whole affair upon which we have built so many hopes must fall through.'[3] Then hope revived: 'Quarry business looks better today . . . influential gentleman from Yorkshire whom we had asked to join the Board . . . has at last consented and will put money into it.'[4] But the Yorkshire gentleman soon withdrew, regarding the venture as 'too risky'.[5] Unsuccessful attempts were also made to raise capital in Liverpool. Towards the end of September Lloyd George feared that the game was up and that he must look out for something more promising. Unless the quarry-owners would agree to reduce their price and accept part-payment in shares, the project would have to be abandoned. Rather touchingly he mentions Micawber and says that he believes something

1. D.L.G. to M.L.G., 6 August 1897 (N.L.W.).
2. D.L.G. to M.L.G., 23 August 1897 (N.L.W.).
3. D.L.G. to M.L.G., 25 August 1897 (N.L.W.).
4. D.L.G. to M.L.G., 26 August 1897 (N.L.W.).
5. D.L.G. to M.L.G., 9 September 1897 (N.L.W.).

else will 'turn up' soon.[1] The owners must have been wise enough to realise that part-payment in shares, granted the people they were dealing with, would be almost the equivalent of no payment. The negotiation came to nothing, and 'Micawber' had to look elsewhere.

The following summer he was at it again. A friend of his was staying in London 'to put those businesses through'. £10,000 was needed, and £6,000 was available 'on my terms'. But a man who promised to find the balance was 'away holidaying', and would in any case advance the money only 'on terms which don't quite fit in with my views'.[2] It turned out to be 'another disappointment' – but by then he was involved in 'some queer business' with Dalziel.[3] Towards the end of the year he begins to refer to some insurance affair in which he is interested, and this is still occupying his attention in the summer of 1899. 'I am here [London] now on Insurance business. We want another Director. Did I tell you that there was a Scotch chap on the Board of Directors I didn't care for? He is now bust up. Luckily we discovered it just in the very nick of time. . . . He is now off the Board.'[4] Very soon he is writing of 'that troublesome Insurance business',[5] and then it disappears from his letters until seven years later when, having meanwhile become President of the Board of Trade, he writes: 'Thornton (of the Insurance Co. – you remember the Insurance Co. I helped to found . . .) tells me he should very much like me to come with the Directors to Paris over a great insurance deal. As I want the office to prosper so as to have something to fall back upon I mean to go.'[6]

While speculating relentlessly in the hope of making a fortune, Lloyd George did not spurn a more respectable and prudent method of protecting his family against financial adversity. In 1894 he insured his life for £500 with the Northern Assurance Company, at an annual premium of £34 16s 0d.[7] He also decided, at least once, that it would be wiser 'to stick to building up [his] legitimate practice' before he took to 'guinea-pigging in business' which he did not understand.[8] There were times when his legal work seemed to be prospering to his satisfaction. 'Curious

1. D.L.G. to M.L.G., 21 and 22 September 1897 (N.L.W.).
2. D.L.G. to M.L.G., 12 and 15 August 1898 (N.L.W.).
3. D.L.G. to M.L.G., 6 October 1898 (N.L.W.).
4. D.L.G. to M.L.G., 22 July 1899 (N.L.W.).
5. D.L.G. to M.L.G., 8 August 1899 (N.L.W.).
6. D.L.G. to M.L.G., 7 September 1906 (N.L.W.).
7. Hugh Lewis to Lloyd George, 23 December 1894, and Northern Assurance to Lloyd George, 31 December 1894 (N.L.W.).
8. D.L.G. to M.L.G., 25 February 1898 (N.L.W.).

how one gets business from Wales with a London office which one would never get if I had an office a few miles from them at Criccieth. . . . So you see business is alright.'[1] Yet he continued to hanker after a quick killing, which would enable him to forget about money and devote his whole mind to politics.

Eventually he did achieve financial independence, partly because as Prime Minister he had, in the honours system, what could be described as a licence to print money – an opportunity which was proof against even his ineptitude as a businessman. He was not the first or last Prime Minister to abuse the system, but he abused it in a cheerful, eighteenth-century manner. Moreover, when he fell from power, he managed to retain control of the Coalition Liberal share of the proceeds. Moralists may note with grim pleasure that, while he was financially insecure he was politically successful, and that when his ill-gotten wealth brought him financial security his political fortunes went into eclipse. Others, however, will never cease to lament the fact that the most creative of modern British politicians should have been distracted from his true vocation by chronic worry about money, from which he was able to free himself only by an expedient which gave his enemies their deadliest weapon against him.

1. D.L.G. to M.L.G., 28 July 1899 (N.L.W.). He nearly always spells 'all right' in one word.

EIGHT
Leading the Leaderless

The story of Lloyd George's financial problems and business speculations as a young man has taken us well ahead of the point reached in his political career. After the 1895 election the Liberal Party was paralysed and prostrated. The leadership deadlock which had made the party unable to govern effectively since Gladstone resigned was more ruinous still in opposition, because whereas power confers a semblance of solidarity upon even the most divided party, the removal of power exposes all its weaknesses and divisions. Rosebery, in spite of a typical, self-pitying gesture of pseudo-resignation, stayed on as the party's titular chief, while Harcourt, though defeated at Derby, was soon returned by another constituency (West Monmouth) to the Commons, where his primacy was hardly open to challenge. The chronic inability of these two men to work together, following the more elemental Gladstone–Chamberlain rift, destroyed for a time the party's credibility as a party of government. But the situation was not without advantage for Lloyd George who, over the next few years, was able to capture more of the limelight than he could have hoped to do under normal conditions.

Immediately after the election, however, he had a slight setback, which could also be regarded as a blessing in disguise. On 26 July 1895, he collapsed while speaking in the Assembly Rooms at Amlwch, at a meeting to celebrate Ellis Griffith's election as M.P. for Anglesey. Ellis Griffith was prominent among the younger Welsh *élite* before he got into Parliament. At Cambridge he was President of the Union and took a First in Law, before becoming a Fellow of Downing College. Lloyd

George was respectful of his gifts, but tended also to be irritated by him, because he was a bit of a snob, rather too polished a speaker, and an excessively uxorious husband. As a barrister and Cambridge intellectual he, in turn, was apt to be resentful of Lloyd George.

At the Amlwch meeting, speaking in a hot room, Lloyd George suddenly came over faint and had to be taken to a nearby cottage. He then went home to Criccieth where he had a fortnight's complete rest. Never one to make light of any indisposition, he would later refer to the incident – privately – as a breakdown. The term suggests something far worse than he can possibly have sustained, or it would have taken him longer than a fortnight to recover. The chances are that he was simply overtired and in need of a short period of quiet, which the Amlwch incident made obligatory. By mid-August he was back in London, unaccompanied by Margaret, for the three weeks' session which inaugurated the new Parliament. He might, he said, have stayed at Criccieth 'had it not been for keeping in with *Guardian*'.[1] In fact, he was feeling quite himself again and in no mood to linger at Criccieth.

In Parliament he was quick to recapture the delights of opposition. 'I am at it busily obstructing . . . have already spoken twice on the salaries of the officials of the House of Lords.' He divided the House and 'for the first time reduced the Government majority under 100'.[2] It pleased him considerably that he was elected to the Radical Committee[3], and he was also pleased in another way when Samuel Storey, the defeated Liberal M.P. for Sunderland, briefed him to present an election petition against the man who won the seat. At Storey's house near York he met the ship-owner Sir Christopher Furness, to whom he submitted a project 'for starting a daily newspaper in South Wales'. His intention was to provide an antidote to the *South Wales Daily News*, which he regarded as D. A. Thomas's mouthpiece. Storey, he said, was 'a large speculator in that line. . . . Well if it goes I shall ask for the London letter at any rate. But I am counting chickens before they are hatched – just like me.'[4] The newspaper project led to various negotiations in South Wales, which eventually produced no result. Storey's petition failed, but Lloyd George succeeded in getting his bill of costs reduced from £2,200 to £900

1. D.L.G. to M.L.G., 16 August 1895 (N.L.W.).
2. D.L.G. to M.L.G., 22 August 1895 (N.L.W.).
3. A ginger group of Liberal back-benchers.
4. D.L.G. to M.L.G., dated 'Sunday morning', and obviously 25 August 1895 (N.L.W.). He asks her to show the letter to Uncle Lloyd but not to William – a significant inversion.

Before Parliament rose for the long holiday Lloyd George bombarded the new Government with minor Welsh grievances. Why was there no Welshman among those put forward for membership of the House of Commons Kitchen Committee? Why were there no Welsh-speaking agricultural inspectors in Wales? Why did the Board of Trade have no labour correspondent for North Wales, where there were no statistics on labour movements, wages and other matters relating to the economy? Why was no effort made in the Public Record Office to deal adequately with Welsh historical documents? Should there not be at least one Welsh-speaker on the staff there? When new Ordnance Survey maps of Wales were being prepared, should not each team of surveyors be accompanied by one Welsh-speaking officer, to ensure the correct spelling of local names? To most of these questions the Ministers concerned gave cautiously helpful answers.

Lloyd George was still determined to forge *Cymru Fydd* into an effective instrument of provincial and personal power. To do so, he had to outbid D. A. Thomas in his own territory of South Wales. What could not be achieved by negotiation might, perhaps, be achieved by a trial of strength. On 5 September he told a conference of Welsh nationalists – convened at Llandrindod by Beriah Evans, the Secretary of *Cymru Fydd* – that he would have no objection to meeting representatives from the South Wales Federation again, but that there would be more chance of getting them to see reason and come to terms if preparations were made for a campaign.

> Let us proceed this day to arrange an elaborate campaign for the winter, for the purpose of establishing branches to carry out the idea of a United Wales. I am convinced that Wales is with us. We have six years in front of us. . . . Let us fight if we must. It will breed backbone. I move that we meet the South Wales Federation, but that in the meantime we fight.

It was his favourite technique – adopting a tough stance while remaining ready to negotiate. In this case it did not work. Though the conference at Llandrindod supported his proposal, the task of getting his opponents in South Wales to 'see reason' proved too much for him.

Apart from D. A. Thomas, he had also to reckon with the hostility of 'Mabon', who had given *Cymru Fydd* his backing at the outset but was now convinced that it was a threat to the 'Lib–Lab' solidarity which mattered most to him, as a trade unionist. At the end of October Lloyd

George was invited to address a series of meetings in the Rhondda ('Mabon's' constituency), but the invitation was coupled with two conditions: that he should confine himself to the importance of local organisation and Liberal principles, and that he should make no reference to any national or federal movement. Lloyd George replied indignantly that 'the gentlemen of the Executive' must be joking; they must know that 'any self-respecting Welshman would be ashamed to accept an invitation to any society where the hopes and ideals of his nationality are treated as a proscribed subject'. And he leaked the story to the Press in North Wales.[1] Another difficulty was that the Liberation Society viewed *Cymru Fydd* with suspicion, as likely to injure the cause of disestablishment. Lloyd George strongly controverted this view, and denied that he was willing to 'banish disestablishment to the dim and distant background', sacrificing 'everything else to Home Rule for Wales'. Since Irish Home Rule was 'falling into greater disfavour day after day', the only sensible policy was Home Rule all Round. Once that was adopted, it would be possible to go on to other measures, such as disestablishment. Ideally, Wales should be given the power to disestablish under the Home Rule all Round legislation, but that was hardly to be expected. He claimed that his policy was endorsed by, among others, Rosebery, Asquith, Campbell-Bannerman and Tom Ellis.[2]

In spite of the forces arrayed against him, he felt that his winter campaign, during its early stages, was going well. After addressing 'the night men at the Collieries', he reported that the Rhondda was 'going over' to him 'bodily'. And the reaction of the day men, at a meeting the same evening, was equally heartening: '. . . not in the memory of the oldest inhabitant has anything to equal it been seen. . . . Hundreds of D. A. Thomas' own colliers amongst them. Mabon looked blue. I talked Home Rule for Wales and all the nationalist stuff which the Mabon crew so detest – but the people cheered to the echo.'[3] Yet he had to admit that, in Monmouthshire, 'the audiences in these semi-English districts are not comparable to those I get in the Welsh districts. Here the people have sunk into a morbid footballism.'[4] He later developed this idea into a

1. Conditions laid down in letter from William Evans, secretary of the Rhondda Labour and Liberal Association, and Lloyd George's reply, dated 1 November 1895 (*Caernarvon Herald*, 8 November 1895).
2. Interview with Lloyd George printed in the *Merthyr Times*, 23 November 1895.
3. D.L.G. to M.L.G., 20 and 21 November 1895 (N.L.W.).
4. D.L.G. to M.L.G., 19 November 1895 (N.L.W.).

distinct ethnic theory, according to which the Welsh were 'a nation of Church and Chapel goers and Sunday school lovers', whereas the English were 'a nation of footballers, stock exchangers, public-house and music-hall frequenters'. The Jewish nation had clung to its traditions, language and religion through the ages, and so had remained in existence while 'the Babylonians, the Syrians, the Roman and Greek empires had sunk into insignificance or passed away'.[1]

Meanwhile he had suffered, in Monmouthshire, a reverse which decided the fate of *Cymru Fydd*. Very early in the New Year he invaded South Wales again 'to fight the Federation'.[2] He paid another visit to the Rhondda which, for the occasion, was swamped with *Cymru Fydd* propaganda. (He even boasted of having written two letters himself.)[3] In the Rhondda *Cymru Fydd* had a 'grand victory', but when the South Wales Federation met a few days later at Newport Lloyd George was denied a hearing on the crucial issue – should there be a single Federation for the whole Principality? The meeting, he said, was 'a packed one'. 'Associations supposed to be favourable to us were refused representation and men not elected at all received tickets. There were two points of dispute between us. By some oversight they allowed me to speak on one and we carried it . . . because they went to the vote immediately after my speech. . . . I simply danced upon them. So they refused to allow me to speak on the second point. The majority present were Englishmen from the Newport district.'[4]

It was true that the procedure was rigged against him. After the first resolution (that the National Federation should have a paid secretary) was unexpectedly carried thanks to his advocacy, the chairman ruled that he might not speak on the more comprehensive question; and the ruling was followed by a vote that he should not be heard. It was perhaps the greatest compliment ever paid to him as an orator, but it also showed that the South Wales bosses would defend their position, by fair means or foul. *Cymru Fydd* never recovered its momentum. Lloyd George still did not despair of uniting the Welsh in a solid bloc, but what happened at Newport on 16 January 1896 made him more than ever aware that he

---

1. Speech at Cardiff, as president of the annual music festival of the Welsh Nonconformist choirs, 5 February 1896. But was it for him to use 'stock exchangers' as a term of abuse? Within a fortnight he was writing Margaret one of his optimistic letters about the Patagonian Syndicate.
2. D.L.G. to M.L.G., 10 January 1896 (N.L.W.).
3. D.L.G. to M.L.G., 12 January 1896 (N.L.W.).
4. D.L.G. to M.L.G., 15 and 16 January 1896 (N.L.W.).

could not rely on purely Welsh issues, or purely Welsh support, to carry him on towards his ambitious goal.

The Government obliged him by introducing a bill which was national in scope, but also calculated to arouse the anti-landlord prejudice which was much stronger in Wales than in England, and even stronger in Lloyd George than in most Welshmen. This was the Agricultural Land Rating Bill, which proposed that the rates payable on agricultural land should be reduced by half. For the past thirty years British agriculture had been in a state of deepening depression – the consequence of Free Trade, aggravated by the ever-growing food production of the New World and by faster and cheaper transport. Within a decade the average price of wheat had dropped from 31s in 1886 to 23s 1d in 1895. But while prices were dropping, farm wages were going up, so that farmers were hit both ways. By the end of the century the acreage under wheat was little more than half what it had been thirty years before, and during the nineties alone the number of agricultural labourers fell by eighteen per cent, in spite of higher wages. In 1896 the Royal Commission on Agriculture set up by the last Gladstone Government recommended (though not unanimously) that agricultural land should be partially derated; and in its final report the following year it stated that 'over a very considerable part of [the] country true rent has entirely vanished, since the owners are not receiving the ordinary interest upon the sum which it would cost to erect buildings, fences, etc., as good as those now existing'.[1] The Salisbury Government's derating bill was, therefore, a measure intended to help a gravely distressed industry, and in a manner recommended by a Royal Commission appointed by Gladstone.

To Lloyd George, however, the rates relief offered in the Bill was simply a present from Tory Ministers to their natural supporters – indeed to themselves. Of the £1,550,000 involved, members of the Government would, he said, receive a total of £67,000. The Prime Minister would benefit by £2,000, Balfour by £1,450 and the Duke of Devonshire (Lord President of the Council) by £10,000. Henry Chaplin, President of the Local Government Board, who introduced the Bill, would be enriching himself by £700. (Chaplin and Walter Long, President of the Board of Agriculture, were both ideal butts for Lloyd George, since they were specimens – even caricatures – of the squirearchical type with which he loved to identify the Tory Party.) Economically he was on a bad

1. Cmd 8540 of 1897, quoted in R. C. K. Ensor, *England 1870–1914*, ch. IX.

point, because landlords were, in fact, subsidising the land.[1] But the line
of attack was excellent politically. £2,000, though of no account whatever to a very rich man like Lord Salisbury, seemed a lot of money to
the man in the street. And Lloyd George was able to contrast the apparent
tenderness shown towards landlords with the continued neglect of the
urban poor. If he could not drive a wedge between English landlords
and English tenant-farmers (between whom there was a traditional
solidarity), he could appeal to the English town-dwellers' resentment of
the landed interest. In Wales, moreover, tenant-farmers were inclined to
share his prejudice, disliking landlords not simply because they were
landlords, but above all because they were anglicised. And the Royal
Commission on Welsh land problems, which also reported at the beginning of 1896, helped him even on the economic side by a majority
recommendation that rents should be fixed judicially, by county courts.
This proposal was never implemented and gradually went out of fashion,
but in the short term it fitted in well with Lloyd George's attack on the
Land Rating Bill.

In the Second Reading debate, on 30 April, he asserted that land had
not been improved materially by its owners, and had increased in value
merely because of the trade and industry which had been created in the
towns. The poor rate had gone down because the increased commercial
activity in the towns had provided employment for the surplus population, which would otherwise have been a burden on the land. Yet it
was proposed to tax the industries of the country to relieve agriculture.
In fact, however, it was not agriculture which was being relieved, but
the landlords. If this relief were not forthcoming, rents would inevitably
go down. The rent burden per acre was 25s, whereas the rates burden
was only 3s 2d. Was it not commonsense to relieve the bigger burden
first? And what about another heavy burden – excessive railway rates?
They were not reduced because there were too many railway directors
and shareholders on the Tory benches. Lloyd George clashed with
Chaplin on his personal interest in the Bill. According to Chaplin, he
would not benefit by 'a single sixpence': according to Lloyd George
his estate would benefit – and Chaplin did not contradict him. The capital
value of Ministers' land would, Lloyd George said, benefit to the extent
of two-and-a-quarter millions. Having bled the farmer to the last drop

1. 'Landlords no longer lived in the country to make their money, they visited the country
to spend it.' (Elie Halévy, *History of the English People in the Nineteenth Century*, Vol. 5,
Pt III, ch. 1–translated by E. I. Watkin.)

of his blood, landowners were now seeking to bleed the taxpayers, who were to be driven into the landlords' leech-pond. And he added that there was misery in the Welsh tinplate industry, for which the Government was providing no relief.[1]

He kept up the pressure when the Bill was in Committee. On one occasion, two or three amendments having been disposed of rather more quickly than had been expected, D. A. Thomas was not in the Chamber to move one standing in his name. So Lloyd George had the satisfaction of jumping up and moving it instead. But since he was ignorant of the precise subject-matter of the amendment he just 'began to talk', thinking on his feet. Chaplin then replied with 'a very weak defence', and 'a very respectable old Tory country gentleman' who spoke after him made 'a glaring blunder in law'. Lloyd George corrected him and was able to prove his point by fetching a work of reference. The old Tory admitted his mistake.[2]

It was hardly an exaggeration to claim, as Lloyd George did, that he had 'led the opposition to the measure so far'.[3] In the early morning of 22 May he and four other Members (one of them Herbert Lewis) were suspended by the Speaker for a week for refusing to go into the division lobby – an ostentatious protest against the Government's use of the closure. He at once wired the news to Margaret, and later wrote: 'All the Radicals are delighted beyond measure. Say it is best thing yet happened for cause. It has had one effect which will please you – the ensuring of a longer holiday. First thing that occurred to me when sentence was pronounced was Well at any rate rhen Fagi will be pleased.'[4]

Railway charges, mentioned by him in his Second Reading speech on the Land Bill, had also been one of his themes when he spoke in another Second Reading debate – on the London and North-Western Railway Bill. He complained of the 'exceptional rates and charges . . . sanctioned in respect of [the Chester and Holyhead] line of 2d per mile, the usual

1. Hansard, Fourth Series, Vol. XL, cols 237–42. The crisis in the Welsh tinplate industry was due to the American McKinley tariff, as a result of which the number of mills working was nearly halved between 1891 and 1896, while the labour force shrank from 25,000 to 16,000. The McKinley tariff helped to lose 'the Major' his seat in 1895 because, with his American connections, he shared some of the odium in which McKinley was held. (K.O. Morgan, *Wales in British Politics, 1868–1922*.)

2. D.L.G. to M.L.G., 14 May 1896 (N.L.W.).

3. D.L.G. to M.L.G., 20 May 1896 (N.L.W.).

4. D.L.G. to M.L.G., 22 May 1896 (N.L.W.). 'Rhen Fagi' = 'My old Maggie'.

rate being 1¼d'. Another complaint was that the Company was using its power 'to oust out [sic] the sea trade in particular ports'. There was a branch line to Caernarvon and the Company used its 'maximum powers' to prevent the shipping of slates from Caernarvon harbour and to force the quarry owners to send them 'along the whole length of line to any particular part of Great Britain'. After the main question had been carried, Lloyd George immediately raised a quite different issue on a point of order. Should Sir W. Houldsworth, M.P. for North-West Manchester and a director of the Company, have been allowed to vote on a Bill in which he had 'a direct personal and pecuniary interest'? After a lively debate Lloyd George withdrew his motion when Balfour agreed to set up a committee to consider the question of principle involved.[1]

On the Military Manoeuvres Bill he touched on a matter which is still of concern nearly eighty years later, when he submitted that the military authorities ought not to be able to seize land without coming to the House of Commons. He was defeated by 204 to 46.[2] He seconded Herbert Lewis's resolution calling for an inquiry into the state of piers and harbours in Wales. Fish, he said, had moved further out to sea, so that larger craft were needed and therefore larger harbours. Little towns like Pwllheli could not find the money from their own resources: they had to appeal to Parliament. At Bangor the ratepayers had to bear the cost of a pier which was 'for the benefit of the whole surrounding country'.[3] Another day he suggested to the Government that the Inland Revenue should have an office in Wales as well as in London, Edinburgh and Dublin. And when the Government spokesman sought to embarrass him by saying there had always been some doubt which was the real capital of Wales, and referred to the likely objections in North Wales if Cardiff were chosen, Lloyd George promptly replied that if Cardiff were chosen there would be no objections from North Wales.[4]

Moving a reduction of the vote for royal palaces, he argued that the cost of maintaining royal parks and gardens open to the public should be borne by the ratepayers of London, since they were the beneficiaries. But he conceded that Kew was a national institution.[5] He protested in

1. Hansard, Fourth Series, Vol. XXXIX, cols 852–81, 14 April 1896. The Select Committee on Members of Parliament (Personal Interest), on which Lloyd George himself was appointed to sit, reported in July and recommended no major change.
2. Hansard, Fourth Series, Vol. XXXIX, col. 234 (26 March 1896).
3. Ibid., cols 918–20, 14 April 1896.   4. Ibid., cols 703–9, 10 April 1896.
5. Ibid., cols 712–21, 10 April 1896.

1896 (and again in 1897) against the annual motion that Committees should not meet until 2 p.m. on Ascension Day, pointing out that many members of the Church party would be riding in Rotten Row instead of attending church services. Anyway, if such a remission was to be made for Church red-letter days, why not for days important in the calendars of other denominations?[1] On the Uganda Railway Bill he had the nerve to protest against the speculative nature of the project. No board of railway directors, he said, would dream of embarking upon such an enterprise upon such scanty information.[2] (He could not have said as much for the directors of a certain gold-mining enterprise in Patagonia.)

All in all, the 1896 session was Lloyd George's most successful in the six years he had been in Parliament.

To Mr Lloyd George [wrote the lobby correspondent of the *Daily Chronicle*] . . . must be put the first beginnings of the fight on the Agricultural Rating Bill. . . . He has a remarkable eye for weak points in debate, and his keen criticisms have often been caught up later by the Front Opposition Bench, and been adopted as the main line of attack. . . . He was also largely responsible for the policy of 'enlarged discussion' on small Bills which blocked the Government's path for a long time after Whitsuntide. . . . His policy – always conducted with a grave weight and seriousness far other than obstruction, as it is vulgarly used – was at first looked at rather suspiciously, but at the end of the session it was appreciated by all. Of all the young men on the Liberal side, I should certainly say that Mr Lloyd George has made the greatest mark of the session.[3]

And Henry Lucy (the famous 'Toby M.P.') was scarcely less glowing:

The nearest approach to the establishment of a new reputation during the last session is found in the case of Mr Lloyd George. The Member for the Caernarvon District is not a stranger to the House of Commons. He has sat in Parliament since 1890, and has not been reticent of speech. Early in his career he suffered from the indiscretion of an enthusiastic countryman who hailed him as 'the Welsh Parnell'. . . . But he has disclosed a perfect mastery of the subject, a readiness of force and

1. *Ibid.*, Vol. XL, cols 1262–3, 13 May 1896, and Vol. XLIX, col. 1345, 26 May 9187.
2. *Ibid.*, Vol. XLIII, col. 1102, 30 July 1896.
3. Quoted in Herbert du Parcq, *op. cit.*, Vol. I, p. 177.

resource in debate, much more nearly resembling the gifts of Mr Tim Healy than the earlier stages of his career recalled the manner of Mr Parnell.[1]

Harcourt congratulated him on his 'eminent services',[2] and his best friend, Herbert Lewis, had this to say of his work with Lloyd George in 1896: 'I had the leisure for it because I was free to devote the whole of my time to Parliamentary work, but he made a great sacrifice. He was a poor man with a family of small children, living in a little flat and dependent upon his profession for his daily bread. Notwithstanding this he threw himself heart and soul into Parliamentary work and I did my best to support him.'[3] It was in the same spirit, no doubt, that Lewis decided to join Lloyd George's gold syndicate and to travel with him to the Argentine during the recess.

Lloyd George rounded off the year with a speech at Bangor, which shows him at the top of his form as a platform speaker. He described the achievements of the Parliament to date as aid for landlords and the provision of battleships for the younger sons of nobility (a shamelessly misleading reference to Goschen's naval estimates[4]). And he went on:

> We also found out another source of leakage in our agricultural rack-rents, and we promptly bunged that up. They were bringing Canadian cattle over to our markets. This reduced the British farmers' capacity to pay high rents. . . . Malevolent persons will suggest that it is rather inconsistent on our part to exclude Colonial goods from the market at the very moment that we are bragging so loudly about Imperial Federation and, above all, about our Imperial Zollverein [customs union]. But then that is a superficial view of the matter; when Canadian farmers appreciate the fact that, by being shut out of our markets, they are sharing with us the ineffable honour of contributing to the maintenance of our ancient nobility, their affection for the old country will be stronger than ever.

1. H. W. Lucy, *Diary of the Unionist Parliament, 1895–1900.* Lloyd George would have appreciated being compared with Tim Healy, the sharpest and wittiest debater in the Irish Party. Healy later became the first Governor-General of the Irish Free State.
2. D.L.G. to M.L.G., 30 June 1896 (N.L.W.), reports that Harcourt has written to him in these terms.　　　　　　　　　　　　　　3. Herbert Lewis Papers (N.L.W.).
4. Goschen, Chancellor of the Exchequer in the previous Salisbury Administration, became First Lord of the Admiralty in 1895, and the first estimates that he presented were for £21·8 million, compared with under £13 million in 1886. The increase was vitally necessary for bringing the Navy up to date.

He then used the same weapons of ridicule and irony in a more familiar context:

> I ought to explain, perhaps, though I hardly think it is necessary – it is too insignificant a point – but still I may as well just mention the fact that we have done nothing for the working classes, except, perhaps, to make their meat dearer, but you can't attend to everybody at once; common politeness demands that they should give way to their social superiors.

But it was not all demagogic banter. On the need to overhaul the Parliamentary system he was utterly serious, without being dull. If the Imperial Parliament was too slow to suit the Tory pace in reform, how could it tackle all the work that the Liberal Party was preparing for it? Part of the problem lay in 'the changed attitude of the times towards State interference'. Palmerston introduced hardly any reform measures, but now Parliament legislated upon almost everything, and there was no distinction between the two parties in this respect.

> They both meddle. . . . From the milk that you buy first thing in the morning to the toddy that some of you may drink last thing at night, the Law inspects and examines every article of food. It prescribes dimensions and proportions for every dwelling-house; it enters the factory and the workshop. It even pursues a man with its guardianship beyond the portals of the tomb. The burial laws passed within the last generation would constitute a heavy volume . . . and I will say this for the Imperial Parliament that, however much it may have neglected the interests of some of us during life, nothing can exceed its care of us all when we are dead. So far does it carry its tenderness in this direction that it has expounded a measure of religious equality to the poor carcases which it withholds even yet from the living soul.

State interference he defined as simply 'the concentration of the power of all for the protection of each'.

Unionist Parliaments had suffered particularly from the amount of time devoted to the discussion of Celtic matters, and he therefore advised the Tories to accept Home Rule all Round for their own sakes. In 1887 seventy-nine pages of the Index of Hansard were occupied by Ireland, twenty-two by Scotland, and three by Wales. In the last session more than three pages of the Index were occupied by *two Welsh M.P.s*. 'The Imperial Parliament now legislates upon local questions without local knowledge and thus, like every other bungler, doing its work badly increases instead of decreasing the volume of work. It regulates everything, from the affairs of four hundred million of the Queen's subjects in the Indian Empire to the fixing up of piers in the Menai Straits. I fear it does both equally well.'

His peroration anticipates the great speeches of 1909–11:

> The contrast is too acute between the wealth and luxury of one class and the destitution and degradation of the other. One man works hard and has to recruit his exhausted strength in cramped quarters, breathing an atmosphere vitiated to the point of foeta. . . . Another man who does nothing has allotted to him acres – nay, miles – of breathing ground, all for himself, walled up high, so that he need not share its vitalising properties with those who have helped to create his riches.
>
> One man labours and yet starves; another lounges and still feasts. One set of men strive all the days of their lives in the vineyard, and yet, amid the plenty and profusion which they themselves have helped to produce, sink unhonoured into a pauper's grave. Another set of men enter into the precincts of the vineyard only to partake of its most luscious fruit, and they live and die amid the pomp and prodigality of millionaires. This can't go on for ever.
>
> They may use their wealth to corrupt the manhood of the men who have gathered it; they may use their power to intimidate those whom they can't bribe; they may strike down with the keen edge of calumny a man raised from amongst the people to proclaim their wrongs on the housetops. But as sure as justice and mercy are eternal attributes in the government of the world, that system which macadamises the road to luxury for the few out of the hearts of the many is doomed. . . .[1]

Lloyd George was not a booming orator. His voice carried well – as politicians' voices had to before the microphone age – but it was a light tenor voice which he kept under control, raising it only occasionally and seldom killing a point with excessive vocal stress. His contrasts of tone could be electrifying, and the sibilants in his gentle North Welsh accent enhanced the effect of his quiet, but often deadly, sarcasm. His words were accompanied by a wealth of telling gestures, 'freer' (as one observer put it) 'than those of the ordinary English Member'. He used his hands and arms to emphasise his words, 'throwing out his arm or waving it, and

1. Speech at Bangor, 15 December 1896.

digging the points of his right-hand fingers – very slender fingers – into the palm of his left hand'. Moreover, his eyes were 'quick, clear and very bright'. When he spoke, they shone.[1]

His speeches were very carefully prepared, with the help of Roget's *Thesaurus*. Most of them were written out beforehand and learnt by heart, though he had the main points jotted on small pieces of paper, in case his memory failed. He always did his homework before making a speech, and acted on the principle that 'You must know more than the average before the average will listen to you'.[2] The habit which Uncle Lloyd taught him – of making an immediate written note of any useful facts or ideas – served him very well in the preparation of speeches. He would also use his relations or friends as guinea-pigs. Margaret listened to a trial performance of his first public speech in London (at the Metropolitan Tabernacle), and while he was incubating his speech for the debate on Second Reading of the Welsh Disestablishment Bill he spent a whole day 'in utter seclusion' at the Royal Forest Hotel at Chingford, Essex, with Alfred Thomas as his companion. In the morning he went for a three-and-a-half-hour walk, and later in the day inflicted upon Thomas 'the agony' of listening to his speech.[3] Though he stated at the beginning of his career that his audience was the country, he probably took even more trouble over important Parliamentary speeches than over those which he delivered at big meetings outside. Moreover, whereas anything that he offered to the House of Commons had to be new-minted, he was able, in his platform speeches, to use the same material several times over, in areas served by different local newspapers. For instance, he repeated the Bangor speech just quoted, with only minor changes of wording, four days later at Barry Docks.

Yet the intense care and premeditation that went into his speeches did not rob them altogether of spontaneity. Apart from his superb talent for making a text which he had learnt by heart appear to flow naturally, there was, in his speeches, an unpredictable element characteristic of the work of any first-rate artist. In his old age he was asked by a would-be biographer if it was true that he never knew exactly how a speech was going to work out, when he got up to make it. He replied:

'That is what they say. But don't you believe that, or take it too literally. In most cases I stick to my brief. Only in crises, or when the

1. Alexander MacKintosh, 'Mr L. G., M.P., the Radical Young Man', from *The Young Man*, March 1903.   2. Quoted in Herbert du Parcq, *op. cit.*, Vol. I, p. 120.
3. D.L.G. to M.L.G., 19 and 20 March 1895 (N.L.W.).

meeting I address contains a challenge, do I improvise. Then I feel my way along. I ——'

He dropped the apple he was munching and clutched the air as though to draw a word from the heavens. 'I pause. I reach out my hand to the people and draw them to me. Like children they seem then. Like little children.'[1]

He responded, in other words, to the atmosphere of a meeting, with whatever changes of text or tone might seem necessary. And he was a virtuoso at dealing with hecklers. When he was proclaiming Home Rule for Ireland, Wales, Scotland and England, and a man interjected 'Home Rule for Hell', Lloyd George is reputed to have said 'Quite right – let every man speak up for his own country'.[2] And when he was discussing rates and somebody shouted 'What about German-made goods?', he certainly did reply: 'I will deal with that when I come to Lord Salisbury's foreign policy. That is made in Germany.'[3]

No artistic style is wholly original, and there were two main influences on Lloyd George's style of oratory – the witty invective of Disraeli and Lord Randolph Churchill, and the Biblical imagery and phraseology of the Welsh preachers. Though so different, the two influences complemented and corrected each other. Disraeli–Churchill in him was proof against excessive earnestness, the Welsh preacher against undue flippancy. While he loved making jokes and scoring clever points, he also delighted in word-pictures and the language of commination. John Elias, a very famous Welsh preacher, once described the Almighty shooting an arrow from His bow, and did it so vividly that his audience split in two to make way for the divine shaft. Lloyd George had much the same capacity to play on people's emotions and senses, but he appealed to their humour and worldly intelligence no less than to their idealism. It was more in his style to split them with a laugh than with an imaginary arrow.

His delaying tactics in 1896 had been designed, among other things, to obstruct the Government's Education Bill, and in this respect they were entirely successful. The Bill was a clumsy attempt to satisfy traditional Tories whose main concern was the Anglican schools; Chamberlain,

1. Donald McCormick, *The Mask of Merlin*, pp. 18–19.
2. The story cannot be pinned down in time and place, but is probably true and anyway *ben trovato*.
3. At Wrexham, 24 September 1897.

who was a zealous upholder of the Board school system (established in 1870, under his inspiration); and disinterested reformers appalled at the confusion and patchiness of British education. It was an ill-thought-out measure whose withdrawal, though enforced by Parliamentary obstruction, would in any case have been justified.

In 1897 a more limited Bill was introduced, for the purpose of making larger grants to the voluntary denominational schools. As a sop to Chamberlain and the radicals provision was also made, under separate legislation, for grants to needy Board schools. The Voluntary Schools Bill was a heaven-sent target for Lloyd George. On Second Reading, he contested the argument that the rates would have to be doubled if the voluntary schools were closed. This was certainly not true in Welsh Nonconformist areas. In the district of the Penrhyn quarries there was the largest voluntary subscription in Caernarvonshire. In Lord Penrhyn's own village £440 was subscribed yearly for schooling. In the adjoining Ffestiniog district there was a School Board, and the rate was 1s 9d. If there were a School Board in Lord Penrhyn's parish and he paid the rate in the same proportion that it was paid at Ffestiniog, he would have to pay £2,188. So it was impudent and hypocritical to claim that he was making a sacrifice for religion.[1] Ten days later Lloyd George scored a Parliamentary triumph when his was the only Instruction selected by the Speaker for debate, as the Bill was going into Committee. 'Toby M.P.' (Lucy) commented in *Punch* that this was another step in a successful Parliamentary career achieved by 'sheer ability' and with 'unvaried modesty'. To frame an Instruction on going into Committee had always been a very difficult task. 'Tonight six Parliamentary hands essayed it. . . . The youngest alone accomplished it.'[2] Balfour himself replied to Lloyd George's speech on the Instruction.[3]

The reference in his Second Reading speech to Lord Penrhyn was topical, because in 1896–7 there was a bitter dispute between Penrhyn and his slate quarrymen at Bethesda – who naturally attracted Lloyd George's sympathy, just as a landowning peer naturally aroused his indignation. An elected committee of the quarrymen demanded a minimum wage of 4s 6d a day and the exclusion of outside contractors, whom the management had called in to work parts of the quarry, and

1. Hansard, Fourth Series, Vol. XLVI, cols 465–71, 15 February 1897.
2. *Punch*, 6 March 1897.
3. Hansard, Fourth Series, Vol. XLVI, cols 1156–64, 25 February 1897. In one of his speeches on the Committee Stage Lloyd George remarked that Tory M.P.s were 'grunting', and was made to withdraw the expression as un-Parliamentary.

who were using unskilled labour. The demands were rejected, and Penrhyn would not even recognise the workers' committee. In September 1896, he suspended seventy-one men, and all their mates then came out in sympathy. An appeal for funds was made to other trade unions and the general public, and a sum running into five figures was raised.[1] Lloyd George was one of those who helped to raise it, and he also spoke on the dispute in the House of Commons early in 1897.[2]

By the summer of that year the quarrymen's funds were nearly exhausted and they had no choice but to settle on the best terms available. W. J. Parry, the former union leader, was called in to negotiate a settlement, and he did so with the same acute regard for his own financial interest that he displayed in the Patagonian business. There was little that he could do for the men, because their position was hopelessly weak; but there was something that he could do for himself. Under the compromise that he negotiated the workers' demands were effectively scotched, though nominal recognition was accorded to their committee. Parry himself, however, who was the local agent for Nobel's Explosives Company, demanded as the price of his services that the Penrhyn management should resume purchases from his company which had been discontinued on account of his connection with the union; and his demand was treated more respectfully than the men's. In August he was able to write to the company's Glasgow office: 'For what I have done, Lord Penrhyn's solicitor has promised to do all he can to get me back the quarry order.'[3]

Militants in the union wanted to fight on in spite of their lack of funds and there was dissension among the union leaders – one of whom was D. R. Daniel, Tom Ellis's and Lloyd George's friend. In 1900 the men came out again, and the second strike lasted until 1903. Again, Lloyd George was involved. When there was rioting in 1900 he gave his services as a defence lawyer, and before the dispute came to an end he was suggesting that the State should take over the quarries. All the same, modern socialists are apt to contrast his activity on behalf of a small and devoutly chapel-going community of workers in North Wales with his alleged failure to espouse the cause of the industrial proletariat in South

1. £20,000 according to Halévy, op. cit., £10,000 according to J. Roose Williams (article on W. J. Parry).
2. '. . . never made a more effective speech in the House of Commons . . . roasted Penrhyn.' (D.L.G. to M.L.G., 29 January 1897.)
3. Quoted in J. Roose Williams, op. cit. For a trade union leader Parry lived in rather grand style. His address was Coetmor Hall and he wrote on crested notepaper.

Wales. The charge ignores his frequent and very strong attacks on social injustice generally, and it also overlooks the fact that he was bound to take a special interest in the Bethesda quarrymen, because they lived in the neighbouring constituency to his and had close links with his constituents. Certainly he had no time for doctrinaire socialism, but it is absurd to suggest that in championing the Penrhyn quarrymen he was just a bourgeois Nonconformist averting his eyes from the reality of the class struggle. He was, on the contrary, so preoccupied with wider issues (and so well aware of his preoccupation) that he was all the more anxious, in this instance, to prove that a small-scale, local dispute was not beneath his notice.

Whenever possible, he gave expression to his radicalism on subjects, or in a manner, calculated to appeal to his fellow Welshmen. One aspect of the Conservative policy of killing Irish Home Rule with kindness was a willingness to encourage Roman Catholic higher education in Ireland, thereby securing the tacit cooperation of the hierarchy against Home Rule. In his speech in the debate on the Address, in February 1898, Lloyd George attacked the idea of a specifically Roman Catholic university, speaking ostensibly as a Welsh Nonconformist, but in reality as a secularist.[1] It was reported at the time that, after the speech, Irish Members were temporarily 'not on speaking terms' with him, and passed him in the Lobby 'as though he were transparent'.[2] The following month he moved a resolution on electoral and Parliamentary reform at the meeting of the National Liberal Federation at Leicester. His targets were plural voting and the House of Lords.

> We give one vote, or probably no vote at all, to the man who handles the plough, and ten to the man who handles the hunting-whip . . . one vote to the busy bee, and ten to the devouring locust. . . . It is not the soil of the country, but the soul, which we want represented in the House of Commons. After all, have they not got a House all to themselves, which they guard as jealously as if it were a pheasant preserve?[3]

Later in the year he was attacking Romanising tendencies in the Church of England. The ritualists, he said, were trying 'to substitute for the Protestant doctrine of justification by faith a system of salvation by haberdashery'. Anglican bishops would fight Welsh disestablishment and

1. Hansard, Fourth Series, Vol. LIII, cols 974–80, 17 February 1898.
2. *North Wales Observer*, 25 February 1898.
3. 23 March 1898.

disendowment, but not the Popish practices in their midst. 'They dread poverty more than Papistry.'[1]

Next year the Government brought in a bill to give the Anglican clergy partial relief from the rates levied on the tithe rent-charge. Between 10,000 and 11,000 clergymen were to receive, in effect, a present from the tax-payers amounting in all to £87,000. This was a nakedly partisan measure, inviting opposition of the same character; and no one knew better how to provide it than Lloyd George. His speech on Second Reading was a masterpiece of destructive argument. While admitting that rural rates had gone up – a direct consequence of the Agricultural Land Rating Act – he claimed that many others were suffering besides the clergy.

What is the case of the lodging-house keeper in seaside resorts, as in my own constituency? He lives in a house which is larger than he himself can use, and from which he derives a precarious income, and he is rated upon the value of that house to an extent larger, perhaps, than the income he receives. But the case of the shopkeeper, the lodging-house keeper, the quarryman – all these are forgotten, and only the case of one section of the community is to be considered.

Lloyd George protested against the measure 'as a Welsh Member', though he ended on a more general note. Money was being voted for landlords and clergymen, instead of for the poor. What of the working man, of whom so much was heard at the last election? What of old age pensions? 'Why, the squire and the parson have broken into the poor box and divided its contents among them.' Promises made by the Tories that they would help the old were believed. 'They were spoken . . . in the name of the Throne, and "shall Caesar send a lie?" I say that the men who were promised some provision for old age are still left out in the cold, and the Tammany ring of landlords and parsons are dividing . . . the last remnants of the money between them.'[2]

The language may have been highly coloured, but the rebuke was essentially just and may have acted as a reminder to the Government of its proclaimed interest in old age pensions. Chamberlain, above all, was associated with the idea, and had not ceased to be a radical when he allied himself with the Tory Party (which, in any case, has nearly always been as good – or as bad – a vehicle for constructive change as the party, Liberal or Labour, claiming to be the party of progress; and quite often a better

1. Address at a Congregational church in Nottingham, 29 September 1898.
2. Hansard, Fourth Series, Vol. LXXIII, cols 1066–72, 29 June 1899.

one). In 1897 Chamberlain pushed through an important measure of
social reform, the Workmen's Compensation Act, against the stiff
opposition of a Conservative magnate, Lord Londonderry. This Act was
wider in scope than its Liberal precursor, the Employers' Liability Bill,
which Asquith, for a spurious reason, abandoned. By 1899 Chamberlain's
genuine desire to do something for the old was reinforced, not only by
Parliamentary pressure from radicals like Lloyd George, but also by
external pressures. The New Zealand Government had enacted a scheme
of old age pensions which the philanthropist Charles Booth was able to
quote in support of his own demand for a similar scheme in the mother-
country – that is to say, a scheme based not on the insurance principle,
but on the principle of compassionate relief. In May 1899 a Select Committee of the House of Commons was appointed to look into the question,
and one of the M.P.s invited to sit on it was Lloyd George.[1] In June, while
the Committee was doing its work, he had a long interview with Chamberlain, who was very friendly, listened attentively to what he had to say,
and asked him to come whenever he liked to discuss the subject.

This meeting has a tragic symbolism. In so many ways Lloyd George
was Chamberlain's political son, and at that stage it was only by chance
that they were on opposite sides in the party dogfight – because Gladstone had given Irish Home Rule precedence over his relations with
Chamberlain, and because Wales, when Lloyd George first stood for
Parliament, was emotionally Gladstonian. Very soon they were to be
divided by a controversy in which they became leading antagonists:
even as they spoke, the storm-clouds were gathering. Meanwhile the
barrier between them was still largely artificial. Chamberlain must have
recalled his own younger days, when he was a Liberal firebrand, though he
may also have reflected that he did not have Lloyd George's privilege of
early election to Parliament. For him, the road to politics had been long
and hard. Belonging to none of the recognised English *élites* – landed
gentry, plutocracy, or Oxbridge intelligentsia – he had to make a fortune
in business before he could contemplate a political career. If he had been a
Welshman a generation later, or an Englishman three generations later,
his talents alone would have brought him opportunity and fame as
quickly as they came to the M.P. for Caernarvon Boroughs. But he was
born too soon, and in the wrong place.

The Select Committee, reporting in July, called for relief on the

1. Among its sixteen other members were Michael Davitt and the historian, W. E. H.
Lecky.

New Zealand pattern, and Lloyd George privately claimed most of the credit:

> ... Old Age Pensions is through. ... I have added some millions on to this Bill for them. I am sure I put on 2 or 3 millions yesterday and a similar sum today. Never mind it goes all to the poor who really need it. It has the additional advantage of putting these bandits who are now in power in a nice fix. They can neither carry out these recommendations nor drop them. ... The curious thing is that the Tory members of the Committee are very pleased with me and the Liberals are equally pleased. ...[1]

The claim is corroborated by J. L. Garvin, who says that Lloyd George was, in Chamberlain's view, 'the best of the lot' (i.e. of the Committee); also that he 'carried with him the progressive Conservatives' and converted the Tory chairman, Henry Chaplin.[2]

In the event, the Tories did not carry out the Committee's recommendation, because the Boer War pre-empted the funds and diverted Chamberlain's energies exclusively to the cause of Imperial consolidation, which seemed to him the key to all other benefits. It therefore fell to the Liberals to introduce old age pensions: their scheme was announced and provided for by Asquith in his 1908 Budget, but was implemented by the next Chancellor, Lloyd George – who thus obtained more of the kudos than he strictly deserved. Yet in a sense he did deserve it, because although his own sense of priorities told him that sick or unemployed breadwinners were even harder cases than the old – because whole families depended upon them – yet he was very conscious of what society owed to those who had toiled relentlessly through their active lives only to face poverty and hardship in their last years. His service on the old age pensions Select Committee enabled him to make his first practical contribution towards founding the British Welfare State – a pioneering process in which his own National Health Insurance scheme is the greatest single landmark.

During the years 1896–9 there were important changes in the *dramatis personae* affecting Lloyd George's career. Osborne Morgan died in August 1897, and at the beginning of the new session, in February 1898, the Welsh M.P.s met to elect a new chairman. Alfred Thomas was chosen, but only after an amendment proposing Lloyd George had lapsed because of his

1. D.L.G. to M.L.G., 26 July 1899 (N.L.W.).
2. J. L. Garvin, *The Life of Joseph Chamberlain*, Vol. III, pp. 626–7.

refusal to stand against his friend.[1] The reason was genuine so far as it went. Lloyd George had a soft spot for Alfred Thomas, from whom, indeed, he had received many acts of kindness. But the more important reason was that he did not wish to become too narrowly identified with Welsh politics, since he no longer believed that Wales alone could provide him with an adequate power base. He had never, of course, intended to be 'the Parnell of Wales' in any sense but one – that he wanted to control the Welsh M.P.s and to make use of their corporate power. Doing so, he at first thought, might be enough to bring him the prizes and opportunities which his ambition craved, but experience had taught him that the Welsh Members would never work together consistently, as a body, under his or anyone else's leadership. It was necessary for him, therefore, to muster substantial non-Welsh support, which might not be so readily acquired or held if he seemed to be merely the spokesman for Wales. At the same time he knew that Wales was his *primary* source of strength, and had no desire to sacrifice any of the advantages which he derived from it. With Alfred Thomas as chairman of the Welsh Parliamentary group he was able to make the best of both worlds, because Thomas was almost completely under his influence and never likely to go against him on any significant matter. Thomas's nominal leadership gave him the effective leadership by proxy – and without any of the inconveniences. Besides, he may also have felt that if he stood for the position himself, he might be giving his enemies a gratuitous chance to humiliate him.

All these considerations are reflected in a letter written to him at the time by Uncle Lloyd:

Chairmanship. . . . I thought your chosen Alf. would be best plan of all. . . . Think it rather an unpleasant position for you to be chief supporter, probably of Alf. – and yet your name be given up as candidate for Chair . . . it would be rather awkward position to let name put up, and be outvoted through *mere jealousy*. And may be that the position (even if elected unanimous) would be an obstacle in your way to work your plans out as you could if free. The great thing is to get a *formal* president – a kind of figurehead – which Alf. would be . . . like old Smith as Leader of the House, which all laughed at and scorned at

1. The amendment was moved by Reginald McKenna – no Welshman, but M.P. for North Monmouthshire since 1895 – and seconded by Herbert Lewis. Later, as Cabinet colleagues, Lloyd George and McKenna came to dislike each other intensely.

first, did better than all, by geniality and non-pretentious plain man-hoodism. But, of course, as usual, I well know that you know what course to take thousand times better than I do here. . . .[1]

Needless to say, that was also Lloyd George's view. Uncle Lloyd's comments were welcome, because they chimed with his own thinking. Had it been otherwise, he would have disregarded them.

In October 1896 Rosebery resigned as leader of the Liberal Party, announcing his decision in a letter to Tom Ellis, the Chief Whip, which he wrote and published without consulting his colleagues. For two more years Harcourt soldiered on as leader in the Commons, but then he, too, resigned (in December 1898). His decision was communicated to Morley, who soon afterwards announced his own withdrawal from the Front Bench. The Liberal Party, Lloyd George said, was passing through a 'moulting season', and he thought it would be a great mistake if, whenever Liberal leaders disagreed, they felt it necessary to resign. The party needed men 'of all temperaments'.[2] Just after Harcourt's resignation he spoke of the high quality of Liberal leaders, mentioning in particular Asquith, Rosebery, Grey, Fowler and Harcourt.[3] Oddly enough, he did not mention the man who, in February 1899, was chosen to succeed Harcourt as Liberal leader in the Commons, and whose outstanding merits he was soon to recognize – Sir Henry Campbell-Bannerman.

Campbell-Bannerman was a shrewd, stable, quietly humorous Scotsman, who had inherited a large fortune and whose home, like Gladstone's, was a castle. He was moderately scholarly, drank moderately, and appeared to be a moderate in politics – though in the event he turned out to be more radical than anyone had suspected. For a British politician of his period he was unusually attached to the Continent, speaking French, German and Italian well and spending six weeks abroad every year. He held junior office (under Cardwell) at the War Office, and was also a junior Minister at the Admiralty, before being appointed Chief Secretary for Ireland in 1884. In Gladstone's third and fourth Governments, and in the Rosebery Government, he was Secretary of State for War. Gladstone introduced him to his Cabinet colleagues as 'canny' and 'couthy' – qualities displayed in full measure when he succeeded in removing the Duke of Cambridge, without ill-will, from the post of Commander-in-Chief which he had held since 1856.[4] Though his easy,

1. Richard Lloyd to David and Margaret Lloyd George, 13 February 1898 (N.L.W.).
2. Speech at Ardwick, 18 January 1899.   3. Speech at Swansea, 14 December 1898.
4. For this diplomatic feat he was awarded the G.C.B. – thus becoming Sir Henry.

equable temperament masked a core of toughness ('his bite', it has been well said, 'was worse than his bark'[1]), Campbell-Bannerman did not aspire to national leadership and would have liked to be Speaker of the House of Commons. But the ambition that he lacked, his wife supplied. Childless, she thought only of him, and was more ambitious for him than he would ever have been for himself. Yet once he was in a job he was determined to hold it. He maintained his grip on the Liberal leadership in opposition in spite of multiple difficulties and vexations, and when he was Prime Minister it was only his health that broke – never his will.

Until the Boer War, Lloyd George had little to do with Campbell-Bannerman. When he made his first public speech in London (at the Metropolitan Tabernacle) Campbell-Bannerman was in the chair, and he also presided over the Parliamentary Committee on Law to which the Clergy Discipline Bill was referred, when Lloyd George and S. T. Evans were baiting Gladstone. Apart from those two occasions they hardly ever crossed each other's paths. The Boer War controversy, however, made each aware of the other's merits, and brought them into close alignment politically. Lloyd George supported Campbell-Bannerman as Liberal leader in the Commons (though not invariably to the extent of obeying the Whip), and later profoundly admired his control of the Cabinet during his short term as Prime Minister.

In April 1899 Tom Ellis died, at Cannes. He was only forty and his premature death might seem to have cheated him of the fulfilment which high office in the next Liberal Government would have brought him. But would it? Haldane believed that 'he died in time', because 'his after-career would have been disappointing'.[2] And Haldane may well have been right. Ellis lacked the force of intellect and the almost brutal force of character needed for success as a departmental chief. Yet it was only by possessing those qualities that he could have held his own in competition with Lloyd George. Rivalry between the two would have been hard to avoid, and Ellis would surely have been the loser. It is unlikely, however, that the Boer War would have divided them: Ellis, like Lloyd George, would probably have opposed the war. In any case, dying when he did, he left the memory of a minor but unblemished career, and of a personality admired by all.

Lloyd George always felt for him affection tinged with respect. He was afterwards happy to recall that one of the last letters Ellis received was

1. Alfred M. Gollin, *Balfour's Burden*, p. 213.
2. D. R. Daniel, *op. cit.*

(surprisingly) from himself, and that it made Ellis laugh. The sincerity of his regard is proved by a letter to Margaret in 1895, dismissing criticism by Uncle Lloyd. 'I am surprised at Uncle Lloyd's criticism of Ellis' speech – I thought it admirable. He went as far as he dare go and it will do the cause of Welsh Home Rule incalculable good. Fair play – the gaffer is out of all reason.'[1] Ellis, for his part, certainly had a high opinion of Lloyd George – most evident, for instance, when he defended him against those who accused him of treachery in 1895. Clearly Lloyd George's 'rebellion', and Ellis's responsibilities as Liberal Chief Whip, did not effect a breach between them. But subsequent political pressures might have driven them apart. Ellis's death left Lloyd George incontestably the star figure among the Welsh Members.

In the period immediately preceding the Boer War there is one incident in Lloyd George's political life which stands on its own, and which most strikingly demonstrates his courage and independence of mind. On 19 September 1898 General Kitchener, having crushed the Dervishes at Omdurman, met at a place called Fashoda, further up the Nile, the French Captain Marchand who had led a small mission across Africa from the French Congo. In spite of Marchand, Kitchener laid claim to the Upper Nile territory – ostensibly on behalf of Egypt – and a crisis developed between the British and French Governments. Salisbury was at first prepared to obtain Marchand's withdrawal on terms not utterly humiliating to France, but Chamberlain insisted that his withdrawal must be unconditional, even at the risk of war. British public opinion strongly supported the Jingo line, and most of the Liberal leaders endorsed it. In 1895 Sir Edward Grey, then Under-Secretary for Foreign Affairs, had stated, without Cabinet authorisation but in the spirit of Rosebery's foreign policy, that Britain would consider it an unfriendly act if France entered the Nile Valley. Naturally enough, he reasserted this doctrine at the time of Fashoda, and on 12 October Rosebery himself – speaking, rather incongruously, at a dinner of the Surrey Agricultural Association at Epsom – said that the Salisbury Government's stand against the French was 'the policy of the last [i.e. his own] Government deliberately adopted and sustained'. Even Campbell-Bannerman, who was relatively pro-French, thought that Rosebery was entitled to take credit for foresight in the matter of Fashoda;[2] while Harcourt, the anti-Imperialist, advised the

1. D.L.G. to M.L.G., 15 December 1895 (N.L.W.).
2. 'One rubs one's eyes in reading [C.-B.'s] highly uncharacteristic utterance' at this time. (John Wilson, CB, p. 282.)

like-minded Morley: 'Don't take your coat off but follow my example and put on your dressing gown.'[1]

Lloyd George, on the other hand, did 'take his coat off'. At a meeting in Yorkshire shortly after Rosebery's speech in Surrey he devoted most of his remarks to foreign affairs, beginning with Fashoda.

> If we go to war, what will be the outcome? I know enough about the condition of our Navy to say with perfect confidence that France will be defeated. But that is not all. If we defeat France, we shall be defeating the only power on the Continent with a democratic Constitution. Emperors, Kings and aristocratic rulers will mock at the whole thing – two great democratic Powers at each other's throats, the only countries where you have perfect civil and religious liberty in Europe quarrelling with each other to make sport for the titled and throned Philistines of Europe.

He urged a spirit of concession and compromise.[2]

It would be hard to exaggerate the importance of this intervention. As a young back-bencher Lloyd George was going against a conventional wisdom largely uniting the two front benches, and against a flowing tide of popular chauvinism. He was anticipating the *Entente Cordiale*, and basing it upon democratic principle rather than upon strategic necessity. We are bound to conclude that, in 1914, one motive for his decision to support the war was a feeling of solidarity with France – though the principal motive was his indignation at the rape of a small country, Belgium. Later in his career his affection for France turned to bitterness, when he became convinced that his grand design for Europe was being wrecked by French obduracy and rapacity. But his perception in the nineties of Britain's basic common interest with France is immensely to his credit, and shows how original was his outlook, how genuine his democratic faith.

1. Harcourt to Morley, 10 October 1898, quoted in Stansky, *op. cit.*
2. Speech at Haworth, 24 October 1898. This remarkable passage is not quoted in any study of Lloyd George known to the present writer, though a later speech (at Ardwick, on 18 January 1899), is quoted by Herbert du Parcq, *op. cit.*, Vol. II, p. 212. K. O. Morgan, in *David Lloyd George: Welsh Radical as World Statesman*, makes a puzzling reference to him as 'an aggressive critic of France during the Fashoda crisis in 1898' (pp. 32–3). Lloyd George was certainly critical of the Salisbury Government's general weakness in foreign affairs, and he thought that some *unnecessary* concessions had recently been made to France. Hence, probably, Dr Morgan's apparent misunderstanding of his attitude at the time of Fashoda. It was always his policy to be strong, but also to be ready, at the right moment, to negotiate from strength.

NINE

Mrs Edwards and 'Mrs Tim'

Apart from the *Cymru Fydd* setback, Lloyd George got on well as a politician during the years immediately following the Liberal defeat in 1895. Meanwhile, how were Margaret and he getting on as a couple? They were together for a fortnight at Criccieth after his post-election collapse, and in September they went for a holiday in Scotland with Mr and Mrs Davies, their Acton friends. Herbert Lewis was asked to go with them, but he had lost his wife in June and, as Lloyd George put it to Margaret, felt that 'he would be rendered miserable by the constant reminder which you and Mrs Davies would constitute of his bereavement'. Lloyd George added that it was bad enough for *him* to be alone in Switzerland the year before, when Herbert Lewis and Frank Edwards had their wives with them and he was on his own.[1]

The Scottish holiday was spent at Oban, to which the Lloyd Georges and Davieses travelled by sea from Liverpool. One day they were nearly drowned in a light boat when a storm blew up in Oban Bay, but otherwise the trip appears to have been a success, and it is notable in Lloyd George's life for being the occasion of his learning the game of golf. This game, which has become one of the favourite recreations of modern affluent man, is essentially a walk in open country with a purpose, artificially contrived. From his earliest childhood, when his grandmother took him for long country walks, Lloyd George had been addicted to that form of exercise; and he was, of course, by nature purposeful. Golf, therefore, was a very suitable game for him and he derived much enjoy-

---

1. D.L.G. to M.L.G., 27 August 1895 (N.L.W.). When Herbert Lewis's wife died, Lloyd George went out of his way to be with him and to give him all the comfort he could, hough it was a very busy time politically.

ment from it during the rest of his active life. He was an enthusiastic rather than a good player, with a handicap of eighteen; but his game was steady if not particularly stylish. At Criccieth, a golf course was made on ground which used to be part of his father-in-law's farm, and its existence somewhat mitigated the gloom with which he contemplated a visit to his home town. In London, he liked to live within easy reach of a golf club, and at the height of his career his favourite retreat was a house built for him, and presented to him, by his friend George Riddell, adjoining the golf course at Walton Heath. Golf, however, did him a serious political disservice when, at the Cannes Conference in January 1922, he played a round with the French Prime Minister, Aristide Briand. Briand had never played before, and pictures of him in the Press next day were hurtful to French national pride and precipitated his resignation – which was a blow to Lloyd George's European policy and contributed to his own fall later in the year.

During the autumn and winter of 1895–6 the Lloyd Georges were mostly apart. The Palace Mansions flat was either left empty or – occasionally – occupied by Lloyd George on his own. More often he stayed, when in London, at the National Liberal Club or with friends. He was at Criccieth for Christmas, but apart from that was hardly there at all. One day in February 1896 he wrote from Swansea, pleading that he was only five-and-a-half hours from London, but twelve hours from North Wales (a revealing comment on the logistics of the Principality, and of its relationship with England).[1] Margaret must have sent him a rather sharp reply, because three days later he wrote an apologia:

It is quite true what you say about one getting accustomed even to these periodic separations from one's family – but all the same I get spasms of hiraeth [homesickness]. You know very well that the pressure to bring us together invariably comes from me. I have led a very strenuous and anxious life for the past five years and it is beginning to tell upon me. That has had a good deal to do with my apparent indifference to my home. Other interests have absorbed my mind but I always come back with a sensation of restful delight to Brynawelon. I only wish I could get such a fortnight there as I enjoyed immediately after my election collapse. In spite of my complete physical prostration I never enjoyed my life as I did then. I felt perfectly happy. It is such a fortnight as that I want now to set me up for the Session.[2]

1. D.L.G. to M.L.G., 8 February 1896 (N.L.W.).
2. D.L.G. to M.L.G., 11 February 1896 (N.L.W.).

Yet he stayed on in London, begging her to join him there.

In addition to her usual motives for remaining at Criccieth, she had the excuse that her mother was ill. She was also active in local politics, and he praised her for taking her public duties seriously. 'You must make a good speech one of these days. That will surprise them. I am sure you can do it. You have any quantity of brains of a very good quality if you only set them to work. THINK – that is what you must do.'[1] But he needed her in London. For one thing, he was quite incapable of looking after himself. In March 1896 he was appealing to her – for the third time – to send him his brown boots, 'owing to the hole in my present pair'.[2] It was typical of him to leave them behind (presumably at Christmas), and of her to be slow in packing them off to him. In July he confessed that he simply could not manage by himself at the flat. 'My bread is now so hard that I could hardly cut it with the knife. . . .'[3] He had persuaded the porter's wife to come in and help him, but even so 'It has got into a very untidy state and no one would think of taking it'.[4] Margaret was in London for a week in the early summer, and again for a few days before he left for the Argentine in August. From the ship he gave her *carte blanche* to surrender or renew the lease of the flat.[5] Her decision was to keep it, but to sub-let.

Early in the New Year he was tempted to take a furnished flat in the neighbourhood of Palace Mansions, but settled instead for rooms at the Bingham Hotel, Chancery Lane. Margaret was there in February 1897, but in the early spring she had a miscarriage which gave her yet another reason for staying at Criccieth. Nevertheless he continued to press her to change her way of life. 'Starting business in London [his London law partnership] must involve a fundamental change in our arrangements. You can't leave me in town alone. That would be an act of desertion which I know you are too noble to contemplate. . . . Besides Heaven knows what it might not eventually lead me to.'[6] At the end of May he wrote her a letter reminiscent of the two very tough ones he wrote during their courtship.

> . . . You say that you would rather have less money and live in a healthy place. Well . . . you will not forget that you were as keen about

1. D.L.G. to M.L.G., 15 December 1895 (N.L.W.).
2. D.L.G. to M.L.G., 9 March 1896 (N.L.W.).
3. D.L.G. to M.L.G, 29 July 1896 (N.L.W.).
4. D.L.G. to M.L.G., 31 July 1896 (N.L.W.).
5. D.L.G. to M.L.G., 1 September 1896 (N.L.W.).
6. D.L.G. to M.L.G., 26 May 1897 (N.L.W.).

my starting as I was myself. Then you must bear in mind that we are spending more than we earn. I draw far more than my share of the profits although I don't attend to 1/10th of the work. . . . Now you can't make omelettes without breaking eggs and unless I retire from politics altogether and content myself with returning to the position of a country attorney we must give up the comforts of Criccieth for life in England. As to attending to the business during Session and running away from it afterwards your good sense will show you on reflection that it is impossible. . . . You are not right however that it presupposes living entirely in London. If you prefer we can take a house somewhere in the suburbs. . . . There the air is quite as good as anything you can get in Wales as it is free from the smoke of the great city. Or if you prefer it we could go still further out and live say in Brighton. . . . That would be right on the sea. During the Parliamentary recess I could run down every evening and during the Session we might take a flat and run down to Brighton for the weekends. That would be as satisfactory as possible. Brighton climate is much more sunny and dry than Criccieth. As for friends that could soon be managed. . . . In any event it would be a much more satisfactory life than the present. More pleasant and beneficial for me because it would give me more of my pets' company. Ought to be more happy for you as it will give you more of your husband's society.

Think of it old pet and think of it with the courage of which I know you are capable. . . .

He signed the letter 'Your fond sweetheart who can't live happily without you, Dei'.[1]

Yet the plea went unheeded for over two years, during which Lloyd George was normally wifeless in London. For some of the time he was at Palace Mansions with one or more of the children to keep him company, and a Welsh servant to look after him. But there were long spells when he was left completely to his own devices. Eventually, towards the end of 1899, he moved into a house on the edge of Wandsworth Common – No. 179 Trinity Road – which provided the family, for the first time, with a real home in London. In principle, they were together there throughout the Boer War period. It was a compromise solution, on the whole favourable to Lloyd George. Margaret would never, of course, agree that the air of suburban London was remotely comparable with that of Criccieth, but

1. D.L.G. to M.L.G., 28 May 1897 (N.L.W.).

she had at last – nearly ten years after he became an M.P. – adapted her way of life to suit his wishes. Unfortunately the change occurred too late to save their marriage from the partial decay which gradually overtook it (and which would, perhaps, have overtaken it anyway). Meanwhile her very long absences at Criccieth were asking for serious trouble, and such trouble arose, most notably, in the case of Mrs Edwards, and in Lloyd George's involvement with Mrs Timothy Davies.

On 8 August 1896, Catherine, wife of Dr David Edwards of Cemmaes in Montgomeryshire, was observed by her husband to be pregnant. In the circumstances her condition was surprising, because the couple had not been sleeping together for the past two years. Challenged by Dr Edwards to say who was responsible, Catherine made the following confession, dated 10 August:

> I, Catherine Edwards, do solemnly confess that I have on 4th of February, 1896, committed adultery with Lloyd George M.P., and that the said Lloyd George is the father of the child, and that I have on a previous occasion committed adultery with the above Lloyd George.

Just over a week later – on 19 August – the child was born.

Rumours were soon circulating, and Lloyd George's name was being linked with the scandal, in the gossip of pubs and clubs, while he was far away in the Argentine. A friend of his in Caernarvon wrote to William George alerting him to the existence of the rumours, but assuring him that Lloyd George's supporters did not believe there was 'the slightest truth in the venom'. William wrote his brother a letter, to be received on arrival at Southampton, informing him of what was being said and suggesting that they should meet at once to discuss it, either at Southampton or in London. Lloyd George replied from London denying the charge made against him in Mrs Edwards's confession, and expressing his determination to prove its falsity.[1]

Early the following year Mrs Edwards presented a petition for judicial separation, alleging several acts of cruelty against Dr Edwards, including the charge that he had forced her to sign the confession. But this petition was never heard, because in March 1897 Dr Edwards sued his wife for divorce, citing as co-respondent not Lloyd George, but Edward Wilson, the station-master at Cemmaes Road railway station (a reversal of the rôle allotted to the station-master in a familiar French song). Mrs Edwards

1. *See* William George, *My Brother and I*, pp. 194-5.

denied the adultery and asserted that her husband was the child's father. She also submitted counter-charges of cruelty against him. Edwards said he had done his best to discover who was the father, but without success. He believed, however, that his wife's original statement as to the child's paternity was false, and stated categorically that he was not, himself, the father. Why the station-master was cited was never explained at the time and remains to this day a mystery. At some stage William George, 'by arrangement with the solicitors' to the other parties in the case, interviewed Mrs Edwards 'at her solicitor's office at Machynlleth'.[1] But neither the date of this meeting, nor the substance of the conversation, is public knowledge.

Before the main divorce proceedings there was a preliminary hearing on 19 July, when the President of the Probate, Divorce and Admiralty Division, Sir Francis Jeune, ruled that Lloyd George – referred to throughout as 'A.B.' – need not be made a co-respondent in the case. Lloyd George had written a letter denying adultery with Mrs Edwards 'in very emphatic terms'; there was no corroboration of what she had alleged, and Dr Edwards was now, apparently, convinced of his innocence. The judge rested his decision upon precedent, but went out of his way to mention two rather puzzling features of the case: that Mrs Edwards had at first said her confession was dictated to her by her husband – which, if true, would have meant that he then believed Lloyd George to be guilty – and that 'A.B.', though perfectly entitled to appear in court and clear his name on oath, was evidently unwilling to avail himself of the opportunity.[2]

The main hearing was on 18 November, Sir Francis Jeune again presiding. Bargrave Deane Q.C. and Ellis Griffith appeared for the petitioner (Dr Edwards), a Mr Inderwick Q.C. and a Mr Priestley for the respondent (Mrs Edwards), and a Mr Barnard for the co-respondent (the station-master, Edward Wilson). Before Bargrave Deane opened his case, there were two curious interventions. Inderwick stated that, as he was unable to produce independent evidence in support of his client's counter-charges of cruelty, he was abandoning them; and that if counsel for the petitioner would proceed with a charge that adultery had been committed by Mrs Edwards with a person unknown, he could offer no defence, though he would contest the charge of adultery with Edward Wilson. After this Barnard, for Wilson, stated that he was prepared to fight the case, adding ominously that he had a large quantity of evidence to adduce.

Bargrave Deane, naturally enough, amended his charge to one of

1. *Ibid.*, pp. 196–7.
2. Decisions of the Probate, Divorce and Admiralty Division, 19 July and 12 August 1897.

adultery with a man unknown, and opened his statement with a summary of the background. Dr and Mrs Edwards had been married in 1887 and had one five-year-old child. They had lived together happily until 1894 when, 'in consequence of some trouble – which need not be gone into – they began to occupy separate rooms'. In 1896 Dr Edwards, who was interested in politics, invited Lloyd George to his house, and Lloyd George spent the night of 4 February there, in the course of which Edwards was called away professionally, returning home the following morning. In August, said Deane, Edwards noticed that his wife 'appeared to be *enceinte*, and on his taxing her with being in that condition she became very distressed, and ultimately confessed that she was *enceinte*'. At this point counsel read the text of the confession, but instead of using the code-letters 'A.B.' to conceal Lloyd George's identity, he gave his name openly 'in the interests of Mr Lloyd George himself', since it was better that his identity should not be 'hushed up'.

On 19 August, Deane continued, Mrs Edwards 'was delivered of a full-timed child', of which Edwards was not the father. Counsel on both sides were satisfied that 'the imputation against Mr Lloyd George was without foundation'. Mrs Edwards's confession was 'of a kind not un-known in the Divorce Court, and designed to protect a guilty man by accusing an innocent one'. The 'whole facts' of the confession, and 'the fact that after careful and impartial search no evidence of any kind could be found against Lloyd George', had been laid before the Court on the earlier motion for leave to dispense with him as co-respondent.

After evidence had been heard in support of Deane's case, and after Wilson had denied on oath the allegations made against him, the judge summed up. It had been quite right, he said, not to press the case against Wilson: once Dr Edwards had established his case against an unknown adulterer, Wilson was entitled to the benefit of his denial. Moreover, it had been quite right for Deane to exercise discretion and publish Lloyd George's name. He (the judge) remained satisfied that there was 'no ground whatever' for the imputation against Lloyd George, but if he had wished to appear as co-respondent permission would not have been granted to the petitioner to proceed without him. Lloyd George, however, 'who was a solicitor, by his own express wish was allowed to remain outside the suit'. Mrs Edwards's adultery with a person unknown had been 'clearly proved', and Dr Edwards was given a decree *nisi*, with custody of his own child.[1]

1. Law report, *The Times*, 19 November 1897.

In his decision to stay out of court Lloyd George was acting on strong advice from his brother. After the preliminary hearing in July William wrote:

> . . . it seems to me that the Judge's feeling was that it might be an unfair thing to debar you of the right of denying the abandoned charge on oath seeing that you were expressing your anxiety in the letters to have such opportunity. But since then circumstances have changed to a considerable extent. In the first place the ch[ar]ge itself has been withdrawn and in the second place the vigorous measures which you took at the time with the view of bringing your slanderers to justice has scotched the scandal and you are under no obligation that I can see to resurrect its stinking carcase merely for the sake of giving it a more formal burial. I therefore still think that the right attitude for you is a passive one. . . .[1]

And in October he reiterated the advice:

> It is far more satisfactory in the long run that you should be at hand to give evidence should either party wish to call you, and after that process is over and all the facts are known and have assumed their final shape it will be open for you to consider whether you should not initiate proceedings of your own. All I wd. do would be to hold myself in readiness to go to the witness-box if called on. . . .[2]

Lloyd George did exactly what his brother advised, and it may have been a relief to him that he was never called upon to give evidence or to face possible cross-examination – though when the *Caernarvon Herald* printed a story that he had declined to go into the witness-box, he reacted with indignation and asked his brother to write at once explaining that he was on his way to court to give evidence when the case was settled. William's *démenti*, dated 21 November, appeared in the next issue of the paper.[3] Soon afterwards Lloyd George wrote to the Press himself – to *The Times* – quoting a letter he had sent to the Caernarvon Liberal Association, complaining of the intolerable wrong inflicted on him by Britain's defective law of defamation. Since a wife's confession to her husband did not, technically, constitute publication, it was impossible to make it the basis for any action for libel or slander. He had, therefore,

1. William George to David Lloyd George, 21 July 1897 (N.L.W.).
2. William George to David Lloyd George, 31 October 1897 (N.L.W.).
3. *See* William George, *My Brother and I*, pp. 199–200.

been prevented from bringing his accuser to justice. 'Surely,' he said, 'the law should be placed on a more humane footing?'[1]

Eighteen months later the Edwards affair came up again when Dr Thomas Pugh Beddoes, Mrs Edwards's personal doctor, intervened as a member of the public – under Section 7 of the Divorce Act 1860 – with a plea that the decree *nisi* granted to Dr Edwards should be rescinded. This new case was tried before Sir Francis Jeune and a special jury on 16 June 1899. The same counsel as before, assisted by a Mr Davenport, appeared for Dr Edwards, and the two counsel who had previously represented Mrs Edwards appeared, on this occasion, for Arthur Johnson Hughes, her solicitor on the previous occasion. A Mr Griffiths represented Dr Beddoes, and Bryn Roberts held a watching brief for Lloyd George.

The hearing was confused and at times degenerated into near-farce, but the vital point at issue was whether or not Mrs Edwards had withdrawn her defence at the previous trial because she was promised by her solicitor (Hughes) that all her costs would be covered and all the money she had so far paid out would be returned to her. She made a very poor showing in the witness-box. Bargrave Deane, cross-examining, reminded her that she had written to her husband, after she had left his house: 'Dear David, Do you think you can ever forgive me. . . . I know I have sinned, but I have repented bitterly. . . . I cannot expect you to receive me home yet, and of course the child shall never come. . . .' In the face of that evidence her solicitor had advised her that it was madness to fight the case, and that she should leave it to Inderwick to get the best terms for her he could. Bryn Roberts asked for permission to cross-examine Mrs Edwards, since he claimed to have a correspondence which absolutely disproved her charge against Lloyd George. But the President would not allow him to cross-examine, saying: 'Mr Lloyd George is not a party to this suit. There is no imputation upon him at all.' With this Bargrave Deane warmly agreed, stressing that Lloyd George was 'absolutely free from any blame' in the matter. The jury found in favour of Dr Edwards on all points and the case was dismissed. Three days later the decree *nisi* granted to Dr Edwards in November 1897 was made absolute.[2]

Was justice done? Did the truth come out? Was Lloyd George really quite as innocent as the Court proclaimed him to be? We can only look at all the evidence – positive and negative, direct and circumstantial – and then weigh the probabilities.

1. His letter to *The Times* appeared on 29 November 1897.
2. Law reports, *The Times*, 17 and 20 June 1899.

The first thing to be said is that a good deal of evidence was never presented. Lloyd George's statement to the judge was made by letter (which was never published) rather than by affidavit, and he was never called into the witness-box to give testimony, or to answer questions, on oath. So long as there was any chance of keeping his name out of the case altogether it was entirely understandable that he was unwilling to appear in court, even for the purpose of making a categorical assertion of his innocence. The publicity would inevitably have done him a certain amount of harm, however convincing his evidence; and some people would have been bound to say 'No smoke without fire'. At the preliminary hearing in July 1897, and in Sir Francis Jeune's ensuing decision that Lloyd George need not be cited as co-respondent, his name was never given and he was referred to throughout as 'A.B.' Yet in the event his name was brought into the case, at the main hearing in November 1897. Rumour had, no doubt, been so persistent that it was thought desirable, in his own interests, that his name should be mentioned and explicitly cleared. But would it not have been better, then, for him to have appeared in person and to have stated on oath that he was innocent, and why?

After all, the man who was actually cited – the station-master, Edward Wilson – went into the witness-box to deny the allegations against him, even though counsel for Dr Edwards had meanwhile dropped the charge that he was the adulterer and was arguing instead that Mrs Edwards had committed adultery with a person unknown. Wilson went into the witness-box, and his obvious eagerness to do so contrasts with Lloyd George's reluctance. But apparently Wilson was never given a chance to produce the 'large quantity of evidence' which his counsel had said he was able and willing to produce. Whatever contribution he might have made to a fuller knowledge of the circumstances he was, for some reason best known to the lawyers, never asked to make.

Of course Lloyd George, as a public man, had a motive for wishing to remain anonymous which did not apply to Wilson. In that sense they were in a different position, and Lloyd George's reluctance to go into the witness-box was, at that stage, natural enough. But it is much less clear why, when his name, willy-nilly, was out in the open, he did not come forward as Wilson did. William George's advice that he was 'under no obligation to resurrect' the 'stinking carcase' could be taken to imply that the whole truth might, in some way, have been discreditable to him.

Why did Mrs Edwards make her strange confession, and why, having made it, did she later withdraw it? At first, she maintained that she had signed it under duress – that her husband had taken her by the throat and threatened her with a carving knife. Yet at the main hearing she dropped her charges of cruelty against him. His counsel described her confession as 'an invention of a kind not unknown in the Divorce Court, and designed to protect a guilty man by accusing an innocent one'. But at the same hearing the only identifiable man whom she might have been trying to protect was accepted as being totally innocent, and no alternative adulterer was identified. Dr Edwards seems to have believed her confession at the outset, though we need not assume that he extorted it, by force or otherwise. And if he believed it, must there not have been something inherently credible about it? Must he not have had reasons for regarding it as *prima facie* true?

The Court was told on 18 November 1897, that Dr Edwards was interested in politics, that he invited Lloyd George to spend the night of 4 February 1896 at his house, and that during the night he (Edwards) had to answer a professional call which kept him out until the following morning. Those statements were not, it seems, contradicted at the hearing, though it has since been suggested that Lloyd George produced an alibi – that he was voting in the House of Commons that night, and so could not have spent it at Cemmaes, however chastely.[1] The alibi was demonstrably false, because the House of Commons was not in session at the time.[2] It is surely most unlikely that Lloyd George would have sought to exculpate himself with such a transparent lie, or that intelligent men of the world would have been taken in by it only eighteen months after the event. In any case, it would have rendered otiose a very strong piece of evidence in Lloyd George's favour – which definitely was produced at the hearing – that the child born to Mrs Edwards on 19 August was 'full-timed'. As such, the child could not, of course, have been conceived on 4 February.[3] Lloyd George's letters to his wife give no indication of his

1. 'In November, when the case came up for hearing, Lloyd George produced to Counsel the record of the Parliamentary division lists to show that on 4 February he had been until early morning voting in the House of Commons.' (Frank Owen, *Tempestuous Journey*, p. 88.) '. . . to refute the charge my father was able to produce a record of his attendance in the House of Commons on the 4th February, until early in the morning. . . .' (Richard Lloyd George, *Lloyd George*, p. 63.) This alibi, if given to Counsel, was certainly never advanced in court.

2. 'The second session of the fourteenth Parliament of Queen Victoria was not opened until February 11 of that year [1896]. How then could Lloyd George clear himself on the grounds indicated by Mr Frank Owen?' (Donald McCormick, *op. cit.*, p. 46.)

3. At the 1899 hearing Mrs Edwards was quoted as having said that her husband examined her on 8 August 1896, and pronounced that she was '7 months gone'. It would not, in fact,

whereabouts on that date. He wrote to her from Sunderland on 31 January, and then not again until he wrote from Swansea on 6 February. On the whole, it seems reasonable to believe that he did spend the night of the 4th at the Edwardses house at Cemmaes, though of course it does not follow that he spent any part of it in bed with Mrs Edwards, and still less does it follow that he begot the child to which she gave birth on 19 August.

Margaret Lloyd George (according to her son, Richard) remembered Catherine Edwards – who was, in fact, a cousin of hers – as 'a pretty, pert, amiable young woman . . . with a carefree disposition'.[1] One letter from her to Lloyd George survives, though it has never before been published. It was written on black-edged paper from Cemmaes, and addressed to him at the National Liberal Club. The envelope is postmarked 15 February 1894. It reads:

Dear Mr Lloyd George

I sent you the Newtown paper yesterday and am sending the Oswestry today trusting they will get into your hands in good time. We showed your portrait in the Newtown paper to Baby and she immediately said 'Uncle Yu d'ydywo'n ghos'!! ['Uncle, isn't he sweet?']

Miss Annie Thomas called here yesterday. She asked very *tenderly* after you, it is quite possible she expected to see you. I believe Mr Thomas is delivering the last of those lectures on Church History this evening, I have not been to one of them yet, must go tonight for fear I shall lose the privileges of our *club*!!

My Colonel went up to town by the 9.22 yesterday morning so as you may imagine it is rather dull here at present, he ought to have given me time to get over the loss of your charming society. I shall send some fresh eggs tomorrow and a letter to Maggie.

You must come to spend either Easter or Whitsuntide with us, I have been told that Carno people are going to ask you to speak there, in that case it can easily be managed.

---

have been medically possible for him to make such an accurate estimate of the stage that her pregnancy had reached. In the report of the original hearing in the *Caernarvon Herald* – in some ways fuller than that in *The Times* – there is no specific reference to the number of months, though Dr Edwards said in his evidence that, when he examined his wife, he 'found she was far advanced in pregnancy'. The phrase 'full-timed', applied to the child when it was born, occurs in *The Times* but not in the *Caernarvon Herald*.

1. Richard Lloyd George, *Lloyd George*, p. 62. Mrs Edwards's maiden name was (according to her marriage certificate) Catherine Owen. Her father was William Owen, a farmer of Mathafarn.

I am addressing this to the Club and the minute you have read it please commit it to the fire, I shall not expect an answer until you write to tell me you are going to spend a few days with us again. Mr Evans the Ship is coming up to consult an oculist next week, poor man he does not look so well these days. They have pulled down the whole of that fence at Cwmlline Common put up by Sir Thomas Frost and Major Bonsall!

Poor old Mrs Gilvach died on Sunday, she will be buried tomorrow.

No more news, you may expect some trout from me in April, I shall send as many as I catch to Maggie and you and if my basket is not sufficient to supply your larder the Dr must help.

Excuse such an untidy letter and with my kind regards

> Believe me
> Yrs very sincerely
> Kitty Edwards.[1]

This letter has been quoted in full, because only thus can its very curious and suggestive character be grasped. Flirtatious it certainly is. Above all, the instruction to burn the letter the minute he has read it surely implies the existence of an intrigue, or the desire to create one. But as well as the flirtatiousness there is an undertone of possessiveness. Mrs Edwards writes as though Lloyd George's connection was specifically with her, rather than with Edwards and her as a couple. She would not expect an answer until he wrote to tell *her* that he would be visiting them again. There is also a hint of conspiracy in her references to Margaret, and an innuendo that she was better able than Margaret to supply him with creature comforts.

On the purely factual side, the letter is conclusive evidence that Lloyd George was no stranger to the Edwardses' home when he stayed with them on 4 February 1896. He had clearly been staying with them two years earlier, during the Montgomeryshire bye-election,[2] and there are, indeed, three letters written to Margaret from Cemmaes at that time, whose only interest is that they confirm that he was there and show that

1. Catherine Edwards to David Lloyd George, dated 'Thursday', post-marked 15 February 1894 (S. T. Evans Papers.) How this letter came to be preserved by S. T. Evans can only be guessed at, but Lloyd George may have shown it to him as a connoisseur in such matters, and then have forgotten about it.
2. *See* above, p. 147.

his visit was of at least three days' duration.[1] Moreover, the date of Mrs Edwards's letter may have a special significance, in that it was in 1894 (according to Dr Edwards's counsel at the divorce hearing) that the couple became estranged and began to sleep in separate rooms. The cause of their quarrel was not revealed: it was merely described as 'some trouble – which need not be gone into'. But the coincidence of dates, and Mrs Edwards's accusation two years later – believed at first, if not dictated, by her husband – almost compel the speculation that it may have been jealousy of Lloyd George, aroused when he was a guest at their house in 1894, which turned Dr Edwards against his wife. This may have been the 'previous occasion' of adultery mentioned in her confession, but she was never required to specify the date, because by the time the case came into court her confession was withdrawn.

We are left, after three-quarters of a century, with a puzzle to which no convincing solution can yet be offered. Information may one day come to light which will enable us to understand what really happened. For instance, it would be most interesting to have a full account of the interview between William George and Mrs Edwards which took place before the divorce hearing in 1897 – or at any rate a fuller record than that contained in *My Brother and I*. It is possible that such a record may exist in the files, as yet inaccessible to historians, of the firm of Lloyd George and George. Descendants of Mrs Edwards may be able to produce fresh evidence, or there may be other families in which relevant documents are preserved. Meanwhile the case certainly appears to have been rather oddly conducted. Sir Francis Jeune (later Lord St Helier) was an eminent judge who cannot be suspected of any political prejudice in favour of Lloyd George. He was the son of an Anglican bishop, had served as chancellor of the diocese of St Asaph (among others), and had once stood for Parliament as a Tory. He may have been over-anxious to avoid any semblance of bias *against* a public man whose views he disliked; yet it may also have been very difficult for him to act otherwise than he did, granted the bewildering representations that were made to him by the parties, through their counsel. In one way or another, the lawyers appear to have arranged matters so that Lloyd George, at any rate, would emerge unscathed. It may be that they were doubtful of the truth, and simply gave him the benefit of the doubt. Whatever their motives, the outcome

1. D.L.G. to M.L.G., 9, 10, 11 February 1894 (N.L.W.).

was very fortunate politically, because it would have been an immeasurable disaster if his career had been ruined at such an early stage. If the case was rigged, Britain was the gainer.

The interpretation which seems most likely to the present writer is that Lloyd George did sleep with Mrs Edwards on 4 February 1896, and on a previous occasion, but that he was not the father of her child. Had he been totally innocent, it is surely inconceivable that he would have run the risk of staying under Mrs Edwards's roof again, after receiving from her a letter such as the one quoted – the tone of which was so flirtatious that no man would have responded to it who was not either very naïve (which Lloyd George obviously was not) or very willing to avail himself of any favours that might be going. The impression that he was, to that extent, guilty is strengthened by his failure – even when his name was no longer being kept secret – to declare his innocence on oath. (In 1909, when two newspapers hinted that he might be cited as co-respondent in a divorce case, he did go into the witness-box and the newspapers promptly grovelled.) Belief that he was not the father of Mrs Edwards's child depends upon the medical evidence that it was born 'full-timed' on 19 August. If that evidence could be disproved or discredited, his paternity of the child would be most probable. Since he left for the Argentine two days after it was born, it is tempting to see some link between the two events; but his reasons for the voyage are sufficiently clear, without any need for speculation that he was going far afield to escape from an ugly scandal at home. Besides, his escape could only have been temporary: the scandal was bound to catch up with him sooner or later.

Any affair that there may have been between him and Mrs Edwards can have stirred his emotions hardly at all, but may have meant considerably more to her. He had the unintentional cruelty of the male philanderer who does not recognise the different attitude of most women towards sexual involvement. Kitty Edwards, bored with her life at Cemmaes and dazzled by Lloyd George, may have seen herself as another Kitty O'Shea, whose romantic story was in everybody's mind at the time. But Lloyd George most certainly did not see himself as another Parnell. As he had explained to Margaret before their marriage, he was prepared to thrust love itself under the wheels of his Juggernaut if it impeded his progress; and, as he later told Frances Stevenson, no man was entitled, in his view, to sacrifice his political life to a woman. He may also have felt that Mrs Edwards was light of heart, by no means exclusive in the bestowal of her favours, and therefore fair game. (Who was her

'Colonel'?). If the lawyers in the case were satisfied that Mrs Edwards was trying to frame him as the father of her child, their readiness to protect him would be morally comprehensible, even though they may also have been satisfied that he did commit adultery with her. Her ruin had been brought upon herself and there was no justification for ruining him as well, unless he were the father. She was ruined anyway: he was not. Her subsequent attempt to re-establish her marriage is consistent with the hypothesis that she hoped, in 1896, that Lloyd George would marry her.[1]

While there is no documentary evidence of Margaret's feelings towards Mrs Edwards, we know just how jealous she was of another woman – Mrs Timothy Davies. In February 1896, Lloyd George mentions the possibility of taking lodgings in Putney. 'Dalziel says I might get a sitting room and bedroom at the house where he puts up. They are decent Scotch bodies Putney way – £1 1s a week. Golf links within ten minutes' walk.'[2] Even then, there may have been other attractions to the idea of living in Putney, besides Dalziel and golf. In June of the same year he writes from the home of Mr and Mrs Timothy Davies in Oakhill Road, Putney.[3] The house was called 'Pantycelyn' after the famous Welsh poet and hymn-writer.[4] It was to become a home from home for Lloyd George, and 'Mrs Tim' was for some time his favourite female companion in London, during Margaret's absences in Wales.

Timothy Davies was the son of a prosperous miller in Carmarthenshire. At the age of fourteen he went to Liverpool, where he was apprenticed in the drapery trade. In 1875 he came to London, and ten years later opened his first shop in Walham Green. Long afterwards, he described the scene: 'It was one Saturday afternoon in February 1885, when I walked to Fulham from South Kensington. There were only two shops

1. After the divorce, Mrs Edwards was at some stage remarried – to an Englishman – but the details of her subsequent history are not known even to some people who might particularly be expected to know. Dr Edwards also remarried, and his second wife died in 1911. In the same year he was presented with a motor-car, a bicycle and a substantial cheque, in token of his neighbours' affection and regard for him. He died in 1923. His daughter (by Catherine) was brought up by her stepmother, married happily and is still living. The child born in 1896 is said to have died within a few years, though clinching evidence on this point is not available.
2. D.L.G. to M.L.G., 20 February 1896 (N.L.W.).
3. D.L.G. to M.L.G., 13 June 1896 (N.L.W.).
4. William Williams of Pantycelyn (1717–91), chief hymn-writer of the Methodist awakening in Wales.

completed in the Broadway. Walham Green Station was there . . . and the trains were steam-driven. My first shop was No. 9 the Broadway and I believe the only other shop there was a fish shop.'[1] Davies's shop grew to be the leading drapery store of south-west London. He also became active in local public life, serving on the Fulham Vestry (later Borough Council) and on the London County Council. He was Mayor of Fulham in 1901, and Liberal M.P. for Fulham from 1906 to 1910. Then, until 1920, he sat in Parliament for Louth.

References to his wife are hard to come by. He did not mention her in his *Who's Who* entry, but at the time of his death an old friend recalled: 'His young and brilliant wife supported him in all his endeavours. I remember going with some friends to his Putney home where the whole family was gathered, a true picture of what British family life should be.'[2] In Richard Lloyd George's book on his father she goes under the name of 'Mrs D.' and is described as 'a lively, attractive creature, rather loquacious, very stylish, perhaps a little flamboyant . . . and she wore a fragrance like a basket of carnations'.[3] Richard claimed to have become aware that something was going on between her and his father when he was taken, one day, to 'Pantycelyn' and noticed that Lloyd George 'began to play some sort of silly game with the lady. He seemed to be eating her fingers.' When Richard told his mother, in all innocence, what he had seen, his parents had a row.[4]

According to the same witness, the affair with Mrs Davies 'continued for longer than most of father's gallantries' – in fact, 'for many years'. Though she tried hard to ingratiate herself with the older Lloyd George children, who saw quite a lot of her, 'her blandishments were proof against' Richard's 'inarticulate and tightly-contained antagonism'. Timothy Davies he regarded as 'a colourless personality', whose political career was furthered by Lloyd George.[5] However the affair first came to

1. Obituary notice of Timothy Davies in the *Fulham Chronicle*, 31 August 1951, quoting an interview given by him the year before. He was ninety-four when he died.

2. J. H. Palmer, J.P., writing in the *Fulham Chronicle*, 7 September 1951.

3. Richard Lloyd George, *Lloyd George*, pp. 60–1.   4. *Ibid.*, pp. 53–4.

5. *Ibid.*, pp. 60–1. Richard's account of Mrs Davies, and of the children's attitude towards her, is broadly corroborated by Lady Olwen Carey Evans, who understood and resented the situation herself, but never discussed it with her sister, Mair. How much, if anything, Mair understood of it cannot be known. No doubt Lloyd George's support was helpful to Timothy Davies, but he would probably have been elected for Fulham without it, in view of his local influence. Richard's statement that Lloyd George later 'awarded Mr D. a government post' is misleading. Davies was never a Minister, but was appointed an Income Tax Commissioner in 1917.

her notice, Margaret was soon, on her own admission, 'a prey to the green-eyed monster', and reproaching Lloyd George for neglecting the Davieses of Acton in favour of the Davieses of Putney. Between 1897 and 1899 there are several bitter exchanges. For instance, in August 1897 Margaret hears through a servant that Lloyd George has received 'a very early visitor' at Palace Mansions, and reflects that if she hears of one such meeting accidentally, how many more must there be of which she hears nothing. She would sooner be told straight when he has met Mrs Tim than have him write affectionate letters intended to mislead. 'This business I tell you comes between you and me more so than you imagine and is growing, and you know it and yet you cannot shake it off. It pains me to the quick, and I am very unhappy. If you must go on as at present I don't know where it will end. . . . Beware, don't give place for any scandal for the sake of your own personal self and your bright career.'[1] He replies fiercely: 'You threaten me with a public scandal. Alright – expose me if that suits you. One scandal the more will but kill me the earlier. But you will not alter my resolution to have neither correspondence nor communication of any sort with you until it is more clearly understood how you propose to guide your course for the future. I have borne it for years and have suffered in health and character. I'll stand it no longer come what may.'[2]

Alarmed, she must have sent him a mollifying telegram, because two days later he writes:

My sweet but stupid Maggie,

That telegram just saved you. Your letter this morning made me wild. There was the same self-complacent self-satisfied Pharisaism about it, as ever. . . . A wise woman who loved her husband well and who knew herself well-beloved by him, would not write foolish letters arguing out the matter with him and doing that badly – she would rather *put these things together ponder them well* and resolve at all costs to redeem the past. Be candid with yourself. . . and reflect whether you have not rather neglected your husband. I have more than once gone without breakfast. I have scores of times come home in the dead of night to a cold dark and comfortless flat without a soul to greet me,

1. M.L.G. to D.L.G., from Criccieth, dated 'Wednesday' but placeable in time because of Lloyd George's reply (Earl Lloyd George collection).
2. D.L.G. to M.L.G., 19 August 1897 (N.L.W.). This letter was written between the preliminary and the main hearing in the Edwards divorce case. Hence the reference to 'one scandal the more'.

bedience – yes in a matter any other wife would have been only too delighted to obey him in.

You threaten me with a public scandal. Alright – Expose me if that suits you. One scandal – the more will but kill me the earlier. But you will not alter my resolution to have neither correspondence nor communication of any sort with you until it is more clearly understood how you propose to guide your course for the future. I have borne it for years & have suffered in health & character. I'll stand it no longer come what may.

4. Facsimile from Lloyd George's letter to his wife, dated 19 August 1897 (see previous page)

when you were surrounded by your pets. I am not the nature either physically or morally that I ought to have been left thus. . . . You have been a good mother. You have not – and I say this now not in anger – not always been a good wife. I can point you even amongst those whom you affect to look down upon – much better wives. . . . My soul as well as my body has been committed to your charge and in many respects I am as helpless as a child. . . .

The letter ends on an affectionate note, but not before he has warned her that if she makes him miserable he will seek – and find – consolation elsewhere.[1]

Lloyd George was susceptible to Mrs Tim not only because she had potent sex appeal (to which he could never be indifferent), but also because she kept a good house and created an atmosphere of comfort in which he could relax. Margaret, even when she was with him, did not always minister very effectively to his 'luxurious nature'. She was a very good gardener, but a poor housekeeper. Without being exactly mean she was certainly parsimonious, and she lacked the gift, which does not depend upon wealth and which many rich people do not possess, for making a house warm and welcoming. Lloyd George liked to come home, in winter, to glowing fires. He liked food to be plentiful, and more especially he liked to have an abundance of fresh fruit. These amenities Margaret did not always provide.

In another undated letter she shows her detestation of Mrs Tim.

I am very angry with Mrs T. for persevering so much with you. Fancy coming over to a man like you, so superior to her Tim, and thinking it was an honour to you to see her off. I am very disgusted to tell you the truth. The idea. I am more angry than ever with her for her presumption. I would not dream of going to any friend to expect anything of the sort. . . . She had no business to do such a thing, and if I see any inclination on her part to make you *cheap* I shall some way or other make her understand that I will not have it . . . you are inclined to allow people to make too freely with you. Supposing that I did so freely with Herbert Lewis for instance. I know you would denounce me, although I would have more claim on Herbert than that woman has on you. But it shows how she thinks you ought to be at her beck and call. They have judged her right, she is very gracious

1. D.L.G. to M.L.G., 21 August 1897 (N.L.W.).

indeed so long as she gets more attention than anybody else, if she is treated like any other ordinary woman she immediately strikes. Fancy Tim allowing her to. . . .[1]

Davies seems, indeed, to have been a very different sort of husband from Dr David Edwards.

In September 1898 there is a particularly nasty flare-up. Lloyd George writes to Margaret that it is all very well to sneer at him for preferring 'Pantycelyn'.

So would anybody. Mrs T. with all her defects – and these I am not blind to – is at least fairly interesting. By the way I hear she is seriously ill. T. just been on the telephone wanting me to go for a drive with him this afternoon. Says Mrs T. rather bad. Has to undergo an operation. What it is I don't know. He had just seen the Doctor and was rather despondent. That will please you I suppose.[2]

Margaret is indignant:

I am surprised you should think I would be pleased to hear of Mrs Tim's illness. I am never pleased to hear of people's misfortune however much I might dislike them. I suppose you were too despondent to sleep after hearing it, that's the state you are in no doubt. I am just as sorry for her as I would be for any other woman I know, I am not like you that I treat her as I would any other person, but to you she is different. You sneer at me when you say she is ill. I can't help it. I wish I could suffer in her place, to relieve all round. . . .[3]

Mrs Tim's illness did not put an end to her, or to her friendship with Lloyd George. But Margaret's decision to spend much more time in London, when the Trinity Road house was acquired at the end of 1899, gave her a chance to defeat her rival – and was doubtless influenced by the desire to do so. For several years her jealousy persists and is reflected in studiously reassuring asides in Lloyd George's letters. 'Tim and I went to a theatre last night and reached Putney after midnight. I am sorry Mrs T. makes him ridiculous by boasting about his prospects of a parliamentary career. She is going about it the right way to destroy his chances.'[4]

1. M.L.G. to D.L.G., dated only 'Sunday' (Earl Lloyd George collection).
2. D.L.G. to M.L.G., 8 September 1898 (N.L.W.).
3. M.L.G. to D.L.G., dated just 'Friday' but obviously an answer to the above (Earl Lloyd George collection).
4. D.L.G. to M.L.G., 19 October 1900 (N.L.W.). The words 'after midnight' are in Welsh in the original.

'Returning from Lewes where I have been having a game of golf with . . .
Tim – no Mrs Tim she has gone to Llandrindod with her kids.'[1] All the
same, Lloyd George did not completely drop Mrs Tim, to please either
Margaret or, later, Frances Stevenson.

Frances Stevenson, however, was more tolerant of his philanderings
than Margaret could ever be. Where Margaret could not help showing her
injured feelings, Frances was able to conceal hers – or perhaps her feelings
were not quite the same. In April 1915 she records: 'In the evening he
[Lloyd George] took Mr and Mrs Timothy Davies out to dinner, she
being downhearted as she had not seen him for a long while. I think he
is very kind and nice to her, and I would not have it otherwise.'[2] And
in February 1916: 'D. managed to find time . . . to go to tea with
Mrs Timothy Davies. He does not go there often, but he says she has
been a good friend to him, and he does not wish to appear to neglect her.
He always tells me when he is going, so I don't mind so much. I don't
care for her so much – she is too pretentious, and I don't think she is very
sincere. However, I don't like to think badly of D.'s friends, as I like to
think that he has good taste!'[3]

Those words help to explain why Margaret, in a sense, lost him, and
why Frances won him. Yet he could never escape from the special
intimacy of his relationship with Margaret, or from the power of her
proud, fastidious spirit.

The Argentine trip did nothing to diminish Lloyd George's zest for
travel. On the contrary, it seems to have stimulated it, because over the
next three years he travelled very extensively. During the Christmas
holiday of 1897–8 he visited Rome with Timothy Davies and D. R.
Daniel. Early in the morning of 22 December 1897, after a night train
journey from Paris, he sent Christmas greetings to the family at Criccieth;[4] and the next day he wrote another letter in the train, which
expresses his passionate response – akin to Vincent van Gogh's – to
Southern sunlight and the Mediterranean scene:

Crossing the Apennines this morning from Turin to Genoa we passed
through vineyards and orchards. But when we left Genoa we forgot

1. D.L.G. to M.L.G., 13 August 1901 (N.L.W.).
2. Frances Stevenson, *Lloyd George: A Diary*, entry for 22 April 1915 (p. 46).
3. *Ibid.*, entry for 9 February 1916 (p. 96). 'Mrs Tim' lived on for a considerable time,
though she appears to have pre-deceased her husband. The author has failed to elicit information on her later years from those who could give it.
4. D.L.G. to M.L.G., 22 December 1897, 8.30 a.m., 'On the frontier, Savoy' (N.L.W.).

all past beauty. The Mediterranean as blue as Wil bach's [Gwilym's] eye – and as sparkling as Llwyd bach's [Olwen's] – as placid as my old Maggie's face. The sun shining brightly. . . . Daniel wanted me to give up writing and look at the surrounding scenery. . . . It is glorious. From Genoa to Spezzia we travelled along the seaboard. The Apennines dip their feet in the Mediterranean. We have 80 tunnels between Genoa and Spezzia. So one moment we fly along passed [*sic*] beautiful villas through gardens and orange groves – with yellow and green fruit growing on them – the blue sea peeping and twinkling through the foliage. The next moment we plunge into the darkness of a tunnel. In less than a minute's time a beautiful deep blue bay bursts into view with white villas hanging on the rocks about it. . . .

You must come this way. I shan't be satisfied until I bring you along.[1]

In Rome, the three Welshmen stayed at the Grand Hotel de Russie et des Iles Britanniques. On the 24th they saw 'the Forum – the Coliseum – the palace of the Caesars and generally the ruins of ancient Rome – the rostrum from which Cicero delivered his great orations – the spot where Caesar was assassinated'. Lloyd George felt that he was 'in a dream'.[2] From Tim Healy he had an introduction to Monsignor Kelly of the Irish College, through whose good offices he and Davies were able, on Christmas Day, to attend mass in the Pope's private chapel at the Vatican. They were 'the only strangers present. The rest were the Pope's immediate retinue.'[3] The Pope was the veteran Leo XIII, author of *Rerum Novarum*, and both he and the occasion appealed to Lloyd George's sense of theatre. Many years later he told Herbert Lewis that it was 'the most impressive service he had ever attended in his life'. Leo was 'a marvellous figure and, although over 90 years of age, his voice was quite strong, and the fervent pleading note in it deeply impressed'.[4] Most of Lloyd George's Nonconformist admirers would have been utterly scandalised if they could have pictured him in such surroundings, and reacting to them as he did.

Davies went down with 'flu – caught, supposedly, in the Vatican – but recovered within a few days. The other two maintained a vigorous routine of sight-seeing (in which they had the assistance of Sir George Trevelyan, whom they chanced to meet in Rome). Lloyd George's letters

1. D.L.G. to M.L.G., 23 December 1897 (N.L.W.). The party had spent the 22nd in Turin and travelled on next day.
2. D.L.G. to M.L.G., 24 December 1897 (N.L.W.).
3. D.L.G. to M.L.G., 25 December 1897 (N.L.W.).
4. Herbert Lewis diary, entry for 22 October 1920 (Herbert Lewis Papers, N.L.W.).

to Margaret, though vivid, are markedly shorter than on previous foreign trips. He was back in London on 2 January, and telling her that Davies had pressed him to go to Putney, but he had declined.[1] A few days later he went to Criccieth for a week or so, but the presents that he had bought in Rome for the family were smashed 'by careless packing'.[2]

In the summer of 1898 he spent a holiday in Scotland, without Margaret. It was a 'driving trip', which he described as 'a trying ordeal for tempers'. 'You are couped [sic] up with three other people for 6 or 7 hours a day – face to face – in a very narrow crib. But never was there a more pleasant party.'[3] It seems to have been organised by Storey, the ex-M.P. for Sunderland, who collapsed with a bilious attack in the Trossachs. There were eight people in all, divided between a dogcart and a landau. One member of the party was a married woman travelling on her own, a Mrs Moore, who poured herself out to Lloyd George, saying that her husband never told her what he was doing. How different from *us*, was Lloyd George's pious reflection in a letter to Margaret.[4] They visited Dunbar (where he was interested in the battlefield), Edinburgh, Bridge of Allan, Kinross, Aberfoyle, the Trossachs, Callandar, Stirling and Haddington. He was impressed by the Wallace monument and the Forth bridge, but did not confine his attention to the 'sights': all the time he kept an appraising eye on his companions. '. . . We are all now in a private sitting room [at the Trossachs Hotel, Loch Katrine]. Some reading – the engaged pair spooning – another couple of whom I fear more will be heard hereafter are out of the room – I suspect not out of the house and in no public room. . . . It is a bad business and the old man is beginning to have an inkling of it. . . .'[5] The group was hardly of a type to inspire Margaret's confidence, and she evidently viewed it with suspicion, because he begins another letter – from the same address – 'My dear suspicious old Maggie'. He then gives further details of life at the Trossachs Hotel.

> Granny Newton accompanied me to the Music Hall. Miss Storey was with Gilchrist – a married man of 45 with 5 grown-up daughters. . . . There is mischief I feel certain. Mrs Blythe is a widow – young, pretty and genial. *Are you scared stiff to hear this, old Maggie? Well, you needn't*

1. D.L.G. to M.L.G., 2 January 1898 (N.L.W.).
2. D.L.G. to M.L.G., 4 January 1898 (N.L.W.).
3. D.L.G. to M.L.G., 4 September 1898 (N.L.W.).
4. D.L.G. to M.L.G., 22 August 1898 (N.L.W.).
5. D.L.G. to M.L.G., 29 August 1898 (N.L.W.).

be. She worships the memory of her dead husband and can think of nothing else. She is not vicious. *She is very religious. I wonder what else you want to know, my darling. I have been gazing at the moon and it has brought great nostalgia to be in my love's arms. I was thinking this afternoon as I sat alone – no, Granny Newton was there. . . . What a pity old Maggie wasn't here. I've said that to myself a thousand times. They all know how fond I am of my Maggie. They see me writing letters when that is difficult. . . . Gilchrist never talks of his wife and children, but I do often.*[1]

This letter is likely to have created more anxiety than it allayed. There was subsequently a misunderstanding when he wrote that Miss Storey and another woman had given him a rug out of their housekeeping allowance, and Margaret misread 'rug' as 'ring'![2]

At the end of the year he left for a cultural cruise in the Mediterranean (organised by Henry Lunn's travel agency). He was accompanied, again, by Timothy Davies, and by another Welsh friend, the Rev. Gwynoro Davies. Gwynoro was a Methodist minister at Barmouth in Merioneth-shire, who was also deeply implicated in Welsh radical politics and Welsh education. He sat on countless committees and was for many years chairman of the Barmouth urban district council. Like D. R. Daniel, he was a friend of Tom Ellis, who had become attached to Lloyd George as well. The party sailed from Marseilles on the s.y. *Argonaut* shortly before Christmas. 'When we got out of the train this morning we stepped into beautiful sunshine and walked underneath cloudless blue skies.'[3] On Christmas night they were nearing Gibraltar. 'We have enjoyed an exceptionally pleasant voyage so far. . . . Amongst the strangers my biggest chum is Miss Hughes (Cambridge). . . . She is Church but a strong Radical. . . . She heard me at Ipswich. I have today attended no end of services on board so that I feel quite good.'[4]

They went ashore at Tangier and the three Welshmen visited the bazaars. 'The Moorish women hid their faces as we passed but I could see their bright black eyes peeping curiously at us. Female curiosity was stronger than their social convention.'[5] When Dr Alex Hill, Master of Downing College, Cambridge, lectured on Tangier in the ship's saloon,

---

1. D.L.G. to M.L.G., undated, but from the Trossachs Hotel, Loch Katrine (N.L.W.). The passages in italics are written in Welsh.
2. The mistake is corrected in D.L.G. to M.L.G., 9 September 1898 (N.L.W.).
3. D.L.G. to M.L.G., 22 December 1898 (N.L.W.).
4. D.L.G. to M.L.G., 25 December 1898 (N.L.W.).
5. D.L.G. to M.L.G., 27 December 1898 (N.L.W.).

Lloyd George was asked to take the chair. The following day most of the passengers landed at Tetuan, but '. . . I had seen quite enough of the Moors and their manners yesterday to last me a lifetime. The horror and inhumanity of the whole thing quite sickened me . . . so we three remained on board and whiled away the time playing quoits and drafts or reading.'[1] At Tunis they saw the ruins of Carthage, which took Lloyd George 'back to the time when as a boy at Llanystumdwy I used to read and re-read the story of the wars of the Carthaginians and the Romans. And how I sympathised with Hannibal and wished him success. . . .'[2]

They reached Malta on the last night of the year, after a stormy passage during which they sailed 'past the bay where Paul was shipwrecked'. Safely in harbour, many of the passengers had settled down to a whist drive, but Lloyd George was sitting apart and writing his letter. 'You know I hate cards so I haven't joined.'[3] From Malta they went on to Naples, where Lloyd George climbed Vesuvius. He asked Margaret to tell the children about the mountain. 'Even as I came down into the smoke room to write the lava stream which has been gradually crawling down ever since 1895 glows in the darkness of the night. . . . T[im Davies] and I went up with Miss Hughes and another old maid – Miss Dobell – who is a schoolmistress in South Wales. . . . I have had a long talk with both as to the education of Mari bach [Mair] . . . they think she should be sent to a girls' school SOON. Had a talk also about Dick but naturally they know less about that.'[4] Another of the lecturers on the trip was Oscar Browning, Fellow of King's and former Eton master – brilliant teacher and fashionable radical – who later claimed to have predicted that Lloyd George would become Prime Minister.[5]

As the 1899 session of Parliament was drawing to a close Lloyd George's first idea was to go to the Continent with Dalziel for his summer holiday. But he changed his mind (partly because he and Dalziel had 'rather fallen out'[6]) and instead decided to go much further afield – to Canada. His principal companion on this important trip was Llewelyn Williams. 'Llew' (as his friends called him) was a fairly rich young man, with an

1. D.L.G. to M.L.G., 28 December 1898 (N.L.W.).
2. D.L.G. to M.L.G., undated (N.L.W.).
3. D.L.G. to M.L.G., 3 January 1899 (N.L.W.).
4. D.L.G. to M.L.G., 6 January 1899 (N.L.W.).
5. W. Watkin Davies, op. cit., pp. 197–8.
6. D.L.G. to M.L.G., 26 July 1899 (N.L.W.). Lloyd George seems to have disliked the woman with whom Dalziel was currently going around, and also to have felt that his 'sudden access of wealth [had] become a curse to him'.

Oxford history degree, who had made his name as a journalist in London. Recently, however, he had been called to the Bar and had embarked on a second career in which he was to prove equally successful. He was a strong supporter of *Cymru Fydd*, but in other respects a Liberal of the old-fashioned sort, whose friendship for Lloyd George turned to bitter enmity during the First World War. He sat in Parliament for the Carmarthen Boroughs from 1906 to 1918 (when the seat was abolished), and in 1921 was defeated by a Coalition candidate at a bye-election in Cardiganshire, which aroused an exceptional degree of acrimony.

Two others travelled with Lloyd George to Canada – William Griffith, the Canadian Government's Agent in Wales, and W. J. Rees, a prominent Welsh Tory. The trip was suggested and paid for by the Canadian Government, in the hope that the visitors would be so impressed by the splendid prospects that Canada had to offer that they would act, on their return, as evangelists for emigration. Shortly before they left Griffith wrote to Clifford Sifton, Canadian Minister of the Interior (and sent a copy of the letter, for information, to the Prime Minister, Sir Wilfrid Laurier):

> . . . It would be difficult to select a more influential Delegation. Mr Lloyd George M.P. is the leading Welshman of today – admittedly the [best?] orator and readiest debater in the House of Commons – and there is little doubt that he will be a member of the next Liberal Government. Mr Llewellyn [*sic*] Williams, Barrister, ex-newspaper Editor, author and public man is also very desirable from our point of view. . . . In Welsh circles it is understood that upon the retirement of Mr Abel Thomas, Q.C., M.P. which is shortly expected Mr Ll. Williams will succeed that gentleman in his Parliamentary seat. Mr Williams also acted on behalf of the farmers of Carmarthenshire before the Parliamentary Commission on the Welsh Land Question. This gentleman's writings are at the moment commanding eulogistic comment from the critical literary journals of London. . . . Mr W. J. Rees, ex-Mayor of Swansea, Newspaper Director, foremost land valuator in Wales, agent of Sir Jno Llewellyn, who is much consulted by farmers as to the future of their sons &c. – is a Tory and an English Churchman, a man of the highest influence and of great wealth, he represents his interests with all the grace and dignity of his class, and he will be particularly acceptable to Canadians. . . .[1]

1. William Griffith to Hon. Clifford Sifton, 18 August 1899: copy sent to Sir Wilfrid Laurier, 19 August (Laurier Papers, Public Archives of Canada). Griffith's confidence that Lloyd George would be a member of the next Liberal Government is worth noting.

The party was seen off from Liverpool on 24 August by Herbert Lewis and several members of the local Welsh colony. They were travelling on the s.s. *Bavarian* and at first, because of their late booking, were installed in a cabin for four; but, when Lloyd George made an 'awful row' about this, he and Williams (and presumably the others as well) were each given 'a deck cabin – first rate'.[1] They reached Montreal on 2 September (a Saturday) and early the following week were in Ottawa, where they had a meeting with Sifton. After a brief visit to Toronto they then travelled out West. At Winnipeg they were 'taken in hand' by a Mr Speers of the Immigration Department, who was to serve as their guide while they investigated the possibility of 'settling 500 Welshmen in the North-west'.[2] From the Hotel Leland, Winnipeg, Lloyd George wrote to Margaret: 'Arrived here after two days and two nights in a railway train. It was luxurious travelling and I enjoyed it immensely. Most of the time we passed through dense forest – fancy a forest that it took the best part of two days to get through travelling at the rate of 30 to 40 miles an hour. I saw an Indian and a squaw paddling their canoe along one of the forest rivers.' There were occasional clearings, with small hamlets of log cabins, in one of which he 'saw a number of children dancing and prancing out of a timber schoolroom . . . full of delight at their temporary emancipation'. These reminded him of his own children.[3] He told her that he would not be 'anywhere within reach of civilisation for another 6 days'.[4]

A week later he wrote, from Regina, a long letter describing his experience of the prairie:

> . . . It is stupendous. There seems to be no end to it. Now and again we came to a fairly settled part . . . with a farm dotted here and there. Then we drove into country into which plough has never entered. Their method of locomotion here is generally by buggies and what is known as democrats – buggies on a larger scale. We had the latter. They are very light but with strong springs – a very necessary precaution. Roads there were none – trails was the best we could hope for – mere tracks made across the prairie by Indian waggons and perhaps also by parties such as ours. . . . One evening after sunset our track came to an end and Llew[elyn Williams] and I had to leave the

1. D.L.G. to M.L.G., 24 August 1899, and 'Thursday night' (N.L.W.).
2. *Winnipeg Free Press*, 8 September 1899.
3. D.L.G. to M.L.G., 7 September 1899 (N.L.W.).   4. *Loc. cit.*

democrat in order to feel in the dark for another trail. At last we got it and in another hour we drove straight into a small prairie hamlet of half a dozen houses and we put up at the hotel. Hotel indeed! Imagine a log or rather a lumber barn – a hut built say out of railway sleepers. Inside a table and four rough chairs. Upstairs poky little rooms – no washstand – no anything but a gwely gwellt [straw pallet], forming the only densely populated spot in the whole country. I couldn't sleep so lit up and read until the morning came. The lamp had also the incidental advantage of forcing the fierce and aggressive inhabitants of my straw pallet to retire into their fastnesses and at any rate to leave my face unmolested. [The following night they slept at a farmhouse] two a bed. These were clean but Llew was bad – the food at the prairie hotel having upset him. He became quite feverish . . . and my slumbers here were consequently somewhat broken. . . . I forgot to tell you that I insisted on bringing out a 'broncho' with us to ride occasionally on the plains . . . the ride was perfectly delightful – canter and gallop. Llew would have nothing to do with him . . . but when he saw how I was enjoying myself . . . he wanted a turn and as I overdid it first day – riding 4 hours until I was so sore that I could hardly sit down – I was only too glad to give Llew room for repentance. . . . The loveliest part of our trip was the drive across the moose mountains. Timber lakes black with wild duck . . . the trees now beginning to don their autumn garments of gold and precious stones. . . . We spent another night at a small 'hotel' on the shores of a mountain lake . . . our straw pallets were clean and the food was wholesome – fried eggs – wheat cakes – stewed berries from the woods – a jelly made out of a little hardy cherry which tastes like a sloe – and tea to wash it down with. Excellent cream. One day a huge wolf started out of . . . a clump of stunted trees . . . and scampered right away across our path. . . . But tell the little pets that I'll reserve my prairie stories until I return. . . . Tonight we go on to Banff. . . .[1]

At Banff they were met by a carriage and pair and by two policemen in uniform, the Police Commissioner of the North-West Territory having sent word of their arrival. At the Hot Springs Hotel they were able to have sulphur baths, and Llewelyn Williams and Griffith played billiards after dinner, while Lloyd George wrote his letters home. The scenery of the Rocky Mountains entranced him. 'It is Alpine in its

1. D.L.G. to M.L.G., 14 September 1899 (N.L.W.).

magnificence with this point in its favour that the foliage is much more variegated than in the Swiss valleys and the colours are therefore much finer'.[1] The pristine quality of the country made a strong appeal to him, whereas in the mind of Rupert Brooke, fourteen years later, it created a deep uneasiness.

> The maple and the birch conceal no dryads, and Pan has never been heard amongst these reed-beds. Look as long as you like upon a cataract of the New World, you shall not see a white arm in the foam. A godless place. And the dead do not return. . . . There walk, as yet, no ghosts of lovers in Canadian lanes. This is the essence of the grey freshness and brisk melancholy of this land. And . . . it is the secret of a European's discontent. For it is possible, at a pinch, to do without gods. But one misses the dead.[2]

Lloyd George's reaction was different. While he could and did respond to the magic of a great historic site (the Roman forum, for instance) he was insensitive to the vaguely numinous atmosphere of 'old' countries, and positively disliked the atmosphere of old houses.[3] In his make-up there was more of the adventurer and pioneer than of the traditionalist, and he could do without ghosts as cheerfully as he could do without gods. This was his strength – though also, in a sense, his weakness.

After a brief visit to Vancouver the Welshmen made a quick return journey across Canada, spurred by news from England. They were at Winnipeg again on 27 September, whence they left for Ottawa. On 4 October they sailed from Montreal, again on the *Bavarian*. It had been a valuable experience for Lloyd George, though as usual he was an absent-minded traveller, leaving things behind him at almost every stop. 'I left three pairs of breeches at the Hotel at Montreal – I placed them under the mattress to keep them straight and forgot all about them. I left my new grey overcoat in the train. I lost my amber cigar holder – no idea where and now my P & O trunk is wandering about somewhere.' So he

---

1. D.L.G. to M.L.G., 14 September 1899 (N.L.W.). Either this or the previous letter must have been mis-dated. From other evidence it would seem the date should be 16 September.
2. Rupert Brooke, description of the Canadian Rockies, first published in *Letters from America*, edited by Edward Marsh (1916); republished in *The Prose of Rupert Brooke*, edited by Christopher Hassall (1956).
3. 'His spirit resented the atmosphere of preceding generations which seemed to cramp and encroach upon the essential independence of his nature which refused to be contained. It was something instinctive and innate and primeval which made him recoil from anything resembling the shackles of the past.' (Frances Lloyd George, *The Years that Are Past*, p. 183.)

wrote from Banff on the way out, and how many of the missing items he was able to recover before returning to England we do not know. What is certain is that he took away from Canada an impression of its huge size and emptiness, of its limitless potential, and of the strength of a free people's attachment to the British Crown.

TEN
Imperialist with a Difference

As Lloyd George was making his way towards the far west of Canada, at another extremity of the Empire the last steps were being taken towards a famous and fateful conflict. On 7 September he wrote from Winnipeg: 'One can't get an idea from the telegraphic news in the Canadian papers as to how things are going about the Transvaal.'[1] But on 18 September, from Vancouver: 'The news from the Transvaal threatens to alter my arrangements. War means the summoning of Parliament, and the former seems now inevitable. The prospect oppresses me with a deep sense of horror. If I have the courage I shall protest with all the vehemence at my command against the outrage which is perpetrated in the name of freedom.'[2]

What was the outrage in question? The Cape of Good Hope, colonised by the Dutch in the seventeenth century, became a British colony after the Napoleonic wars; and a few years later another British colony was established in Natal. The Dutch settlers (Boers) found British rule at the Cape irksome, more especially after the abolition of slavery in 1833, and many of them trekked northwards to establish two new States which were virtually independent – the Orange Free State and the Transvaal. Schemes for federating the British and Dutch territories came to nothing, and in 1880 the Boers claimed absolute independence. A force sent against them

1. D.L.G. to M.L.G., 7 September 1899 (N.L.W.).
2. David Lloyd George to William George, 18 September 1899, quoted in *My Brother and I* (p. 177). At a meeting at the Guild Hall, Caernarvon, on 6 October, the message was read out by the chairman, but with the wording slightly altered: 'The prospect oppresses *us with sorrow*, and I shall protest with all the vehemence *I can* command against *this blackguardish action* which is perpetrated in the name of human freedom.' (Author's italics.)

was destroyed on Majuba Hill, and in the 1884 Convention of London the second Gladstone Government appeared to relinquish the British claim to suzerainty, retaining only the control of external relations.

Meanwhile the discovery of vast mineral wealth had given the South African problem a new dimension. To secure the diamonds of Kimberley Britain annexed the territory east of the Orange Free State, known as Griqualand West; and the diamond king, Cecil Rhodes – a young man of genius to whom Anglo-Saxon Imperialism was a religion – gradually extended that power, through the medium of a chartered company, over the wide area north of the Transvaal which still bears his name. In 1886 gold was discovered in the Transvaal, on the Witwatersrand, and within a decade a community of foreigners (Uitlanders) had sprung up there, equal in number to the Transvaal Boers, who thus saw their isolation and Biblical way of life threatened. Paul Kruger – sly, autocratic and deeply conservative – became president of the Transvaal Republic and resisted the demand of the Uitlanders – who provided nine-tenths of the revenue of his State – for political rights, the granting of which would have been bound to undermine his own power, if not to corrupt his nation.

In December 1895 an attempt was made to solve the problem by a revolutionary stroke. Rhodes, at the time Prime Minister of the Cape as well as chairman of the Chartered Company, sought to engineer an uprising of the Uitlanders at Johannesburg, who might at a suitable moment be joined by a flying column of the company's police under his close friend, Dr Jameson. Chamberlain, the new Colonial Secretary, was well aware of the plan and would have given it his blessing if it had succeeded. It was, however, a calamitous failure. Jameson moved too soon and had to be disowned, while the Uitlanders, who had talked very freely (too freely) of the impending rebellion, proved unable, when the time came, to go through with it. The net result was a humiliation for Britain even worse than that of Majuba.

Rhodes immediately fell, and the confidence which he had done much to promote between Britons and Boers in Cape Colony was shattered. Foreign Powers were delighted – the Kaiser, in particular, sending a telegram of congratulations to Kruger. At home, a Parliamentary inquiry into the Raid was scandalously rigged and only served to intensify anti-British feelings abroad. Chamberlain was completely whitewashed and Rhodes, though censured for the plot, was left in undisturbed control of the Chartered Company which, in turn, lost none of its privileges. The Boers naturally assumed that it was only a matter of time before another attempt was made to subjugate them. They started to arm themselves to the teeth and in 1897 the two republics signed a convention of 'perpetual alliance'. In the same year Chamberlain sent a new High Commissioner to South Africa, a man of strong faith and unbending will – Sir Alfred Milner.

Like Chamberlain, Milner was a man of the Left whom circumstances later forced into association with the Tory Party. His first job was on the radical *Pall Mall Gazette*, and before joining the Civil Service he stood as a Liberal candidate. As Chairman of the Board of Inland Revenue, he was the chief influence behind Harcourt's scheme of death duties. His friends included several leading Liberals, including Asquith[1] and Haldane, but in many ways he had less mental kinship with bourgeois democrats of their type than with Fabian Imperialists such as the Webbs.[2] He was not indeed a democrat at all, but a despot and an ideologue, who could be enlightened, yet also at times dangerously limited. He arrived in South Africa with a fixed determination to reassert British suzerainty over the Boer republics, and with an obstinacy more than equal to Kruger's. Between two such men compromise was impossible, and after 1897 only a miracle could have averted the war for which both sides were preparing.

In the late spring and summer of 1899 the principals met twice, at Bloemfontein and Pretoria. On the first occasion Milner demanded enfranchisement for the Uitlanders on terms which Kruger rejected. At the second conference Kruger appeared to accept Milner's franchise demands, but insisted that Britain should renounce all claim to suzerainty over his republic's internal affairs, and that future disputes should be referred to arbitration. Milner would not abandon the suzerainty claim, and on 26 August Chamberlain made a hectoring speech at Birmingham, in which he said that Milner's demands were moderate – some might say too moderate – and that the sands were running out. Next day he sent a note to the Transvaal Government in which an even harder line was taken than Milner's at Bloemfontein. Kruger then withdrew his proposals and on 9 October issued an ultimatum which no British Government could have accepted. Two days later the British Empire was at war with the Boer republics.

1. In spite of Milner's being a rejected suitor of Margot Tennant whom Asquith married, as his second wife, in 1894. Milner, like Asquith, was a Balliol man.
2. As a concept, the Webbs' '*élite* of unassuming experts' bears an obvious affinity to the Milner Kindergarten.

During the long sequence of events which culminated in the outbreak of war the Liberal Opposition's attitude towards the South African problem was uncertain and equivocal. It was not only that some of the party's leaders were out-and-out Imperialists: even among those who belonged to the Gladstonian tradition there were mixed feelings. Harcourt, for instance, admitted the need for internal reform in the Transvaal. He was also attached to Chamberlain personally, and this made him ineffective on the Parliamentary inquiry into the Jameson Raid. When Milner came on the scene, he too (as we know) had his friends and admirers among the Liberal leadership. Kruger, in any case, was not a man who could easily be built up as a Liberal hero. Finally, Cecil Rhodes was a subscriber to Liberal Party funds, and some of the younger Liberals, including Tom Ellis, were enthralled by his ideas.

Until war was imminent Lloyd George took little interest in South Africa. It was not one of his subjects. The Jameson Raid moved him to ridicule rather than indignation. 'In South Africa, a small republic, with an army the size of that of an ordinary German principality, has been able to defy the power of Great Britain.'[1] Chamberlain's discomfiture amused him: 'The Govt have had a snub from old Kruger the Boer and Chamberlain has met his first reverse as a Minister.'[2] But he did not make a serious issue of it. In 1897 he seems to have thought of visiting South Africa, but the plan – if it was a plan – lapsed.[3] He did not serve on the Committee of Inquiry into the Raid: had he done so, he might have become more concerned about British policy in South Africa and would probably have joined Labouchere in recording a dissentient opinion. In a general way, he denounced Chamberlain's brand of Imperialism. 'Some people talk as if they have the British Empire in their back yard. They put up the notice: "No admittance except on business", and set up Chamberlain there and say: "Beware of the dog". Let him bark! . . . If there is one thing that the Liberals want, it is a man on the Front Bench to unmask the pretensions of this electro-plated Rome, its peddling imperialism, and its tin Caesar.'[4] In another attack on Chamberlain, at the end of 1898, he specifically referred to the Transvaal, but only as one place among a number where Chamberlain's methods were having a bad effect.[5] It

1. Speech at Penarth, 28 November 1896.
2. D.L.G. to M.L.G., 14 February 1896 (N.L.W.).
3. 'Mr Lloyd George proposes to take a voyage to South Africa, for the benefit of his health, after his recent efforts in the House of Commons.' (Report in the *Caernarvon Herald*, 2 April 1897.)
4. Speech at Cardiff, 4 February 1898.   5. Speech at Swansea, 14 December 1898.

could not be said that he anticipated the crisis of the following year, and the news that reached him in Canada obviously came as a surprise.

Why did he react so vehemently, committing himself in advance, and from a great distance, to total opposition to the war? His motives need to be analysed with some care, because they have been much misunderstood. The key to his message from Vancouver, expressing deep horror, is surely that he had become convinced – by what precise piece of evidence we do not know – that war was being deliberately provoked in South Africa. This, to him, was the basic outrage. For all his pugnacity, and for all his interest in the history of war, he regarded war itself as a terrible calamity, which statesmen should never enter into 'unadvisedly, lightly or wantonly', but 'discreetly, advisedly, soberly' (like marriage, according to the Book of Common Prayer). If he was never a pacifist, he was also never a warmonger. He had none of the romantic illusions about war which many British civilians were able to cherish until the mass slaughter of 1914–18. Whereas the prevailing opinion on both sides was that the issue in South Africa would be decided quickly, one way or the other, he predicted from the first that the struggle would be long and costly. He knew, moreover, that it would be a setback to the cause of social reform. Every lyddite shell exploding on the African hills was, as he vividly put it, carrying away an old age pension.[1]

Thus his primary objection to the war was that it was unnecessary and wasteful, but he was also strongly influenced, of course, by the fact that the Boers were a small pastoral community, like Wales before the Industrial Revolution. His sympathies were with them, as later with the Belgians, because he was angered by the spectacle of a mighty empire riding roughshod over small nations, and because the David-and-Goliath motif could never fail to appeal to his imagination. To that extent he was a pro-Boer, and in one of his last letters to Margaret from Canada he said that he hoped the English would 'get a black eye', though he warned her not to make the sentiment public.[2] His emotional response to the Boers' courage – if not to Kruger's political and religious outlook, which he certainly did not share – was combined with a rational belief that they would be very hard to beat. As a boy he had read Motley's history of the Dutch republic, and it seemed to him more than likely that

1. Speech at Carmarthen, 27 November 1899.
2. 'Hope you judiciously selected your extracts of my views on the Transvaal for the press. They were not intended for publication but I don't object so long as my hopes that the English will get a black eye are omitted. I am still at boiling point. . . . It is wicked.' (D.L.G. to M.L.G., from Winnipeg, 27 September 1899, N.L.W.)

the descendants of those who had successfully resisted the power of Spain would give an equally good account of themselves in resistance to the power of Britain.

While he respected the Boers, he had nothing but contempt for the Uitlanders, and this was due, unfortunately, in large part to anti-Semitism. One of the more striking ironies of his life is that he, who made possible the Jewish nation's return to Palestine, and some of whose best friends were, later, Jews, should have had a distinct, even a venomous, prejudice against Jewry. 'The people we are fighting for, those Uitlanders, are German Jews – 15,000 to 20,000 of them. . . . Pah! fighting for men of that type!' Most of them, he said, ran away when the trouble started.[1] He shared the popular Gentile belief that the Jews were natural cowards. In 1916 he said of Edwin Montagu, who succeeded him as Minister of Munitions, that he 'sought cover as was the manner of his race, grew hollow-cheeked under the strain'.[2] As well as being prejudiced against them on ethnic grounds, Lloyd George may have had another, but subconscious, ground for resentment against the Uitlanders. They were, after all, men who had struck lucky with gold, and to one of the promoters of the Welsh Patagonian Gold Mining Syndicate their prosperity must have been galling.

In his stand against an Imperialistic war – undertaken, as he saw it, for vainglorious reasons, without regard to Britain's vital interests, and from which only sinister, alien, commercial elements could hope to benefit – Lloyd George was not opposing the British Empire as such. He was an Imperialist himself, but with a difference. The argument between him and Chamberlain was not between a Little Englander and an Imperialist, but between two men whose judgements differed on what was best for the Empire. Chamberlain stood for · the maximum integration and consolidation, Lloyd George for the maximum variety and local autonomy. His formula for the Empire, as for the United Kingdom, was responsible self-government in all matters not strictly relevant to maintaining effective central power: in other words, Home Rule all Round. As for the Boers, both in Cape Colony and in the republics, he thought that their allegiance to the Empire might be won by conciliation, not by coercion. He believed that freedom could hold the Empire together,

1. Speech at Carmarthen, 27 November 1899.
2. *The Political Diaries of C. P. Scott, 1911–1928*, edited by Trevor Wilson, p. 239. Incidentally, Lloyd George's anti-Semitism did not prevent his being a Dreyfusard, presumably because, when the choice was between supporting a Jew and supporting the traditional French officer class – aristocratic and Roman Catholic – he was obliged to prefer the former.

but that force never could, and no doubt he was strengthened in that belief by what he had seen in Canada. Yet he cared for Imperial unity just as much as Chamberlain did, and he also shared Chamberlain's relative unconcern for the interests of all those subjects of the Crown, in South Africa and elsewhere, whose skins were not white.

Writing from Toronto, on his return journey, Lloyd George summarised the Government's dilemma: 'If they go on the war will be so costly – blood and treasure – as to sicken the land. If they withdraw they will be laughed out of power.'[1] As he expected, they did not withdraw and by the time he got back to England the war had begun.[2]

Parliament was recalled on 17 October, 'to deal' (in the words of the Queen's Speech) 'with an exceptional exigency'. The purpose of the session was to enable the Reserve to be called up, and to vote supplies. Lloyd George would have preferred not to have to speak so soon after returning from Canada, and before he had had time to brief himself thoroughly, as was his habit. Yet he knew that he should not remain silent, and on the 27th he intervened at the end of the Third Reading debate on the Consolidated Fund (Appropriation) Bill. With unerring flair, he put his finger on one of the weakest spots in the Government's position. Since the true reason for going to war – to establish British supremacy in South Africa – had only the flimsiest legal justification, and no moral justification, the Government was laying most emphasis upon its moral duty to secure democratic rights for the Uitlanders. This, however, involved it in logical absurdities such as Lloyd George was particularly good at exposing. He asked whether those who supported

1. D.L.G. to M.L.G., from the Queen's Hotel, Toronto, 2 October 1899 (N.L.W.).
2. According to a report in the *North Wales Observer* (27 October 1899), Lloyd George returned without a moustache. This may be the origin of Richard Lloyd George's story of the shaved-off moustache (*see* above, pp. 192–3). He may have been confusing the Argentinian trip with the Canadian. The *North Wales Observer* stated that 'his friends in the House failed at first to recognise him. . . . However, his shining eyes and characteristic gait soon revealed his identity, even to those who did not hear his unmistakable voice. To cut off a moustache requires courage, but Mr George received the banter of his friends with smiles.'

A. J. Sylvester is probably referring to the same occasion when he says that once, when Lloyd George was abroad, he decided to grow a beard, but decided it did not improve his appearance, so shaved off the beard, and, along with it, his moustache. 'Shaving off his moustache was a bigger mistake than allowing the beard to grow. . . . With the moustache gone, so altered was he in appearance that when he entered the House of Commons cleanshaven, the constable on the Members' Entrace door challenged him, and the Speaker failed to recognise him when he rose to address the House. There were no more experiments.' (A. J. Sylvester, *The Real Lloyd George*, p. 14.)

the war realised that within seven years every Uitlander would have had the right to vote for two Chambers. And when Chamberlain interrupted him to say that Kruger's franchise offer 'was accompanied by a whole cloud of difficulties – registration qualification and so on', Lloyd George rejoined:

> I have some experience of registration, and the condition of things in this country is a good deal worse than . . . in the Transvaal. . . . In this country it takes three years before a man can get a vote; and I know of a case where an alien resident in this country for very many years never has become an elector because he cannot pay naturalisation fees. We have two Chambers in this country, but a man, although he may be a permanent resident, cannot get a vote for one Chamber; while for the other if he lives for ever he will never get a vote.[1]

Lloyd George's speech was the last of the debate and the last of the session. After it, the Bill was read a third time and Parliament prorogued.

A month later, at Carmarthen, he made his first comprehensive attack on the war. He reminded his audience that the country had been practically unanimous for the Crimean War, against which John Bright protested. But that war was now regretted. He compared the casualties in individual battles with the numbers lost in colliery disasters – a skilful device to enable the audience to feel more intimately what the cold figures meant. He did not say that under no conditions should they fight, but he did say that the case for fighting had to be overwhelming. There was no justification for this war, which had been deliberately provoked just as Napoleon provoked us by sending his Grand Army to Boulogne. They were now fighting 'a little country, the total of whose population was less than Carmarthenshire – the British Empire against Carmarthenshire!'[2] On New Year's Day 1900, at a concert in Criccieth, he began his speech: 'I was in Carthage a short time ago, and saw the place where it had been. No trace of it was left – no sign. This people had become great in their day and afterwards went forth, as they thought, to conquer the world. They were defeated.' The same could be said of Rome, which he had also visited. He hoped that the Welsh people would not commit the same error[3] – sentiments which echoed Kipling's *Recessional*.

1. Hansard, Fourth Series, Vol. LXXVII, cols 782–4.
2. Speech at Carmarthen, 27 November 1899 (in which he also made the remarks, already quoted, about lyddite shells and old age pensions, and about the Uitlanders).
3. Speech at Criccieth, 1 January 1900.

Between Lloyd George's speeches at Carmarthen and Criccieth 'black week' occurred, when news came through of a series of defeats sustained by the British forces under the inept command of Sir Redvers Buller. The overall military situation was, in fact, less disastrous than it seemed, because the British had merely committed gross tactical blunders, whereas the Boers – by invading Natal rather than Cape Colony, and by wasting much of their effective strength in operations against the beleaguered garrisons of Mafeking, Kimberley and Ladysmith – had committed a fundamental error of strategy. Yet to a public which was expecting the campaign to be a walkover, the news of British defeats was stunning. To reassure the public, and to reverse the military tide, the Government appointed Britain's two most illustrious soldiers – the veteran Lord Roberts as commander-in-chief, and Lord Kitchener, the victor of Omdurman, as his chief of staff. Roberts swiftly grasped the need for more mounted troops, and for a drastic reorganisation of the transport system. Within two months of his arrival the British were advancing, Kimberley and Ladysmith were relieved, and a large Boer force had surrendered at Paardeberg. In mid-March he entered Bloemfontein, capital of the Orange Free State; in May Johannesburg fell and Mafeking was relieved; in June Pretoria, capital of the Transvaal, surrendered. By the end of the summer Roberts had won the war so far as it was possible to win it. The Boer republics had been annexed and Kruger had fled to Europe, where he was given a cool reception by Continental rulers who, much as they disliked and resented Britain, had little interest in an apparent loser. In Britain, the public mood had swung from the shock and dejection of 'black week' to the mindless euphoria of Mafeking night.

Throughout this period Lloyd George maintained his political opposition to the war, unaffected by the course of military operations. Very wisely, he concentrated upon the policy of the war, rather than upon its conduct: the Colonial Office, not the War Office, was his target. Of course, he felt secret *Schadenfreude* at the initial British reverses, and was well aware that British victories would make the going even harder for him.[1] But in public he defended himself against the charge that he was the enemy of Britain's fighting men, and he hit upon a clever means of doing so when he pointed out that regular soldiers from the home country

1. On 3 November 1899, he said in a letter to Margaret: 'Our losses on Monday were great and *I fear* the Boers must have lost heavily.' (N.L.W.) And on 26 May 1900, to his brother: 'Roberts crossed the Vaal on the Queen's Birthday. No Boers met anywhere. Brave Boers – *I feared* they might be caught between Bobs and the river.' (*My Brother and I*, p. 181. Author's italics.)

were paid only 1s 3d a day, compared with the 5s a day paid to Colonial volunteers. He expressed admiration for the performance of British troops, more especially of the Welsh contingents, while at the same time deploring the waste of good British lives in a rotten cause. From this standpoint he could claim to be the soldiers' friend.

Before Parliament reassembled after the Christmas holiday he addressed the Palmerston Club at Balliol College, Oxford.

It is true [he said] that at the end of this war we shall miss millions from our coffers. We shall lose much of that deference which has always been paid to the masters of many successful legions. We shall miss many a gallant name from the roll-call of our warriors. But there is something infinitely more precious . . . that we shall miss, and that is the distinction of being the hope and shield of the weak and the oppressed in all lands, which was once the brightest gem in Britain's glory. No Liberal would have bartered that for all the gold in the Rand.

He reviewed the pseudo-virtuous pretexts on which the war was being fought, including the claim that it was being fought on behalf of the 'natives'.

Here, I will admit, if it were true, there might be a great service rendered to humanity. There might be something magnanimous in a great Empire like ours imperilling its prestige and squandering its resources to defend the poor, helpless black. Unhappily, here again is a fiction. The Kaffir workmen of the Rand are better treated and have better wages and more freedom under the dominion of the 'tyrant' Kruger than they enjoy at Kimberley and in Matabeleland, where the British flag waves under the benignant patronage of Mr Cecil Rhodes.[1]

It was a telling point, but on the racial issue Lloyd George was, unfortunately, no less hypocritical than the Government. He gave very little thought to the Africans – or to the Indians in South Africa, whose leader, the young M. K. Gandhi, was supporting the British war effort. To Lloyd George, the war was a contest between British top dog and Boer underdog, whereas in fact it was between two white top dogs, vying for hegemony in a country where the real underdogs were black and brown.

On 6 February 1900, in the debate on the Address, he made a speech which prompted Harcourt to compare him with Grattan. Referring

1. 27 January 1900.

to the charge of 'intolerable oppression' in the Transvaal, he asked how many British workmen realised that the wages of Transvaal miners were four times as high as their own, and that an eight-hour day was enforced by law in the Transvaal. How many knew that mining royalties, which were fifty per cent under British rule in Rhodesia, were only one-half per cent under the Transvaal Government? While disputing the argument that Kruger had made no concessions, he pointed out that a more liberal regime than Kruger's would almost certainly have been elected but for the effect upon Boer opinion of the Jameson Raid. It was our own fault that we had Kruger to deal with; yet even Kruger had come quite a long way to meet us. Lloyd George ended with a fierce denunciation of the Uitlanders.

> I should have thought that [their] greatest pride . . . would have been to take part in this conflict and fight for their supposed rights. But how many have availed themselves of the privilege? They prefer to lounge about the hotels of Cape Town while English homes are being made desolate on their behalf. Seven thousand of the Uitlanders are fighting for their intolerable oppressors. How many are fighting for their rights? Barely a battalion out of the whole 80,000, and the remainder are living in security, grumbling about their losses, and without turning a thought to those who are suffering in the war . . . such men and their grievances are not worth a drop of British blood.[1]

With the news of Roberts's victories, Lloyd George's anti-war line became increasingly unpopular. Even in Wales he represented the minority view. Most Welshmen, especially in the first year of the war, supported it no less enthusiastically than the English or the Scots. Among the politicians there were curious realignments. Thus, while it was natural enough that Herbert Lewis and Frank Edwards should go with Lloyd George, it was surprising to find him joined, in opposition to the war, by Bryn Roberts, who was his implacable opponent on Welsh Home Rule. Lloyd George's view of the war was also shared by Humphreys-Owen, a very 'conservative' Liberal on the subject of Welsh

---

1. Hansard, Fourth Series, Vol. LXXVIII, cols 758–67. Lloyd George was speaking to an amendment moved by a Liberal M.P., Lord Edmond Fitzmaurice, regretting 'the want of knowledge, foresight and judgement displayed by Your Majesty's advisers, alike in their conduct of South African affairs since 1895 and in their preparations for the war now proceeding'. The amendment was, of course, defeated, but Campbell-Bannerman voted for it. Balfour, who wound up the debate, made no attempt to answer Lloyd George's speech.

nationalism. On the other hand, Beriah Gwynfe Evans, the secretary of *Cymru Fydd*, was strongly pro-war, and so was Ellis Griffith, another keen nationalist. Opinion was divided in the Caernarvon Boroughs, as elsewhere, and for a time Lloyd George's tenure seemed more than doubtful. At Criccieth itself he was burnt in effigy, along with his brother and Uncle Lloyd. When he spoke at Bangor, on 4 April 1900, he was interrupted throughout his speech, and after the meeting, as he was walking away, was struck over the head with a bludgeon. Fortunately, his hat took the impact of the blow and, though stunned, he was able to take refuge in a café, guarded by the police.

It was obvious that the Government would hold an early election, to take advantage of the favourable turn in the war, and of public enthusiasm for it: obvious, too, that Lloyd George would have difficulty in holding the Boroughs. Lloyd George knew that he would need to draw heavily on his credit as a constituency Member, and throughout the session of 1900 was at pains to add to that credit. As well as speaking repeatedly on the war, he intervened on any matter which had a local bearing. Thus, when the election came, he was able to boast that he had saved the ratepayers of Caernarvon £18,000 (by forcing the Local Government Board to pay for a water scheme); that he had preserved Conway's dignity (by scotching a plan to move police headquarters from there to Llandudno); that he had helped Pwllheli in a number of ways (most notably by securing Government aid for the establishment of a harbour of refuge there); and that he had obtained for Nevin the prospect of doing well as a tourist centre (by winning approval for a light railway to the town).[1] In July he complained that Wales had no representative on the Public Works Loans Commission, and did it so persuasively that soon afterwards he was appointed a Commissioner himself.[2]

Meanwhile it was not only at Bangor that he experienced a violent reaction to his unpopular views on the war. He had earlier faced a rowdy meeting at Glasgow,[3] and on 5 July, at Liskeard in Cornwall, a meeting at which he was speaking ended in pandemonium. Forty or fifty young roughs stormed the platform and occupied part of it, while a soldier in

1. 'What has Mr Lloyd George done for his constituents?' (*North Wales Observer*, 28 September 1900.) This anonymous article was clearly inspired by Lloyd George, and the style suggests that he probably wrote it.
2. Speech in debate on Public Works Loans Bill, 11 July 1900 (Hansard, Fourth Series, Vol. LXXXV, cols 1235-7). His appointment to the Commission was reported in the *Caernarvon Herald* on 3 August 1900.
3. 6 March 1900.

khaki was carried shoulder-high from end to end of the hall and ladies in the front seats escaped hurriedly by way of the platform door. Still Lloyd George went on with his speech, until chairs were flying in all directions. Only then did the platform party leave.[1]

Any hesitation that the Government may have felt about going to the country in 1900 must have been overcome when, on 25 July, the Liberal Party split three ways in a division on the Colonial Office vote. A motion to reduce the vote by £100 was supported by thirty-one anti-war Liberals, including Lloyd George, while Campbell-Bannerman and thirty-four others abstained, and forty 'Liberal Imperialists' voted with the Government. The term 'Liberal Imperialist' was applied to Rosebery, Asquith, Grey, Haldane and others, who were broadly in sympathy with the Government's policy in South Africa. It was and is a misleading term, implying that Liberals who opposed the war were anti-Imperialist, which Lloyd George, for one, emphatically was not. He was so anxious to remove the false impression that he even put it around that on all topics other than South Africa he was 'of the school of Lord Rosebery', and that in South Africa he desired the supremacy of British rule as much as anyone, only differing from the Government and its Liberal fellow-travellers in believing that the desired result could have been 'attained by pacific methods'.[2] He also made adroit use of the potentially embarrassing fact that substantial help for the war effort was being provided by the self-governing Colonies. This, he said, merely proved his point. The Colonies were giving unprecedented help to the mother-country precisely because they were more independent than they had ever been. The same freedom should, therefore, be given to the Transvaal and Orange Free State: 'to assert supremacy was the very worst way to achieve it'.[3] Yet for all his protestations the Little Englander and pacifist labels stuck to Lloyd George, bringing him some approbation, and much odium, that he did not deserve.

Just before Parliament rose in early August – nobody doubting that its dissolution was imminent – Lloyd George and Chamberlain were involved in a tingling duel which set the tone for the ensuing election. When Bloemfontein fell to Roberts's army the Orange Free State archives were captured, and in them were discovered a few letters from British

1. The chairman was Arthur Quiller-Couch, the man of letters.
2. From the 'London Letter' of the *Western Mail*, 6 April 1900.
3. Speech at Bangor, 11 April 1900. By the end of the war Canada had contributed (in round figures) 5,800 volunteers to the Imperial forces in South Africa; New Zealand, 6,100; Australia, 15,500.

M.P.s to President Steyn and other Boer leaders. The Colonial Office announced the letters' existence, but with only a vague indication of their contents, and without identifying their authors. Suspicion therefore rested upon every M.P. opposed to the war, and for electoral purposes Chamberlain was well content that they should all be suspected of treasonable correspondence with the enemy. On 8 August he defended his withholding of information on the ground that he had written to the authors of the letters, asking if they were genuine. For all he knew they might be forgeries, and it would be wrong for him to publish them until he was quite sure they were authentic. Meanwhile he could only say that, in his opinion, they were 'not proper letters to have written', but he did 'not wish to exaggerate' their turpitude.[1]

Lloyd George spoke next and 'went for Joe' with a vengeance. The letters had not been published, but their purport had been quoted. 'If giving the actual words used would have been more damaging to the reputation of hon. Gentlemen on this side of the House, I venture to say that the right hon. Gentleman would have done it.' At this, Chamberlain intervened to say that, since rumour had 'greatly exaggerated the purport of the letters', he wished to give their true effect. Lloyd George quickly underlined the admission that he had given the letters' purport. That was what he (Lloyd George) complained of. Real news was censored – even the despatches of generals – but the moment any letter was found which could implicate any critic of the Government, it was released not in its true form, but in an exaggerated form. 'If it has been exaggerated who did the exaggeration? It must have been exaggerated by someone in the Colonial Office.' Chamberlain, he said, had taken very good care to communicate with the authors 'at a time when no reply could possibly be given before the rising of the House'. As a result, all those who opposed the war were being sent to their constituencies under a cloud of suspicion.[2]

Having registered his protest, he struck a retaliatory blow. If he and his friends were to fight the election under a cloud, he would see to it

1. They were eventually published on 23 August, and did not amount to much. As might have been expected, Lloyd George was not among the authors. Labouchere had written: 'Don't for goodness sake let Mr Kruger make his first mistake by refusing this; a little skilful management and he will give Master Joe another fall.' But the rumour of what was in the letters was far more exciting than the reality.

2. He might have added that suspicion would be minimal in his own case, since his constituents knew how reluctant he was to write letters even when there was no risk of their being used as evidence against him.

that Chamberlain did the same. A special committee appointed to examine the placing of War Office contracts had just issued its report, and had shown that 'a certain firm which had sent in the highest tender was told that if they reduced their tender a large order would be given to them'. This firm had been 'practically made by the War Office'. The House was entitled to ask, would the recommendations of the committee be carried out 'ruthlessly'? At the moment, Members could only proceed by innuendo.

Chamberlain: Hear, hear! By innuendo.
Lloyd George: They were taking a lead from the right hon. Gentleman, who insinuated treason, insinuated impropriety of language, and, above all, insinuated that he treated hon. Members in a gentlemanly manner by offering them an opportunity of which they could not avail themselves.

Lloyd George's short, deadly speech ended with the comment that a Government so anxious to purify the administration of the Transvaal should endeavour to do the same at home.

Chamberlain was allowed to reply, and he took it for granted that Lloyd George's innuendo was 'perfectly well understood by the House'. The firm in question was Kynoch's, of which his brother, Arthur Chamberlain, was chairman. He had not seen the committee's report, so would say nothing about its contents. But he could say that he had 'no interest, direct or indirect, in Kynoch's or in any other firm manufacturing ammunition or war materials'. He had never spoken to anybody in the War Office about contracts, nor had he ever discussed them with his brother. 'I have nothing whatever to do with his private concerns, any more than he has anything to do with my public concerns, and it is a gross abuse to attack a public man through his relatives, for whom he is not responsible.'[1]

Kynoch's was not a new theme for Lloyd George. He had mentioned the Chamberlain family's connection with the firm during the 1895 election, when the 'cordite vote' gave him an excuse for doing so. He had also referred to the matter in his speech at Bangor in April. It may be assumed, therefore, that he would have raised it again in his 1900 election campaign, even if Chamberlain had not invited such tactics by his questionable behaviour over the Bloemfontein letters. The timely report of the Contracts committee, however, and the fact that Chamberlain

1. Hansard, Fourth Series, Vol. LXXXVII, cols 1005–14.

seemed to be casting a slur upon the honour of all opponents of the war, combined both to justify Lloyd George's attack and to give it an air of spontaneity.

Parliament was formally dissolved on 17 September and the 'Khaki election' followed. If Chamberlain had had his way it would have been held in June or July, and Lloyd George was expecting it at that time.[1] But other Ministers were not then as confident as Chamberlain. Since 1895 the Government's majority had dropped from 152 to 128. Would 'patriotism' be 'enough'? The Tories of Caernarvon District were among those who trusted that it would be. Their candidate was a retired Army officer, Colonel Platt, who gave four reasons why the electors should vote for him:

1. BECAUSE he champions the rights of his own country.
2. BECAUSE he supports a Government which has given us good Laws and better Trade.
3. BECAUSE he will not allow the Blood and Treasure spent in the South African War to be sacrificed in vain.
4. BECAUSE his opponent has been on the enemy's side throughout the War, and has insulted the Generals and Soldiers of the Queen.[2]

Three of these four reasons amounted to a charge that Lloyd George was unpatriotic. At his adoption meeting on 19 September he flung the accusation back: 'The man who tries to make the flag an object of a single party is a greater traitor to that flag than any man who fires at it.' In the same speech he said that, while he personally believed that the war could have been prevented, he knew that 'two out of every three electors in the Boroughs' did not agree with him. It was an M.P.'s duty, however, to give his constituents honest advice, not always to tell them exactly what they wanted to hear. He praised Captain Lambton, a Liberal candidate just returned from South Africa, who was denouncing the war and whose ancestor, he said, gave freedom to the French in Canada.[3] The

---

1. On 29 May he wrote to Dr R. Parry at Caernarvon: 'The prevailing idea here is that we are in for a dissolution in July if Roberts captures Pretoria during the coming month.' (He did) '. . . The business now is to manœuvre into positions where it will be difficult to attack us. I think we'll give them as good a thrashing as they ever had. I feel quite eager for the fray already and I hope it will not be postponed.'
2. Election leaflet, in English and Welsh. (A copy, defaced by some Lloyd George sympathiser, is among the Lloyd George correspondence at the National Library of Wales.)
3. The ancestor in question – Durham – actually envisaged the extinction of a separate French culture in Canada and the assimilation of French Canadians to their English con-

principle of liberty prevailed throughout the Colonies, 'save India perhaps'. Hence their loyalty. There was no need to fear applying the same principle in the Transvaal, for it was the bridge that would 'span over the differences between the British and the Dutch'.[1]

On Chamberlain's behalf a letter was written to Colonel Platt, denying the 'ungentlemanly' insinuation that Chamberlain had 'used his position for the profit either of himself or of his relatives'. Lloyd George, for his part, denied that he had ever been in communication with the enemy, or that he had ever insulted British soldiers or generals. On the latter point, he challenged the colonel to a public debate – but only in the last week of the campaign, when it was unlikely that he would accept.[2] Apart from giving plausible instances of his own active concern for the soldiers' welfare, and contrasting it with alleged Tory indifference, Lloyd George did not spend much time answering his opponent. His campaign was throughout offensive rather than defensive, but his fire was directed at Chamberlain and the Government, not at Platt (who received only a light peppering). Early in the campaign he wrote to Herbert Lewis: 'You are fighting a brewer and I a ghost. . . . I have had one or two good meetings. For all that I have great difficulties to surmount. Men who have speculated heavily on South Africans threaten my life. I mean politically. However I believe we'll lick them all. But a man who putteth on his armour should not boast as he who is taking it off. (How's that for Scripture?)' And he added the beguiling postscript: 'I am going for Chamberlain and everybody in the hope I may distract attention from my own iniquities.'[3]

His main line of attack was that the Government was using the war as a cover for its lack of constructive policy at home. There was no promise

---

querors. This aspect of his famous Report did not, however, determine the future course of events and has been mercifully forgotten. What people remember is his nostrum of responsible self-government within the Empire.

1. Speech at Caernarvon, 19 September 1900.
2. The challenge was made in a speech at Caernarvon on 2 October, and in a letter from Lloyd George's agent, R. O. Roberts, to Platt's agent, H. Lloyd Carter, which appeared in the Press before Carter received it. He replied on 3 October that it was too late to alter Colonel Platt's arrangements, and that anyway the proposed meeting 'might develop into rowdyism' (N.L.W.). Lloyd George must have welcomed the reply. For all his superiority as a debater, he would not necessarily have gained from the encounter, in which Platt might have appeared to be David to *his* Goliath, and which would certainly have given much gratuitous publicity to a relatively unknown candidate.
3. David Lloyd George to Herbert Lewis, from Conway, 20 September 1900 (Herbert Lewis Papers, N.L.W.).

of domestic reform, 'unless Mr Balfour's proposal to renew the Landlords' Relief Act at the expense of the heavily burdened town ratepayer [could] be counted as such'. Yet if South Africa was really the only issue, then why were the Tories 'attacking seats held by Liberals who approved their South African policy, wherever the Liberal majority at the last election was so small as to inspire the hope that they might be captured?'[1] He insisted that the election should be seen not as a referendum on the war, but as the choice of a new Parliament for general political purposes. In one speech he admitted that the war might be 'nearly over';[2] but, if so, it was all the more important for voters to make up their minds on the issues of peace.

Of course, he did not soft-pedal his opposition to the war, but he sought to unite Liberals against the Government's inflexibility towards the Boers, instead of harping on the war's origins – which he was prepared to treat as ancient history, on which good Liberals could agree to differ. Kruger was 'a Tory', whom the British Tories were helping, in spite of themselves, by their policy of annexation. Joubert, Botha, Meyer and others were 'Liberals . . . working in the direction of reform'.[3] Occasionally, he appealed to pacifist sentiment, as in the much-quoted peroration: 'See here now – five years ago you handed me a strip of blue paper to give to the Speaker as your accredited representative. If I never again represent these Boroughs in the House of Commons I shall at least have the satisfaction of handing back to you that blue paper with no single stain of human blood upon it.'[4] But these familiar words do not convey a true impression of his handling of the war issue during the campaign. They represent a deviation from his considered line, which was more subtle and less emotional.

The Boroughs voted on 6 October and the result was:

Lloyd George	2,412
Platt	2,116

Lloyd George's majority of 296 was over a hundred more than in 1895, and the largest that he had obtained in four elections. There were delirious scenes when the poll was declared just after midnight. On the balcony of the Liberal Club in Caernarvon he 'clasped his faithful partner in his arms

1. Lloyd George's election address, 1900.
2. Speech at Pwllheli, 17 September 1900.
3. Speech at Criccieth, 21 September 1900.
4. Speech at Nevin, 15 September 1900.

and gave her an affectionate and impassioned kiss in the sight of the cheering multitudes'.[1] When he spoke, it was to commit another (but, one must repeat, untypical) lapse into sheer emotionalism: 'I am more proud of my countrymen tonight than ever before. While England and Scotland are drunk with blood, Wales is marching with steady step on the road of liberty and progress.' The sober, steady people of Caernarvon continued to celebrate until about 3 a.m.

It was an important, but not an isolated, victory. In Wales, of ten Liberal candidates hostile to the war, nine were returned. Herbert Lewis was elected by more than twice his previous majority. Humphreys-Owen increased his nearly tenfold. Frank Edwards, defeated in 1895, was re-elected in 1900. Nor was it only in Wales that anti-war candidates triumphed. Labouchere, probably the strongest English opponent of the war – who, moreover, *had* corresponded with the enemy – got in again comfortably. John Burns slightly increased his majority at Battersea, while in Scotland every major critic of the war, including Campbell-Bannerman, was returned. The suggestion that England and Scotland were 'drunk with blood' is not borne out by the facts. Indeed, it is a complete fallacy to interpret the election result as a mandate for Jingoism. The Unionists won, but they only gained six seats compared with their strength at the dissolution, and their overall majority was eighteen fewer than in 1895. In the popular vote Liberals alone (not counting their Labour and Irish Nationalist allies) scored 1,568,141, against a Unionist total of 1,797,444 – and 163 Unionists were returned unopposed, compared with only 22 Liberals.

Those figures provide the true explanation of what happened. The Liberals were beaten because they were disunited and hopelessly disorganised. The war certainly added to their confusion, but this was already so flagrant that they were virtually bound to lose, war or no war. The Government also had the advantage of improved trade since 1895, which the war helped to turn into a boom. All things considered, the Liberals did remarkably well, and if they had been in a fit state to put even approximately their normal number of candidates into the field, it is quite possible that they would have won.[2] War fever,

1. *Caernarvon Herald*, 12 October 1900.
2. One newly elected Unionist M.P. had a shrewd awareness of the Liberals' latent strength. 'I think this election, fought by the Liberals as a soldiers' battle, without plan or leaders or enthusiasm, has shown so far the strength, not the weakness, of Liberalism in the country.' (Winston Churchill to Rosebery, 4 October 1900 – quoted in Robert Rhodes James, *Rosebery*, p. 418.)

which might have been an overwhelming factor if the election had been held in June or July, cannot be said to have determined the result in October. In his colourful phrases after the declaration of the poll Lloyd George helped to popularise a view of the 'Khaki election' still widely held even now, but legendary.

When the new Parliament met in December, Lloyd George expanded his attack on Chamberlain's business connections. In the debate on the Address he moved an amendment that 'Ministers of the Crown and Members of either House of Parliament holding subordinate office in any public Department ought to have no interest, direct or indirect, in any firm or company competing for contracts with the Crown', unless such precautions were taken as might 'effectually prevent any suspicion of influence or favouritism in the allocation of such contracts'.

Lloyd George's speech was very long, but for the most part very telling. He reminded the House of Chamberlain's own objection when the former (Liberal) Government appointed as High Commissioner in South Africa a man who had held Rhodesian shares, even though he had sold them before his appointment. Chamberlain had argued then that the Queen's representative should be not only pure, but, like Caesar's wife, above suspicion. His own attitude and conduct must be judged according to the standard which he himself laid down. Kynoch's was by no means the only case in point, though it was the only one which had been investigated by a committee of the House of Commons. There was also the case of Hoskins and Sons Ltd, a firm described on its own bill-heads as 'contractors to the Admiralty', in which Chamberlain's son, Austen – Financial Secretary to the Treasury, and until recently Civil Lord of the Admiralty – held £3,000 worth of shares. And there was also the case of Tubes Ltd, in which Austen Chamberlain and his father were both interested as shareholders in an investment trust, and of which – like Kynoch's – Arthur Chamberlain was chairman. Lloyd George maintained that this company was doing very badly when Arthur Chamberlain took it over, but that he had revived its fortunes by obtaining a contract for making the weldless tubes for water-tube boilers needed by the Admiralty. An M.P. interrupted: 'And they all burst.' 'Oh yes,' resumed Lloyd George gaily, 'but what is far more to the point here is that they saved this company from bursting.' Instead of losing at the rate of £4,000 a year, it was now making a profit of £10,000 a year.

After mentioning one or two other firms to which the 'Caesar's wife' principle might be applied, Lloyd George considered the Kynoch's affair in detail, showing how that firm had received preferential treatment from the War Office, though its products were competitive neither in quality nor (initially) in price, simply – as he alleged – because of the 'unconscious influence' of 'a powerful personality'. Cleverly echoing Chamberlain's words about the Bloemfontein letters, he submitted that the relationship between public and private interests that he had been describing was 'not treasonable but improper'.

Chamberlain's reply was as vague and generalised as Lloyd George's speech was specific. Only one point in the indictment was effectively rebutted. Lloyd George had gone too far in hinting that Boer prisoners might have been sent to Ceylon so that a firm in which Chamberlain held shares could build huts for them there. It was only a hint, but a scornful reaction to it was justified.[1] For the rest, Chamberlain's tone of outraged virtue was inadequate morally, however appropriate it may have been tactically. He never answered the substantive charge, which was not that he had been corrupt, but that he had been negligent and disingenuous. No doubt he had tried to liquidate his own direct, personal interest in any company which might have dealings with the Government, and it was bad luck that he had not wholly succeeded. But how could he pretend that the interests of his family were no concern of his – that he had no responsibility for ensuring that Chamberlain-dominated firms received no preferential treatment from Government departments? It was just not good enough to disclaim all knowledge of his brother's affairs (while at the same time, incidentally, asserting his perfect integrity). Chamberlain relied upon impugning his critics' motives, upon flaunting his own high-mindedness in the service of the State, and upon the *reductio ad absurdum* that if he were censured no Minister of the Crown should be permitted to hold, for instance, railway or shipping shares.

1. Chamberlain did hold a few shares in the Colombo Commercial Company, which had received a small contract from the Government for building huts for Boer prisoners. But the shares were not quoted on the Stock Exchange, so he could reasonably claim that it was difficult for him to dispose of them; and the contract involved was on such a modest scale that nobody could suspect it of having influenced the decision to send Boer prisoners to Ceylon. On the other hand, Lloyd George did score when he referred to a Colonial Office regulation that no Colonial servant in Ceylon should be allowed to engage in commercial pursuits, and that no land there should be held either by a Colonial servant *or in the name of any member of his family*. The relevance of this to Lloyd George's main argument was inescapable.

By accepting the amendment, the House would be 'practically prohibit-ing anyone in future from being a member of a Government who has any money whatever outside the salary of his position'. The malice of his enemies had 'made it more difficult for honourable, sensitive men to serve the State'.

Austen Chamberlain followed his father with a much briefer, but equally unconvincing, apologia, and Balfour later endorsed Chamber-lain's specious defence with the characteristic quip: 'Wanted, a man to serve Her Majesty, with no money, no relations, and inspiring no general confidence!' From the Opposition benches Campbell-Bannerman sup-ported the amendment in somewhat guarded terms, Haldane rather bumblingly, and McKenna very incisively. When the House divided, Asquith (though not Grey) joined Haldane in voting for it, and another 'Liberal Imperialist' who voted for it was Ellis Griffith. It was, of course, defeated – by 269 votes to 127.[1]

Yet the honours of the debate unquestionably went to Lloyd George. With formidable application and forensic skill he had raised an issue which deserved the attention of Parliament and public. Was he, however, the right man to raise it? In the whole perspective of his life the answer must be No. The 'Caesar's wife' doctrine which he used against Chamberlain was not one which conspicuously guided his own conduct, when he was in power. Even in 1900 he might have recalled that his political prestige had been used to entice small shareholders to risk their money in Welsh Patagonian shares, and the memory should have given him pause. Was he, even then, so blameless that he could afford to point the finger of blame at Chamberlain? At the end of his speech he unctuously invoked the 'purity' of British statesmanship, and said that the Chamberlains had 'established precedents which, if . . . followed, would lead to something infinitely worse'. These words make distasteful reading, in retrospect. If Lloyd George had confined himself to his attack immediately before the election, when his political life was at stake – and when Chamberlain was making unscrupulous use of the captured letters – he would hardly be open to criticism. But the detailed, cold-blooded indictment after the election, brilliantly though he con-ceived and executed it, would have come better from another man.

1. Report of debate: Hansard, Fourth Series, Vol. LXXXVIII, cols 397–476, 10 December 1900. It was on another occasion that Ellis Griffith made the remark most often quoted as an example of his (rather laboured) wit: 'The more the British Empire expands, the more does the Chamberlain family contract.'

The war, meanwhile, was entering its last phase, of a duration and nastiness that very few anticipated. The Boer republics were occupied and annexed, but the Boers went on fighting in guerrilla groups, or commandos, whose members wore no uniform and were sustained by the civilian population living on scattered farms. Roberts came home in December 1900, but before leaving South Africa he had instituted the strategy of farm-burning which Kitchener, who took over from him, developed into a systematic war of attrition. Gradually, the commandos were deprived of their bases of support, as tens of thousands of men, women and children were herded into concentration camps. The wide spaces of the veld were traversed with lines of blockhouses and barbed wire. Even so, small detachments of Boers continued to harass British troops and to carry out daring long-range forays.

To Lloyd George, at least, it was no surprise that the Boers were proving hard to beat. He had predicted a long war, and it seemed to him that the policy of unconditional surrender was likely to prolong it indefinitely. A few days after the election he was saying that the war would last longer than people imagined,[1] and early in November he foreshadowed, with remarkable accuracy, the dire consequences of an all-out anti-guerrilla strategy. 'Lord Roberts has written to General Botha to say that where the railway near Boer farmhouses is damaged the farmhouses will be destroyed, and all cattle and supplies will be removed within an area of ten miles around. Is it civilised warfare to starve women and children? The remedy is to abandon the call for absolute surrender.'[2] At the end of November, speaking in Liverpool, he asserted that 'military necessity could not justify wrongdoing', and asked the audience to consider what would happen in England if the Germans invaded. Resistance, he said, would go on in Derbyshire and the Welsh hills 'long after the keys of Birmingham had been handed over to the enemy'. If the Liverpool–Warrington line were cut, 'the German Lord Roberts would burn every house in Liverpool, Warrington and St Helen's'. At this he was interrupted, but swiftly disposed of the heckler: 'Perhaps the gentleman who interrupted would only object to the burning of the public houses.' While Lloyd George was speaking people came to blows in the gallery, and the meeting ended in chaos.[3]

1. Speech at Newtown, 9 October 1900.   2. Speech at Bangor, 7 November 1900.
3. Meeting at the Picton Hall, Liverpool, 30 November 1900. It is interesting that he conjured up the spectre of a *German* invasion.

Just before the New Year he told an audience in his constituency that it was no longer profitable to discuss the origins of the war. The need was simply to end it. After the capture of Bloemfontein the Boers would have accepted 'any terms which left them their freedom'. Instead of this, 'a second war had been started upon – a ghastlier war, a war more expensive, degrading and dishonourable for Britain'. He committed himself to the view that it would not be over until the following April, adding that 'there would be years of sniping and guerrilla warfare afterwards'.[1]

At about this time he was clinching a deal which brought substantial reinforcement to the anti-war cause. When the war broke out, one of the two London Liberal penny newspapers – the *Daily Chronicle* – denounced it, but the proprietor took the opposite view and insisted that editorial policy must conform to his. Rather than betray their convictions, the editor, H. W. Massingham, and several of his colleagues resigned, taking refuge on the *Manchester Guardian*, the outstanding anti-war newspaper in the country. The other Liberal penny daily in London – the *Daily News* – was, under the editorship of E. T. Cook, genuinely Milnerite, so that, after the *Daily Chronicle's* defection, the anti-war school had no authoritative organ in London to counteract the influence of *The Times*, the *Daily Telegraph* and the *Morning Post*. (The *Westminster Gazette* was an evening paper, and the *Morning Leader* had a different sort of readership, selling at a halfpenny in competition with the militantly pro-war *Daily Mail*.) This was the state of affairs which, towards the end of 1900, Lloyd George made it his business to remedy.

His method was to organise an anti-war syndicate to take over the *Daily News* which, he knew, was in financial difficulties. Previous failure as a syndicate-promoter did not deter him, nor did his unsuccessful attempt, in 1895, to secure control of a newspaper in South Wales, with Storey and Furness providing the money. He was right to be undeterred, because over the *Daily News* he scored a triumph as astonishing as it was complete. The key figure in the syndicate was George Cadbury, the Birmingham cocoa manufacturer and pioneer of social reform. Cadbury was already the owner of four weeklies in the Birmingham area, but he had no desire to become a national Press lord and was noted for strictly discriminating, rather than lavish, generosity. A devout Quaker, he was

1. Speech at Conway, 28 December 1900.

believed to be in the habit of saying: 'Liberalism is too high and sacred a thing for money. But I will pray with you.'[1] From this unpromising source Lloyd George obtained £20,000, and he did so by the (for him) improbable method of writing letters. By the same means he extracted another £20,000 from J. P. Thomasson of Bolton, but Thomasson's interest in the project was short-lived: a year later he withdrew and Cadbury became sole proprietor.

Harold Spender describes Lloyd George reading him 'two very careful letters' – one to Cadbury, the other to Thomasson – 'over the coffee and cigars' at Gatti's:[2] a rather comical scene, because Cadbury never touched alcohol or tobacco, and in his early years would not even allow himself to drink coffee. His mental picture of the correspondent who was urging him to part with such a large sum of money for the sake of humanity may not have been that of a cigar-smoking man of the world sitting in a London restaurant, but rather of a puritan idealist like himself. In any case, Lloyd George persuaded him that it was his duty to capture the *Daily News*, and shortly before Christmas 1900 he wrote from Bournville, asking to be excused a trip to London: 'Just at this time of year I am overwhelmed with work. . . . All you want is the money and that I have promised. . . . We do not want any cranks as shareholders, as the venture is not likely to pay unless commonsense and business capacity are combined.'[3] It was, in fact, to cost him a great deal more than he expected in the years ahead, both financially and in nervous wear-and-tear. But the immediate effect of his intervention was a change of editorial policy on the *Daily News* which, according to Cadbury's biographer, A. G. Gardiner – who soon became the paper's editor – 'gave a powerful impulse to the cause of peace'.[4] E. T. Cook, following Massingham's example, would not change his line to suit the new regime and made a dignified exit, becoming chief leader-writer on the *Daily Chronicle*; and then, with an almost balletic symmetry, Massingham joined the *Daily News*. By mid-January 1901 the palace revolution had been carried out. One morning members of Cook's staff found Lloyd George in possession of the office in Bouverie Street. 'Henry had broken into the spence with a vengeance and turned the

---

1. From E. T. Cook's diary, 7 January 1901, quoted in J. Saxon Mills, *Sir Edward Cook, K.B.E.: a Biography*, p. 196.
2. E. H. Spender, *The Prime Minister*, p. 123.
3. George Cadbury to David Lloyd George, 18 December 1900 (N.L.W.).
4. A. G. Gardiner, *Life of George Cadbury*, p. 217.

monks, or a few of them, adrift.' But it was 'perfectly fair war' and the obligations of the old and new proprietors were fully, 'even generously', met.[1]

For any student of Lloyd George's career the paramount importance of the *Daily News* deal is, surely, that it shows how influential he had become among *English* Nonconformists. Cadbury was one of the most respected members of the English Nonconformist establishment, and it is indeed striking that he should have responded so readily when Lloyd George appealed to him on behalf of anti-Jingo, radical Liberalism. It cannot have been simply that Lloyd George wrote a very persuasive letter: his name, too, must have carried weight. In the absence, since Gladstone, of normal party leadership on the Liberal side, Lloyd George had acquired the reputation of a national leader, and had come to represent in the eyes of men like Cadbury not merely Wales, but all that was best in the English Liberal tradition. The enlargement of his political base was apparent to at least one of his Welsh colleagues. In March 1901 Humphreys-Owen wrote to Rendel: 'George is now . . . a below the gangway English radical – nothing more – and is doing that work admirably. . . .'[2]

The *Daily News* under its new management did not, as some Liberals hoped, show a tender regard for the susceptibilities of 'Liberal Imperialists'. Its unequivocal view was that ending the war was a more urgent task than reuniting the Party. On 18 February Lloyd George spoke with unabated force in the debate on the Address, though he did not move the amendment which stood on the Paper in his name, calling for the immediate cessation of hostilities and 'full local autonomy' under the Crown 'within the several areas of South Africa'. Winston Churchill, who rose next to make his maiden speech, was able to suggest that the amendment was too moderate for Lloyd George's liking – the moderation being that of his 'political friends and leaders', while the bitterness of his speech was 'all his own'.[3] In fact, it was by agreement with Campbell-Bannerman that he had decided not to move the amendment. Campbell-

---

1. J. Saxon Mills, *op. cit.*, p. 199.
2. Humphreys-Owen to Rendel, 23 March 1901 (Glansevern Papers, N.L.W.). In the same letter Humphreys-Owen said that the Welsh Party 'committed suicide when it put that worthy old pantaloon Alfred Thomas into the chair', and that the Welsh M.P.s 'made an irreparable blunder in not taking Lloyd George'. If pressed, Lloyd George would probably have accepted the chairmanship, but the Alfred Thomas arrangement really suited him better (*see* above, pp. 218–20).
3. Hansard, Fourth Series, Vol. LXXXIX, cols 397–407, 18 February 1901.

Bannerman judged that 'it was not in the interest of peace and good feeling that such a reasonable amendment should be . . . rejected', as it inevitably would be. But he had no objection to a strong speech from Lloyd George. 'I am convinced that . . . the centre of gravity is palpably shifted forward. I have no complaint to make of the way I have been met even by the extremest men – Lloyd George' (and he mentioned four other names).[1] Peace talks with the Boers were imminent, and it was of these that he was thinking when he referred to the interests of 'peace and good feeling'. As a by-product, however, of the momentary hopes of a settlement, the pro- and anti-war factions did make an effort to appear united when the Committee of the National Liberal Federation met at Rugby on 27 February.

Next day, at Middelburg in the Transvaal, a meeting took place between Kitchener and Botha which, if the British general had had a free hand, would probably have resulted in peace. Kitchener was willing to agree that Afrikaner rebels in Cape Colony and Natal should be amnestied, but Milner and the British Cabinet were obdurate and it was on that single point that the negotiations broke down. Afterwards, Botha returned to his demand for independence, which Chamberlain cited as evidence that he was never prepared to accept British sovereignty. Lloyd George, however, had good grounds for maintaining that it proved nothing of the kind. In a Parliamentary debate later in the year he reacted sharply when Chamberlain interrupted him to say that Botha demanded independence again after Middelburg.

Of course he did. General Botha afterwards issued a fighting circular to his burghers, and the right hon. Gentleman [Chamberlain] knows himself the difference between the two things – of holding up an ideal to your men, and sitting round a table to settle a compromise. When he makes speeches in the country he holds up the principle of 'Ransom'; when he comes to practical operations he whittles it down to three acres and a cow. There is a vast difference between holding up an ideal and sitting down to negotiate what is practicable. . . . General Botha said that the negotiations had failed, and now they had got to fight. Do you imagine that [he] would issue a circular asking his burghers to fight to the death for Sir Alfred Milner and a nominated executive with an advisory board? Surely no man with his wits about him would

1. Campbell-Bannerman to Lord Ripon, 16 February 1901 (quoted in J. A. Spender, *op. cit.*, Vol. I, pp. 321–2).

do that. If General Botha was appealing to his men to sacrifice their lives he would use such words as 'independence' and 'freedom', for those are the words that rouse men.[1]

Some will read that passage as an example of Lloyd George's cynicism, others of his realism. Certainly it reflects his own idea of leadership – pugnacity and audacity, with an ever-open eye to the chances of compromise. If his reading of Botha's conduct is correct, Kitchener's may be similarly explained. After the breakdown of negotiations he, who had been so conciliatory, asked for authority to shoot Cape and Natal rebels out of hand, and to confiscate the property of all Boers who failed to surrender within a time-limit. He, too, had to think of the morale of his men.

The war went on, and by early summer the horrifying consequences – which Lloyd George had foreseen – of the anti-guerrilla strategy were becoming obvious even to supporters of the war. In the concentration camps, where about 60,000 Boers were interned,[2] the average mortality was 117 per thousand. In one camp the mortality among children was nearly 500 per thousand. Between January 1901 and February 1902, over 20,000 people died in the camps. One passionate Milnerite wrote subsequently that too little allowance was made 'for the helplessness and ignorance of elementary sanitary rules on the part of women who had always lived in isolated farms, nor for the tremendously rapid growth of the camps', with the result that the 'death-rate from measles and enteric, especially among children, was at one time terribly high'.[3] Milner himself was admitting privately, by the end of 1901, that the camps had been disastrous, though he did so in a tone of self-pity rather than of self-reproach. (How could he be expected to attend to *everything*?)[4] Chamberlain, meanwhile, had assumed responsibility for the camps, which were originally under the War Office, and improved administration brought the death rate down to a tolerable figure.[5]

The collapse of the peace talks, and above all the scandal of the camps, had the effect of pushing Campbell-Bannerman and the Liberal Centre into alliance with the pro-Boer 'extremists'. The division between them had never been wide. Campbell-Bannerman was always an opponent of

---

1. Hansard, Fourth Series, Vol. XCVIII, cols 1135–50, 2 August 1901.
2. Later, the camp population reached a maximum figure of nearly 118,000.
3. L. S. Amery, *My Political Life*, Vol. I ('England Before the Storm, 1896–1914'), p. 162.
4. Milner to Haldane, 8 December 1901 (Haldane Papers, National Library of Scotland).
5. Twenty per thousand by the end of the war.

the war, though he expressed himself less forcibly than Lloyd George and would not join him in denouncing the policy of annexation, holding that the dual system in South Africa would have to be ended. By the beginning of 1901, however, Lloyd George was no longer treating annexation as a live issue, and his outlook and Campbell-Bannerman's were almost identical on the war, even before Middelburg and the camps brought them together in a very active and militant unity. At the National Liberal Federation meeting at Bradford, on 15 May, Campbell-Bannerman took his stand on the principle of an amnesty for rebels. And on 14 June, after he had listened to Emily Hobhouse's first-hand account of conditions in the camps, he made his one really famous speech, asking 'When is a war not a war?' and providing his own answer 'When it is carried on by methods of barbarism in South Africa'.[1]

The phrase 'methods of barbarism', used not by an unofficial leader (Lloyd George had been speaking in similar terms for months) but by the official leader of the Liberal Party in the Commons – and an ex-War Minister to boot – provoked a furious outcry in which Campbell-Bannerman was execrated as a traitor to his country. The abuse distressed him, but he did not withdraw the phrase, even though it separated him decisively from the Liberal Imperialists – a separation which was marked, three days later, by his voting for an adjournment motion on the subject of the camps, moved by Lloyd George, which the Liberal Imperialists did not support.[2] The divided state of the Liberal Party was ridiculed by Henry Lucy as 'war to the knife – and fork', since the rival factions seemed to have a preference for expounding their views at banquets. But in spite of the publicity thus given to party dissension Campbell-Bannerman held the loyalty of the Centre, as well as that of the pro-Boers, in Parliament, and among Liberals in the country the backing for him was even more solid.

There was, however, an alternative to be reckoned with. Liberal Imperialists – and some disenchanted Unionists – looked to Rosebery who, in the latter part of 1901 and early 1902, re-emerged as a potential national leader. Free alike from the taint of being a Little Englander or a pro-Boer, and from any responsibility for recent frustrations in South

1. Speech at a dinner of the National Reform Union, Holborn Restaurant, London.
2. Hansard, Fourth Series, Vol. XCV (17 June 1901), Lloyd George's speech, cols 573–83. In the debate C.-B. explained and justified his description of the camps as barbarous: Haldane deplored it. In the division fifty Liberals abstained, while seventy followed C.-B. in support of the motion – the actual wording of which was so innocuous that refusal to vote for it was manifestly a demonstration against Lloyd George and C.-B.

Africa, he was able to offer himself as the man for the hour. Yet he did so, characteristically, with such vagueness and ambivalence that the opportunity came and went. The high-water-mark of this particular Rosebery revival was his speech at Chesterfield in December 1901, which was eagerly awaited and briefly admired, but whose contents were found, on closer inspection, to lack substance. He tried to have it all ways – reaffirming his support for the war while condemning Milner and Chamberlain, deprecating any approach to the Boers while hinting that peace talks should occur 'at a wayside inn', rejecting traditional Liberal policies (which he termed 'fly-blown phylacteries')[1] while proclaiming efficiency (whatever that might mean) as a panacea for the nation's ills. It was not a convincing programme. All the same, he remained a focus of disloyalty to Campbell-Bannerman, though he failed to attract steady loyalty to himself. The Liberal League, which was founded in February 1902 with Rosebery as president, and with Asquith and Grey as vice-presidents,[2] was more anti-Campbell-Bannerman than pro-Rosebery. It was never a separate party, nor even a coherent party within a party; but it enabled ambitious politicians to reinsure with Rosebery, and to show their disapproval of the existing leadership, without incurring the penalties of schism.

Throughout 1901 Lloyd George was tireless as a platform speaker. In May, at the National Liberal Federation meeting at Bradford, he used the war as an argument for female suffrage, which he had long favoured. If women had had the vote, 'there would have been an end of all this bloodshed'. On the same occasion he said: 'We must remember that there is nothing deeper than race, and anybody who excites racial prejudices is exciting passions more difficult to allay than even religious passions and prejudices.'[3] At Oswestry a few days later someone interrupted his speech by singing the National Anthem. 'That is an insult to the King,' was his quiet retort. 'It is an insult to sing so badly, to begin with.'[4] He paid many compliments to Campbell-Bannerman. For instance, when he attended a meeting at Pontypridd in July, Lloyd

1. Campbell-Bannerman's private comment on this phrase was typical. 'What is a 'fly-blown phylactery'? Fly-blow is the result of a fly laying the egg from which maggots come in meat: no fly out of Bedlam would choose a phylactery (if he found one) for such a purpose.' (Letter to Herbert Gladstone, 18 December 1901, quoted in J. A. Spender, op. cit., Vol. II, p. 14.)
2. A third vice-president was Sir Henry Fowler, later Lord Wolverhampton – a Cabinet Minister under Gladstone and Rosebery.
3. 15 May 1901.   4. 18 May 1901.

George, moving a vote of thanks to him, said: 'It is a healthy thing in these days, when people seem to be ready to apologise for principles, to hear the leader of the Liberal Party proclaiming them boldly and without faltering.' The remark was greeted with loud cheers, and some counter-cheers. He added that Campbell-Bannerman was 'a leader with a cool head and a stout heart'.[1]

A recurrent theme in his speeches was that Chamberlain had sabotaged the peace talks between Kitchener and Botha. He 'strolled among his orchids six thousand miles away from the deadly bark of the Mauser rifle' and 'stopped Kitchener's peace'.[2] Chamberlain was 'a smart townsman dealing with an old Transvaal farmer'.[3] In November, Lloyd George gave a notable address on Imperialism at Birkenhead. Did the modern advocates of Empire mean Empire on the Roman model? If so, he would say that it was 'absolutely impossible under modern conditions'. When Rome established her Empire she was practically the only civilised power and there were 'hardly any free communities'. But in two thousand years human character had changed. Slavery had been abolished. 'Mommsen said of Rome that it was a city of millionaires and beggars. That is what the Empire cost Rome in spite of its free corn and millions of tribute.'

Turning to the British Empire, Lloyd George said that his conception of the best Imperial policy was one which, while diminishing the burdens of Empire, increased its strength. A great Empire must be 'fearlessly just' and must use its strength to protect the weak. 'I suspect the call of Empire when it shirks Armenia, but goes straight forward to force freedom on goldfields.' And there must be no 'racial arrogance'. If the Empire was to be kept together it must be on the basis of national freedom. 'We ought to give freedom everywhere – freedom in Canada, freedom in the Antipodes, in Africa, in Ireland, in Wales, *and in India. We will never govern India as it ought to be governed until we have given it freedom.*'[4]

When the General Committee of the National Liberal Federation met at Derby in early December, Lloyd George was received by the delegates with enthusiasm. He urged them not to elaborate their peace terms, but simply to declare that they were in favour of negotiations; and his

1. 12 July 1901.   2. Llanelly, 7 October 1901.   3. Leigh, 7 November 1901.
4. Speech at Birkenhead under the auspices of the Ruskin Hall Debating Society, 21 November 1901. (Author's italics.) The reference to Armenia was a dig at Rosebery, who had resigned the Liberal leadership in 1896 ostensibly because Gladstone had made a speech calling for action against the Turks on account of their latest Armenian atrocities.

advice was accepted.[1] The purpose of this adroit formulation was to close ranks within the party, more especially in view of Rosebery's imminent speech at Chesterfield. Lloyd George's genuinely warm regard for Campbell-Bannerman did not exclude admiration for Rosebery's talents, or agreement with at least some of his ideas. Soon after the Derby meeting Lloyd George stressed, at Wrexham, the appalling cost of the war, and the extent to which it was pre-empting resources needed for social reform. He quoted the prediction of a *Daily Mail* correspondent that it would last another two years. This would mean a total cost of £300 million. Did his audience know what Wrexham's share would be? He calculated that their share would be £120,000, and that the cost of garrisoning South Africa after the war would impose a further four shillings in the pound. He also estimated that of the seven thousand children who had died in the camps, Wrexham's share was six children. So £120,000 had been added to their town debt, plus £13,000 a year which they would have to find in hard cash – 'per contra six little graves in Africa'.[2]

A few days later he nearly went to his own grave. Throughout the war he faced rowdiness and occasional violence at his meetings, but the Birmingham Town Hall meeting on 18 December 1901 was in a class by itself. It was planned as a demonstration of Liberal Party solidarity, in the spirit of the Derby conclave. The Birmingham Liberal Association organised the meeting, which was to be for ticket-holders only, and a Liberal Imperialist, Alderman William Cook, was to take the chair. Partly to emphasise the fraternal theme, but also partly for prudential reasons, the organisers went to some lengths to explain that the meeting would not have an anti-war character. Nevertheless two Liberal Unionist papers, the *Birmingham Daily Mail*, and the *Birmingham Daily Post*, did their best to ensure that there would be a riot, by saying over and over again that one was likely and by blaming the Liberals for the consequences of inviting 'this most virulent anti-Briton'. Publicity was also given to a statement by the Lord Mayor that the Liberal Association had accepted responsibility for any damage done to the Town Hall.

By the time Lloyd George arrived in Birmingham, during the afternoon of 18 December, the atmosphere was charged with menace. A large crowd was waiting for him at New Street station, and he was lucky to pass unnoticed from there to the house of some Welsh friends in Hagley Road, a destination which had been kept secret. There he was

1. 4 December 1901.   2. 12 December 1901.

told that Alderman Cook would not, after all, be taking the chair. Elderly and rather shaky in health, he had been receiving threatening letters and a mob had surrounded his house. His doctor had insisted upon his crying off, but another Liberal Imperialist, A. C. Osler, was to substitute for him. Lloyd George also received a telephone call from the Chief Constable, urgently repeating warnings previously given of the risks involved in holding the meeting. In spite of these portents the villain of the piece decided that it would be shameful to disappoint his public, and at about half-past six he arrived in a carriage at the Town Hall, where 350 policemen were confronting a crowd of 30,000, many of whom were armed with sticks, hammers, knives, stones or bricks tied round with barbed wire.

It was providential that Lloyd George managed to get into the building, and even more providential that he ever emerged from it. When the doors were opened the surge of humanity was so overpowering that any attempt to keep non-ticket-holders out was doomed from the start. Before long pandemonium reigned inside the Hall, and when Lloyd George appeared on the platform the tumult reached fever-pitch. After he had spoken a few sentences, for the most part inaudibly, there was a rush towards the platform from the body of the Hall. The assailants were held off by the police, but the platform was pelted with missiles, while from outside stones and bricks were hurled through the windows, and even the glass dome of the building began to fall in. At that stage, Lloyd George complied with the Chief Constable's request to leave the platform, and as the wounded were attended to in the basement he was smuggled out of the building amid a detachment of police, disguised as one of them.

The riot continued for some time before the crowd dispersed under the combined impact of a snowstorm and a truncheon charge. Two people, including a policeman, lost their lives and nearly forty were detained in hospital. Lloyd George spent the night, under guard, at Hagley Road, and from there telephoned Harold Spender in London, who immediately wrote to Margaret at Trinity Road and Uncle Lloyd at Criccieth, with the news that he was safe. Next day he returned to London, unscathed and more than ever a household name.

The ferocity of his reception in Birmingham should not be taken as indicating that popular support for the war had increased. On the contrary, there was much disillusionment on the subject, and many who believed that the war itself was right had been shocked by the rate of mortality in the camps. At the same time the relatively wholesome Jingoism of the Mafeking period had given way to nastier, more bitter feelings among those who still supported the war without reservation. Moreover, in Birmingham, hatred for Lloyd George was a function of loyalty to Chamberlain, whose services to the city were incomparable. People hated Lloyd George not only for having denounced their hero's policies, but, more intensely, for having besmirched his personal honour; and Chamberlain's own resentment may have caused him to turn a blind eye to the campaign of provocation in the Birmingham Liberal Unionist Press before the meeting (in which Conservative papers did not join). While there is no evidence of his having instigated the riot, there is equally no evidence of his having made the slightest effort to prevent it, though his word was virtually law among the Liberal Unionists of Birmingham. And afterwards, when a fellow Member asked him why Birmingham had allowed Lloyd George to escape, he allegedly replied 'What is everybody's business is nobody's business'.[1] He never ceased to respect Lloyd George as an adversary, and Lloyd George never ceased to respect him. But the war completed the work that Gladstone, unwittingly, had begun – of driving the two outstanding radical politicians of modern Britain into opposite camps. And apart from the war there was a human element in their mutual antagonism. Lloyd George envied Chamberlain his wealth; Chamberlain envied Lloyd George his youth.

At Bristol on 6 January the authorities took no chances when Lloyd George spoke at the Vestry Hall of St Philip. The doors and windows of the hall were barricaded, police barriers were erected outside, mounted police were held in readiness and a fire hose was placed on the steps of the hall. These precautions may have contributed to the success of a meeting which was noisy but never violent. Lloyd George naturally referred to his recent experience at Birmingham. 'After centuries of struggle in this country we are yet in the position that argument is thrust aside and we are to trust to sheer brute force – not to the mind and intellect which God, in a greater or lesser degree, has endowed all of us with. . . . It was necessary that we should hold this meeting at all hazards, to stand up for a great principle.'

When Parliament reassembled towards the end of January 1902,

---

1. Quoted in the *Review of Reviews*, October 1904. The remark, however, was not necessarily made in deadly earnest, since the question was put to Chamberlain light-heartedly by a friend of Lloyd George, W. S. Caine, M.P.

OUR PARLIAMENTARY INDIANS PREPARING FOR THE WAR-PATH.

"Little Minister" plainly means business, to the horror of the White-'eather or Ma-Jubah T-ibe.

Br-n R-b-rts.   C.-B.   Ll-yd G-rge.   H-rc-rt.   M-rl-y.   F-wl-r.   R-s-b-ry.   B-lf-r.   Ch-mb-rl-n.   S-l-sb-ry.
                                          Asq-th.

5. 'Our Parliamentary Indians preparing for the War-Path', by E. T. Reed, *Punch*, 15 January 1902

Lloyd George soon made it clear that the eirenic approach to intra-party differences which he had shown at Derby in early December was now a thing of the past. A Liberal back-bencher, Frederick Cawley, moved an amendment to the Address designed to facilitate a united vote by the Opposition.[1] The amendment had Campbell-Bannerman's support, but Lloyd George did not vote for it. Instead he voted for an amendment to the amendment, moved by John Dillon, which forthrightly condemned the war and made no reference to its effective prosecution. Moreover, in the debate he attacked the Cawley amendment and poured scorn on his leader. The amendment, he said, 'meant that one set of gentlemen were asked to support what they regarded as a criminal enterprise as an inducement for another set of gentlemen to vote for a proposition they did not believe to be true'. Campbell-Bannerman had been captured by the Liberal Imperialists and 'had been treated by his captors as the Boers treated their prisoners – he had been stripped of all his principles and left on the veld to find his way back the best way he could'. In the vote on Cawley's motion, Lloyd George was one of five anti-war Liberals who abstained.[2]

His apparent injury to Campbell-Bannerman gave deep offence to middle-of-the-road Liberals and even to some who opposed the war no less fervently than he did. H. J. Wilson, for instance, wrote to him next day, as one who had watched his career with interest and expectation, and who agreed with him on all important issues:

> When you got up last night I expected to hear a justificate of the grounds on which some of us found we could not vote for Cawley's amendment, put forward in a spirit of *regret* . . . and with a tribute of respect for C.-B., who has not fully shared our views about the war, but who has . . . deserved our confidence and our thanks. . . . That being so, I was pained and shocked at your language more than I should like just now to describe. . . . It seems to me impossible that you should in calmer moments approve of it yourself. It must do great harm to the anti-war, radical section of the party.[3]

---

1. 'That this House, while prepared to support all proper measures for the effective prosecution of the war in South Africa, is of opinion that the course pursued by Your Majesty's Ministers and their attitude with regard to a settlement have not conduced to the early termination of the war and the establishment of a durable peace.'
2. Hansard, Fourth Series, Vol. CI, cols 537–43, 21 January 1902.
3. H. J. Wilson to Lloyd George, 22 January 1902 (Lloyd George Papers, Beaverbrook Library). Wilson was Liberal M.P. for Holmfirth, Yorks.

Wilson's indignation was understandable, but naïve. Lloyd George's line in the debate could hardly have been more helpful to Campbell-Bannerman even if it had been agreed between them beforehand. Nobody was likely to believe that he had been captured by the Liberal Imperialists, but there were plenty of people who believed – since his 'methods of barbarism' speech – that he had been captured by Lloyd George. To be assailed as a backslider, and accused of veering towards the opposite faction, by Lloyd George of all people, was exactly what Campbell-Bannerman might have wished to happen, and one newspaper comment shows how he gained from the speech: 'A number of Liberals who had intended to imitate Sir E. Grey's action in abstaining from the division altered their minds after hearing Mr L. G.'s speech, and voted with Sir H. C.-B. It was a speech therefore which achieved the rare distinction of influencing votes, for, had it not been delivered, the Ministerial majority would have been even greater than it was.'[1] There is no evidence of collusion, but Campbell-Bannerman, having gently reproved Lloyd George in his own speech, showed no ill-will towards him afterwards, and his private comment on the incident shows that he, at least, was aware of the benefits accruing to him: 'On the whole I think we did well. . . . Lloyd George's outburst has greatly angered the party generally. . . . I see nothing to regret in the whole thing. The centre of the party is enlarged and consolidated. . . .'[2]

From his new position of strength Campbell-Bannerman issued a challenge to Rosebery, with whom he had tried, in vain, to re-establish working relations after the Chesterfield speech. Was he, or was he not, inside the Liberal tabernacle?[3] Rosebery promptly replied, in a letter to *The Times*, that he disagreed with Campbell-Bannerman on Irish Home Rule and on the war, and was therefore 'outside his tabernacle, but not,' he thought, 'in solitude'.[4] It was this exchange which led to the formation of the Liberal League, signifying that Rosebery held the (doubtful) allegiance of the Liberal Imperialists, but had alienated the Centre and 'Left' of the Party. Lloyd George was one who might have supported him, but for whom, by the New Year, the spirit of Chesterfield had evaporated. No 'wayside inn' negotiations had taken place, no end to the war was in sight; and meanwhile Rosebery, instead of making

1. *Liverpool Daily Post*, 23 January 1902.
2. Campbell-Bannerman to Ripon, 24 January 1902 (quoted in J. A. Spender, *op. cit.*, Vol. II, p. 25).
3. Speech at Leicester, 19 February 1902.
4. 20 February 1902.

further gestures to the anti-war faction, had reverted to the stance of a pro-war Imperialist. On Irish Home Rule he and Lloyd George were of roughly the same mind: they both stood for Home Rule all Round, and against the exclusive Gladstonian commitment to Ireland. Yet on the war, which was the immediate issue, they differed profoundly. Besides, Lloyd George knew that a great majority of Liberals in the country, if they had to choose between Rosebery and Campbell-Bannerman, would unhesitatingly choose the latter. In December he had hoped that there would be no need for such a choice, because reconciliation seemed to be at hand. But when he saw that the war was dragging on, and that the leaders were drifting apart again, he resumed his normal 'outside Left' position. There was nothing reckless or out of character about his rebellion on the Cawley amendment.

To the end he maintained a relentless opposition to the war. In his last major speech on the subject in Parliament, on 20 March, he clearly assumed that there was no prospect of an early peace.[1] Margaret was at Criccieth, awaiting the birth of their youngest child, Megan, and he wrote to her there about the speech:

> Your sweetheart made a proper job of it last night. Several have told me it was the best I ever delivered in this House. The Tories behaved on the whole very well considering it was like salt in the wound to them. There were only just one or two who interrupted unfairly – the rest listened intently. Crowded benches of them. Dilke just telling me that this morning he thought I was like Shelley's Adonais. I had at last through toil and trouble got to fame. I haven't got the quotation but you can see it in Shelley's Adonais.[2]

He was staying with Sir Charles Dilke at Shepperton when the news came through that the war was over – at long last, but sooner than he expected. 'The first intimation I received of the news was after I went

1. Hansard, Fourth Series, Vol. CV, cols 638–55.
2. D.L.G. to M.L.G., 21 March 1902 (N.L.W.). Words in italics are translated from the original Welsh. It is impossible to say which lines in Adonais Dilke was thinking of, but such relevance as the poem may have to Lloyd George derives from the fact that Shelley was thinking of himself, rather than of Keats, when he wrote it. Keats did not wage contention with his time's decay or dare the unpastured dragon in his den – except in the very loose sense that all artistic endeavour may be so described. But Shelley saw himself as a crusader and emancipator, which Lloyd George, up to a point, actually was.

to bed last night when I heard the church bells of Shepperton ringing – shots fired and the sound of cheering crowds in the distance.' It was, he thought, an honourable peace. 'They are generous terms for the Boers. Much better than those we offered them 15 months ago – after spending £50,000,000 in the meantime.'[1]

What were the terms? In return for acknowledging British sovereignty, the Boers were allowed to keep their rifles and go back to their farms, for the restoration of which they were to receive £3 million from the British taxpayer, and, if necessary, further aid. The use of their own language was guaranteed in schools and courts of law. Representative government was soon to take the place of military rule. The question of amnesty for the Cape and Natal rebels, on which the Middelburg negotiations had broken down in February 1901, was settled by a face-saving device. No amnesty for them was included in the peace treaty of Vereeniging, but a collateral assurance was given that only leading rebels would be punished at all, otherwise than by disfranchisement, and that even they would not suffer the death penalty. It was a compromise, affecting only two or three hundred people. Had it been worth prolonging the war by fifteen months for such a modest symbolic gain? Lloyd George was surely right in thinking that, in more substantial respects, the Boers were better off with the Vereeniging terms than with those on which the war might have been ended at Middelburg. Britain had won, at best, a Pyrrhic victory.

In Lloyd George's considered view it was not a victory at all, but defeat disguised as victory. One day in 1915 he was telling Frances Stevenson about his experiences during the Boer War, and the risks he had run by mocking at British defeats and saying they were just retribution. 'But,' she asked, 'you were glad that we *won*?' '*We didn't win*,' was his emphatic reply.

The Boers – the Dutch – are the rulers in South Africa. We had to give them back their land to rule – for us! And more – for whereas they had ruled the Orange Free State and the Transvaal, they were given in addition Cape Colony and Natal to rule. Had we not done this, we should now have been driven from South Africa. C.-B. was wise enough to see that safety lay in giving them autonomy. Had we not done so, Botha and others would have gone back to their farms, and waited for the moment – this moment – when all our energies

1. D.L.G. to M.L.G., 2 June 1902 (N.L.W.).

were wanted elsewhere, to drive us from South Africa. We didn't win the Boer War![1]

When he spoke of giving the Boers Cape Colony and Natal to rule, Lloyd George was referring to the Union of South Africa which came into force in 1910, after the Liberal Government of which he was a member had granted responsible self-government to the Transvaal and Orange River Colony. The Union was freely negotiated between the British and Boer leaders in South Africa, but the first Prime Minister of the Union was Louis Botha and the country has been dominated throughout its existence by the Afrikaners. They accepted membership of the British Commonwealth as a light price to pay for mastery in their own house. In both world wars South Africa was a combatant at Britain's side, but her contribution was less impressive than that of the other Dominions, and on the second occasion it was touch-and-go that she came in at all.

Meanwhile the Boer philosophy of white supremacy was being rigorously applied in the Union. From the first this was endorsed, with slight reservations, by most British South Africans. Insofar as the British complained of racial discrimination, it was mainly of Boer discrimination against themselves. They objected to the Afrikaners taking their jobs, but had little or nothing to say of the systematic denial of political rights to Asians and black Africans. One 'loyalist' wrote to Milner in England, while the Union was being negotiated: 'It is Dutch, Dutch, everything Dutch. . . . It is just about at the stage that nobody but Dutch need apply. When you left in this district all the officials were English with the exception of one. Now they are all Dutch.' And another wrote, at about the same time: 'Not a single Boer I have ever met, or ever heard of, admits that the English were victorious. We left them unbeaten, we then treated them with ridiculous magnanimity which they interpreted as weakness or fear and, perhaps worst blunder of all, we agreed to give the fullest official rights to their language. . . . South Africa to many is no longer British.'[2]

Milner might argue that the Liberals sold the pass when they were in power after 1905 – that they gave the Boers self-government too soon. But the 'ridiculous magnanimity' of which his correspondent complained had already been shown by the Tory Government, in the treaty of

1. Frances Stevenson, op. cit., entry for 25 January 1915, p. 24.
2. Quoted in Evelyn Wrench, Alfred Lord Milner: the Man of No Illusions, p. 272.

peace. It was the Tories who left the Boers 'unbeaten', and who gave 'the fullest official rights to their language'. As for the timing of self-government, would it really have been possible for any British Government to delay it much beyond the moment when the Liberals conceded it? Were the Liberals, in fact, as generous as they believed (or as irresponsible as their opponents believed)? Is it fair to claim anything more for them than that they made a virtue of necessity? On Lloyd George's view of the war's result, Britain had no choice but to enter into arrangements highly advantageous to the Boers, because they were essentially unbeaten and any renewal of hostilities against them was unthinkable. It would seem, on the whole, that he was right.

Certainly, his attitude to the war was from first to last consistent, and he stuck to it with admirable tenacity. No episode in his whole career shows him in a better light. When his courage and resourcefulness were tested by terrible emergencies in 1914-18, he was a powerful Minister with the machinery of the State at his disposal and public opinion strongly sustaining him. In the Boer War he was a back-bencher asserting his private judgement against the rulers of the country, who were supported by an influential section of his own party and by a majority of the people. Apart from the anti-Semitism which appears in his attacks on the Uitlanders, and apart from the regrettable lengths to which he carried his 'Kynoch' vendetta, it cannot be denied that he kept the argument at a high level. Though the focus of his criticism to some extent changed as the war progressed – centring first upon the arrogance and mishandling which caused the war, then upon the policy of annexation, then upon that of unconditional surrender, then upon the scandal of the camps – it was always on issues of policy that he arraigned the Government, not on strictly military issues. Moreover, in all phases of the war he continued to stress the damage that it was doing to the cause of social reform at home, and to Britain's credit in the world.

To Lloyd George the Boer War seemed as injurious to the British Empire, in which he believed, as it was unjust to a small national community with which he instinctively sympathised. He opposed it as a nationalist, but he also, and no less sincerely, opposed it as an Imperialist, since it appeared to confirm the philosophy of Empire which he had held since he was a boy, and to which, as Prime Minister, he later tried very hard to give practical expression. In his efforts to consolidate the Empire as a Commonwealth of free nations he came to rely upon some of Milner's young disciples – notably Philip Kerr, Lionel Curtis and

Edward Grigg. There was no paradox in his reliance on them, or in their admiration for him, because on the principle of Imperial consolidation there was never any difference between him and Milner (or between him and Chamberlain). The difference was as to means, and the apparent success of South African Union, achieved by methods of pro-Boer Imperialism, led some of the younger Milnerites to look to Lloyd George, rather than to Milner himself, for the implementation of their dream.

Was the dream ever realisable, or was it a mirage? Apart from the natural forces which would anyway have tended – as de Tocqueville foresaw – to make the United States and Russia pre-eminent in the world, there were two big problems to be overcome: India, and the centrifugal pull of Colonial nationalism. As regards India, Lloyd George was handicapped by racial prejudice. Widely travelled though he was, compared with most British politicians of his day, he had never visited India[1] and had no personal acquaintance with Indians. It is fascinating (though profitless) to speculate how his thinking might have developed if he had travelled to India, as well as Canada, before his years of power. His receptiveness to ideas, and above all to atmosphere, might have enabled him to grasp the vital significance of the Indian National Congress, and the need to do business with it as the movement through which India might become self-governing within the Empire, while remaining united. During the Boer War he twice gave tantalising hints of the way his mind might have moved. In September 1900, when referring to the 'principle of liberty' prevailing throughout the British Empire, he added the pregnant qualification 'save India perhaps'.[2] And in November 1901, lecturing on the Empire at Birkenhead, he declared that Britain should give 'freedom everywhere', including India.[3] Yet he did not champion the rights of Indians in South Africa, nor did he ever make an issue of Indian freedom, as of Boer freedom. When he was Prime Minister (admittedly dependent upon the Conservative Party) he was responsible for a policy which disappointed legitimate hopes and drove the most Anglophile Indian leaders into opposition to the Raj. At

1. It is an astonishing fact that between the Duke of Wellington and Ramsay MacDonald – that is to say, between 1831 and 1924 – no British Prime Minister had first-hand knowledge of India, a country upon which British power largely depended.
2. Speech at Caernarvon, 19 September 1900 (*see* above, p. 271).
3. Birkenhead, 21 November 1901 (*see* above, p. 285). Yet it is perhaps revealing that he expressed himself in paradoxical terms: 'We will never govern India as it ought to be governed until we have given it freedom.'

heart, he did not fully accept the case for Indian self-government, nor did he ever rid himself of the feeling (characteristic of Northern white Protestants) that 'coloured' people were inferior.[1]

On the possibility of reconciling Colonial freedom with effective Imperial unity he was, as a Welshman, over-sanguine. The Welsh nationalism that he knew and represented was not centrifugal (except to a very limited degree) for two main reasons: first, because the Welsh economy had become inextricably linked with that of England, and secondly, because the Welsh, with their distinctive cultural tradition, were not dependent upon political or economic independence for the satisfaction of national pride. Even before the Industrial Revolution, Welsh patriots had felt perfectly free to be British patriots as well. After the Industrial Revolution, they were in no realistic sense free to be Welsh patriots *unless* they were British patriots, because the development of South Wales had made Wales and England virtually inseparable. Yet this increased dependence had coincided with a revival of Welsh national feeling, of which Lloyd George was both a product and a prophet. It was, therefore, natural enough for him to regard Colonial nationalism – which he equated with Welsh nationalism – as compatible with a wider Imperial unity; natural, but mistaken, because the conditions that applied to the one did not apply to the other.

The British self-governing Colonies were not, like Wales, contiguous to England, but separated from the mother-country by vast tracts of ocean. Moreover, their economies, though at first dependent, were capable of independent development. All that they needed were population and capital, which time would supply from sources by no means exclusively British. Chamberlain was probably right in believing that closer political union of the Empire would not occur unless it were preceded by closer economic union. But the currents of self-interest, both in Britain and, to some extent, already in the Colonies, were against the formation of an Imperial *Zollverein*. Above all, the Colonies needed to be completely independent, because it was only by being independent that they could convince themselves or anyone else that they were nations at all. They lacked altogether the marks of nationhood that Wales conspicuously possessed – a language, a literature, ancient monuments, a folklore. Possessing such things, Wales could afford to do without sovereignty: lacking them, the Colonies had to become sovereign

1. In one of his early speeches (at Rhyl, 16 November 1894), he not only used the word 'niggers', but used it to describe Indians.

States, and to assert their sovereignty in deeds as well as words. For this reason more than any other the 'white' Commonwealth was bound to disintegrate, as a power bloc, sooner or later.

Its disintegration was a slow process, however, and the unity of the Empire in 1914 and 1939 seemed a vindication of Lloyd George's form of Imperialism. Meanwhile he emerged from the Boer War with a strong sense of having been proved right, not least as an Imperialist. In every way his self-confidence was enhanced. Before the war he always acted on the assumption that he was capable of national leadership: thereafter, he could feel that he was a national leader. On an issue of the first importance he had pitted his judgement against that of leaders experienced in statecraft when he was a child; yet it appeared to be his judgement which had turned out to be correct. Not yet forty, and still a stranger to office, he could feel himself the equal of Salisbury and Chamberlain. Moreover, his view of himself was now more widely shared than it had ever been before. In Parliament – the decisive arena for any British politician – he was listened to eagerly and, by his opponents, with grudging respect, throughout the war. Whereas some of his meetings in the country were broken up, the House of Commons never failed to give him an attentive hearing. This was a tribute to the institution, certainly, but also a tribute to him. Among Liberals, he was now accepted as an all-round party leader and man of the future.

With the ending of the Boer War the triumphant period of Lloyd George's life is about to begin. He stands on the threshold of twenty years of influence and power such as few men, before or since, have ever achieved. He is also on the threshold of middle age.

Note on Sources

Since this book is not a doctoral thesis, there is no need to pretend that the author's reading for it has been exhaustive. Many things have been left unread which might have been read, and some, no doubt, which ought to have been read. All the same, the footnote references supplied throughout the book may have shown that the research for it has not been desultory, and that a serious attempt has been made to describe and evaluate Lloyd George's early career in the light of the best available evidence. This Note will merely indicate the principal sources on which the author has drawn, discussing, where necessary, the extent of their reliability and mentioning a few incidental matters of interest.

A politician has to be judged, above all, by his public record, and the public record of Lloyd George's early life is mainly to be found in the Press and the Parliamentary Report (Hansard). But supplementing the contemporary printed evidence there is now, in the National Library of Wales, a large collection of manuscript letters, many relating to the early period of Lloyd George's life. Among two thousand or so from him to Margaret (his first wife), more than a thousand belong to the years before 1902. These letters provide a fascinating counterpoint to his public utterances and activities, revealing much that was previously unknown, and illuminating what was already known (or, at any rate, knowable). A general description of the letters has already been given in the text,[1] but it is worth emphasising that they are a specially rich source for Lloyd George's first decade in Parliament, when Margaret

1. *See* above, pp. 61–3.

spent much more of her time at Criccieth than in London, and when he still had the leisure and inclination to write to her very frequently and, often, at length.

In addition to the letters to Margaret, the collection includes other relevant material: correspondence with Lloyd George's children, with other members of the family, with outsiders; a diary for the year 1887; notebooks and notes for speeches; albums of Press cuttings; and miscellaneous documents, many trifling but some of considerable value.

Dr K. O. Morgan has recently (March 1973) published some of the National Library's Lloyd George material in *Lloyd George Family Letters, 1885–1936*. This, as the title implies, consists almost exclusively of correspondence, reproduced in chronological order with editorial notes and a historical introduction to each section, as well as a general introduction. Though quite a lot has been deliberately omitted (more especially nearly all of Lloyd George's early letters from abroad), the book is a very useful source. It should not, however, deter serious researchers from making the journey to Aberystwyth to consult the whole Lloyd George collection there, which is vital for any proper study of the man, and above all for studying the first phase of his career.

Another vital source on the young Lloyd George is the D. R. Daniel memoir, also in the National Library of Wales. Composed in Welsh, it was translated for the present writer by Dr Prys Morgan. In form, it is more diary than memoir, the entries dating from the period 1908–16. But the contents have, essentially, the character of a biographical study of Lloyd George, since the author ranges backwards in time and gives a very full description of the man he first got to know in 1887. Daniel writes diffusely, but with close personal knowledge and often with keen psychological insight. Both for information and judgement the work is immensely helpful, deserving, perhaps, to be published in its own right. (The D. R. Daniel Papers at Aberystwyth also include a number of early Lloyd George letters.)

The main collection of Lloyd George Papers, in the Beaverbrook Library in London, contains comparatively little relating to his early career. As a young politician, living for much of the time on his own in London, he neither bothered to keep a file of correspondence himself nor employed a secretary to do so. Margaret fortunately kept the letters which he wrote to her – now the prize of the Aberystwyth collection – and Frances Stevenson, when she became his confidential secretary in 1912, immediately began to preserve all his letters and papers, so laying the foundation of the great archive which he bequeathed to her at his death, and which, in 1950, she sold to Lord Beaverbrook.[1] Deficient though it is in early Lloyd George material, the Beaverbrook collection does, however, contain a few political letters dating from the period covered by this book, as well as a most useful file of speeches, Press interviews and Press comment.

Among the few books on Lloyd George that deal extensively with his early career, two are outstanding: *My Brother and I* by his brother, Alderman William George, and *The Life of David Lloyd George* by Herbert du Parcq. These two books share the crucially important distinction of quoting extracts from the diary which Lloyd George kept as a boy, and from letters to Richard Lloyd and William George – sources not available to other biographers.

William George's book has, moreover, the unique advantage of being written by one who grew up with Lloyd George, who worked with him as articled clerk and solicitor, and by whose efforts he was sustained financially during his early years in politics. On the other hand, it was published long after most of the events described (in 1958, when the author was in his nineties) and is unmistakably an old man's book. Yet, in spite of a tendency to ramble – as well as an understandable tendency to be reticent on some matters of legitimate interest to posterity – it does present a first-hand, detailed, authoritative account of Lloyd George's home background, upbringing and political emergence. Without it, much that we need to know about the young Lloyd George would have been lost for ever. William George also published, in 1934, a Welsh-language biography of his uncle and guardian, Richard Lloyd, which contains some useful information not reproduced in *My Brother and I*.

Du Parcq's *Life* – still in many ways the best – appeared over the period 1911–13 in four volumes, long since out of print. The first two volumes cover Lloyd George's career to 1899 and 1904, respectively; the third takes the story on to 1912, and the fourth consists of a selection of speeches. The author was, at the time, a young barrister of strong Liberal sympathies. He was given access to material which no outsider has since been allowed to see, and he wrote on a scale adequate to the subject. But he also wrote under supervision, and in the knowledge that his work was intended to be hagiographic. It is a tribute to his intelligence and skill that he managed to do what was required of him while at the same time producing a work of enduring merit.

1. It is now the property of the First Beaverbrook Foundation.

In later life, however, Lord du Parcq (as he eventually became) took no pride in this important literary and historical achievement of his youth. On the contrary, he seems to have been so ashamed of it that he did his best to ensure that there should be no reference to it in any record of his career. In the 1920s, before he became a judge, he did not mention it in his *Who's Who* entries;[1] when he died, in 1949, it was not mentioned in *The Times* obituary of him; and, most astonishingly of all, it is not referred to in the article on him in the *D.N.B.* According to his daughter, the subject of Lloyd George was unmentionable in the family during her childhood, though she never knew why.

Apart from his brother William, two other members of Lloyd George's family have written about him – Frances Stevenson (Frances Lloyd George), and his elder son, Richard Lloyd George.

Frances Stevenson's books are an autobiography, *The Years that are Past* (1967), written under her married name, and a volume of extracts from her diary, edited by A. J. P. Taylor (1971). Of these the *Diary* is by far the more valuable source, though the autobiography contains some useful information. Neither book has very much relevance to the first phase of Lloyd George's life, of which the author was not a witness, but there are some interesting allusions to it, together with retrospective comments by him on a variety of topics, and comments by the author on his character. When she refers to his family, and more especially to his first wife, allowance has to be made for her inevitable prejudice.

Richard Lloyd George also contributed two books, of even more unequal merit. The first, *Dame Margaret* (1947), is a life of his mother which at the same time tells us much about the family background and about his own life as a child. In spite of occasional inaccuracies, a rather muddled structure and a few palpable errors of interpretation, this book has charm as well as substance. The same cannot be said of *Lloyd George* (1960), which was ghost-written at a period when Richard himself was in no fit state for authorship, which reflects in an extreme degree his tortured attitude towards his father, and which was clearly published with a view to sensation. It should not be totally discounted, however: a son's evidence has to be reckoned with, and Richard's book on his father contains some flashes of light.

The best all-round account of Lloyd George's career before the First World War is *Lloyd George: 1863–1914*, by W. Watkin Davies (1939).

1. He first appears in *Who's Who* in 1927.

Davies's father was the Rev. Gwynoro Davies, who accompanied Lloyd George on his Mediterranean cruise in the winter of 1898–9. He is a native of Criccieth, knew Lloyd George well, and writes clearly, if with a Welsh bias. His book also suffers slightly from being written while the subject was alive.

The same applies to *David Lloyd George* by J. Hugh Edwards (first published in 1913[1]), and the *Life Romance of Lloyd George* by Beriah Gwynfe Evans (1916) – both the work of Welsh journalists well acquainted with Lloyd George. There is also a short Welsh-language biography by E. Morgan Humphreys (1943).

E. H. Spender's *The Prime Minister* (1920) is the work of an English journalist who became very closely attached to Lloyd George. It has considerable value in spite of being wholly uncritical.

Of Lloyd George biographies published since his death the best on the early period is Frank Owen's *Tempestuous Journey* (1954). This has been somewhat unfairly criticised. Its defects are its style (an amalgam of Welsh *hwyl* and *Daily Express* journalese), and the fact that it is not written on an adequate scale for what purports to be a study of 'Lloyd George, his Life and Times'. But it was not for nothing that Mr Owen got a First in History at Cambridge. His knowledge is wide-ranging and he is not often wrong on vital points.

By contrast, *David Lloyd George: the Official Biography* by Malcolm Thomson (1948) is a rather pedestrian effort. It was written in collaboration with Frances Lloyd George, and has a long Introduction by her. A. J. Sylvester's *The Real Lloyd George* (1947) is revealing of some aspects of Lloyd George's character. The author was his secretary during the latter part of his life, but when he writes of earlier times he can be naïve as well as inaccurate. *The Mask of Merlin* by Donald McCormick (1963) is subtitled 'A Critical Study of David Lloyd George', which is an understatement. The author's technique is slapdash, and his allegations and innuendoes should be treated as critically as he has tried to treat Lloyd George. His book, however, is not devoid of interest.

Other books on Lloyd George have virtually nothing worthwhile to say on his early life. The extreme case is *Lloyd George* by Thomas Jones C.H. (1951), which, though profoundly informative on the years when Dr Jones knew him, dismisses the whole of his career before 1914 in 45 (out of 290) pages.

1. In four volumes, with 'a Short History of the Welsh People'. Edwards's shorter, two-volume, Life appeared in 1930.

Lloyd George's colleagues during his first phase in politics have so far been rather ill-served by history. T. E. Ellis has done best, with a biography in Welsh by his son, T. I. Ellis (1944), another by Wyn Griffith (1959), and a very recent one in English by Neville Masterman, entitled (in an obvious allusion to Lloyd George) *The Forerunner* (1972). The T. E. Ellis Papers at the National Library of Wales contain some moderately important letters from, and about, Lloyd George.

Lord Rendel's papers, also at the National Library, are of much greater interest. Some of them have been published in *The Personal Papers of Lord Rendel*, edited by F. E. Hamer (1931) – but only some. There is no biography of Rendel, and no article on him in the *D.N.B.*

Herbert Lewis's papers at the National Library are an important source. They include a type-written diary and numerous letters exchanged between Lewis and Lloyd George during the period covered by this book. There is a study of Lewis in Welsh by his daughter, Mrs K. Idwal Jones (1958); otherwise no biography.

Unfortunately, very few of D. A. Thomas's papers survive, but J. Vyrnwy Morgan published *The Life of Viscount Rhondda* (1918), and a book on him was produced by his daughter, Lady Rhondda, and others – *D. A. Thomas, Viscount Rhondda* (1921). There is also an article on him in the *D.N.B.* by Harold Begbie.

S. T. Evans is another important figure most of whose papers have been lost, but those that remain (in the possession of his daughter, Miss Gwendollen Evans) include, within the period, the letter from Catherine Edwards to Lloyd George quoted on pp. 235-6. Evans's entry in the *D.N.B.* is by J. L. Brierly.

The papers of Alfred Thomas (Lord Pontypridd) are preserved at the Central Library, Cardiff, but they are not very exciting. Among the few letters from Lloyd George none is really important.

The W. J. Parry (Coetmor) Papers at the University College of North Wales, Bangor, are of greater value. They naturally throw light on the Penrhyn quarry dispute, and they also contain correspondence on the Welsh Patagonian Syndicate, as well as an account by Parry (in Welsh) of his trips to the Argentine in 1893-4.

E. J. Griffith's life was written, in Welsh, by T. I. Ellis (1969), but his papers at the National Library – anyway a small collection – contain virtually nothing of interest to students of Lloyd George.

Memories (1927), by Lloyd George's clerical friend and antagonist, A. G. Edwards (Bishop of St Asaph and later Archbishop of Wales), is an informative book, and so is *The Early Life of Bishop Owen* by Eluned E. Owen (1958).

The *Dictionary of Welsh Biography* is of value only as a source of bare facts and dates. It provides none of the detail and colour for which the *D.N.B.* is justly famous.

Among general works on the period the author has derived most benefit from *A History of Modern England* (1906), Volume V, by Herbert Paul; *England: 1870–1914* (1936), by R. C. K. Ensor; and *Imperialism and the Rise of Labour*, the fifth volume of Elie Halévy's *History of the English People in the Nineteenth Century* (1926, translated – by E. I. Watkin – 1929).

Ambitions and Strategies (1964) by Peter Stansky is useful as a blow-by-blow account of the 'struggle for the leadership of the Liberal Party in the 1890s'. An even more recent study which has been read with interest is *Liberal Politics in the Age of Gladstone and Rosebery* (1972), by D. A. Hamer.

Much has also been learnt from the biographies of major figures, such as Gladstone, Rosebery, Balfour, Harcourt, Campbell-Bannerman and Chamberlain.

On the Welsh side, *A History of Modern Wales* (1950) by David Williams is clear, competent and balanced, and as a detailed study of Welsh politics during the Lloyd George era *Wales in British Politics: 1868–1922* (1963) by K. O. Morgan is unique and indispensable.

For the background to Lloyd George's Patagonian venture *Y Wladfa* ('The Colony') (1962) by R. Bryn Williams is of interest.

Index